CHICANA TRIBUTES

ACTIVIST WOMEN of the
CIVIL RIGHTS MOVEMENT

Stories for the New Generation

Edited by Rita Sanchez and Sonia Lopez

Montezuma Publishing
San Diego

Published by
Montezuma Publishing
Aztec Shops Ltd.
San Diego State University
San Diego, California 92182-1701
619-594-7552
www.montezumapublishing.com

Publishing Manager: Kim Mazyck

Design and Formatting: Lia Dearborn

Cover Design: Duane McGregor and Lia Dearborn

Quality Control: Jasmine Baiz

iii

CONTENTS

♦ CONTENTS ♦

EDITORS' PREFACE

This book documents the experiences of sixty-one women who flourished in the ferment of the civil/ethnic/women's rights movements of the late twentieth century and beyond. While each life is unique, collectively they demonstrate the benefits gained when a community and a society unleashes and fosters the potential of women who create, organize, and lead. Conversely, an undetermined degree of loss may accrue to societies that suppress or discourage the freedom of women to shape their destinies.

When women come together with a collective intention, powerful things happen. Simultaneously, but separately, in 1972–73, at San Diego State University and at Stanford University, and having never met, two of us had the same idea, to propose and design a course about Mexican American women. The idea for this book also has a history. In those days, both of us wanted to contribute to the development of Chicano studies. The Mexican American voice, so much a fabric of U.S. history was missing from the dominant English narrative and the women's presence was nearly absent from Chicano literature and history. Chicanas acted to change these injustices, thereby adding new energy to the Chicano Movement and to other liberation discourse. At that time, as graduate students, we had the opportunity to teach a Chicana women's course.

Such a course had never been taught at either university. While women instigated change at different colleges, in those years Chicanas/Latinas appeared to be anonymous. And although Anglo women around the country had already started addressing women's needs, they did not include the new diverse student population that was entering the universities.

Civil Rights Activism

Many people had become aware of their rights written in the U.S. Constitution. They made demands for equality in education, voting, and employment. Most affected were Blacks, Chicanos, Native Americans, poor whites, and women. As many of the narratives in this book from that time period will attest, these were tumultuous times. All kinds of different people gathered in protest and spoke up for the first time about their deepest concerns as Americans after feeling for so long like they had not been heard.

By 1972-73, our proposed college courses were added to the curriculum. We found ourselves among the first to teach Mexican American women's once-buried history, as well as their contributions to U.S. society. For the first time, Mexican Americans and other under-represented students on our campuses were able to learn about themselves in college courses; at the same time, others in academia were now exposed to the diversity truly representative of the country's population.

Now, more than forty years later, as teachers and co-editors of this book, we are proud to have contributed, along with many others like ourselves, to filling an academic void that existed on college campuses across America; but more than that, to be part of something monumental, the awakening of a generation of voices daring to act for change.

Our goals also seemed similar in that we both hoped to see Chicana/Latina writings in print. We wanted to see ourselves in the required readings. Eager to capture Mexican American women's experiences and bring them to our students, we encouraged our classes to write. We knew that the lack of publications about women like us represented solid neglect. Our students, nearly our age, submitted work that we prepared for publication. We researched and wrote along with our students, sharing our once unwritten histories and contributions.

It was during the fervor of the Chicano Movement that some women began calling themselves "Chicanas" to address gender as well as ethnicity; some of us chose the name, controversial as it was, to show self-determination, and to acknowledge the power that came with it, refusing labels provided by others, while intent on affirming our Hispana/Indígena identity, so as not to exclude the Indian mother, and exposing other contradictions such as sexism in the Chicano Movement.

Chicana Publications Needed

We submitted writings for publication as we also presented our thoughts orally at seminars and conferences, along with other women. These efforts stemmed from specific goals by Chicano movement activists to end stereotypes of Mexicans as a group, most of whom were U.S. citizens, and to demand equality in education and the workplace. Knowing other women's actions and their stories led to publishing them in this book. We realized how important their stories were. These narratives represent San Diego women, some of the first Chicanas to stand up for change, documenting a generation of activism.

Over forty years have passed since our college days. Now we have come together to produce this book at San Diego State University where we have both, at different times, taught the Chicana course. We can now pay tribute to the many other Chicanas, some who have also been the first in their families to go to college; they have broken barriers for future generations. The narrative voices of women in this book, some of whom were yet to call themselves Chicanas or feminists, are preserved here for the next generation to know of their courageous actions and how they bettered conditions for the future. The publication of this work is long in coming, a tribute to the many Mexican American women who have not been fully acknowledged for their contributions or the benefits of their actions.

Chicana Diversity

Most of the women in these stories soon began calling themselves Chicanas as a term of empowerment in solidarity with others. It often meant standing up for themselves in the community or the workplace, where many acted alone in a climate lacking in diversity. The stories compiled here will, therefore, use the term "Chicana" as it represents activists for positive change, the ones who worked to create it in their communities over the past forty years. These *Chicana Tributes* represent the diverse faces of women in San Diego, activists from the civil rights movement to the present.

The idea for this Chicana tribute came from different sources; one came from a younger generation. In 2012, Patricia Aguayo and Zerina Zermeño proposed a celebratory event to honor Chicanas who had served their communities for so many years and had not been recognized. Inspired by their idea, this book is a continuation of their efforts. They wanted to reach out to the people of San Diego and together acknowledge them. They called the event *Chicana: Una Decision Conciente*. It was held in the *barrio* of Logan Heights, a San Diego community, with a high population of Chicanos and Mejicanos who still have not been given effective access to their own history and culture in the public schools or media. These two dynamic young Chicanas were among the first ones we invited to author a story for the book.

An Idea is Born

Their innovative celebration revealed the need to come together to honor Chicanas who came before them. Hundreds of community activists and their cohorts, artists and poets, gathered one night for an evening of art, music, culture, *teatro*, *danza indigena*, and performances by *Mujeres en Resistencia*. All paid tribute to Chicanas in San Diego. Visuals of every kind filled the senses, along with the sounds, the sights, the colors of the culture including biographies and photographs of Chicanas taken by the young women sponsoring the event. Young artists Bernice Badillo and Patricia Aguayo, poet Zerina Zermeño, brought the walls of the building and the streets to life with color and consciousness. Importantly, many Chicanas were recognized that day.

In 2013, at another event, photographic portraits and biographies paid tribute to San Diego Chicanas once more. This time it was part of a benefit organized by early activists with the assistance of young Chicanas to preserve Chicana history in the San Diego State University Archives. The fundraiser, called *Chicana Conciencia: Past Present and Future*, also paid tribute to Chicanas with poetry, *teatro*, *danza indígena*, and *mariachi* music. A featured honoree was Gracia Molina de Pick, known for her years of dedication and mentorship of Chicanas. A Chicana "Tribute Wall" of photographs and biographies graced a prominent wall at the Centro Cultural de la Raza, some from the previous event and other new ones. About thirty Chicana activists were recognized, many for the first time. Many people admired the wall of tributes but hoped to see it broadened so others could view it in more permanent form. Then and there, the idea for this book was conceived. The "Tribute Wall" of women's voices was a powerful concept opposing the idea of border walls meant to keep people out.

Chicanas Honored

Since then, both of us have volunteered our efforts. We persuaded some sixty-one authors to write stories of women nominated for this book. They are presented here, stories of activist women, written by authors inspired to preserve Chicana/activist narratives. Each author has written a story of an honoree, while providing a brief biography of her own work. As it turned out, the authors' bios are as powerful as the stories they have written. Some of the women honored here have contributed their personal papers to San Diego State University Special Collections Library for the Chicana and Chicano Archives to be preserved for students, scholars, and younger generations. Others have been acknowledged as KPBS (public broadcasting) heroes; given the Cesar E. Chavez Humanitarian Award; or inducted into the San Diego County Women's Hall of Fame. Still others continue to be active in their communities working for causes important to them. This book will allow many to know their stories.

A central theme in the activists' ongoing narrative has always been community and what that means. Together we felt a longing, a desire to search for a lost history, and only together could it be recovered. Community means the varied stories told by different people in different ways, not just one version; and so each story is unique. Each story brings empathy, different notes and sounds, new music, poetry, art, adventure, scholarship, and action, but always something dynamic to build on, a community that is continually growing, with each generation.

Twelve Representative Chapters

Each of the twelve chapters provides a brief history of four to six women, placing the woman where she has most noticeably served. Chapters One and Two begin with *Mujeres Presentes*, that is, the women who have passed away but whose presence lives on as their actions continue to affect the lives of others. Chapters Eleven and Twelve highlight educators whose work builds on that of earlier mentors and their actions. The chapters between include: Three and Four, "Early Activists;" Five and Six, "Chicanas in the Arts;" Seven and Eight, "Chicanas in Education;" Nine and Ten, "Chicanas in Public Office." Each chapter includes a brief introduction, but the women's narratives are the core of the book; their stories easily stand on their own.

This collection may be considered a starting point and by no means represents the entire Chicana/Latina community in San Diego. As it turned out there were many more women than the sixty-one women presented here. The hope is that others may read the book and decide to author a future edition. All women ought to be honored for their efforts and receive the recognition they deserve.

Acknowledgments

We wish to thank the many people who have made this work possible. Chicanas in various fields—those who continue to be community activists, retired volunteers, or professionals—all agreed to provide their biographies. These narratives exude much power, to heal, to motivate, and to incite further action. The honorees conferred with an author they either knew or who knew of them. All are busy people, mothers or grandmothers, community workers, or both; they are professionals, or retired persons. Each brief author biography acknowledges the writers; it tells a small story, revealing the author's own life work and dedication, adding to the ongoing narrative.

Special Thanks to All Who Contributed

Thank you to those who commented, inspired, designed, transcribed, filed, proofread, edited, or thus, supported our project. Among them, most prominently are our families, whether a spouse, a sister, a brother, a son or daughter, who waited patiently for us to finish the work. Thank you Montezuma Publishing:

Kim Mazyck for her prefessionalism and dedication to our project; and to Lia Dearborn for her hardwork, beautiful interior design and cultural sensitivity. Special thanks to Bertha Hernández for proofreading the entire manuscript; thanks to her, and to Rosalie Schwartz for their excellent commentary and suggestions, adding immensely to our work; to Duane McGregor for all the cover designs and for all her patience; to Richard Griswold del Castillo for all his love, technical support, and for organizing the computer files, a complicated task at best; to the Women's Museum of California and its director, Ashley Gardener for previewing some of the narratives from our book in the museum's exciting exhibition, "Shoulders To Stand On: the Chicana Narrative," and to those who curated it, designed it, and introduced it, Duane McGregor, Tina Clarke, Leticia Gomez, and Charla Wilson. Thanks to Celia Sotomayor Moody, Connie Puente, and Karl Schlatter for their generous contributions.

The best part of this project came with the opportunity we had to gather with the women, whether authors or honorees. It gave women the chance to open up new dialogue, and exchange stories. Our many visits, gatherings for coffee, or simply drop-bys, created new alliances and treasured camaraderie.

While we spent countless hours reviewing the manuscript to ensure accuracy at every level, any errors you may find are ours alone.

As we were completing this anthology, the political climate in the nation changed radically. The 2016 presidential election brought many new challenges for our nation relative to women's rights, voter suppression, migrant and refugee rights; affordable healthcare; and water rights on indigenous lands. This new political reality also brought out many to speak against injustices. After the inauguration, over 500,000 women marched in Washington D.C. and nearly 40,000 marched in San Diego. These actions have given us a renewed commitment to sharing the stories of women, affirming that "Women's rights are human rights." They show that women will continue working to resist injustice, challenging any threats to civil liberties. Their narratives affirm women's courage, resilience, and empowerment proving that "standing down is not an option." We hope that their voices may be a guide in shaping a society that values social justice and shared humanity

This book is dedicated to our families with love.

Respectfully,

por la causa y la educación,

Rita Sanchez and Sonia Lopez, co-editors

January 2017

PART I: THE PAST

CHICANA MATRIARCHS: A TRIBUTE TO WOMEN WHO HAVE PASSED

CHAPTER 1

TINA C. DE BACA

LAURA RODRIGUEZ

FAUSTINA SOLÍS

MARTA SOTOMAYOR

CHAPTER 1

Mujeres Presentes:
A Tribute to Women Who Have Passed

In this chapter, Chicana Matriarchs represent strong women leaders who have left their mark on U.S. Civil Rights history. Recognized here are ones who have passed; they are more than a celebration of notable Chicanas; their actions helped change the way women live in the world and the way the world views them. They changed themselves and they changed the world around them when they stood up for equal rights, cultural identity, and the right to work as active leaders. By taking risks, despite criticism for breaking tradition, they decided that they no longer wanted to be seen in the background. In the end, their actions have advanced society, providing the younger generation with countless stories, documenting their lives to pass on to their children and grandchildren.

At many Mexican memorial services for a significant person, the loved one's name is called out. The congregation responds, ¡Presente! to affirm that the person, although passed from this life, remains a living presence. ¡Mujeres Presentes! in chapters one and two, represent Mexican American activist women who fought for justice and equal rights at a crucial time in America. Chicanas Concientes, they were awakened to higher consciousness, and then awakened others. In Chapter One, Laura Rodriguez, Tina C. de Baca, Faustina Solís, and Marta Sotomayor stood up for equal rights for workers, students, or community members. Chapter two includes the artists/activists who passed away. They had equal passion and dedication. Since the 1960s and 1970s, these women devoted much of their lives to helping others. It is on their shoulders we stand, because of the foundation they have left behind.

"Shoulders to Stand On," became the title of the Chicana exhibit, at the Women's Museum of California, honoring many of the women in this book. The 2016 program read, "From roots of self-discovery, strong branches blossomed with Chicana literature, art, and activism for equal rights in politics, education, and the work place. San Diego's Latina women drew on the strength of their ancestors and their own experiences."

The stories in this book prove the results of these women's activism, some in the face of exclusion and discrimination; they challenged traditional roles often defined for them by others, confronting problems with a spirit of self-determination and courage against all odds. They entered positions in the work place never before given to women. In San Diego, they advocated for basic human rights, a park, a cultural center, a health clinic, almost simultaneously, even while they had to place themselves in harm's way. Beyond that, they made great strides outside their communities, at colleges and universities in the state and in the nation. Their stories reveal the outcome of their actions. One can see the dramatic results when women chose to rise up, breaking all barriers, for the good of their families, communities and larger society.

In this chapter, Laura Rodriguez's story is a prime example of how one woman came to be called the mother of Chicano Park. She protested the City of San Diego's attempt to build a highway patrol station where the people of Logan Heights had been promised a park. Laura placed herself in front of a bulldozer to prevent its progress. She also chained herself to the doors of Neighborhood House to fight for a people's clinic. These extreme measures reveal the extent to which Laura and others like her were moved to effect change in their communities.

Other women like Tina C. de Baca stood up for the rights of the people, whether at her church as a member of the Catholic Diocese board of directors, or in the community where she worked to ensure people's need for basic services. Her profound actions changed many lives at a time when women were not commonly members of boards. Tina's story also represents the diversity of these women, some whose U.S. heritage like hers dated back for generations, while others were recent migrants. The term "Chicana" exemplified the bond between the two that erased all borders.

One of the first Chicana Ph.D.s in Social Work in the United States, Marta Sotomayor initially worked with *Trabajadores de la Raza*, addressing employment discrimination and the need for Spanish-speaking social workers and services; she graduated from college, and went on to help found the National Hispanic Council on Aging in Washington, D.C. The tradition for men in lead roles suggested that women must remain in the home. Marta fought for more than a job, or for breaking a glass ceiling, she fought for the rights of the most vulnerable, the aged in our communities.

The first Chicana/Latina provost at UCSD at the School of Medicine, Faustina Solís advocated for the poor, dedicating her life to improving social conditions in underserved communities. Her priority in academia was to reach out to students in need. She benefitted society and the university immensely when she brought the concerns of the most needy to the forefront, before her own concerns as provost.

¡Mujeres Presentes! Their actions live on.

TINA C. DE BACA (1933–2012):

COMMUNITY RIGHTS ADVOCATE
Leader and Pioneer in the Chicano Movement

BY DOLORES C. DE BACA

When I think of Anton Chico, New Mexico, the place where my mother was raised, I am in awe of her even more. Tina C. de Baca, born Maria Celestina Marquez on July 16, 1933, would not only lead the coolest pack of "chicks from Anton Chick," but would also go on to marry a war hero; move half-way across the country to San Diego in 1949; give birth to five children; and subsequently become a leader and pioneer in the Chicano Movement. How could this dynamic, influential, and commanding Chicana that I knew have such a modest beginning and yet accomplish so much?

Tina C. de Baca, at the height of her activism. Courtesy of Vincent Z. C. de Baca.

During the Great Depression, my mother endured many hardships. Despite the hardships, Tina and her two sisters, Gloria and Pearl—all part of the coolest group of girls from Anton Chico, the "Anton Chicks"—lived happily with their grandparents, poor farmers, Pedro J. Sanchez and Aurelio Lucero, on their small *ranchito* along the Pecos River. Tina's mother, Petrolina Sanchez, one of their nine children, left her three daughters when Tina was one year old. Tina's father, Bonifacio Marquez, an influential man, had Petrolina admitted to the state hospital where he was the manager. There, Petrolina was subject to the cruel treatment of the day. As she grew up, Tina surely listened to those stories about her mother and was saddened by them.

Although her grandparents survived droughts, floods, crop failure, and severe poverty, life was good on the ranch where they raised their grandchildren and the girls had very satisfying childhoods.

In 1940, when Tina was a still a child, her father moved his three daughters to Las Vegas, New Mexico, to live with him and their new stepmother, Emma Banos. There Tina helplessly observed her mother laboring on the hospital's farm near the manager's three-story house. At the age of 16, Tina married my father, John Herman C. de Baca of Mora, New Mexico, who was a World War II marine combat veteran.

By 1949, Tina and John were expecting their first of five children and on their way to San Diego, California. My father enrolled at San Diego State University on the G.I. Bill and got a job at Convair, an aircraft company. My father's mother and brothers joined in the big move westward as well as my grandmother's siblings with their families. My brother Vince was born in 1950, quickly followed by my sisters, Claire and Letty. Soon there was a large extended family of C. de Baca's in San Diego and they lived it up with frequent gatherings, camping outings, parties, and poker nights.

John and Tina agreed on most political ideologies, such as supporting Mexican American groups like the Mexican American Political Association, the Viva Kennedy Clubs, Reies Tijerina's Alianza, and Cesar Chavez' United Farmworkers movement. Tina's philosophical and political conversations with family members and friends moved some to join the cause and others to resent her knowledge and radical stance on civil rights and educational reform.

Not only did Tina ensure the best education possible for her children, but she also joined many Catholic committees urging the church to improve educational opportunities for all people. She knew she could do better for herself, her family, and Latinos all over the world, despite the fact that she was not formally educated beyond the 10th grade. Informally, however, she never tired of educating herself. Her favorite subjects included music, world and local politics, poetry, civil rights, literature, art, and contemporary anything.

Tina and John's family continued to grow into the late 1960s, with the birth of Alma in 1966 and Dolores in 1967. A few years later, they adopted Arru from a family member and raised her as their daughter.

By 1968, my brother Vince was working with groups such as MAYA/ MEChA, the Brown Berets, and the UFW Grapes Boycott. In late 1969, Vince was arrested during the *Católicos por la Raza* takeover of the Catholic Church property at Camp Oliver in Descanso, California. My mother made phone calls, getting people to picket Bishop Buddy's home; she also joined the call for the Catholic Church to address the needs of the Chicana/o community and give Chicana nuns and Chicano priests equal voting power when adopting Catholic policies within their own dioceses. This event solidified my mother's commitment to *La Causa*.

San Diego in the 1960s was a central location for Chicano politics. My mom was a pivotal character in the progression of the *movimiento* at that time; she was always planning, always raising money, and always connecting one person to another. She was a formative agent in a system known as "The Drum," where telephone communication was the mechanism of the era to transmit information about meetings, protests, and other important issues. She helped spread the word that a Barrio Logan lot intended for a community park was going to be turned into a police substation; people responded from all over California. That lot was to have historical significance well beyond that day and a few hours of phone calls.

One of my first memories is of that day when my sister and I placed the first two foundation stones for Chicano Park on April 22, 1970. I was almost three then and my mom already understood that she would have to usher in future Chicanas early. Obviously, I was only one in a long line.

The Chicano Movement progressed, as did our family until the untimely death of my father on August 28, 1973, which shocked the family in San Diego and throughout New Mexico. John C. de Baca died in his sleep of a myocardial infarction at the age of 47, leaving behind a wife and six children. Now 40 years old, and suddenly a widow and single mom, Tina needed help. Luckily, her three eldest children were in their early 20s, but the three youngest were then 8, 7, and 4 years old. Despite many new obstacles, she managed to send the young girls to Catholic school from first grade through high school.

Throughout the 1970s, 80s, and 90s, Tina continued to wield her politicism, intelligence, and influence to level the playing field for the disenfranchised wherever she could. In one instance, she might be protecting children in orphanages in Tijuana; another might have taken her to Washington, D.C., to speak out about the injustices plaguing the Chicano community; yet another would find her raising endless dollars for the causes she supported. She was an integral agent in so many organizations, including founding board member of *La Prensa* newspaper and board member on the Committee on Chicano Rights (CCR). However, those events that were more descriptive of her as a heroine were the picket lines, the late-night letter stuffing, the endless phone calls, the football games, the carnes asadas, the ubiquitous meetings with anyone and everyone at any time. These events included life-long relationships that she could instantly build with people around the globe.

On April 5, 1996, in another heroic act, Tina brought Petrolina to San Diego to live with her, sacrificing much of the political work she was doing so she could take care of her mother. Petrolina loved being with family, but longed to return to her beloved ancestral homeland of New Mexico; one day she would. Tina took care of her mother in her home for fifteen years until the day Petrolina died in 2011 at nearly 100 years of age.

In 2012, after more than a decade of retirement, Tina went into the hospital at the age of 79 for reasons that should not have led to her demise; however, after several complications, she ultimately succumbed leaving us on October 14, 2012. Tina C. de Baca, faithful wife and mother, devoted daughter, and activist woman for the disenfranchised, now rests in a tiny, peaceful cemetery in Anton Chico, New Mexico, alongside her mother and countless other ancestors.

My brother, his wife Rosario, my son Jett, and I watched as they placed the stones on the gravesites for them both. As I stood there staring disbelievingly at my mother's place in the earth, with an angry darkened monsoon sky beckoning in the distance, I thought of her amazing and otherwise impossible journey where she came full circle from that modest old west New Mexico town to the world and back again.

About the Author:

DOLORES C. DE BACA, Tina C. de Baca's daughter; Dolores has a B.S., Bachelor of Science in Biochemistry/Cellular Biochemistry from UCSD, and an M.Ed., Master of Education, Multiculturalism in the Classroom. Presently, Dolores is a science teacher in the San Diego Unified School District and a science instructor and curriculum writer with Upward Bound, and teaches math and science at Southwestern College. Dolores wishes to acknowledge her brother, Vincent C. de Baca for his contribution to their mother's story.

LAURA RODRIGUEZ (1909–1994):

THE MATRIARCH OF CHICANO PARK

A Grandmother Who Became An Activist

BY MARIA E. GARCIA

Laura Rodriguez has come to be known as the matriarch of Chicano Park, a historical landmark in San Diego. In 1970, the land was taken over during the Chicano Movement to address the people's need for a park. Laura was very much a part of the San Diego effort to acquire the land, as long as it meant the betterment of the people who lived there. First, it was Chicano Park she fought for; then it was the Neighborhood House that became her central concern.

On October 5, 1970, Logan Heights resident Laura Rodriguez chained herself to the Neighborhood House doors, setting in motion what has come to be known as "The Occupation." This action was to awaken the public to the area's need for a health clinic. The fearless 61-year-old grandmother chose this very public display of activism to force a decision on the future of Neighborhood House.

Laura Rodriguez, has an elementary school, and a wing in the Logan Heights Health Clinic, named after her.

Courtesy of Timothy Fraser,
Family Health Centers of San Diego.

The services that Neighborhood House had provided to the community for decades had been first reduced and then eliminated. Laura and Logan Heights activists wanted the space returned to its original purpose, as a community resource to benefit the people. This story traces her life from her Logan Heights beginnings to the years she lived at the historical Marston House in Balboa Park; her return to Logan Heights in the Mexican American Community; and the takeover of Chicano Park and Neighborhood House.

Laura was born in 1909 to Amelia Fox and John Gallo, an Italian immigrant. Her mother moved out when Laura was four years old, leaving Laura, her sister Lugina, and her brother John, to be raised by their father. John Gallo was blind and made his livelihood as a newspaper seller in downtown San Diego, in front of the Lewis shoe store at Fifth and C Streets. His obituary describes the devotion of his young daughter Laura, who "would lead him to the corner in the morning, go to school, then return in the evening, and lead her father to their home at 1740 Main Street."

Laura's Early Childhood

Laura told me this story about her early childhood. When she was around ten years old, her father became very ill and knew that he would not live to raise his children. He made the decision to place the girls in an orphanage in Los Angeles. At this point, Laura's brother John had ditched school one too many times and had been placed in a boys' group home. Thus, their father was concerned about his children's future.

On the train ride to Los Angeles where the children would be placed in a home, both girls cried continuously; or, as Laura put it, "We wailed all the way up there." Her father could not leave the two sisters at the orphanage, so they all returned to San Diego. Mr. Gallo then spoke to Miss Mary Marston, the daughter of San Diego businessman and philanthropist George Marston. He owned the Marston Department store and was very active in social and political activities throughout San Diego. Laura's father explained his situation, adding the story about the Los Angeles train ride.

As Mary and her sister Helen Marston were involved with the operation and ongoing funding of Neighborhood House, Mary assured Mr. Gallo that when the day arrived that Laura and Lugina needed a place to live, they would come and live with the Marston family in their home. Thus, at the age of 12, Laura left the *barrio* of Logan Heights to go live at the Marston house on Seventh and Upas, on the north end of Balboa Park.

During her early childhood, Laura had many responsibilities in a family with financial struggles. In her new home there were cooks, maids, and chauffeurs. Laura once described the view from her bedroom window: "I could see Roosevelt Junior High out my window and across the canyon. Her ties to Neighborhood House had gone from using the services provided there, to being a part of the Marston family that supported those services.

Laura Marries at Age 16

By age 16, Laura met David Rodriguez at a dance at the old Pacific Ballroom and later married him. The Marstons begged her not to get married at such a young age and assured her that they would send her to college. Laura declined their offer and married David. Although she did work outside the home at one of the aircraft plants, most of the first 40 years of Laura's marriage were spent as a wife and mother on Newton Avenue in Logan Heights. Her life was raising kids, cooking, sewing, not at all the life of an activist.

A momentous year in Logan Heights was 1970, with the recently created community of Barrio Logan where Mexican American families made their homes. Interstate 5, constructed in 1963, served to separate the area that is known today as Barrio Logan to the south, from the rest of the Greater Logan Heights communities. With this great intrusion into the people's lives, by her late fifties, Laura had become a community activist.

The sudden eruption of activism came with the takeover of Chicano Park in April, then followed six months later at Neighborhood House. The roots of discontent began when the people's neighborhood was split in two, first by a freeway and then by the Coronado Bridge. The people were feeling the injustice. They had lost their services at Neighborhood House and were made a token promise of a park underneath the newly constructed bridge.

Laura described it this way. Walking to the store one day in April 1970, she saw the earthmovers on the land that is now Chicano Park. She asked what was going on and was told that a highway patrol substation was to be built on land that had been promised for a park. She used to say, "After that, I never went home," much to the chagrin of Mr. Rodriguez.

Laura Joins the Protest

Laura joined with the people of Barrio Logan to protest the building of a highway patrol station. She was one of the people who lay down in front of a bulldozer to keep it from breaking ground for the substation. This transformation, from the housewife who obeyed whatever her husband said, to the Chicana activist, Laura Rodriguez, was a metamorphosis of unforeseen scope.

The occupation of Neighborhood House followed soon after that of Chicano Park. The need for a health clinic was one concern constantly discussed by residents, and a natural next step for Laura. A decision was made to "take back" the building and restore the services that once made Neighborhood House the heart of the community.

The Neighborhood House of 1970 was not the one of Laura's childhood. Laura's youth had been spent at Neighborhood House where she learned to cook and sew. Medical services were available there since her childhood. They included visiting nurses, well-baby clinics, nutrition services, and tonsillectomies on site. Generations of young men were introduced to sports at Neighborhood House and played on its team. The heart of the barrio had now been reduced to administrative offices. The services Laura had known as a child were no longer offered. The few that were left were limited in scope.

The night before the occupation, Laura, José Gomez—who is immortalized in a Chicano Park mural wearing a white tee shirt and holding a pick ax—and I, met to discuss what could possibly go wrong. A general agreement among the three of us was that this action would be quick and easy. This was not how it turned out. Neighborhood House had assumed that the change to an administrative office—now referred to as the Big Neighbor—would not be a problem for the people. But the community disagreed. The people had Head Start programs since 1964, along with funding for these policies, and now the people were feeling the loss.

The occupation would be announced on a Monday night at the Community Action Council (CAC) meeting held at Lowell School. On that particular night, there were some surprised people, but I don't remember any real objections to the takeover. After I left the meeting, I joined Laura on the steps of Neighborhood House. I remember the fearless, 61-year-old grandmother turned barrio activist, chained to the front door of Neighborhood House. Earlier that October 1970 evening, the case had been made at the Barrio Logan CAC meeting that Neighborhood House must once again provide services to the community as it had for so many decades in the past. Laura had also been advocating for its use as a badly needed community health clinic.

The showdown happened that very evening. Laura did not attend the CAC meeting, but had requested the keys to Neighborhood House under the pretense of holding a meeting there, not an unusual request, since the community continued to hold meetings there. I joined Laura there after leaving the CAC meeting. Joe "Kiki" Ortega, José Gomez, Tommie Camarillo, and David Rico had already entered the building, where they would continue the occupation inside.

Laura Rodriguez is the central figure on the Twenty-fifth Anniversary Poster of Chicano Park. The poster entitled "Laura," by artist Mario Torero in 1995, he also dedicated to Florencio Yescas, the maestro from Mexico who introduced Aztec dancing on this side of the border. The original work is in the permanent collection of the U.S. Library of Congress.

Courtesy of Mario Torero.

Then Laura, chained to the door, informed me that she was going to spend the night there. I agreed to stay with her.

The steps were cold and hard, and I am embarrassed to say I went home around two in the morning. Laura stayed there to make sure that the police did not storm the building and remove those who were inside. What cop was going to rush a building with this little grandmother wearing her trademark bandana while chained to the door? Cops did circle the building and there were several of them parked on the corner, but not one tried to make an arrest.

A Victory for the People

After the occupation, the old Neighborhood House actually did become the Centro de Salud, the health clinic that the community so desperately needed. Laura considered the security of the building her personal responsibility. She lived directly behind the building, on Newtown Street, and could hear the security alarm. If the security alarm went off at two a.m., she would put on her coat over her pajamas and walk to the clinic to see exactly what was going on, her trusted partner Bianco, a German Shepherd, walking at her side.

When the clinic went into operation, Laura was willing to assist with any clinic task. She mopped floors and cleaned toilets countless times to assure that the clinic would be as germ free as any other doctor's office. I remember the smell of Clorox and pine sol in the kitchen, bathrooms, and hallways. Marian Anne Rodriguez collected stories about her grandmother, revealing in one that Laura's cleanliness was also carried out at home with equal enthusiasm—she washed groceries but she also washed the money.

Laura's love and work for the clinic continued in many ways. Along with several other women, she would make what seemed like millions of tamales to be served at the fundraising luncheons held in support of the clinic. These monthly "Spirit of the Barrio Luncheons" extended into the 1990s and attracted a who's who of San Diego's political and social world. One luncheon accommodated 700 guests! It could be said that Laura worked her behind off for the clinic, but that would not be accurate. What Laura did was an act of love, love for the *clínica* of her childhood and love for the Neighborhood House itself.

Laura Receives an Award from the President of the United States

In October 1991, Laura was awarded one "Point of Light" of "One Thousand Points of Light," presented by then President George W. Bush. She had been designated as the 595th Daily Point of Light. President Bush visited the clinic in 1992 to kick off a national childhood immunization campaign and to meet Laura, the clinic's founder. She greeted the President wearing her bandana. This was one of countless awards Laura received for her work in the *barrio*. Her activism for just causes never ended.

Laura Rodriguez passed away on September 17, 1994. Over twenty years have gone by since her death. Laura hasn't been forgotten and can't be forgotten. Her face gazes out from her beloved *barrio* in a Chicano Park mural by artist Mario Torero. A *corrido*, a musical ballad, by Pepe Villarino immortalizes her in song. In 2010, Laura was inducted into the San Diego Women's Museum Hall of Fame.

But it is Laura's love for the children of Logan Heights, a devotion to her community, and her faith that things could be better, that remain her lasting legacy. That legacy lives on at Chicano Park, in the Logan Heights Family Health Center, and in the Laura Rodriguez Elementary School. On October 11, 2007, the San Diego Unified School District held a ribbon-cutting ceremony there. Laura would be very proud to know that a school has been named in her honor. And her Barrio Logan neighbors will forever treasure her as their matriarch.

About the Author:

MARIA E. GARCIA received a BA and MA from SDSU in 1972; as a public school principal, she has implemented successful mentor programs for at-risk students, helped to establish a language-arts magnet program in San Diego, and has actively lobbied for bilingual education. She has received awards, including the San Diego Save Our Heritage (SOHO) preservation award for her interviews and narratives of Logan Heights residents; and in 2016 was inducted into the San Diego County Women's Hall of Fame by the Women's Museum of California.

Faustina Solís, memorial photo; it honored the UCSD Provost at her passing in 2014.

Courtesy of Dan Solis.

FAUSTINA SOLÍS (1923-2013):

UCSD PROVOST, PIONEER IN PUBLIC HEALTH

Educator/Activist for the Underserved

A Mexican Corrido chanting from fire-pits of inequity
A Mayan temple silhouette standing tall and dignified
A vibrant Zócalo even when the goddess of water poured out rain
A farmers' market filled with healthful edibles wild flowers & birds
The Revelle Plaza clapping in the Sixties for the arrival of Peace.

~Teresa Gonzalez-Lee

BY JADE GRIFFIN

Faustina Solís—an educator and pioneer in public health—was the second provost of the University of California, San Diego's Thurgood Marshall College. A UC San Diego ermitus, Solís was also the university's first Latina provost.

One of 12 children of parents who fled from Mexico to escape the chaos of the Revolution in 1911, Solís was born in Compton, California, on April 28, 1923. Her father attended English classes at night school after a 10-hour workday. Solís earned her undergraduate degree in sociology from UCLA, followed by her master's degree in social work from the University of Southern California in 1954.

She served as provost of the university's Thurgood Marshall College (then known as Third College) from 1981 to 1988, and taught at the UCSD School of Medicine beginning in 1971. She established public health coursework for undergraduates and medical students, following many years in social work focused on healthcare for underserved populations. Solís' contributions were honored in 1990 when the Thurgood Marshall Lecture Hall on the UCSD campus was renamed the Faustina F. Solís Lecture Hall.

"Without bold leaders like Faustina Solís, UC San Diego would not be the world-class university it is today," said Chancellor Pradeep K. Khosla. "She was a beloved campus leader who helped establish the foundation of excellence on which the university has been built."

During her years as provost of Marshall College, Solís promoted mentoring programs and aimed to engage new students, particularly from minority backgrounds. She was once quoted about her experiences with her students: "They weren't left to fly by themselves. Freshmen and transfer students can feel very lost in a large university. They need support and assistance in every way possible, whether financial, social, or counseling."

Solís helped solidify Thurgood Marshall College's mission of developing students as scholars and citizens who value social responsibility and academic excellence alike. She also encouraged her students to participate in community outreach efforts in local neighborhoods.

"Faustina Solís was one of the first emerging female leaders at UC San Diego who gave vision and necessity to public service and excellence in undergraduate education," said Allan Havis, Thurgood Marshall College's current provost. "Our college is so honored by her superb contributions and we all benefit by her generous legacy."

Because of her extensive background in public health, Solís was the first full professor without a medical degree or doctorate at the UCSD School of Medicine. She introduced ethnic content into the medical school curriculum, based on her experiences in social work and the development of healthcare services for California's migrant farmworkers. She also served as an assistant chancellor during her time on campus.

Over the course of her career, she served as deputy director of the public health division of the California State Department of Health, and was coordinator and director of the Farmworkers' Health Service Program with the State Department of Public Health from 1967 to 1971. In 1975, she was elected president of the California Association for Maternal and Child Health, the first lay person to head the organization which had traditionally elected physicians to the post. She was also directly involved in the establishment and operation of community health programs for Latinos in San Ysidro and San Diego County, and held consultation appointments in Mexico Venezuela, and Ecuador.

Faustina Solís died on August 4, 2014, in San Diego at the age of 90. She is survived by two brothers, two sisters, and many nieces and nephews. A celebration of her life followed on August 24, which brought together many friends and family to honor her.

In Faustina's honor, Teresa Gonzalez-Lee dedicated this poem to her friend:

Dama de Espíritu/Lady of Light
She had an eloquent voice
when in motion she flowed like river waves
her footprints witnessed loving serpentine steps
empowering others
here and there
mentoring the different
everywhere.

A daughter of migrant workers
in the Californian orchard fields
Faustina's growing up was Providential
a nugget extracted from the entrails of the Earth.

Inspired by her Tarahumara spirit
of Integrative Health and Healing
she carried forth with Olympic impetus
a torch of excellence to the thresholds
of UCSD School of Medicine
awakening thus every conscious soul
to the human dawn of social inclusion.
Rest in Peace. *Dama del Espíritu.*
Lady of the Spirit. Rest in Light.

About the Author:

JADE GRIFFIN, Associate Director for Marketing and Communications; University Communications and Public Affairs at UCSD, with the Solís family, wrote the homage to Faustina Solís, presented at Faustina's Memorial, offered here along with a poetic eulogy by Teresa Gonzalez-Lee.

About the Poet:

DRA. TERESA GONZALEZ-LEE, Ph.D, Literature, UCSD; Chilean-American poet passed away shortly after her friend Faustina, July 2015; born in 1942, she came to the U.S. as a Fulbright Scholar; she credited Faustina for helping her accomplish placing medical terms into Spanish for professional use. She taught English abroad in Korea, followed by Spanish—her mother tongue; lived on the East Coast of the U.S. until she became a professor of languages at MiraCosta College and as a gifted bilingual poet, published her poetry in San Diego.

Marta Sotomayor pictured in 1993, not long before she was invited by President Bill Clinton to serve as a member of the White House Conference on Aging. The photograph was a gift to her son Karl Schlatter.

Courtesy of Ben Zweig, photographer.

MARTA SOTOMAYOR (1932–2013):

FOUNDER, NATIONAL HISPANIC COUNCIL ON AGING

First Chicana Ph.D. in Social Work

BY ANA MARIE PUENTE

When asked in a *La Prensa* interview about the ups and downs in the life of their sister Marta Sotomayor, her sister answered, "She did not have any ups and downs; her life was a straight line. Since she was little she was a leader. At school, at church, at home, she grew up leading others."

Throughout her life, Marta Sotomayor was a steadfast advocate for Latina/os and the elderly, working on their behalf until her passing on June 24, 2013. As a born leader, it is not surprising that she accomplished many "firsts" in her life. In 1955, she was a first Chicana/Latina to receive a bachelor's degree in social work from the University of California at Berkeley and a master's degree at Smith College; she was the first Chicana professor of social work at San Diego State University; and in1973 she became the first Chicana Ph.D. in the United States when she graduated from the School of Social Work at the University of Denver. She also wrote the first doctoral dissertation on the Hispanic elderly. She was lauded for it in 2009 when the dean praised "her leadership in advocating for the vulnerable and oppressed" throughout her career.

Marta Sotomayor was born in Mexico City, the youngest of five sisters who grew up in San Diego. When she was eleven years old, her family decided to return to the United States where their mother was a teacher. In school, Marta excelled in math and spelling, although she did not speak English well at first. It was in high school where she experienced injustice in the selection of awards. Although Marta had one of the highest grade point averages upon graduation, she was bypassed because she was Mexican American and the scholarship was given to an Anglo American student. Marta was hurt and disappointed, but decided to prove to herself and others that she was a deserving student. With the support of her parents, with various stipends, and with money she made working during vacations, she went on to graduate from the UC Berkeley School of Social Work in 1955.

Marta returned home to San Diego with a desire to help her community. As a young girl she had learned the value of education from her mother. As a student at a missionary school, education was profoundly impressed on her mother and her sisters. At the same time, Marta understood from her upbringing the importance of helping others. She began to work for a short time as a social worker. She joined an advocacy group called IMPACT, composed of community leaders representing sectors of San Diego County, among them, Councilman Leon Williams, Gracia Molina de Pick, Petra Glenn, and others. During this time she was also involved as a supporter of Cesar Chavez and the United Farm Workers' grape strike. Some of these experiences early in her career set her on a course of becoming a tireless advocate for Chicano/Latino communities with a voice for social justice.

Even so, Marta always felt the need to pursue higher education. In addition, she wanted to reach a silent impoverished group: the Latino elderly, especially women who as widows and homemakers ended up with little or no benefits.

She won a scholarship to Smith College in Massachusetts, and in 1960 went on receive a master's in social work. Today she is considered one of their most distinguished alumnae. In 2008, she was awarded the Day–Garrett Award. To that end, Smith College established the Marta Sotomayor Fellowship to address issues regarding racism and other aspects of social oppression.

While Marta was doing an internship in mental health at a Detroit hospital, she was introduced to a young handsome accountant of German descent, Edwin Schlatter. Their friendship blossomed into a serious relationship, which lead to marriage. Happily married, Marta wanted to return home to San Diego where her parents and sisters lived. Several years later, Edwin and Marta had a little boy, Karl Schlatter, their only child.

A new career developed for her at San Diego State University where Marta became the first Chicana to teach in the School of Social Work. This was also a period of activism and she was able to contribute her time to other causes such as working for *Trabajadores de la Raza* and advocating for Chicano Studies on the SDSU campus.

Her persistent drive to reach out to a broader group in her professional career led her to apply for a scholarship at the University of Denver's Ph.D. program. She thus became the first Chicana/Latina in the United States to earn a doctorate in social work in 1973. As a doctoral student, she conducted her fieldwork as a Fulbright Scholar in Bogotá, Colombia, studying its higher education system. This time, she traveled alone with her son and mother while her husband stayed behind. The couple had decided to continue their personal and professional careers apart as they were moving in different directions. Marta was now a student, a single mom, and a devoted daughter.

Dr. Sotomayor was honored in 2009 by her alma mater, the University of Denver Graduate School of Social Work, with its first Notable Scholar Award. The award honors doctoral graduates whose social work scholarship and leadership represent excellence and includes the generation of innovation and evidence-based practices and advancement of social justice. In presenting the award to Dr. Sotomayor, Dean James Herbert Williams noted that Marta wrote the school's first doctoral dissertation on the Hispanic elderly. He also cited the impact of a book she later co-authored, *Elderly Latinos: Issues and Solutions for the 21st Century*. As a doctoral student at the University of Denver's Graduate School of Social Work (GSSW), Marta was lauded for conducting her fieldwork as a Fulbright Scholar.

During the 1970s, Marta's life continued to move forward in the direction she had planned and dreamed. She became Dean and Associate Professor at the University of Houston's Graduate School of Social Work. From there she moved to Washington, D.C. She later served as a senior policy advisor to the U.S. Department of Health and Human Services (HHS) Secretary's Task Force on Minority Health.

Dr. Sotomayor served on several national boards, including Americans for Democratic Action and the National Council of La Raza (NCLR). She became Chair of NCLR's Executive Board during a difficult period when NCLR was transitioning from a predominantly male board to a half male/half female board. During her tenure as Chair of the Board, Marta saw NCLR grow from an organizational force for social movement into a solid institution. Having had one of the longest terms on the NCLR Board, Marta decided it was time to move on; she resigned from the board and went on to work full time with the National Hispanic Council on Aging (NHCOA). Marta was one of its founders, "a group of Hispanic researchers and educators who conceived of it in the late seventies to enhance the quality of life of older adults and their most pressing needs."

Dr. Sotomayor's involvement with the National Hispanic Council on Aging (NHCOA)—a membership-based, nonprofit advocacy organization concerned with all issues affecting the Latino elderly, families, and communities—began in its formative years. She started out on a volunteer basis as the president of the board of directors, leading the organization through many challenges associated with its growth and development. In 1978, during a crucial period of unrest, Marta called on President Jimmy Carter for a Conference on Hispanics, "And if we don't get it," she added, "We'll call for one ourselves."

Dr. Sotomayor's rise to advisor for President Clinton's White House Conference on Aging in the 1990s began some ten years before he invited her to serve on the committee. Her U.S. Federal Government service took shape first as an assistant to the director of Alcohol Drug Abuse and Mental Health (ADAMHA) and later as director of the Agency's Office of Special Populations. In 1979, Dr. Sotomayor was appointed to the U.S. Commission to UNESCO. By the 1980s, she played a key role coordinating the resettlement of 125,000 Cuban refugees. She became senior policy advisor to the HHS Secretary's Task Force on Minority Health , while she served on several national boards.

After retiring from federal government service, Dr. Sotomayor became the organization's full-time president and chief executive officer. During her tenure as president, Dr. Sotomayor helped expand the organization's chapters. In 1991, she assisted with founding the Texas Hispanic Council on Aging (TXHCOA). Under Dr. Sotomayor's leadership, the NHCOA conducted several studies to help elucidate elderly Latino issues. Among these are "Elderly Latinos: Issues and Solutions for the Next Century" and "In Triple Jeopardy, Aged, Hispanic Women: Insights and Experiences." Also under her leadership, NHCOA was able to purchase and develop a senior housing facility in Washington, D.C. In 1996–1997, Dr. Sotomayor was invited by President Clinton to serve as a member of the White House Conference on Aging Policy Board, ensuring Latino elderly concerns were addressed.

In her later years, Dr. Sotomayor lived in Corpus Christi, Texas, close to her son, daughter-in-law, and grandsons. In between spending time with her son and grandchildren, she established the Latino Education Project, the LEP, a community-based, nonprofit, advocate organization promoting problem solving through coalition and partnership building. One of several successful projects conducted by LEP was addressing the high rates of diabetes among midlife and older Latinos in Corpus Christi. The activities were conducted, in part, with a grant from the Centers for Disease Control and Prevention REACH (Racial Ethnic Approaches to Community Health) project. The LEP project is published in an article titled "Building Community Capacity for Health Promotion in a Hispanic Community." In 2013, Dr. Sotomayor was honored as "One of Corpus Christi's Greatest Treasures," an award by the City of Corpus Christi Senior Community Services Division and the Mayor's Council on Aging.

In reality, Dr. Marta Sotomayor never fully retired. Besides teaching at San Diego State, she taught at other universities: San Jose State University School of Social Work; University of Denver; Howard University School of Social Work in Washington, D.C; and the Baylor School of Medicine in Houston. Her writings were based on scholarly research studies, with thoughtful analysis and innovations contributing to the body of knowledge about the Chicana/Chicano experience.

In Corpus Christi, she continued to look for better housing for the Latina and Latino elderly and disabled. Her main concerns were always for this neglected group of society. She was former dean and an associate professor at the University of Houston's Graduate School of Social Work at the time of her passing. Marta Sotomayor's illustrious career speaks strongly of her generosity and activism for social justice.

For me, more than an aunt, Marta was a cheerful encouraging person who gave me hope for the future. She was a role model for hundreds of women who sought to improve conditions for Mexican Americans.

About the Author:

ANA MARIE PUENTE, Connie Puente's niece, retired in 2012 with the rank of Captain (06) after a 30 year career with the U.S. Public Health Service/Commissioned Corps. She resides in Washington, D.C. She received an Exceptional Capability Promotion and the HHS Secretary's Award for Distinguished Service (under President Clinton). She has also collected data for the Migrant Health Program, authoring an agency publication *Assuring a Healthy Future Along the U.S.-Mexico Border*, and managed projects on farmworker pesticide exposure in the border area, and in 2004 presented at the United Nations Commission on Sustainable Development in New York.

CHAPTER 2

HERMINIA ACOSTA ENRIQUE

AIDA MANCILLAS

DELIA MORENO

DELIA RAVELO

LIN ROMERO

CHARLOTTE HERNANDEZ–TERRY

CHAPTER 2

Mujeres Presentes:
Women Who Paved the Way in Art and Culture

This chapter continues to recognize *Mujeres Presentes*, that is, women who passed away and left a legacy in the arts. Their actions in the 1960s and 70s deserve recognition for accomplishing something truly monumental at a given moment in history when women were not recognized for their art. Chicano movement visual and performing artists, challenged the *status quo* for their basic rights, eventually questioning the colonial mentality that left out Mexican American history and culture in schools, colleges, and media.

Soon after, Chicana artists asserted their own opposition in art, poetry, murals, music, and *teatro*. It was a new day. This form of resistance women understood. Chicanas actively supported the takeover of the land in their neighborhood for Chicano park under the Coronado Bridge, for a cultural center, a clinic, and a senior center in their neighborhood.

In 1968, two of the first Chicana artists/activists were Herminia Enrique and Delia Moreno. Both of these women took part in the growing desire by Chicano artists for a culture center at the Ford Building in Balboa Park, now the Aerospace Museum, a temporary space used by Salvador Torres that he and others hoped to acquire. The women wanted a place to perform and teach their unique art forms, *danza y musica*. Herminia used the space for workshops and rehearsals, teaching dance that evolved into the Ballet Folklorico en Aztlán with an exploration into the people's historical Mexican and Indigenous roots.

Delia Moreno, a talented musician and single mother, saw a way out of the confines of daily struggle. She taught her daughters musical performance, and in 1968 joined with other artists/activists at the Ford Building. The artists called themselves *Toltecas en Aztlán*, eventually establishing a permanent space as the Centro Cultural de la Raza. From there, the Trio Moreno blossomed, and the Ballet Folklorico and other Chicana artistic developments grew.

At that time the women, a few among several men, are to be commended for acting for change, rebelling against exclusion, a condition that kept them homebound, and for taking advantage of the opportunity to do something about it. Such qualities represent the courage that helped them win victories that led to the founding of a permanent space at the Centro Cultural de la Raza, a venue that also inspired poetry.

Poet Lin Romero, one of the first "Taco Shop Poets" prospered at the Centro Cultural. She challenged the people to recognize their Indigenous roots, "Planta Mas! Raza." In spoken word and in a first Chicana chap book published by the Centro, Lin spoke to women of their high culture and new possibilities to celebrate it, to build, to plant, and to fight back against injustices.

In 1965, with the fervor surrounding the United Farm Workers Movement— followed by the high school walkouts in 1968 called the East L.A. Blowouts—in 1969 several Chicanas joined the National Chicano Youth Liberation Conference, and traveled to Denver. Controversial as they were, Chicanas instigated dialogue about their condition as women experiencing sexism in a male dominated society and *machismo*, within the Chicano Movement. Although different sides did not agree on all points, new debates were initiated that changed the lives of many. In San Diego, women began to break out of their expected roles, entering the new energy that filled the air with protest music, dance, poetry, *teatro*, and visual art.

In 1971, Chicanas participated in the First National Chicana Conference in Houston, Texas, and in 1975, in the United Nations International Women's Conference in Mexico City. San Diego women traveled together, among them, Charlotte Hernandez-Terry, who had touched lives at home, but like many other Chicanas she now traveled for the first time to other cities. A single mother, she left her six daughters well cared for at home while she journeyed to reach larger audiences with her musical compositions. Her resounding messages, "Living in the Barrio" and "Mama works hard everyday/Mama works hard for her weekly pay," belted out a kind of chant in her passionate vibrato, to the beat of her guitar. She eventually traveled to Washington D. C. for the bicentennial and to the Women's Folk Art Festival in Lansing, Michigan, spreading the message of Chicanas everywhere.

At San Diego State University, Delia Ravelo, a co-founder of Teatro Chicana, with her friend, Felicitas Nuñez, brought new life to agitprop theatre by introducing Chicanas' struggles against injustice to the public. In 1970, Delia wrote the first skit "Chicana Goes to College," performed at SDSU for a mother's tea, introducing their parents to the new life and new ideas that forever changed them. From there, the women in the theatre group went on to form the Teatro de las Chicanas, an innovative art form that gave women a voice and a platform for issues dear to them, addressing Chicana poverty, the need for better education and healthcare, touching the lives of many young women away at college for the first time.

Visual artist, Aida Mancillas, left a strong mark at the Centro Cultural as well as the entire city of San Diego in the visual arts. In 1985, she was one of the first Chicanas to exhibit her art at the Centro when few women were acknowledged. In response to the Border Arts Workshop/Taller de Arte Fronteriza (BAW/TAF) a Chicano exhibit, in 1990, she founded a multi ethnic women's group, a collective of artists, writers, and teachers. Members of the group participated in the making of the large-scale women's installation/exhibition, *La Vecindad*, a multi-media visual and performing arts production at the Centro Cultural that eventually went on tour. Over a twenty-year period, Aida taught, exhibited, co-founded Las Comadres, and became president of the Board of Directors at the Centro. She crossed boundaries into the broader community as co-designer of North Park's community children's play yard and co-designed the 400-foot Vermont Street Bridge in Hillcrest. As a gallery co-owner and innovator, Aida became a Commissioner of the Arts in San Diego. An LGBT activist, she became known throughout San Diego and in the arts community. Hillcrest residents still refer to her as "One of the Women who Changed San Diego and Our Neighborhood."

Chicanas did not wait to ask what to do or how to do it. In the late sixties, with the support of one another, these artists/activists designed their own dreams in the visual and performing arts, exhibiting and performing art of struggle and revolution, at the Centro Cultural, Chicano Park, Voz Alta, or Taco Shops. For the first time in history, new art forms and new possibilities unfolded for women. Since then, a new generation of Chicana artists continue to gather, to create, to rehearse, perform, and perfect their craft.

Heminia Acosta Enrique, c1939, in her "Hollywood audition photo," San Antonio, Texas, before she married.

Courtesy of Viviana Enrique Acosta.

HERMINIA ACOSTA ENRIQUE (1919–2009):

MAESTRA DE BALLET FOLKLÓRICO

Tecihtzin Wise Woman Storyteller, Spoke Out for Indigenous Rights and Culture

BY VIVIANA C. ENRIQUE ACOSTA

Herminia Acosta Enrique Tecihtzin has been honored in many ways for her nine decades of activism preserving the Indigenous arts and culture as an Indigenous elder role model. For these enduring qualities, she was awarded the prestigious Jesse Bernard Wise Woman Award from the Center for Women Policy Studies in Washington, D.C., especially for her life's work in social advocacy, and for teaching folkloric dance and the arts. In 2004, she was inducted into the San Diego County Women's Hall of Fame. Many of her photos and files of her accomplishments over the years at the Centro Cultural de La Raza in San Diego are housed in the Special Collections Library at the University of California at Santa Barbara.

Herminia Acosta Enrique Tecihtzin has been a lifelong culture and social justice activist, preserving and teaching Indigenous history through culture, dance, and the arts. Tlatoani Tecihtzin, her Indigenous name, has been recognized as the Chicano Nation Elder and Storyteller. Since childhood in the 1920s, Tlatoani Tecihtzin creatively inspired her family and community, taught folklore, designed costumes, composed plays, and produced local musical theatre productions. Today, she is best known as the founder of the Ballet Folklórico en Aztlán (1967) and as a cofounder of San Diego's Centro Cultural de la Raza (1969).

Herminia Enrique grew up in San Antonio, Texas, where she faced blatant racism in the elementary schools at an early age, whether as a judgment about the food she ate, the way she dressed, the way she spoke, or the way she wore her hair. She recalled that students at her elementary school were not allowed to speak their own language and would be fined up to 25 cents if they spoke Spanish. If it got to that point, the parents were called in and asked to explain why their children were continuing to speak Spanish when they had been informed the language was forbidden to be spoken in the schools. Herminia further described the treatment of their food—the tortillas, rice, and beans that their parents had lovingly provided for them to eat for lunch—as cultural culinary racism. "If the teachers caught us eating tortillas, they would take them away from us and throw them in the trash," she recalled.

The saddest intrusion of all was when she was only six years old, a story she told to a narrator from the Media Arts Center for the San Diego Teen Producers Project. The team video documented her story, "Defendiendo Mi Cultura," in Tecihtzin's *Voices of Change*. She recalled when one day as a child, the students had to stay inside the cafeteria because it was raining. Herminia remembers her teacher walking up and down the aisles of the long tables where the students were cutting paper designs. When the teacher got to Herminia's table she stopped. There she began interrogating Herminia as if testing her ability to answer in English. "Where are we?" she asked. "Texas," Herminia answered. "And where in Texas?" Herminia answered again, "San Antonio." As the teacher asked each question, she grabbed the long, single braid Herminia wore, and gave it a tug, as she challenged her to answer another question. "And where is Texas?" Herminia answered her correctly, "In the United States." The teacher persisted, "And where are you now?" When Herminia answered, "In the United States," the teacher said, "Right! Then we're not in Mexico." She laughed as she pulled Herminia's hair and tried to cut off her braid with scissors. When the scissors did not work well enough, she asked the students for other pairs of scissors and continued cutting while the students began to laugh along with the teacher. After trying three pairs, "She cut off my braid and threw it in the trash." Herminia was mortified.

The memory stayed with her and she felt the same *sentimiento* and anguish she described as the "San Antonio Incident" to the youth videographers, as they tried to keep a dry eye during the videotaping of the project. "It hurt me so much," Tecihtzin intoned, as she struggled to hold back a tear, bringing all on the set (which happened to be at the Centro Cultural de la Raza) to an even more alert attention. She implored with that single sentence a sentiment that "such an act should never have happened to me, a young girl, and much less to the other youth." It was because of Herminia's social activism efforts that such racist behavior became known and considered unconscionable. Herminia said that her mother, Carolina, consoled her that day long ago by "fixing my hair, cutting it evenly, and making me a new dress."

Tecihtzin never truly grew her hair long again after the San Antonio Incident, as a reminder and marker of what had happened. She wanted to ensure that those who chose to wear long braids should be able to do so without ridicule. That incident became a cultural conundrum for the community to coalesce over.

whether or not to maintain their Indigenous identity and, if in doing so, they should be able to retain self-respect and not have to completely assimilate into a racist regime that could, with such facility and ease, cut off a child's braid.

Tecihtzin, or as she became known, "Wise Woman Storyteller," counseled many and held council with many Indigenous Elders, offering insight for the journey ahead through 2012. She spoke of her years of journey on the Red Road—the right life path— and of enduring the challenges of a dark-skinned woman. She was adopted into the Raven Clan and the stories she told, and the ones that can still be told about her legacy, could fill several books. During an interview, her philosophy became evident as she said, "We have sun, but we also have shadow," reminding her audience that "you have to make your own way out of the shadow." She then laughed heartily when she said, "And you have to do it on your own. No one is going to do it for you."

Herminia and Julio M. Enrique and family came to California in 1967 at the height of the U.S. Civil Rights Movement. In San Diego she became one of the most influential activists of the time. She and her children were also active participants in the founding and arts production of the Centro Cultural de la Raza. Her lifelong social advocacy work has been preserving culture through dance, poetry, writing, and performance art as well as actively engaging in her own culture. She gave birth to and raised 11 children, many of whom have continued with her work of preserving Indigenous culture.

One of the areas Herminia especially enjoyed was teaching the significance of the different regions of Mexico and what they signify in Mexican Indigenous history. The *vestuario* or vestments of Danza de los Quetzales she often referred to, signify the freedom the Indigenous people are seeking. "The fringe over their faces will not go away until all the Indigenous people are free," she told the narrator during the video shoot. Until then we are all behind bars; the significance of the gold fringe also represents the greed of the gold the Europeans were seeking on Indian land. Her name Tecihtzin also means Wise Old Craftswoman, and helps create a proud identity, one that stands unwavering in community awareness.

Señora Enrique, Doña Enrique, or Tecihtzin challenges everyone to participate in change. "You can't pretend everything is all right when it's not." She reminds us that there are two sides to everything: "You can be light and carefree if you want to, but this is not the way to fight injustice." She added emphatically, "Get involved!"

In 1978, she was invited to participate in the Smithsonian's Folklife Program in Washington, D.C., with storytelling sessions on Mexican folktales, myths, legends, and superstitions. She was also a facilitator of Mexican games and participated in exhibits on the many varieties of chile and salsa, some derived from her own culture. She was guest lecturer at the Houston Museum of Art, offering insight into the last emperor of Michoacán for their exhibit. Also, she was a volunteer, working as a Chicano Federation board member, the National Health Systems Agency, the National Council on Aging, and The Esperanza Peace and Justice Center Board of Directors. Besides that, she has been involved in numerous local and international theatrical, dance, and storytelling organizations.

Tlatoani Tecihtzin is the author and illustrator of *Chia: A Powerful Recuerdo* (1996); several research studies about folkloric dance and Indigenous culture and history; and numerous short plays, songs, and performance art works. She was also recognized as a brilliant installation artist, and for her work with clay and pottery, as well as *couture*, being the originator of the "Sun Dress." She was known as a skilled designer and visual artist, able to quickly sketch, draw, paint, and turn those sketches and designs into 3D manifestations of costumes or sculptures materialized with fabric and clay from her surrounding landscape. She was a frequent speaker in San Diego, California, and San Antonio, Texas, about Southwest folktales, traditional morality tales, and the history of Indigenous rights and ceremony, providing insight and counsel to activists across the world. She was a keynote speaker for many Chicano symposiums and for Chicano Park Day, San Diego. She has also been featured in videos and has taught folkloric dance at the San Diego State University Chicana and Chicano Studies department.

She is honored annually by the Ballet Folklórico en Aztlán's production of The Herminia Tribute, Flor y Canto. Tlatoani Tecihtzin has shared her stories and wisdom in libraries, schools, Old Town, theatres, the Centro Cultural de la Raza, and Chicano Park. She has offered her energy, dancing in the local Sundance Ceremony. She was always, and continues to be, a role model for artists and activists organizing and participating in Chicano rights marches and ceremonies. Tlatoani Tecihtzin has passed on cultural treasures to generations and has helped to create and preserve a proud identity for thousands.

About the Author:

VIVIANA C. ENRIQUE ACOSTA, Herminia's daughter; Artistic Director of the Centro Cultural de la Raza in 1999; promoter of Danza Indigena, Ballet Folklorico en Aztlán; and known as San Diego's only *Voladora*; she runs her own studio, Muévete Dance Studio; and in 2015 she was inducted into the San Diego County Women's Hall of Fame as Cultural Guardian and Historian by the Women's Museum of California.

AIDA MANCILLAS (1953–2009):

PROFESSOR, COMMUNITY ARTIST, LGBT ACTIVIST

Creative Force That Believed in Merging Art and Life

BY BLANCA GONZALEZ

Written for the San Diego Union-Tribune, Feb. 16, 2009.

A creative force and vocal advocate for public art, Aida Mancillas left an imprint throughout the community.

From the cobalt-blue Vermont Street pedestrian bridge in Hillcrest to her work on an affordable-housing complex in Poway and her dedication to local arts organizations, Ms. Mancillas' endeavors reflected her belief in merging art and life.

A past commissioner of the San Diego Commission for Arts and Culture and past president of Centro Cultural de la Raza, Ms. Mancillas also helped start Public Address, a public-art advocacy group, and Las Comadres, a multinational women's collective of artists, educators, and critics.

Ms. Mancillas died of brain cancer February 3 at her North Park home. She was 55. Friends and colleagues said she was passionate about the concept of "the citizen artist." She believed arts could and should be a vital part of community planning and development.

Local artist and teacher Ruth Wallen said Ms. Mancillas fervently believed that "artists have the ability to imagine different futures and the ability to symbolically express those possibilities."

In her weblog, Ms. Mancillas wrote: "The artist is an important contributor to society because we help people find the feast. It's our role, and it's an important one.

We're not entertainers, although some of what we do will entertain. We're not gadflies, although some of our work will prod and poke. We're not decorators, although some of our work will dazzle with its skill. We are meaning shapers in a world that desperately needs us."

Aida Mancillas, community activist, and author of an essay "The Citizen Artist," in the book with the same title.

Courtesy of Andrea Villa.

While painting was her main medium for several years, Ms. Mancillas was equally creative in writing, sculpture, and public-art design.

She was awarded a $20,000 artist fellowship from the National Endowment for the Arts in 1991. After working as a solitary artist, she began to work collaboratively and with community groups and agencies on large-scale public-art projects.

In the mid-1990s, Ms. Mancillas was part of a trio of artists, which included Gwen Gomez and Lynn Susholtz, commissioned to meld art into the refurbished Vermont Street pedestrian bridge. The elevated walkway that unites

University Heights and Hillcrest features quotations about walking from such famous people as "Dr. Seuss" and architect Irving Gill. The team also designed pillars at each end to complement the architectural styles of the two neighborhoods the project bridged. The project was honored with an Orchid Award from the American Institute of Architects and an award from the American Planners Association.

Other projects include one known as The Playground of 100 Frogs, the first phase of a major redesign of an urban park in the North Park area, and the design of a playground and plaza for an affordable-housing development in Poway.

Ms. Mancillas was proud to work on projects that connected people to the spaces where they lived, said Andrea Villa, her partner of three years. "She was a visionary. She was always creating, designing, and coming up with new ideas," Villa said.

In addition to her work with various city and arts groups, she was a state representative to Marriage Equality USA and a member of the Latino Services Advisory Committee of the San Diego LGBT Center.

Aida Mancillas was born February 28, 1953, in Los Angeles to Manuel and Consuelo Mancillas. The family moved to Oceanside when her father was stationed at Camp Pendleton. She graduated from Oceanside High School in 1971. She received a bachelor's degree in visual arts from Humboldt State University in 1985 and a master's degree from the University of California, San Diego in 1988.

Editors's note: Aida was survived by a son, Eamonn Doyle.

About the Author:

BLANCA GONZALEZ, community opinion editor for the Union Tribune San Diego. In 2010 she was a contributor to Sign-on-San Diego and before that was as assistant business director for the *Sacramento Bee Newspaper*. She is on the Board of Directors of the National Association for College Admission Counseling; and has served with others on the Chicano/Latino Advisory Committee to the San Diego Union-Tribune.

Delia Moreno (right), performing with The Trio Moreno, including daughters, Delia (Chica) Moreno (left), and Maria Moreno (center) MEChA-UFW rally; Indio, Ca., 1973.

Courtesy of Carlos LeGerrette.

DELIA MORENO (1928–2013):

CHICANA WARRIOR, FOUNDER OF THE TRIO MORENO

More Than a Musician, She Was an Ethnomusicologist

BY GLORIA ANDRADE

This is an open letter to the Spirit of Delia Moreno.

Although we never met, while researching your story, I learned of your incredible dedication to *El Movimiento Chicano*. You came to San Diego with all the armor needed for the fight ahead: a woman of strong and spiritual energy; a single mother who carried the values of love for community with an awareness of our ancestor's sacrifices for a better life; and cognizant of the essential need for future generations to know their history. You used your artistic and musical skills as weapons to fight against the injustices and inequalities of our civil rights. When the call went out for warriors, you were ready to join without hesitation. This was your fate, and you are one of the many unsung Chicana heroes who deserve acknowledgment and appreciation for your outstanding contributions and sacrifice. With gratitude and respect, I begin your story of a Chicana Warrior: the right woman, in the right place, at the right time.

Delia Parra Moreno was definitely the right woman. She was born on November 9, 1928. She was the daughter of Francisco Meza Moreno and Gertrudis Parra of Sonora, Mexico, who raised her and her six siblings on their Buena Vista Ranch, just 35 miles outside of Tucson, Arizona. Early on, Delia demonstrated her gift and love for music and learned to play the guitar as a child, although the guitar was not considered then an acceptable instrument for a girl. Delia looks back at when "it was a sin for women to play guitars. At that time, it was more ladylike to play the piano." Delia recalls that she was criticized "for walking around with a guitar in my hand, which I did constantly back in the early 40s." And so, she says, "I was gossiped about a lot."

It is apparent that Delia was a bit of a rebel, which served her well in her adult years. As an adult, she would use this gift to pursue her personal goals. Besides that, she was raising two daughters on her own, Delia (la Chica), and

Maria Francisca. As the Trio Moreno, the three actively fought for social justice to support the idea of Chicano self-determination in the Chicano Movement. However, long before that, Delia was perfecting her craft in Tucson at the Blue Moon Ballroom with musicians like Henry Corral and Lalo Guerrero, the famous composer of Mexican American music known as the "Father of Chicano Music."

In the late 1960s and 70s, Delia, along with others, found herself immersed in a feeling of general unrest regarding the discrimination exhibited against people of color in the United States. The Black community was marching and demonstrating for civil rights and equality. In the Chicano community, Cesar Chavez and Dolores Huerta were organizing farmworkers to unionize and establish a strong unified voice in order to change the poor working condition for those who labored in the fields. At the same time, a disproportionate number of Chicanos were fighting and dying in the Vietnam War. It seemed that those who were labeled as the nation's "minorities" were considered expendable. Delia Moreno was ready at the right time and able to be of service.

In the 1960s, it was clear that change had to come or the United States would not have peace in the homeland, at least not until justice was served. On the campus of San Diego State University, a student group that called itself MEChA—Movimiento Estudiantil Chicano de Aztlán—organized demonstrations to demand justice for the presently unheard voices of the people. Even though Delia was not a student, she decided to join this extraordinary group of highly motivated students speaking out for justice. Her enthusiasm was matched by the many young activists who wanted change.

In 1969, the center of action was the Ford Building in Balboa Park. Delia was about to enter that world. The artistic/activist movement leader, Salvador Torres, had just returned home as a college graduate in the arts, and was given permission to use the building (now the Aerospace Museum). Described in the 1985 Centro Cultural book, *Made in Aztlán*, "By 1969, the Ford Building became a major center of activities for San Diego's Chicano artists. What had been offered by the city as a temporary studio space for six months had been transformed into a focus of cultural activity." There were painting and culture studios where artists worked into the night. Rehearsal spaces soon blossomed for ballet folklórico, teatro, music, and other classes in performing arts.

Delia and her daughters began to use the building as a rehearsal space for the Trio Moreno. The group of artists/activists banded together to formally organize under the name Toltecas en Aztlán, using the term to indicate the indigenous group, master craftsmen of precolonial Mexico. It was an appropriate title for the artists, credited to the poet Alurista, author of the definitive *Plan Espiritual de Aztlán*. Another artist, Guillermo Aranda— famous for his murals at San Diego State University, the Centro Cultural de la Raza, and Chicano Park—invited Delia to be a member of the notable arts group Los Toltecas de Aztlán, which soon became the title of her signature song.

The green light was flashing, and it was obvious that Delia was at the right place to let her positive energy soar. Delia's idea to include her daughters in this historical undertaking, teaching the girls to play guitar and sing, was a labor of love. In 2012, both daughters were able to speak about their growing up. Maria talked about how she and her sister Chica, also named Delia—after her mother—always had music throughout the house; they went to sleep and woke up to all different kinds of music—a beautiful family tradition they shared and enjoyed.

The daughters also tell this story. The work of the Trio was a priority. They were expected to be ready for a performance, even if it meant missing school for the day. "The schoolwork could always be made up" Maria recalls in an interview with Sonia Lopez. Their mother saw her musical talent as a tool or, better yet, a weapon to be used in the fight for self-determination and Chicano Power. She stressed acknowledging past struggles and sacrifices made by their ancestors. She encouraged everyone to know their family history and that of their homeland. Chica remembers visiting a soldier of the Mexican Revolution with her mother. "He gave my mother a Mexican flag with the bullet holes from the war." The Trio Moreno performed everywhere they could during peak moments in Chicano Movement history "to inspire the people working for justice and equality and to educate future generations so they would know what had gone before them," so no one could become complacent about past struggles as some still exist today.

Delia began offering guitar music lessons to other youth. One of her students was Richard Saiz from SDSU. Richard remembers performing with Delia at the opening of the Community Center in Logan Heights. He recalls Delia's generous spirit, pride in her Mexican heritage, especially as a Catholic woman dedicated to her faith. He remembers, "Delia had so much heart; although a very traditional feminine woman, she had a strong attitude and political beliefs." Delia taught Richard how to play Huapango music, and he tried his hand at composing songs because of her. He said, "Delia's sense of identity as a Chicana didn't just happen because of the Chicano Movement, it was already within her."

As editor of *La Verdad* newspaper, Ricardo honored the work of El Trio Moreno in an article. "Los Toltecas en Aztlán, the La Verdad staff, and the Chicano community are fortunate to have a group like El Trio Moreno . . . that uses culture as a weapon towards Chicano self-determination."

More than just a performer, Delia was engaged at every level to make sure the dream of a cultural center became a reality. She attended city council meetings to fight for the Ford Building. When that was no longer attainable, she helped inaugurate the new space the city offered them in Balboa Park. Another excerpt from *La Verdad*, captures the spirit of the Trio's participation, artistic talents, and volunteer work: "These three Chicanas were deeply involved in the organizing necessary to build a successful Centro Cultural de la Raza. At last Sunday's Inauguration (1971) they each displayed beautiful art work . . . made with their hands while also entertaining the more than 500 Chicanos. The Trio now works full time at the Centro Cultural. Delia "grande" conducts a guitar workshop from 9 to 5 on Wednesday. Maria and "Chica" perform secretarial duties."

The Trio Moreno were important members of *La Verdad's* newspaper staff: they wrote articles, typed copy, and helped lay out the issues. "Very few individuals or groups contribute more to the unifying of our Raza than las tres Morenos," La Verdad continued. "Wherever the Morenos have gone, they have left a message deeply implemented in the hearts of La Raza. Singing and playing their own songs like "La Bandera de Aztlán," "Mañanitas de Azltán," "Ya Llegaron Los Toltecas," and many more." Linda LeGerrette recalls the music jam sessions at her home with Richard and her husband Carlos, "I mostly remember her spiritual side." It seems Delia had great wisdom and insight.

In the peak year of the Chicano Movement, "El Trio Moreno has demonstrated through music and struggle of our people our willingness to survive culturally, politically, economically, and socially. Their hardworking spirit should serve as an example to all of us." To add to the many accolades showered on the Trio, a highest of compliments came from Professor of Chicano Music at SDSU, José "Pepe" Villarino. "Delia Moreno was more than a musician," he said, "She was an ethnomusicologist."

The 1990s took Delia back to her hometown of Tucson. Apparently, she tried to bring some of the fervent spirit of her activism in San Diego to the people of her home state. In 1991, it seems that she wanted to fight for a cultural center there too. Her dream was "to help create a center of international culture" in her hometown. In an interview with an Associated Press reporter (*Prescott Courier*, December 20, 1991), she said that she already had her eye on a building "in the Old Pueblo to be used as a hub of art and music classes, art exhibitions, poetry readings, concerts, theater, and other activities." Soon after her 1990s visit to Tucson, Delia returned to San Diego.

The Trio as Delia dreamed it, had to change as times changed. Both of her daughters were now married, and Delia was a grandmother. La Chica and her family remained in San Diego, and Delia resided with them. Maria had since moved to Nebraska where she met and married a young lawyer and had two sons, while Chica and her husband cared for her mother who remained in their home until the day she died.

In 2000, Delia was honored at the 30th anniversary of the Centro Cultural de la Raza, where she performed her signature song, "Ya Llegaron Los Toltecas en Aztlán." Introduced by Viviana Enrique, the artistic director, Delia sang out her words and music with passion and sentiment for a time past. Surely, memories flooded as she performed her composition, and one can only imagine her now in the way she used to dress, as the AP article described her, "in a sequined dress radiating a thousand colors."

In 2013, the news came of her passing. She was 85 years old. A *corrido* was dedicated to Delia by Dr. Villarino, "Homenaje a Nuestra Amiga Delia Moreno." In it, he laments how the people "went on their knees for their sister who they loved so much" when they heard the news of her passing. Among the many were her good friends, Ramon "Chunky" and Isabel Sanchez. Dr. Villarino leaves us with his final words to Delia, "You are waiting for us with your guitar in hand en *La Gloria.*"

This is the partial story of a faithful Chicana Warrior in the fight for human rights and self-determination in the Chicana Movement. She is just one of so many who lived and fought for a better world so that future generations could stand proudly and continue carrying the torch—Delia Moreno ¡Presente!

About the Author:

GLORIA ANDRADE grew up in San Diego, attended Kearney High School, and graduated from the University of California at Riverside; known for her innovative research on Teresa Urrea, "La Niña de Cabora," co-authored with Richard Rodriguez, and published in 1973 in *Quinto Sol*; she is an intern at the Centro Cultural; a member of Danza Azteca under Mario Aguilar; and she is also Chair of a committee to preserve the original Logan Heights Library as a historical site.

TEATRO DE LAS CHICANAS

Se Presentan

3 de Mayo, Jueves
Montezuma Hall
11-12 noon
San Diego State

Teatro de las Chicanas Poster, c1973. (From left to right) Top row: Delia Ravelo, co-founder; Maria Pedroza, and Lupe Perez. Bottom row: Felicitas Nuñez (co-founder) and Peggy Garcia.

Courtesy of SDSU, Special Collections Library, Chicana/Chicano Archives; Sonia Lopez Papers.

DELIA RAVELO (1952–2000):

CO-FOUNDER, TEATRO DE LAS CHICANAS
She Fought for an Education for Herself and for Others

BY MALINA GOMEZ

She was full of adages. I heard so many over the years that I became numb and eventually very few seemed meaningful. As I get older, they come back to me. I find myself regurgitating them on a regular basis: "The early bird gets the worm." "Never burn your bridges." I realize now they are bite-sized portioned life lessons. I think I was thirteen or fourteen when I heard my favorite one. My dad was in a particularly bad mood that day and spoke to her in a short, rude tone before he walked away. She told me in a loud voice, "Just because everyone is being an asshole doesn't mean that you have to be one too." She looked at me and said, "Remember that." I do.

Delia Ravelo was born in 1952 in Kenosha, Wisconsin. Her father worked on the assembly line at General Motors; her mother was a housewife who spoke broken English. Both had immigrated to the United States. Her father entered through the Bracero Program and her mother left Zacatecas to join her then fiancé. They married and lived in a predominantly Italian neighborhood. Delia was the oldest of their three children and lived a normal middle-class existence. In 1958, her father died of a sudden heart attack at work. Unbeknownst to Delia at the time (she was six), her mother was battling breast cancer.

Delia's mother moved with her three children to San Diego, California, to be near her mother and brother who lived in nearby Tijuana. She bought a small house in National City, the house where Delia and her siblings would grow up. Her mother died in 1959. Delia was seven.

She was raised by her grandmother and her uncle, who spoke no English. Delia had spent her life speaking English. Her grandmother taught her all the things she thought a girl needed to know. Delia learned to cook, clean, sew, and prepare freshly slaughtered animals into meat for cooking. And, yes, she learned Spanish.

She continued her schoolwork in the United States and spent weekends across the border in Tijuana, Mexico. These abrupt changes in her life left an intense impression on her that remained for the rest of her life. She was always acutely aware of cultural differences and inequalities.

She often spoke about her school experiences: the way teachers were always impressed that she spoke perfect English and had no accent; the way it was assumed that she had no intelligence. She was constantly enrolled in remedial courses until one teacher in junior high noticed she read at a high level and enrolled her in honors courses.

The first six years of her life had shown her that not everyone had to live such a difficult life. She knew things could be different. She was also a huge Beatles fan despite the disapproval of her grandmother and uncle. She surreptitiously learned everything about the group. Though she was a diehard Paul McCartney fan, she greatly admired John Lennon's intellectual persona. He had written one book and attended college. The combination of these two factors led her to the decision to attend college. The high school counselor told her she would not be able to get admitted. It was the fall of 1969. She knew that several programs had been recently implemented by colleges, including EOP. She applied to San Diego State University because her best friend was also applying there. They both got accepted.

Lifelong Friendship

Once in college, she was finally free. Leaving home had been a struggle. She escaped with a couple of bags during a heated argument with her uncle who refused to let her go, and was told she could never come back. For the most part she did not, though she kept in contact with her siblings. She lived in the dorms. During this time, many of the EOP students were housed together. Delia met several of the women who eventually became known as Las Chicanas, including Felicitas Nuñez, a lifelong friend and collaborator.

She took several classes in her major, English, as well as Chicano studies. These classes gave her the tools to understand and recognize the inequalities and injustices occurring in society. She also joined MEChA, the Chicano student organization. She took a *teatro* class, taught by Ruth Robinson, with several of her friends. They learned acting and writing techniques for performances. The teatro's foundation was based on raising awareness of social injustice.

They began as a class and formed into a group. Their first performance was given for their mother's at a mother's tea in 1970. My mother did not perform the piece they presented, called "Chicana Goes to College." She did not have a mother who could attend, but she helped write it and was very involved behind the scenes. However, when they gave their second presentation, she performed and continued to perform through all the incarnations of the *Teatro de las Chicanas*.

The *teatro* was pivotal in the lives of so many of the women involved. It gave them a voice and a platform to express the inequalities between the sexes in the Chicano Movement. They could also advocate for other issues, such as women's healthcare, poverty, and education.

When she spoke of her college years, it seemed like a blur of traveling to MEChA events, protests, performances, conferences, and trips. I'm not sure when she ever went to class. She was also one of the student supporters of the creation of Chicano Park. She also became involved with Ralph Gomez, whose brother, Jose, led the Chicano Park Steering Committee. During their tumultuous relationship, she managed to keep active in the *teatro*, the Chicano Movement, and attend school. She had a baby with Ralph in 1975. She returned to school and graduated the following May with a bachelor's degree in English and a minor in Marxist Economics. Soon after, she began working at San Diego Gas and Electric. Her relationship with Ralph ended and she spent the next few years working and raising her daughter. She met and married Michael Reyes and had two more children, a boy and a girl.

A New Incarnation

Soon after she married, Delia and Felicitas started a new incarnation of *Teatro de las Chicanas*. They called it *Teatro Raices*. They co-wrote several scripts and performed them with a few other women, including Evelyn Diaz. They practiced every Saturday in Delia's garage. I used to love to watch their process from beginning to end. From the beginning stages, when Delia and Felicitas would discuss an issue and toss ideas around until something clicked for the both of them, to the arduous writing process, to the rehearsals where I would see the women's reactions as they gave their input on how a character should be portrayed, and, finally, to a performance. It was magic to me. The messages they delivered were important and changed lives—I know they changed mine.

Delia also began taking classes at San Diego State University again, working toward a master's degree in Latin American literature. This endeavor combined her three loves: learning, structure, and books. She continued working and raising a family, so it was several years before she completed her courses. The classes she took and her reading and writing critical papers were on several Latin American writers. Due to her example, her children all have a knack for writing papers.

She noticed that several of her classmates were ESL teachers in public schools and most were not Latino. This inspired her to do a class project where she mimicked a situation she had seen frequently in elementary school. Teachers would often belittle and shame students who were not native English speakers, seating them in the back of the classroom. The native speakers would sit in the front. Her original idea was to recreate the situation with her as a student and a Caucasian classmate as the teacher. Felicitas suggested they reverse roles to make more of a statement. Delia agreed and made the presentation with the Chicana as the teacher. She went through the whole class and critiqued their Spanish. She made it clear that her Caucasian classmate, playing the student, was the example of how not to speak Spanish. Delia was shocked by the reaction she received. Her classmates were outraged and actively defended the student. They became very upset with Delia and confronted her on her discriminatory actions. Delia then revealed that she and her classmate were performing a scene to expose the kind of discrimination students feel when they are criticized for their imperfect English. The class fell silent. They realized that they were manipulated into confronting their own internalized prejudices.

Delia Ravelo, (far right) with her family, c1984. Michael Reyes, her husband, is holding their daughter Isela; their son Michael is standing next to his mother. Delia's eldest daughter Malina Gomez is on her left.

Courtesy of Isela Reyes.

During the nineties, Delia became more involved with volunteer activities. She joined the Contrib Club at work and became a part of the group that decided how to distribute funds to nonprofit organizations. She also discovered a small school in Tijuana. It was in a small section called Colonia Esperanza. It was an incredibly poor area. The school was designed by James Hubbell, a San Diego artist/architect. She and her children began working with Hubbell, making mosaics along classroom walls. Soon she began to talk to the parents and children who lived nearby. She started to spend more time with the mothers. She began to collect things for them, such as clothing and school supplies. She was soon receiving beads and yarn. She started to hold informal arts and crafts classes. They made necklaces and bracelets out of chunky plastic beads, but they progressed together, making small sculptures out of clay. She learned to knit and implemented that into the class. She became friends with many of the families and regularly communicated with them.

Meanwhile, in San Diego, she and Felicitas had come up with a new idea. Breast augmentation had become popular. They wondered how men would react to a similar concept. Their skit, called "Bola Job" was presented in the style of an infomercial. They sold the idea of men augmenting their testicles, of having larger, more attractive balls, similar to the way women are taught to want beautiful, voluptuous breasts. The skit was quite successful. It was also hilarious; they really displayed the ridiculousness of society's standards of beauty. They performed it at several gatherings.

Throughout all this time, Delia was an extremely attentive and involved mother. She imparted her hard working, multitasking, relentless pursuit-of-everything attitude onto her children. They also picked up her love of literature and art, and her ability to see the world beyond its surface.

In 2000, Delia was diagnosed with stage 3 cancer of the perineum. She changed her diet dramatically and began chemotherapy. She lost a tremendous amount of weight and began to lose her hair. She shaved her head; Felicitas shaved hers too in solidarity. She took about a year off to undergo treatment and recuperate. She then resumed working and volunteering at the school in Tijuana. The cancer returned. She decided to undergo a second round of treatment while working. One day she collapsed at work. Two days later she died of heart failure. She was 50 years old.

Some might say Delia lived a simple life; she married, worked, and had a family. She was a dynamic woman who inspired those around her. Through her interactions and volunteer projects she was able to share her story. It let people know they can always change their situation with hard work. She was full of ideas and constantly acting on them and moving forward. She was persistent, goal oriented, powerful, intense, reliable, relentless, and she is my mother.

About the Author:

MALINA GOMEZ, Delia's daughter, is a relentless seeker of truth with an incredibly soft spot for the underdog. She has inherited these qualities from her mother and spent her life recovering from the consequences. She received a B.A., Bachelor of Arts in Drama at Mills College. She became legally blind at 31. She runs a blind theater group; and is on the Board of the Blind Community Center of San Diego.

Lin Romero in her activist days in San Diego.

Courtesy of Mariana Raquel Acevedo.

LIN ROMERO (1955–2006):

PUBLISHED POET AND TACO SHOP POET
¡Planta Más Raza! Was Her Rallying Cry

BY MARIANA RAQUEL LYDIA ACEVEDO

Lin Romero was a great voice for courage and never giving up. She had the conviction and determination of a strong woman, as a leader, artist, poet, and writer. What most stands out in Lin was her courageous spirit. She was always speaking out against the injustices committed in our society. She sometimes roared like a lioness so that we could hear and feel the injustice. Lin was a champion for human rights. Her causes were for women and children. She was a true activist of her time and she spoke best in poetry.

Born and raised in México, D.F., Lin was educated at California State University, Los Angeles. She began writing as a child. She was already writing poetry in the sixth grade and continued to do so ever since. Foremost a poet, she was also a community worker within the Juvenile Justice System. She was the mother of a 22-year-old daughter then who attended the University of California at Los Angeles (UCLA).

Lin worked with families of young adults who were growing up among chaos, who were in trouble with the law, and who were powerless in the schools. More than ever, Lin wanted to help them. She worked in the Chicano/Latino communities as a counselor and probation officer. She was also a poet–artist, instilling hope and inspiration through poetry workshops and writing. Lin also wanted to reach the parents of the students she worked with. She was bilingual and so she had no problem communicating with the parents and the children. Being able to speak Spanish with the parents was very important to her. She knew that parents would often feel at a loss for lack of not knowing the English language. Lin worked with them as well, offering parenting classes they could attend to understand the struggles of their children.

Lin expressed her activism through poetry like a pro. She was loved in San Diego for her ability to articulate injustices through her voice. She performed in California and México, and was published in various Chicano literary journals.

Lin had the distinct honor of being the first Chicana in San Diego to publish a book of poetry at the Centro Cultural de la Raza, San Diego's center for arts and culture. The artistic publication, *Happy Songs Bleeding Hearts*, was a chapbook she subtitled, "A series of Indigenous Xicana Journeys Rostros de Amerindia by a Woman Creadora" (San Diego: Toltecas de Aztlán, 1974). It was described as "A fiery Carnalista's heart burns the copal of her creation in the first of a series of *Rostros Amerindios*. She brings the transient urban life of Mexico City and East Los Angeles to look into the ephemeral eyes of modern woman."

It was also one of the first times that Chicana artists saw themselves in print. As a result of her talents and her ability to reach youth, Lin was hired as a "Poets-in-the-Schools Teacher." She also worked as a Neighborhood Arts Project Teacher and as a Poem-College Workshop Teacher. She was one of the first members of the original Taco Shop Poets, and a Word Sound & Power Collective, Creator Flying Heart Productions. But it was in Taco Shop Poets where her woman's voice resounded loud and clear.

The Taco Shop Poets

The Taco Shop Poets were an innovative group of artists and poets in the 1990s, exhibiting the spoken word with unique talent, at times giving voice to the voiceless, and doing it with bold power. They have been credited with helping to "revive, redefine, and revolutionize" the spoken word in San Diego and elsewhere. Their history tells it well: "They employed a very aggressive style of guerilla style poetry, central to which are its improvisational nature and combination of punk and hip hop influences." The collective's legacy reaches far beyond Southern California and has "spawned numerous copy-cat groups across the USA." For their generation, they were unique. Mostly men, Lin was at first their only woman, and woman she was. Her strength resounded.

Much of the beauty of her poetry was that it was bilingual. In *Ondas Chicanas*, Lin uses both Spanish and English to strengthen her message:

I live in this movimiento bosque de la vida aquí hay maíz vivo aquí
hay frutas maduras aquí los árboles cantan en montañas se oyen poemas
como besos gotas de lluvia rayos de sol aquí la gente es madura
rellena de amor aquí brotan vidas.

Lin also wrote in English, but the spirit of her language always shined though. In *man y festo*, the title is in Spanish but the text is in English:

SHE SAID TACO HE SAID SALSA HE SAID NO ONE REMEMBERS SHE SAID
SHE DID THE POET IS NOW THE DRUMMER THE CRIES DREAM IN LOVE
WORDS LOVERS DREAM AWAY FROM IT ALL TO FLY INTO THEIR ARMS
WAVES NOTES SEND RHYTHM WORDS TO LIFE.

Lin's use of Spanish and English mixes together in a creative and unforced
way. This was her style, always ease and grace. And she was an innovator of that
poetic style, executing the mix.

Others have written about her. In 2013, Nieves Pascual Soler and Meredith
E. Abarca, in *Rethinking Chicano Life Through Food*, comment about her work
in their essay, "Reading the Taco Shop Poets." Fascinated by her combined use
of Spanish and English, they talk about what that means and how Lin used it
so effectively. "Rhetoric derived from the movement appears in *Who Invented
the First Taco?* A poem from Lin Romero, one of the group's collaborators in the
1990s."

who invented the first taco? who first said zás orale
simón que onda pues who in verdad ate the first taco?
were you invited to the cracking of el Plan de Aztlán?
are you on the phone tree? planta mas baby you got to move
and be sure your raza is here to live in justicia & peace
move on raza who invited you to the operation of the mind on death row?
the squad invaded the people are on the corners doing dope deals
barrio deals death deals bail deals what is up raza?
answer please before the taco becomes extinct.

The authors notice, "The poem directly refers to *El Plan Espiritual de Aztlán*
by poet Alurista from the early days of the movement and mines the cadences of
the Chicano idiom and Spanglish enabling Romero to provide a mesmerizing call
to her audience to continue movement and struggles in a new era." The authors
further recount that Romero's linguistic approach using the mix of language,
points to the mix of cultures, a struggle where Chicanos are at the center, placed
there by the contradictions they were born into, and speaking Spanish in a land
that nearly outlaws it. Lin's poetry allows people, themselves called mestizos or
mixed bloods, to talk about it.

Lin moved from the venues of the Taco Shops to Voz Alta, a space for
open-mike offerings in downtown San Diego that encouraged the voices of
women. But Lin's greatest gift was that she helped youth to become productive
citizens in this harsh society; she instilled hope in them to keep going forward
no matter what. She gave them courage through tough love and the youth could
feel and see that this woman, Lin Romero, really cared for their well-being and
the plight of all human beings against racism, suffering, abuse of women and

children, and war. In her mind, there should not be any strife or killing of one another.

Lin held life dearly. That is why it was so hard to see her die so young. She was barely over fifty years old when she discovered that she had the deadly cancer, and she died shortly after. Lin as a friend of 33 years was more like a sister to me. She always praised my efforts as a mother and daughter, always told me not to give up, and not to take all the responsibilities of the home entirely upon myself. As an artist, she could see that I was a dreamer, like her, and that I wanted to paint and write as well as parent. Lin wanted to help me fulfill my dreams. And she did. She helped me to see my potential as an artist and as a woman. She truly inspired me in my personal life.

Now that she is no longer with us, we, her friends and followers, are continuing in her footsteps, stepping up to take action in spite of all the chaos. We are also remembering the other women who never give up and who continue their fight for justice with words and actions of wisdom, love and grace, not of anger. Lin Romero was one of these women. Because of her, we must not forget ourselves as women who are here to inspire humanity now, yesterday, and tomorrow. We cannot forget that we hold the torch; we hold up half the universe; we are sacred; we are creators; therefore, we are divine mortals. Thank you for teaching us this, Lin Romero.

About the Author:

MARIANA RAQUEL LYDIA ACEVEDO, a graduate of SDSU, was born in Lima Peru. She came to the U.S. with her parents, brother, and sister in 1960. Her father Guillermo Acevedo, a great artist, was headed to New York, but the tuna boat's last stop was San Diego; it reminded him of his beloved city Arequipa where he was born. Mariana's mother, Lydia Acevedo, was a great story teller, singer, dancer and wonderful cook. Mariana feels like she inherited all these wonderful qualities combined from her two parents.

CHARLOTTE HERNANDEZ-TERRY (1937-2010):

CHICANA MOVEMENT SINGER, COMPOSER, ARTIST

Called "Angel of Mercy" for Her Many Generous Actions

BY CHRISTINE CLAUSNER

All Charlotte Hernandez-Terry wanted to do was sing her heart out for the people of the world, while working for the benefit of her family in public service jobs that ministered to the needy. She wouldn't take just any job; she cared too much about others, exhibiting her generosity of heart and compassion of soul. One of her daughters remembers her composing songs in the middle of the night; another one painted with her at Chicano Park, witnessing her mother become one of the first women to paint on the park pillars of the now designated historical monument under the Coronado Bridge; another one accompanied her to the border to see her administer medication to the infirm. All these telling actions say something about the character and personhood of Carlota, their mother's given name.

My name is Christine Clausner, fifth in a family of six girls, Teresa, Rebecca, Deborah, Charlotte, Leslie, and me, Christine, the surviving daughters of Charlotte Hernandez-Terry, Chicana activist. I knew my mother as a different person other than her stage persona. She was charismatic, inspirational, and captivating on stage. She gave the world something they had never experienced before. Her music taught them about life at its most profound level. Her songs pierced the heart because she had lived each one as surely as she had written them. One of them, "Living in the Barrio, Life is Just Like That," spelled out a kind of determination she hoped might change the conditions of the poor in her own neighborhood. Another song, a sort of chant, "Mama Works Hard Everyday/ Mama Works Hard for her Weekly Pay," she sung to the beat of her hand on the face of her guitar. The tune lamented the workday drudge. Set apart from her children in an attempt to make a living wage to feed them, the song paid homage to the working class mother. It certainly rang true for Charlotte who, without receiving any child support from the father who abandoned his children, still managed to simultaneously put food and laughter on the table. But you knew from listening to the words of her songs that it wasn't easy for her; the lyrics and tone spelled it out. Other Chicanas identified with her; but her compassion for struggle and her hopeful spirit in the music is what still speaks every day to countless women just like her.

Charlotte Hernandez-Terry, "Mama Works Hard Everyday," the title of her signature song; mural painting the Chicano Park Logo, 1974 (design by Rico Bueno).

Courtesy of Helen McKenna.

She performed her songs at community rallies, in Chicano Park, and at the Centro Cultural de la Raza. She also traveled to unexpected places, for someone who grew up so distanced from middle-class culture. She was proud of being the first Latina invited to perform professionally in a special engagement at The Ford Theater in Washington, D.C., for the United States bicentennial celebration in 1976. She proudly accepted an invitation to perform for Mexican diplomats at the International Women's Annual Conference in Mexico City in 1975, also conducting a music workshop at the conference; and, before that, she performed at the Women's Folk Festival at East Lansing, Michigan. All were far from home, but she was proud of what she had accomplished, mostly because of the people she could reach to hear her message.

Charlotte Hernandez-Terry was born April 13, 1937, in San Diego to Jessie Ferrer and Gorgonio Hernandez, whose genealogical history extends in California to the early 1900s. Hernandez passed on to his only child, a home the family purchased in 1953 in National City; Charlotte continued to maintain and live in it until her death, which came much too soon. When she died in 2006, even the California State Senate stopped what it was doing to honor her. A message sent to her family read: "In Memoriam: the California State Senate on June 26, 2006, adjourned in memory of Carlotta Hernandez-Terry." Initiated by the honorable Senator Denise Moreno Ducheny, her signature affixed, and representing the 40th District in San Diego, it read, "On behalf of the California Senate, may I express our deepest sympathy." Other letters, accolades, and awards had come to Charlotte in her life. One was from Bonnie Dumanis, District Attorney of San Diego County, congratulating Charlotte for her appointment to the Committee on the Status of Women; another letter in 1977 announced her as a National Endowment for the Arts Teacher in School Grant recipient.

The Charlotte Hernandez-Terry Papers are now housed in the Archives of San Diego State University Special Collections Library. Her personal papers were processed and her famous guitar was exhibited in 2010 and placed on public display along with others for the *Unidos de La Causa* Exhibit and Reception at the Malcolm Love Library, SDSU. There, one can access her files—preserved for

perpetuity—showing the technical skill she applied in her drafting course at San Diego City College in 1974 to prepare the Chicano Park mural. She was only one of two women in the class of 20 men who completed the technical course.

Honoring her in obituaries, her daughters said Charlotte would have been pleased to know that her story came out in three newspapers in one day. Reminiscent of earlier times, they also recalled what their mother said the day that the front-page headline in the *San Diego Union-Tribune* told her story. More than a Chicana activist, a mural artist, a performing artist, composer, musician, and single working mother of six children, she is described in the feature story as an "Angel of Mercy." She laughed when she read that and told everyone with a wry smile that she had "made front-page news along with the president of the United States." In reality, Charlotte was

Charlotte Hernandez-Terry, c1970, strumming her famous guitar.

Courtesy of Sonia Lopez.

indeed an angel of mercy as the news feature described her; as an AIDS patient health care provider; as an AIDS Counselor for *Horizontes*; as a conservationist working with at-risk young adults for the California Civilian Conservation Corp; and as a health aide for The County of San Diego health and human resources in the tuberculosis unit where her job was to reach non-compliant tuberculosis patients.

As her daughter, I knew she needed me. I remember driving with her one day to the U.S.-Mexican border to contact a patient. I watched her administer him his medication, so he would not transmit the disease to other unsuspecting victims, mainly his wife and infant child living with him. In 1991, my mother received a Certificate of Appreciation "for dedicated service to the programs and goals of the County of San Diego Department of Health Services." She was proud of that. And we were proud of her.

As a performer, her stage presence was professional; at home, she was excited, demanding, and hilarious. Drinking too much coffee and talking about world events or even about the neighbors was always a pleasure with my Mom. Her sense of humor, her intriguing stories, and her funny gossip always kept me at the edge of my seat. We amused each other daily with our different lifestyle choices. I was in an accounting field; she was a performance artist. She always wished that we, her daughters, were more like her, musically inclined. What stands out most about her is that she taught me to be honest, hardworking, to "take no shit...," and to do so all with a smile on my face.

And so my mother was not the typical mom. I remember as a child, many hot summer nights, falling asleep as she serenaded us with her songs and her kisses, lying on bunk beds, sleeping bags, or all piled up together in her bed. We woke up each and every day with music all around us. Her spirit was filled with colorful, beautiful music. Her songs were her stories, her strength, and her courage, courage to brave life as a Chicana folk artist, an educator, and a struggling mother of six. As adults, we shared and understood each other's frustrations and pleasures, as much as we also felt each other's pain and excitement. We always supported each other. She was not only my mother and father; she was my sister and a great friend.

My mother lived life on her own terms. She was a fighter first and foremost; we all knew that. In a letter we found in her personal papers, an administrator challenged her work performance. My mother responded eloquently in a formal letter with a judgment on the institution's "lack of training and personal attention provided for the workers who depended on, and had many times requested assistance." She was a true fighter for the people. She answered that fact with compelling one-liners. Her ultimate statement was, "This is my Last Revolution," words she grandly articulated before she died. And she chose her time too. Her friends and family were able to enjoy Carlota, as she was also named to Hispanicize the Charlotte Terry and to show pride in her heritage. Over the last ten years she was blessed with the grace of God, caring daughters, modern medicine, and an immense will to live.

I could never fully express her life's meaning or put a value on what she meant to me in a speech or essay about her. We were all lucky to have her touch our lives in so many ways, some luckier than others. All I know is that my mother was larger than life and would have been thrilled to know that she had so many admirers, as well as knowing that she is in our hearts forever. To you Mom, I will say this: You always said that you worked so hard to make life easier for us girls and for others; well, you did it Mom. I will remain on the edge on my seat until I hear your voice again.

Charlotte Hernandez-Terry lost a hard-fought battle with breast cancer three years after she was diagnosed in 2003. Survivors include daughters Teresa Hernandez of Santee, Rebecca Rose of San Diego, Deborah Riegel of Chula Vista, Charlotte M. Terry of Las Vegas, Christine Clausner of Dana Point, and Leslie Aguirre of Chula Vista; nine grandchildren; and three great-grandchildren.

About the Author:

CHRISTINE CLAUSNER, Charlotte's daughter was born and raised in San Diego, the fifth of six girls; she was a regular fixture at her mother's shows where she performed throughout her life. Her mother made sure that her children knew the sacrifices and history of her people as the Chicano movement spread throughout California. Today Christine, an accountant, makes her home in Southern California and enjoys sharing her mother's history with close friends, family, and the next generation as they come of age.

PART II: THE PRESENT

CHICANA ACTIVISTS
STILL AT WORK

CHAPTER 3

TOMASA "TOMMIE" CAMARILLO

IRENE MENA

GRACIA MOLINA DE PICK

CONSUELO "CONNIE" PUENTE

LILIA VELASQUEZ

CHAPTER 3

Community Activists for Chicana and Chicano Causes

Chicana activist leadership developed in response to a society that denied Mexican American people's history. For more than 150 years, following the United States takeover of Mexican land as a result of the 1848 Treaty of Guadalupe Hidalgo, the Mexican people who remained and those who would come later from Mexico were relegated to second-class citizenship. They endured racial discrimination, economic impoverishment, and political disfranchisement. In this chapter are stories of early as well as present day activists, who have been pushing their way past cultural, economic, and political barriers to make a difference in their communities. For many it was during the Civil Rights Movement of the 60's and 70's that their activism addressed exclusion and discrimination in education, politics, art, mental health, law, and other fields.

These women have shown their courage and commitment to changing an unjust society. In time, they brought about change in many areas, demanding that the Mexican American people be included as contributors to the historical development of this country and that they be given the rights they deserve.

Through their stories one is able to glimpse the different contexts in which Chicanas navigated, bringing to light how different institutions manifested policies of discrimination against Chicanos/Latinos and other under-represented populations. These women, whether raised in poverty or in a more economically advantaged environment, shared the values of our common humanity and justice. Many of the early activists did not realize they were making history as they demanded basic rights for themselves, for their children, and for the communities in which they lived.

This was the case when Josie Talamantez, Angie Avila, and Tomasa "Tommie" Camarillo participated in San Diego's historic Chicano Park takeover on April 22, 1970, when the community defied injustice. They stood with others to make a community space for their neighborhood, fighting for a park, not a highway patrol station.

Crossing the border from Tijuana, Mexico, with her mother and three siblings, Tomasa "Tommie" Camarillo lived much of her childhood at a dairy in Mission Valley where her mother worked. In 1970, as a young woman, Tommie participated in the take over of Chicano Park. She became a member of the Chicano Park Steering Committee (CPSC). As caretakers responsible to oversee and negotiate with local and state authorities, CPSC helped transform the area into a space celebrating Chicano art and culture. Along with local artists, they helped transform the park into an open air art gallery with its murals and sculptures for the community to enjoy. Chicano Park Day which has been celebrated for the past forty-six years, represents the quality of leadership of Tommie and the CPSC.

Irene Mena, mother of ten children and a life long resident of Barrio Logan, is known as *La Generala* and the "Grandmother of the Brown Berets of San Diego." A Chicano militant organization of the times, the San Diego Brown Berets, founded by Arturo Serrano in 1968, was regularly at the forefront in organizing and implementing community action regarding different issues, from police brutality to anti-war protests. Irene rallied for and became a member of the Brown Berets in support of their efforts, including the takeover of Chicano Park. At any meeting, rally, or protest in which the Brown Berets participated, Irene was present, sometimes along with some of her children.

In the late 1960's, Gracia Molina De Pick, one time activist in the feminist movement in Mexico, and a professor at San Diego Mesa College, was key to organizing faculty and students in the effort to establish Chicano Studies at Mesa College, one of the first such departments in the nation. Gracia attended the historic University of California at Santa Barbara Conference of 1969 that put forth *El Plan de Santa Barbara*, that called for the implementation of Chicano Studies in the colleges and universities throughout the state of California. Later, at the University of California at San Diego, she was active in the process that instituted Third College (now Thurgood Marshall) for Black and Chicano students.

Born in Los Angeles and raised in Mexico City, Connie Puente returned to the U.S. as a young woman. Connie became the first Chicana business woman to secure a concession in Old Town San Diego and opened her own restaurant, "El Fandango." From the very start, she supported Chicano/Latino involvement in the political process, providing a meeting space and financial backing to such organizations as the Chicano Democratic Association, the San Diego County Latino Association, and the Early San Diego Regional History Collaborative.

Lilia Velasquez became known as *La Flama*, The Flame of Justice, in San Diego legal circles. Specializing in Immigration and Nationality Law, Lilia, an immigrant herself, assists not only her paid clients, but those she serves *pro bono*. She is a staunch immigrant rights advocate, especially when it comes to defending women's rights, including undocumented victims of domestic violence, sexual abuse, and forced prostitution. Lilia has been recognized for her community commitment with many prestigious awards which include the California Women Lawyers Association Fay Stender Award and the San Diego County Bar Association Community Service Award.

These are only a few of the activists who have made significant contributions to the Chicano/Latino communities, as well as to the overall San Diego area. We acknowledge their courage and perseverance.

Tommie Camarillo and David Rico with Flag of Chicano Park.
Courtesy of Chicano Park Steering Committee.

Tommie Camarillo, Chair, Chicano Park Steering Committee; 2012, in front of the kiosko in Chicano Park.

Courtesy of photographer David Avalos.

TOMASA "TOMMIE" CAMARILLO:

CHAIR, CHICANO PARK STEERING COMMITTEE
Indefatigable Defender of Chicano Park

BY ANNIE ROSS

Tommie Camarillo has been, and continues to be, the indefatigable defender of Chicano Park and, in turn, of the Chicano community throughout Aztlán. The passion and dedication she brings to this lifelong work is beyond the scope of most people's motivation. Tommie is a stunning example of the enormous impact one person can have in our world.

Tommie was a single parent of a two-and-a-half-year-old daughter when she joined in the occupation of the small piece of land under the Coronado Bay Bridge. She stood on the land while negotiations were under way and activists demanded that the property be donated to the community. They wanted the land for a park where the people could express their Chicano culture through art. And she is still here today, now with her children and grandchildren. As she says, "Since the takeover of Chicano Park, I have been involved and I have never gone away."

On Wednesday, April 22, 1970, after twelve days of occupation and negotiations, the land was claimed for the community. The next day, the Chicano Park Steering Committee (CPSC) was formed to direct the community effort to build a park and deal with state and city authorities.

The CPSC continues as a grassroots organization comprised of individuals who all volunteer their time, talents, and energy. They ensure that the original stated goals for the development and expansion of Chicano Park are never forgotten or abandoned. The mark of Tommie's leadership, generosity, patience, and persistence in the struggle is evident through time and space. She has proven to be an extraordinary leader and organizer for more than four decades. From 1970 to today, she hasn't missed a beat in between. Tommie is an icon in the San Diego Chicano Movement in its never-ending quest for social justice and self-determination. In describing her participation in the takeover, she said, "I was just here as a worker. That's what I've done my whole life."

As the leader of the CPSC, Tommie provides a space where every voice is heard; yet, she is unmoved by any argument that does not put Chicano Park and the *comunidad* at the forefront of what is best for all. She doesn't sweat the small stuff unless it would adversely affect the park. Then, no amount of time or effort is too much, nor the matter too small. She rises above the cacophony of noise that can frequently plague community meetings to highlight the crux of a given issue and move forward.

Since its inception in 1970, one of CPSC's goals was to transform the grey concrete and rock-hard dirt that once dominated the area, into a glorious place of beauty that would mirror and showcase the beauty, culture, and spirit of the Chicano people. Today, the murals in Chicano Park are world famous, included in the National Register of Historic Places. They constitute (along with various sculptures, including the Zapata statue) one of the world's largest outdoor art galleries. Chicano Park has received international recognition as a major public art site for these commanding murals that depict past and present struggles of Mexican and Chicano history. All of this has been accomplished without any funding and, for the majority of the time, under Tommie's leadership.

Tommie came as a young child from Tijuana to San Diego with her mother and three siblings. For much of her childhood, Tommie lived at the dairy in Mission Valley where her mom worked. Her mom remarried and had 9 more children. At 15 years old, Tommie went to live with her beloved older sister, Diana. She then lived on her own in Logan Heights for many years.

She worked for 13 years with the Chicano Federation, before she resigned and took a position at the U.S. Grant Hotel in downtown San Diego. She worked more than 20 years at the hotel, primarily as a pantry cook, until the property was purchased by Sycuan. The staff was laid off and the hotel was closed two years for renovations.

There is never any doubt that Tommie will be present and fully prepared in any given situation. As an archivist, her skills are innate. Chicano Park's history and legacy is packed into her house in binders, boxes, and cases. In the early 70s, Tommie started clipping newspaper articles and keeping a daily log of events concerning Chicano Park. She said, "In some of the meetings I noticed that nothing was being documented. Somebody could later just say, 'You're full of it; that did not happen.' I don't know why, that's just the way I am; but you need to have backup of what you say and what has been discussed." And her archives are used nearly daily today. "Just like I don't like to go speak at some event when I don't know everything about the topic." Although she knows that not everything has backing, she believes it is needed as much as possible. Tommie explains her reasoning well, "I feel it's very important to have everything documented. That's what backs up history. It backs up what you say. You know I can say whatever I want, but if I don't have the documentation, it means nothing. To this day I have boxes full of notebooks with my daily logs. I can go back and refer to those."

She says, "I started putting together binders on topics such as this one on the mural restoration project. I started making binders with all leaflets, agendas, and notes; I always took minutes in whatever meetings I went to and included pictures, but lots of paperwork. For example, I have a binder for all correspondence to the Chicano Park Steering Committee from 1970 to today. I also have one on the meetings, including agendas, minutes, notes and other supplemental documentation." Her CPSC archives include a binder on the *kiosco*, including blueprints from the city; a binder on the *placita*; one on the long ordeal related to the retrofitting of the bridge pillars; one on the fight for the Zapata statue; on the struggle for the Aztlán rocks; and undoubtedly of other struggles to come. The community can rest assured that Tommie will preserve every scrap of paper, every voice. And in her role as the reference librarian for the park, she regularly refers to her archives to answer questions about various aspects of the park.

Archives are very important to Tommie. Archives have an incredible power to expand the range of people and stories we know and the experiences in which we can share through another's life. They also create a neighborhood without boundaries of place or time. The power of historical records serves to teach us and others. Tommie has an extraordinary capacity to organize huge amounts of information. As an archivist, Tommie has built on her innate skills.

Tommie emphasizes that Chicano Park is not just for Logan residents: "It is not just for this community. I always say that because, through all of the development of this park, so many people have volunteered. In the more than 40 years, a lot of people have come at some point in their lives to be a part of this. Maybe for months, maybe weeks, maybe for years, but they volunteered their time here and came to Chicano Park to help. That's why I never think of it as just for Logan. It's not. It's for the community, and the community is all over."

For many years, Tommie not only worked long days as a professional cook at the U.S. Grant hotel, but she then poured countless more hours of work into preparing for the annual Chicano Park Day celebration, which attracts tens of thousands of visitors. In addition, Tommie leads CPSC members, the park's caretakers and watchdogs, on all political and social issues affecting it. They learned from each other and their elders, and are passing on that pride in the park to younger generations. Tommie's children and grandchildren are active members and custodians of the park as well. And the younger generations are charged with a sense of responsibility for preserving and enhancing the park and its art.

As Chunky Sanchez, another of the Park's leaders stated, "The formation of the Chicano Park Steering Committee was equivalent to the formation of an indigenous tribal council to oversee their people, their land, and their cultural existence. For forty years, this committee has functioned with community members from all walks of life that have been dedicated to the 'labor of love' for a small park that has symbolized the importance of struggle and sacrifice for the betterment of humanity and respect for others."

Tommie has been a tremendous contributor since the beginning through her dedicated leadership and work on behalf of the Chicano Park. Her unwavering commitment is evident throughout the community. With a passionate spirit, she is at the forefront of continuous struggles and countless hours of work that it takes, year after year, day after day, to maintain and develop Chicano Park for the community.

According to Tommie, "People recognize the park's true value and importance to the community. And I get tired from the work, but never tired of it." Her dedication knocks away any complacency from those around her. As one reflects on the history of those who struggled to create and maintain Chicano Park, there's gratitude for all who play a part and continue to do so. Although the monumental murals are usually what come to mind when one says "Chicano Park," for me it's hard not see Tommie in my mind too.

About the Author:

ANNIE ROSS is a graduate of UCSB with an M.A. from UCLA in Folklore and Mythology. She has worked at the Library of Congress as a librarian and editor in the Hispanic Division on *The Handbook of Latin American Studies*; as a writer/editor for arts magazines; bilingual observer for the *Civil Rights Monitor*; Spanish software linguist, and as an employee of the UCSD Geisel Library. Annie is also a long-time member of the Chicano Park Steering Committee.

IRENE MENA:

GRANDMOTHER OF THE BROWN BERETS

Known to Her Community as "La Generala"

BY ADELINA PERLA LOPEZ

Irene Mena is referred to as *La Generala* by her friends and comrades. She is also known as the grandmother of the Brown Berets de Aztlán, San Diego's National Chapter. As an original member of the Chicano Park Steering Committee and the Brown Berets, she has the honor of saying she has been instrumental in the "takeover" of Chicano Park; of the Neighborhood House, now known as the Logan Family Health Center; and of the Ford Building that led to the opening of the Centro Cultural de la Raza in San Diego. It was the 1960s, people were demanding their rights, and Irene Mena was at the center of the action.

Irene Mena (left) with her daughter Adelina (right).
Courtesy of Adelina Perla Lopez.

Irene Mena began her life in San Diego, California, as Irene Alice Perrariz at San Diego County Hospital, on June 3, 1929. Her family home was on Julian Avenue, only two blocks from Logan Avenue in historic Logan Heights. She attended Burbank Elementary School, Logan Elementary School, Memorial Junior High School, Riverside Junior High school, and San Diego High School when it was still the old grey castle covered with vines. Irene is proud to say she received her diploma from San Diego High School, along with her family members, Debbie, and Mona. She then continued her education at San Diego City College. Irene worked hard for her education and at many different jobs.

In 1949, Irene got her first job at Convair Aircraft and received a Certificate "B" as a cutter for airplane parts. In 1964, she had progressed as a working woman, wife, and mother. She received a training certificate for a nurse's aide and orderly from San Diego Mesa College.

By 1969, the Chicano Movement was in full swing and she knew she wanted to work to help her people progress. She took a job as bilingual teacher's aide at Memorial Junior High School during the same period that she worked at St. Jude Church for the Chicano Federation as a senior aide for senior citizens. These efforts on behalf of the people were in her own neighborhood and close to home. Irene lived across the street from Chicano Park. She also worked in a facility on 21st Street and Logan Avenue, in the heart of the neighborhood that provided special programs for residents. For example, located upstairs from her was Henry Collins, the supervisor of a drug rehabilitation program, called NEPSI, Narcotics Education and Prevention Services. These memories invoke Irene's work career which continued to promote her heartfelt compassion for her people, especially the ones who benefitted from these services. She continued working at other jobs, one as security guard at San Diego Convention Center. Irene recalls those days when there were concerts that successfully promoted Mexicano music, so important to raising the spirits of working people. She also fought for the rights of workers in downtown San Diego with the Services Employees International Union. As a canvasser for the union, she learned a lot about her city, community organizing, and campaigning.

Irene has campaigned for many important candidates, such as Peter Chacon, for councilman, who later became the first Latino elected to the California Assembly in 1970; for Gilbert Robledo, for mayor, who was then a professor of Chicano Studies at San Diego City College; and for Maureen O'Connor who won the election in 1986 and became the first woman mayor of San Diego. Irene was an original member of the Raza Unida Party. She also worked hard for voter registration and proudly continues to encourage La Raza to vote!

As a leader at the forefront of the Chicano Movement in the 1970s, she assisted in getting Chicano studies bilingual education, and English as a Second Language classes included in the curriculum. She also helped to make financial aid available to veterans and students who otherwise may not have had the opportunity to attend San Diego City College and San Diego State University (SDSU).

Irene spoke of one incident at SDSU that affected her. The newspapers called it a riot, but Irene was present and saw what had actually happened. Students were protesting the loss of their grant money. The administration told them that it did not know where to allocate money for student grants. Although it was money the students had been promised, and needed, the administration was going to return it to the government instead of distributing it. The students said they needed it for books, tuition, and school supplies that they could not afford on their own, but the administration wanted to send it back to Washington.

The people of the community went to the campus to speak to the dean, or the person responsible for losing the students' grants. Irene recalls that "the dean sent a 'patsy,' a person used for his own purpose, to speak to the students, but just to tell them he was not present to talk to them." At the same time, there was a combination of actions taking place. Aside from the student group, there was another group on campus fighting for their needs too. At that point, the crowd became enraged; an American flag went up in flames and that's when the disturbance escalated. Someone else was hanging a dummy of Nixon from a pole and "then all hell broke loose." People that were in the building were now held hostage by one of the groups that demanded that they "wanted answers!" Irene recalls, "That is when we decided to leave." Later that day in another place, five men and one woman were jailed; all went to court to be tried. These were troubled times. Students were recruited to go to college but were not provided the resources they needed to survive. Others distrusted the police system because they had suffered abuse.

Irene remembered the time Chunky Sanchez and Tommie Camarillo, well-respected community members, were arrested and taken to jail for drawing pictures of the police as "pigs." The city and administration did not like what they had done and took them and others to court. Irene said photos of these drawings were published in a newsletter known as *El Chingazo*. It was the 1970s and, during this period, Chunky and Tommie had assisted the Chicano Park Steering Committee as well as the community, helping the people in many ways. Chunky Sanchez, Raul Portillo (RIP), and Sortillon worked with youth in an office in Southeast San Diego. Chunky was a musician and a community volunteer. He worked with a program called STAR, Street Alternative Resource for youth, at the

Barrio Station in Logan Heights. All of these memories emphasize Irene's desire, and other people's desire, to help the community.

Irene spoke of another time when a group of them went to a county building on 43rd Street and National Avenue. She said they knew that representatives were going to be there. She said "We went there to protest a council person who wanted to know who one of the activists was, by the name of Rico Bueno. They started asking questions about him, inquiring who he was, and asking other questions. They wanted information about him and were questioning people." At that time, Rico Bueno's father had run for a certain office. The people that had arrived with Rico did not like the kind of interrogation about him that was going on, nor did they agree with it. So they closed the doors on these officials, stated their demands and community needs, until an agreement was reached. Irene recalls that many community people including the Brown Berets were present and that some of them were jailed that day. These people did not deserve to go to jail. They were standing up for their rights. Irene recalled that some of these people later went on to become lawyers.

Irene asserted, "Nothing was ever given to us. We had to fight for it!" She added, "And it was no one person who did it; it was a collective of people that were concerned about equal rights. We had to organize and go to meeting after meeting to be heard. We marched, protested, and wrote letters for them to listen to our demands for health, education, and community centers." Irene said she did what she had to do in those days "by any means necessary!" And she would do it all over again if she had to.

Irene Mena is now an 85-year-old woman. She says to this generation, "Be educated! Realize you have to fight for what you want. Progress and learn how to reach your goal in life." This is her message to today's youth, coming from a mother, a grandmother, a great- grandmother, and great-great grandmother. Irene Mena is a woman who has stood strong for many of the benefits the people of her community enjoy today. "¡Que Viva La Raza! ¡Que Viva Aztlán!"

Irene Mena (front, far right), c1970s; Brown Berets march in protest against FedMart for their mistreatment of Laura Rodriguez.

Courtesy of Tommie Camarillo.

About the Author:

ADELINA PERLA LOPEZ, daughter of Irene and Alfredo Ochoa, a commercial fisherman (deceased), considers herself a Chicano Park baby, as she was always at her mother's side during the Park takeover. An activist in her own right, she is a graduate of the Chicano Leadership Program at the Chicano Federation; a member of Chicano Park Steering Committee; the National Brown Berets, San Diego Chapter; the Union del Barrio and its Chicano/Mejicano Prison Project. She campaigned for La Raza Unida Party and worked as a health education worker for Horizontes, a program to aid persons with HIV. She has worked as a secretary, teacher's aid, outreach worker, and liaison between unions and employees. Proud recipient of the Presidential Fitness Award, Adelina said, "Being involved in sports kept me out of trouble." She is the mother of five, a grandmother, and great-grandmother.

Gracia Molina de Pick, 2014, honored at the reception for "The Gracia Molina de Pick Glass Gallery at Mesa College."

Courtesy of Olivia Puentes Reynolds.

GRACIA MOLINA DE PICK:

FEMINIST, PROFESSOR, AND MENTOR TO CHICANAS

She Signed the Historical "Plan de Santa Barbara"

BY SARA GURLING

My best memories of Gracia Molina de Pick are from a 2006 Unity League meeting. She came through the bold, rustic doors, and onto the back patio area. A splash of color from the fringe of her elaborate *huipil* assured me it was her. If I were to duck the low-hanging branch of the mature *aguacate* tree, and avoid tripping over Yoyo the dog, I could possibly get to her before the others, who had already seen her arrive and were beginning to wrap up their conversations in order to be the first to greet Gracia Molina de Pick, our guest of honor. I barely made it under the tree as I razed the bark with my hair. At barely five-feet tall, I could pretty much clear that branch. In fact, Gracia and I share this common trait, a gift really. We are little, but determined. When ducking a low-hanging *aguacate* branch, she and I have an advantage over my sister Chicanas who are over five-feet tall—with inches to boot. I made my way to where I spotted her, avoiding other friends and family as I rushed by. My goal was to be first in delivering a welcoming *abrazo* and make a big fuss over the beauty of her *huipil*. I would tell her that she is the only lady on the LeGerrette patio towering over us all. Although she was visibly demure standing there, everyone around her feels the enormity of her presence and a desire to be at her side. That kind of urgency to be in her presence is not something that is unique to me or to the folk gathered at the home of Carlos and Linda LeGerrette. In San Diego's Chicano and Chicana circles, Gracia Molina Enriquez de Pick is our very own living legend, a goddess extraordinaire.

I represent a latent generation of Chicanas with whom Gracia became endeared. But there are Chicanas of older generations who comprise an on-the-spot entourage wherever Gracia goes. Of the most seen among them is the lovely and always radiant Olivia Puentes-Reynolds. She was there that day on the patio. Olivia was keeping an eye on those who were greeting Gracia and enjoying some freshly diced *aguacate con tomate y sal*. Simple and delicious. The patio scene has been playing out in similar fashion with an array of community purposes for more than forty years. Gracia has been a fixture of the gatherings on this Grove Street block. Whether entering through the notoriously red door or keeping a low profile, guests will arrive and start scanning the patio. The reason everyone is looking tonight? Gracia is rumored to be on her way and could be arriving at any moment. Consequently, when awaiting Gracia's arrival, one might make light conversation with the likes of a young woman named Natalie. She is the most beautiful Black Chicana you've ever seen. She's a blaxican, Chicana and Black, representative of our San Diego tradition of Black and Chicano unity in our inner city neighborhoods. She has known Gracia her whole life and is the daughter of Tonantzin LeGerrette, daughter of hosts Carlos and Linda. Together they will accompany Olivia to make sure Gracia has a great time and also to cut a path so she can get to the guacamole. Making their way, the three duck the low-hanging branch as Gracia steps in stride; she moves gracefully past the *aguacate* tree and through the crowd. All who see her will proceed to compete for Gracia's attention. Gracia will leave those she speaks with, marveling at her wit, beauty, and intellect. She is the magnet at the depths of *Chicanismo*.

On the house patio, with the not-so-easy-to-clear *aguacate* branch, a gray-haired woman with a *guitarra* plays a melody to ignite the ever-present spirit of every Chicana woman who fought for her place in community. Thanks to Gracia's Chicana feminist efforts in education, women are better positioned both locally and internationally. Gracia is the most politically astute woman you could ever meet and she has made an impact in the educational, political, civic, and grassroots threads throughout this southwestern city.

At a fancy dinner where San Diegans are requested the pleasure of attendance, it's suggested all too commonly to don eveningwear or business-casual attire. Gracia arrives in a beautiful *huipil*. It is carefully crafted and meticulously stitched. All the same dynamics of the patio politics are at play here. With no low-hanging branch to avoid, people swiftly move through the crowd. Women whisper to each other that, years ago, they had spotted a similar *huipil* in a little Mexican village but the vendor was holding it for some someone else. The women guests at the event begin to murmur. "That's Gracia Molina de Pick," they declare softly to one another. It is then suggested that Gracia is one of the most renowned Chicanas in America and internationally. One lady, with great sheen in her red hair, is deeply intrigued; she pulls out her smartphone and Googles the name all together with no spaces. With one hand on her Chardonnay glass and the other on an Apple 5 phone, she reads off the first few returns from a list of 13,400 search engine hits. The woman remarks as others listen intently, "It says here she was inducted into the San Diego County Women's Hall of Fame by the Women's Museum of California."

Gracia Molina de Pick promoting voter registration among Spanish speakers. The sign reads, "Register Here to Vote."

Courtesy of Daniel Pick.

Those two honorable mentions are absolutely correct. Blessedly, Gracia is also a philanthropist. Her generosity has improved local college institutions. She is a community stalwart of groundbreaking leadership development across all of our neighborhoods. The work she has been lauded for in our region is an extension of her early feminist and political work in her native Mexico City. She has made an impact internationally, yet, concentrated her efforts locally to make transformative change possible. Like the lovely designs sewn on her *huipil*, Gracia has been weaving, joining, and meticulously stitching community into patterns that intersect with one another. She has reached us all. Like her *huipil*, she resonates with and for all of the *colores* and the variations of those *colores*. Like a *huipil*, our community has patterns of campaigns, groups, and organizations that left their mark. The colors and variations of the reds in one square inch of Gracia's *huipil* can easily translate to the levels of chile-red anger and orange-cinnamon resolve we felt and expressed at injustices in our communities. Another pattern of mango-yellow next to *limón*-green expresses a healthy start of a new tomorrow, thanks to the trailblazing organizing and educational efforts of Gracia. Look closely; if a design has a row of black zigzags through it, that will represent the never-easy and never-straight road to achieving the hard work of a woman, an organizer, and a Chicana who runs up against a wall and finds a different but never-ending path to fight on for what she believes in.

In a video interview, Gracia was all smiles and full of that same gracefulness that becomes her. But in her eyes, she expressed the cadence of a person still unsettled by policies she helped to eradicate. Gracia told the story of Spanish-speaking children who had been insensibly labeled "mentally retarded" because they could not pass an English proficiency exam in school. Her reaction when she first learned of this practice was, "No way." Gracia meant "No way is anything going to get in the way of me changing that terrible and unjust practice." Gracia has a careful and methodical way of organizing resistance to the injustice and forcing a policy change so that children are allowed to learn without prejudicial labels based on illogical testing mechanisms. Graceful and feisty, determined and beautiful all the while, that is Gracia.

The San Diego Unity League meeting with Gracia at the table is always interesting. A local institution, the group's origins date back to the 1944 CSO Leagues, the Community Service Organization, that Fred Ross and others organized to establish multiracial unity in cities across the country. Carlos and Linda welcome all to grab their seats because the meeting is about to start. It's 2006 and we're in the thick of an election. The San Diego Unity League has endured, revived its membership, and become highly influential, aided by the mastery of crafty organizing and the determination of Gracia. She is the one who brings sensible logic in times of strife.

Carlos and Linda, our hosts, represent much more than a centimeter stitch on one of Gracia's *huipiles*. She integrated them and others into a movement and provoked a hunger for justice that led the couple to join the farmworker's movement and live as lieutenants in Cesar Chavez's UFW labor organization for twelve years. Now at the table working our way through a full Unity League agenda, Gracia will speak and we all hush to listen.

Her political understanding is razor sharp. Her ability to see through the mud and cut an issue is the stuff of organizing greats. If you didn't know her, you might still see that she was the child of a politically astute family, perhaps a feminist revolutionary in her own right, who cut a path to justice through the founding of a political party for common people, and through the formation of educational modules that changed the way Mexicans in America view their history, especially where women have been cajoled for too long. She's the *alta* Chicana. Like a breathtaking butterfly, all things beautiful, colorful, and full of hope and grace evoke the presence of Gracia Molina De Pick.

About the Author:

SARA GURLING. Mexican-born, Sara is a columnist with *El Latino News* and a radio segment personality on *Uni-radio, La Poderosa* 860AM in San Diego. She's known as a humanitarian, pro-justice labor organizer and activist; has served as executive board president of Border Angels; is a member of the American Federation of Teachers Local 1931; and teaches labor studies at San Diego City College.

CONSUELO "CONNIE" PUENTE:

FIRST CHICANA PROPRIETOR AT OLD TOWN SAN DIEGO
Made El Fandango Restaurant an Activist's Meeting Place

BY CELIA SOTOMAYOR MOODY

Consuelo "Connie" Puente played an integral role in the development of San Diego's Old Town during its formative years. Aside from being a successful business owner, she contributed her efforts to benefit many community members and organizations. Connie is considered a pioneer, visionary, and role model. She appeared on "100 Portraits," a catalog of *One Hundred People of Mexican Heritage*, "men, women, and children who have taken different roads in their lives, but whose paths have all led to a significant contribution that has improved the quality of our lives."

Connie has also contributed significantly to San Diego's history. She is best known for the community gatherings at her restaurant "El Fandango" in San Diego's historical Old Town. Consuelo received a Certificate of Appreciation from the Old Town, San Diego State Historical Park, for her continued commitment to its history and culture. The El Fandango Restaurant site at 2734 Calhoun Street was originally built as the home of one of the early residents in the 1800s. It was once Casa Machado, a home that was eventually destroyed by fire in 1858, and then came to be known as the La Casa Blanca Restaurant. It had fallen into disrepair and in 1982 the California Department of Parks and Recreation solicited proposals for the site. Connie submitted a proposal and because of its merits and her outstanding track record with Casa de Pedrorena, an earlier acquisition, was awarded a 10-year site lease to operate. After a considerable investment of capital, research, planning, and extensive repairs, El Fandango was born in 1983 as a restaurant featuring continental cuisine from the Mexican–American period of 1846 to 1856, a time of great change in California's history for its early residents.

Old Town represents the place where both the Indigenous people lived for hundreds of years and the Spanish colonization followed in the 1700s. Once Mexico, the area went from status of "pueblo, or chartered town," granted by the Mexican government, to being the home of the people after 1848, where most locals gathered and lived after the takeover of their land by the United States. When California was admitted to the United States in 1850, San Diego—still largely limited to the Old Town area—was made the county seat, where Mexican American families lived and thrived.

It was in this Old Town Historic State Park where Connie Puente first experimented with making delicious *churros* at "Bazaar del Mundo." She had great success, as many of the old-timers recall, including the opening of Casa de Pedrorena in 1971. At the urging of then State Senator and Pro-Tem Jim Mills, she took on the adobe structure known as Casa de Miguel de Pedrorena, the home of another of Old Town's early residents. She gained an outstanding reputation over 12-years for its garden-like setting, excellent food, and baked goods prepared in a typical Mexican bread oven or *horno* of brick and adobe that she designed herself. Due to erosion of the adobe walls, it was closed in 1983 by the Department of Parks and Recreation to prevent further damage to the site. Since then, Connie used this success to open El Fandango Restaurant. Soon, Connie opened and owned additional restaurants. Until retirement, she served top-quality traditional Mexican cuisine to San Diegans and visitors alike. She also delighted families by providing marimba music, along with a colorful atmosphere of Mexican folklore and fiesta.

More than that, Connie is known for giving back to the community, and she has done so in many different ways. First, she offered the El Fandango conference room free of charge to people seeking to have a meeting space to discuss concerns similar to hers. Among these concerns was the preservation of Mexican history and culture, as well as providing a sense of pride and identity to the people of San Diego. Many community activities were held in the "upper room," including meetings of volunteer organizations, community service groups, leadership proponents, or Latino community members advocating for equal representation in many different areas. It was also the place where Hispanic candidates knew they could stage strategy sessions. Second, Connie volunteered her nursing skills to Flying Samaritans, served as board member for the Centro Cultural de la Raza in Balboa Park, worked with the Binational Arts Cultural Commission, and helped with the San Diego Regional History Conference.

Connie Puente, c1999, photographed in front of her restaurant, El Fandango, in Old Town San Diego, for 100 Pioneers, Visionaries, and Role Models.

Courtesy of Olga Gunn Photography.

During all of these volunteer actions, Connie became known for her special sense of humor, while at the same time taking the life of a restaurateur as a serious challenge. During one scheduled program by the Early San Diego Regional History Conference, she was asked to cater and deliver lunch to a neighborhood church where the conference was held. To make sure that the drivers found the church, Connie assigned guides to stand at each corner near the church to watch for a small truck that would be carrying the tamales. It was not coming. The guides waited nervously. When the truck finally appeared in the distance, everyone sighed with great relief and let out a big cheer! There was Connie, as if coming to the rescue.

You could always count on Connie to bring in the essentials. As the owner and leader in charge, Connie should have only payed attention to the big things and delegated the small things to others. When Connie arrived at the conference that day, she noticed that there was no coffeemaker available. So, she left the building and came back with a coffeemaker that she had purchased at a nearby store. Nothing seemed to stop Connie! And, the Early California Conference event was a great success!

Connie did manage her restaurant with a strict hand. She demanded punctuality, good manners, good grooming, and honesty from her employees. She also provided instruction to improve their careers in the restaurant business. She praised her employees and always provided a Christmas dinner and party for them and their families. Connie considered this to be the time of the year when everyone should gather together for fun and relaxation, and so should the generous heart who provides it.

Consuelo showed her generosity in many ways. El Fandango Restaurant was also the place where families could enjoy a fiesta. Once, Connie was notified that there were limited funds in the budget to celebrate *Fiestas Patrias* in Old Town. So, the fiestas were not going to be held. Connie refused to let that stop her. She did not take "no" for an answer. Connie offered to have a fundraiser at El Fandango to make sure that the *Fiestas Patrias* would not be ignored. Many community members saw that support for this important annual Mexican cultural activity had been neglected by the larger committees. Connie spread the word and many locals attended the fundraiser, enough money was raised, and the *Fiestas Patrias* continued as planned; in fact, that year they turned out to be one of Old Town's most successful and fun events. There were now enough funds to buy plenty of *papel picado*, hang several *piñatas*, provide supplies for the children's games, and for all that was needed to present the best *Fiesta Patrias* parade that San Diego Old Town had ever seen! With Connie's strong spirit and community support, the Mexican spirit did not die.

This hard-working entrepreneur was born in Los Angeles, California, and raised in Mexico City. During the Depression years, her father lost his business. As a result, her parents decided to move back to Mexico City where her mother had been a teacher. Upon their return, her mother had a teacher's position waiting for her. At this point, Connie narrates the experience of her grandmother, a young widow with three little girls who was offered housing and education for her daughters by the Protestant American Missionaries in the state of Aguascalientes, Mexico. It was an all-girls school, and the students with financial means went home during the summer months. However, her grandmother and her girls— including Connie's mother—remained at this residence for years, since they had no other place to go. However, it was here, at this missionary school where Connie's mother learned the value of a good education, something she always passed on to Connie and her sisters. This is why Connie's mother never forgot to look for the opportunity to return to the United States someday, and that is what she did.

In the meantime, while in Mexico City, Connie and her sisters lived a very sheltered life and seldom left the suburban area where they resided. Even so, Connie remembers fondly her high school years, especially one time when she was able to break away from some of the family restrictions. Commuting to the capital by bus was a new adventure. She made new friends and was able to discover the beauty of the Mexican colonial and historical buildings that surrounded her high school. She still treasures these memories, but she also recalls that the time to leave these experiences was approaching. She was then a teenager and it would be time to start a new life in the United States. Connie's parents had new plans for the family to move. However, for Connie it meant leaving her friends and teachers. Ultimately, it became more than an ending; very soon, it was to be the beginning of a new adventure.

The family soon settled in San Diego where they had relatives who had never left. But, returning to the United States was a period of adjustment for Connie. On the way back from the station, Connie remembers how surprised she was to see all the wooden-frame houses built on hilltops. They were so different from Mexico City, which is built on a flat area and the houses are constructed with brick.

The urgency of learning a new language and finding the correct placement at school followed shortly. Connie knew that education was the key to success. She enrolled and attended school day and night. Soon, she had earned a high school diploma and had completed other requirements for advancement. In her résumé, one can see the list of schools she attended and the classes she completed to better herself and to learn more: the Mercy College of Nursing; San

Diego Community College; American Society of Clinical Pathologists; Registry of Medical Technologists; and more.

Consuelo married, but her first marriage ended and she had to raise four children on her own. If she had any hurdles to overcome, she always managed to move ahead and succeed in her plans. She remarried to James Miller, a well-known San Diego attorney, who loved to grow roses in their Mission Hills home. Now a widow, Connie provided love and care for her mother, and a beautiful place for her to live where grandchildren and friends could visit. Connie's mother lived a long life, almost 100 years. She instilled in all of her daughters the desire to keep learning, the importance of determination, and, most importantly, that education is the key to success. These are the qualities that Connie has lived by, that have guided her life, and that she has so generously passed on to her children and grandchildren.

These are also the qualities that her community—that she has served so graciously over the years—has witnessed in Connie, and continues to hold dear.

About the Author:

CELIA SOTOMAYOR MOODY, now retired, has served The Early San Diego Regional History Collaborative; has worked with Cabrillo National Monument, the Old Town Project; and the Delta Kappa Gamma-ETA-Nu, San Diego Chapter. After retiring from a career in education, she joined her sister, Dr. Marta Sotomayor's non profit organization, The National Hispanic Council on Aging, and managed the San Diego Chapter, *Los Tecolotes*, and several programs: she aided Income Tax for the Elderly; collected data for statistical research; and, under the leadership of Dr. Sotomayor, coordinated The Fellowship Program in Gerontology on Public Policy and Research, funded by The AARP, Andrus Foundation. Most recently, she was awarded "Volunteer of The Year" by Casa de Mexico, The House of Pacific Relations, International Cottages in Balboa Park.

LILIA VELASQUEZ:

ATTORNEY FOR WOMEN'S AND IMMIGRANT'S RIGHTS
Represents the Most Vulnerable and Disenfranchised

BY ANNE HOIBERG

To know Lilia Velasquez is to know one of the most passionate, dynamic, and respected immigration advocates in the country. Known as *La Flama*—"The Flame of Justice"—to her peers, she embodies the zest, humanity, and courage needed to represent the most vulnerable and disadvantaged segments of our population. Her entire career has been committed to providing justice and equality for all, particularly immigrant women and refugees. How did Lilia become this tireless advocate? Her early history provides much insight.

Coyuquilla Norte is the birthplace of a child, christened Lilia Salazar Castañeda. This small town is 200 miles north of Acapulco in Guerrero, Mexico. Lilia was born to Jesús Salazar and Maria Salud Castañeda. Lilia's parents separated, and her mother moved to another town to look for a job. Her paternal grandmother, Sofia, agreed to take care of Lilia. The home was a small, one-room, square adobe structure, without electricity or running water. Life was simple, but Lilia's childhood was happy with her grandmother in the little adobe house.

Lilia's formal education began in an outdoor, wood structure covered with a thatched roof. Children from preschool to the fifth grade were taught in one room by one teacher. After school, Lilia played with her pet iguana, and the two would spend hours swinging in the hammock.

When Lilia was five, her mother came to take custody of her. Sofia refused, claiming Lilia was happy living with her. The authorities came to Sofia's house and told her she had to give Lilia to her mother. Rather than complying with their request, Sofia chased the men with a rifle. Eventually, Maria took Lilia from Sofia; the separation from her grandmother and pet iguana caused Lilia immense pain and endless tears. Lilia was not to see her grandmother again until she was 15 years old. The long separation served to strengthen the bond they shared. Lilia's mother later remarried and had five more children; they lived in Tijuana until the family immigrated to the United States. From the time she arrived in the United States at age 19, Lilia was a goal-oriented person, accepting new challenges with relish, and moving at a speed few can match. Her desire for knowledge led her to San Diego City College, where she enrolled in classes, trying desperately to identify the few English words spoken in class that she knew. Language came quickly as she continued her education. After City College, she enrolled at Grossmont College, earning an associate degree in secretarial science. She then transferred to San Diego State University where she earned a degree in social work.

Lilia did an internship as a social worker at the nonprofit Family Service Association. This group conducted clinics combining the resources of social workers and law students from the University of San Diego School of Law. She observed the power of the law as a means of resolving problems and providing justice to the weak and vulnerable. Thus, she was drawn to a new challenge, shifting her career choice from that of social worker to that of attorney.

Nothing Could Stop Her

Her marriage to Louis and the birth of her child did not stop Lilia from pursing her dream of becoming a lawyer. When she enrolled at California Western School of Law, her daughter Sandra was two years old. And, in her last semester of law school, her second daughter, Elena, was born. Even with the responsibility of caring for two daughters, Lilia passed the bar exam on her first try.

Immediately after Lilia was licensed to practice law, she was hired to direct the Small Claims Advisory Program, under the County Office of Defender Services. After two successful years of running the program, she accepted the position of Assistant Clinical Director at California Western School of Law, where she worked for two years. In the fall of 1985, Lilia decided to take on yet another challenge: going into private practice as an immigration attorney. Since then, her office is devoted entirely to representing immigrants from all over the world. For the last decade, she has focused on defending women's rights, particularly victims of domestic violence, sexual abuse, and forced prostitution.

This amazingly fast accomplishment, from being a non-English-speaking immigrant to being a certified specialist in immigration and nationality law, has affected the lives of everyone who meets her, especially her clients. She has a special empathy with her clients and is all too aware of the difficulties of being in a foreign country and not knowing the language or the laws. Money is frequently a factor for her clients; Lilia understands and generously provides pro bono service. Through numerous daily telephone calls, she frequently gives legal advice to save time and money for the caller. Lilia is also the consulting attorney in immigration law for the Mexican Consulate in San Diego. To her clients, Lilia is a hero!

Lilia's role as a consummate attorney sets her apart from many others in her field. In addition, she also counsels young people. As an adjunct professor, Lilia teaches immigration law at California Western School of Law. Her students acknowledge her not only as a great teacher, but also as a compassionate mentor. Some students experience difficulty with their class assignments or question their decisions to become attorneys. Lilia dedicates a considerable amount of her time at the law school helping these students solve class assignments or resolve their career quandary. Former dean of the law school Steven Smith, in recommending Lilia for the Fay Stender Award, stated, "Beyond the quality of her classroom teaching, her interaction with students outside the classroom has been very impressive. She conveys to our students a strong sense of commitment to client and to justice, and that the two cannot be separated. She is a model of professionalism and commitment. As a role model, advocate and educator, Lilia Velasquez has embodied the high professional qualities of Fay Stender." To her students, Lilia is a hero!

The Fay Stender Award

It is important to know some background about Fay Abrahams Stender. She was born in Berkeley in 1932. She received her law degree from the University of Chicago. Throughout her life she undertook unpopular causes and worked with underrepresented groups and individuals. Her integrity, tenacity, creativity, and compelling sense of justice were legendary. The California Women's Lawyers established the Fay Stender Award in 1983, which is given annually to a feminist attorney who, like Stender, is committed to the representation of women and disadvantaged groups and has demonstrated a courageous ability to effect change. Lilia has said that the Fay Stender Award represents the "Oscar" of her professional career.

Lilia's advocacy on behalf of women is immeasurable. It is not uncommon for clients to tell Lilia, after she wins their cases, "you saved my life." One of these cases involved a 16-year-old Mexican girl, "Reyna," who was smuggled into the United States and forced to engage in prostitution in North County. Her captor, an older man, took her infant son and placed him in the care of his family in Mexico City. One day, while living in North County, he beat her because she refused to work and threw her out of the house. A neighbor called the police, and the federal government began an investigation of the prostitution ring. The American Civil Liberties Union of San Diego asked Lilia to represent "Reyna" who became a material witness in the prosecution of the case by the U.S. Attorney's

Office. The case had a happy ending. Reyna was reunited with her infant son, and Lilia obtained legal status for both, giving them a chance for a new life in the United States.

In another case of a client seeking asylum, Lilia represented a woman from Costa Rica who came to the United States with her three young daughters. For many years, she suffered brutal domestic violence by the father of her three children. She moved to seven different provinces in Costa Rica, but her victimizer always found her and continued the abuse. She tried getting protection from the authorities, to no avail. She was institutionalized several times due to her depression, and once attempted suicide as a means of escaping the violence. When the man attempted to kill her, she fled to the United States. Although domestic violence had not been recognized as a ground for persecution under our asylum laws, the immigration judge granted her and her three daughters relief, allowing them to reside legally in the United States.

Lilia Velasquez, Attorney, specializing in immigration and naturalization law, talks to KPBS about President Obama's new immigration policy in 2012.

Courtesy of KPBS.

Lilia describes her work this way:

My background, language skills, and cultural sensitivity have given me an opportunity to help those immigrants, refugees, and asylees who are most vulnerable: people whose civil rights have been violated, refugee women who have fled gender persecution, victims who have been trafficked, and women victims of domestic violence. When I hear women's stories of personal hardship and survival, I am inspired and motivated. It makes me realize how lucky I am to have the knowledge and ability to help them navigate the legal system and to be able to make a difference in their lives. It is touching to receive their gratitude and small tokens of appreciation, especially when they thought their cases were impossible to win.

Lilia has been recognized as one of San Diego's best immigration law attorneys by the *San Diego Union Tribune*. She has been lauded for her human rights work by California Lawyer magazine and other lawyering periodicals. Her many awards besides the Fay Stender Award, include the Excellence Achievers' Award by Today's Youth Asia; Latina of the Year by South Bay Adelante Mujer; Helen Marston Award by the ACLU; Award by the California Women Lawyers Association; and the San Diego County Bar Association's Community Service Award.

Lilia is an internationally known speaker and lectures regularly on immigration, human rights, refugee, and human trafficking issues. She is featured regularly on national and international news programs. In addition, she trains judges and lawyers throughout Latin America in trial skills, and has taught workshops in media advocacy in Mexico, Chile, Costa Rica, and Nepal. For seven years, she was featured weekly in "Despierta San Diego" of Univision TV on a variety of immigration issues.

Lilia Velasquez inherited her grandmother's strength, courage, and fighter spirit, which she uses to defend the rights of immigrants and women who are victims of domestic violence. She stands out above us all as she moves fast to fulfill her quest of bringing social justice and human rights to all. The flame of justice burns brightly and fiercely.

About the Author:

ANNE HOIBERG. During her 25-year career as a research psychologist with the U.S. Federal Government, Anne published two books and more than 130 scientific articles, book chapters, and reports. Currently, she serves as President of the following: Women's Museum of California, International Museum of Human Rights at San Diego, and La Jolla Pen Women. She is a past president of the League Women Voters of San Diego, United Nations Association of San Diego, and National Women's Political Caucus. She has volunteered as an election supervisor in "emerging" countries (eight missions for the U.S. Department of State) and leads delegations to United Nations' conferences and meetings.

CHAPTER 4

IRMA CASTRO

GLORIA SERRANO MEDINA

RACHAEL ORTIZ

ANDREA SKOREPA

CHAPTER 4

Leaders and Directors of Public Programs

Chicanas played active roles for change as dedicated leaders in public institutions that serve the Chicano/Latino community. Sometimes with little or no administrative experience, Chicanas took on leadership as directors of organizations or programs, like the Chicano Federation, the Barrio Station, Casa Familiar and the Centro Cultural de la Raza.

These organizations were founded to meet the need for various services in the Chicano/Latino community, from working with high-risk students and implementing drug abuse programs to providing child care to low-income women workers. The *mujeres* in this chapter confronted challenges head on, and found the means, methods, and support to make these organizations viable. Today these well-established institutions continue to serve our communities.

With roots in Logan Heights, Irma Castro returned after completing her college education and helped to establish La Escuelita del Barrio in San Diego's Logan Heights neighborhood. A component of then San Diego State College's Centro de Estudios Chicanos, La Escuelita taught English and math to underserved students in the 1970s. She was one of the first Chicana Executive Directors of the Chicano Federation in San Diego and was instrumental in leading many legal battles, including the adoption of district elections for the City of San Diego. She also developed special programs to benefit Chicanas, such as Niñas De Aztlán, Las Madrinas, and San Diego Adelante Mujer.

Gloria Serrano Medina moved with her family from Arizona to Old Town San Diego while still a child. In the late 1960s and early 70s, Gloria often joined her husband, Arturo Serrano, founder of the San Diego Brown Berets in 1968, at meetings, marches and protests. In 1974 Gloria became the first Affirmative Action officer to address the underrepresentation of people of color in the San Diego County work force, and aided in the lawsuit filed by the Department of Justice against the County of San Diego for its discriminatory practices. Gloria was a keynote speaker at the first Chicana conference held at the Chicano Federation.

Rachael Ortiz exemplifies the radical action needed to counter the neglect of youth in her community. Born in 1941 and orphaned as a child, Rachael Ortiz spent her young life in foster care and entangled in the juvenile justice system and became a "chuca" in 1950s. Heroin addiction led to her incarceration. Becoming involved in Cesar Chavez 's farmworker struggle in the Bay Area in 1966 not only changed her, but prepared her to be the leader she became. Returning to San Diego in the 1970s, when the Chicano Movement was in full swing, Rachael was hired as a youth organizer at Neighborhood House and then at the Barrio Station. In 1975, she became its Executive Director. Since then, Rachael's commitment to empowering barrio youth in Logan Heights and her work on behalf of Barrio Logan have been recognized with numerous awards.

Andrea Skorepa remembers watching trains go by in her South San Diego border town of San Ysidro and keeping company with the gypsies that camped on her family's land. At eighteen she joined VISTA, Volunteers in Service to America, and trained as a community organizer. Returning to San Ysidro, she eventually became a teachers' union organizer and then was hired at Casa Familiar, an organization that provides social and cultural services to one of San Diego's poorest communities. After over 30 years, she is now its president and CEO. Andrea's leadership in this organization has been vital to strengthening the community, giving residents a voice in the issues that impact it, from community development to border crossing.

These women activists forged a history of sacrifice and commitment that is important for future generations to know and to be inspired by, a legacy of which they are a part.

IRMA CASTRO:

A FIRST CHICANA DIRECTOR, LEADER, AND MENTOR

A Revolutionary Force

BY MARISOL RERUCHA

Irma Castro is a revolutionary force that has forever changed San Diego, the city where we live and love. She is a powerful woman who has changed the lives of many through her work as an activist, leader, and professor. It is with greatest pride and humility that I share the story of her life through a daughter's eyes.

My mother was born on June 19, 1941, into a poor, but powerful and educated family with deep roots in San Diego. Our ancestors and relatives are powerful because of the impact their work has had on our community. My *abuelita* worked in a fish cannery and my *abuelito* was an auto mechanic. My mom's earliest memories include being taught to read the daily newspaper by her grandfather and walking her first picket line at five years old. Her Aunt Katie, a union organizer for the fish canneries, was one of her greatest influences. Her Uncle Armando Miguel Rodriguez was appointed commissioner of the Equal Employment Opportunity Commission under four different U.S. presidential administrations. Her first cousin is Rafael Rubio, father to Rafael Rubio, Jr., founder of Rubio's—"home of the Original Fish Taco—a San Diego favorite. Her first cousin, Mike Amador owned and operated Mike Amador Market in Barrio Logan for over 50 years. Her first cousin, Elisa Luna Sanchez, served as an assistant superintendent and interim superintendent for Compton Unified School District. In a 1987, Palm Beach Post article, author Leilani Grajeda Higley credits our family for Irma Castro's career, "Though her parents may not have been aware, they were grooming her as a social activist; they gave her the roots and wings necessary for her success."

Although she came from a strong family, my mom still made the choice to dedicate her life to public service. I believe that the reason why Irma Castro is recognized as an influential woman in San Diego is because she is an example of a strong, fearless, and courageous leader who inspires others to take action and be a voice for those who are powerless. Hundreds of people have shared with me that her work has inspired them to finish their university education, become civically engaged, and to serve our communities. While this is something I am extremely proud of, there is more to be learned from her life. My hope in sharing her personal story is to document the way she chose to raise my brother and me and inspire others to courageously choose love, which I believe is the most revolutionary act of her life.

When attending Fresno State University in the sixties, my mother fell in love. One of her childhood friends told me of the shock she endured at witnessing my mother, a young fiery woman, on her knees, lovingly looking up into my father's eyes, as he sat in my abuelita's living room. My father, Abran Quevedo, was a student, activist, and artist. What an amazing pair they must have been. She, the eldest of three children who, as a high school graduate at age 16, declared a chemistry major before discovering her place in the civil rights movement. He was the youngest son of 14 children born and raised in the fields whose high school counselors placed on the university track once his intelligence was recognized. The few pictures in existence show a tall and slender pony-tailed man, with twinkling eyes, and a dark mustache, partnered with a curvy woman with short dark hair, bright eyes, and a smile that welcomed the world. I imagine that he was the ocean; she was the sand, brought together and pulled apart by the moon—the *movimiento*.

Together, they moved to a tiny square-shaped house, next to the small market across from Chicano Park. They started a life together and had their first child, my brother, Abran Alejandro Quevedo. It was at this time in 1970 that their place in San Diego's Chicano history was cemented. My dad's paintbrush was one of the first to touch the cement pillars under the Coronado Bridge. He was among the masters: Salvador "Queso" Torres, Victor Ochoa, and Mario Torero. During this time, they created a circle of friendships, some that were bound through the familial ritual of baptism.

At that time, Irma was asked to apply for a fellowship at MIT in Boston, Massachusetts. For whatever reasons, my dad stayed behind. My mom packed my brother and me into a station wagon and we made the cross-country trip. My only memories are of the cold Boston winter. It was shortly after we returned, a year later, that my parents separated. With a swift betrayal, my dad severed their marriage and violently broke my mother's heart. Regardless of the divorce and her pain, my mom found a way to forgive my father and ensure that he was a consistent presence in our lives. That presence and that of my *abuelita*, and my mom's number one supporter, her sister Yolanda Alicia Castro, or Yoli, formed the home base of our childhood.

When it came to the relationship between my dad, my brother, and me, my mom stood strong against the judgment of her mother, family, and friends. When my dad met my stepmother, Nancy, my mom slowly welcomed her into her home. After they were married, my two moms had a silent agreement to always put my brother and me first. The birth of my brother, Cameron, to my dad and Nancy, cemented our family union. Cameron grew up spending holidays at my mom's house and joining all family celebrations. Today, my mom, Nancy, and Yoli travel the world together. They have formed a beautiful sisterhood, bound by the choice to love. The words "blended family" do not describe what my parents have created. We are family.

Irma Castro, 2013, inducted into the San Diego County Women's Hall of Fame, by the Women's Museum of California.

Courtesy of Eleazar Lopez.

In order to complete this story of my mother's life, it is essential that I share the way Irma Castro changed our community through her work. Her career began in the 1960s as a young woman working with her Aunt Katie answering telephones at the union office. She also worked at Mercy Hospital and then Neighborhood House where she started as a bookkeeper, but learned everything from writing proposals, employee benefits, budgeting, community development, translating, and proposal writing.

Her involvement in the Chicano Movement began in 1964. Her career as a professor started at Fresno State University where she taught Raza Studies. In the mid-70s, she was one of the original professors of Chicano Studies at San Diego State University (SDSU), while founding La Escuelita in Barrio Logan. La Escuelita started as an SDSU project with the goal of teaching English as a Second Language

Irma Castro, Director of Programs at Casa Familiar; (left), presenting a "Girl Scouts San Diego Cool Woman of 2013" award to UFW activist Dolores Huerta. Girl Scouts' annual awards program honors outstanding female role models for girls who raise the standard of excellence through their personal and professional achievements. Castro was a Cool Woman in 2001, the inaugural year of the awards program.

Courtesy of Girl Scouts San Diego.

and basic math in Barrio Logan. It was at La Escuelita where Ramon "Chunky" Sanchez wrote "The Ballad of Chicano Park," during his work with preschool children. Most recently, she was a professor at Springfield College, teaching Activist Movements to multiple cohorts of human services undergraduates over sixteen years.

From 1979 to 1991, Irma dedicated her life and work to being the Chicano Federation executive director. She led them to win three court battles against the County of San Diego regarding the consent decree, a settlement involving long-ignored problems of employment discrimination; monitored the consent decree with the San Diego Police Department to secure equity within the department in terms of hiring and promotion; led a lawsuit against the City of San Diego that led to adoption of district elections in the city; chaired San Diego Dropout Prevention Round Table with San Diego Unified School District; and diversified United Way to ensure more organizations governed and served people of color.

In 1991, Irma left the Chicano Federation to work for San Diego Unified School District (SDUSD), were she remained for over thirteen years. She began as the coordinator for the New Beginnings Project, a collaboration between the City of San Diego, the County of San Diego, the San Diego Housing Commission, and SDUSD. She then became program manager for the Latina Advisory Program, later to become Latinas/Latinos Achieving More Academically (LLAMA), and then Student Advocacy Program. It was there that she developed Las Niñas de Aztlán; the Aspira al Futuro Program; the Adelante Mujer Program; the Hombres del Futuro Program; Las Madrinas, the Aunties program; and Student Advocacy. She worked with principals, counselors, teachers, and instructional assistants to establish Latina/Latino groups like these in over 85 schools.

At the time of this writing, Irma Castro is 73 years old and is the program officer for Casa Familiar, a community-based organization in San Ysidro. At Casa Familiar she has developed new programs, including Universidad Para Padres, the Books Project, Parent *Pláticas*, and summer camps for kids; developed and monitors programs meeting the needs of the Marguerite Casey Foundation; implemented Plaza Comunitaria, a Mexican government program for improving the education of Mexican citizens living outside Mexico; established and implements the internship-volunteer-community service program for Casa Familiar; developed the San Ysidro Community Posada; coordinates the Neighborhood Partnership Program, a communications mechanism for governmental and nonprofit organizations; and coordinates the San Ysidro Centennial Celebrations.

Yes, my mother changed our community, but through her love, she changed the trajectory of my life and that of my brothers. We are three whole adults who have the beauty of four parents: mom, dad, Yoli, and Nancy. We are by blood ties "half" siblings who share a whole family. We are the products of true love, a love that has made others uncomfortable in its truth and purity. This is what I consider a revolutionary love and my mother's most revolutionary act.

About the Author:

MARISOL RERUCHA, born and raised in San Diego, struggled through her teenage years, influenced by the realities of the inner city. As a single mother of two, she earned her BA In English at SDSU; taught middle and high school while earning her MA in Education Leadership at SDSU. She worked as an elementary school assistant principal, then as principal in South Bay Union High School District, and at MAAC Community Charter School. She is currently working with the Juvenile Courts and Community Schools in the San Diego County Office of Education as a career technical educations specialist. Marisol is a passionate mother and educator; she lives with her husband Daniel and their daughters, Carmina, Emilia, and Sophia.

GLORIA SERRANO MEDINA:

EQUAL RIGHTS ACTIVIST AND SAN DIEGO COUNTY'S FIRST AFFIRMATIVE ACTION OFFICER

She Felt an Urgency, Responsibility, and Commitment to Act

BY YVETTE FERNANDEZ

It was the 1960s! The Chicano community had identified many injustices and critical issues to address. These had been lingering for years and now was the time to change and correct the wrongs. The momentum and unity were there to get things done. Being actively involved in those times was indeed important and essentially a must, if you truly cared about equal rights for all people.

The 60s were tumultuous times for everyone and it was no different for Gloria Medina Serrano. There was a fire within her that was fostering the *peleonera*, that feisty spirit that is still there. But, she also acknowledges that the 60s were unique times. "It was the time for change and we definitely felt an urgency, a responsibility, and a commitment to act."

At age 70, Gloria calls herself Chicana. It's a term she immediately felt comfortable with in the early 60s. "I love the term 'Chicana' because it defines me," she added enthusiastically. Although often seen negatively by the older generation, for her it was always positive. For her, "It's what fit; it's what identified me."

Gloria's first language was Spanish, as she lived until second grade in Nogales, Sonora, Mexico. She loved being bilingual and bicultural. But, she recalls, "As an American citizen in my younger years, when I would go to Mexico they didn't call you a Mexican—they called you *pocha*. This term was used for those of Mexican descent born and raised in the United States. Gloria learned quickly about labels. They would become part of the fabric that would create a strong character, define her values, and lead her on a path she still follows to this day.

Born Gloria Luz Fernandez in Nogales, Arizona, at an early age, she and her family moved to what is now Old Town San Diego and eventually to Linda Vista. She attended Fremont Elementary in Old Town and later she and many other children were bussed to Dana Junior High and Point Loma High School. In Old Town, the family lived at her uncle's house at the end of Conde Street, a property that was later acquired by the state through eminent domain.

Her first official job was at the University of Nebraska Library in Lincoln, Nebraska. She went to Lincoln soon after graduating from high school to live with her brother and his family; he was an Air Force pilot stationed there at that time. Here is where she got a taste of discrimination first hand. She realized that the people looked at her dark features as different, and she had a hard time getting a job.

After several years and many jobs, in 1966 she was hired by the State of California Employment Development Department to staff and open up a new facility in Southeast San Diego, the San Diego Service Center. This new project proved her determination and intelligence. It was championed by then Governor Edmund G. Brown to house several state, county, and local government agencies all in one building accessible to the community. It was a success and quickly became the hub of many activities. It was in the basement of this building that the initial meetings to form the Chicano Federation were held. During this time, Gloria's awareness, knowledge, and activism blossomed and she readily got involved in many projects and activities.

That same fire that burned in her to change the world also fostered anger and frustration at the slow process. Admittedly, while there was plenty of reason for anger and urgency, sometimes it may have been misguided. She recalls a time when she and her "crew" decided to protest the dinner of Latino educators, which took place in Mission Valley, because "we considered the leaders to be traitors and sellouts." The word got out that they were serving non-union grapes at the dinner, which to us revealed their lack of consciousness for the United Farm Workers grape boycott by Cesar Chavez." Gloria recalls "walking in strategically to surround the place." Her girlfriend, a well-known public figure, grabbed the microphone. "She got that far!" Gloria exclaims, "Yes, this was truly radical. She picked up the microphone and shouted, '*No tienen huevos, ¡putos! Ustedes no apoyan a los campesinos. No tienen vergüenza*,'" (loosely translated: "The nerve! You are not supporting the farmworkers. You have no shame!"). Soon, the whole place was in turmoil. "They began chasing us out the doors," Gloria continues. "Someone had called the cops on us. We had to get out in a hurry. My girlfriend's niece was with us and a woman was trying to push her. So she grabbed the woman's hair and pulled off her wig. While we were being chased out of the building, we were also laughing out loud!"

During those times, as funny as the fights seem now, they were just as sad because Gloria recalls, "We were also fighting on our own." At the same time,

Gloria Serrano Medina, 1976, when she received the Dama de Distinction Award from the Mexican American Foundation.

Courtesy of Yolanda Avila Coquereau, on behalf of the late Victor E. Avila, photographer.

"we also learned that the way we did things was not always the best way," Gloria asserts. "But we were young and zealous and we felt we were fighting for our rights."

Those were not the only lessons along the way. Gloria had to learn to find the delicate balancing act between fighting for what she believed socially and politically, while protecting her government job and still finding a way to spend time with her family. It seemed as if the marches and protests were never-ending. At one point, she remembers being at a protest, pregnant with her second child, while her husband carried their first child on his shoulder.

Both Gloria and her husband, Arturo Serrano, had the same social and political makeup. He was instrumental in establishing the Brown Berets chapters in San Diego and San Ysidro. They were the power couple, both involved in several significant events like the "takeover" of Chicano Park and the establishment of the

These three women represent Chicana activists during the peak period of the Chicano Movement in the 1970s. Left to right: Rosalia Salinas, bilingual education; Gloria Serrano Medina, affirmative action; and Rachael Ortiz, community youth advocate.

Photo taken with Rachael's camera c1970 by Carlos Manzano.

Chicano Clinic, later named Logan Heights Family Heath Center—a dramatic, untold story unto itself. They were also at anti-war activities; fighting for prisoners' rights; or at the new social services programs that were brought into the community.

Gloria also fought for the women's rights. One of the biggest hurdles of that tumultuous time was sexism. "In the 60s, sexism was present and there was nothing subtle about it," she said. "So in addition to everything else, we also had to take on our own guys." She recalls that there were so many times when she was working so hard organizing, but got little credit because the guys were the ones assigned the lead roles. Unfortunately, the Chicanas fought an additional battle during the feminist movement of that era. Machismo was still very much ingrained into what should have been a more evolved Chicano Movement. Realizing this, the women became more vocal and outspoken and, in the end, stronger.

Still, there was even more to handle in the balancing act in the 1970s. Experience had taught Gloria about the power of intellectually strategizing. And, she learned the valuable lessons of financially taking care of herself and her family. All of those seemingly polarized elements came together. In this decade, the Chicana college students at San Diego City College and San Diego State University organized the first Chicana Conference, held at the Chicano Federation building in Chicano Park. Gloria was honored to be their first keynote speaker.

Also in 1970, at 25, Gloria became a founding member of the Barrio Station in Logan Heights. She has served on that board since its inception, which now marks its 44th year—over 45 years in existence. While working for the state, Gloria was selected to be the first state employee to be "out stationed" at a community agency: the Chicano Federation (housed at what is now the San Diego City College building at Chicano Park). Once again Gloria found herself in the hub of a myriad of community activities. She also partnered with the Chicana Service Action Center in Los Angeles and was able to bring to San Diego four paid apprenticeship positions for women.

In 1974, Gloria became the first Affirmative Action Officer for the County of San Diego and was later promoted to coordinator in charge of the County's internal Affirmative Action Program (AAP). The work of changing the extreme underrepresentation of Latinos at all levels of the county workforce was eventually aided by the lawsuit filed by the Department of Justice against the county for discrimination in 1976.

In 1979, Gloria and several women met to discuss the need for a women's group inclusive of all Latinas. The group worked diligently for about a year, writing the bylaws. Unfortunately, several factors came up in the group and it never came to fruition.

Sadly, on Father's Day in 1985, Arturo Serrano passed away, leaving Gloria with three sons, Armando, age 17; Israel, 15; and Joel, 5, to raise alone. Gloria also raised her niece, Mia. That same year, Gloria joined the Chicano Federation Board of Directors. She ended up serving a total of 16 years as a board member, seven of these as board chair. These years were difficult at times, but also fruitful and productive because of the groundwork she had laid. During this time, the Federation took the City of San Diego to court regarding district elections, and won.

After retiring from the county in 1998, Gloria worked for the Census Bureau preparing for the 2000 Census. She initially worked as recruiting assistant and then as recruiting manager. At the end of Census 2000, she resigned from the Chicano Federation Board to accept a job with the organization.

Gloria remains active. She worked seasonally for the County Registrar of Voters, registering individuals to vote, recruiting bilingual poll workers, as well as assisting with English/Spanish translations. Although she is now retired, Gloria remains on the board of the Barrio Station; on a Chicano Federation committee; and during elections often works as a federal elections observer, under the guidance of the Department of Justice.

After all the accomplishments and setbacks, there is one lesson Gloria feels the younger generation should learn: parents need to teach their children about all the fighting and sacrifice undertaken by the U.S. Civil Rights activists in the 1960s and 1970s in order to achieve what we have today. Clearly, Gloria's passion for justice and equality still burns just as bright. And she will still talk about an issue, and plot and strategize on what should be done. "I think that's something we will always carry with us," she says. Finally, Gloria proudly adds one more important thing when she claims, "I can say, I've lived my life."

About the Author:

YVETTE FERNANDEZ. This article was co-written by Yvette Fernandez, Gloria's niece. Yvette is a former Emmy-Award winning TV reporter, published author and columnist. She has been active in Latino and women's issues. An alumni of the prestigious Valley Leadership Civic organization (Phoenix); she also founded S.T.A.R., a mentorship program for high-school aged young women, and was invited to testify in Washington about the importance of mentorship.

RACHAEL ORTIZ:

EXECUTIVE DIRECTOR, THE BARRIO STATION

A Powerful Advocate for Youth in Logan Heights

BY LUCIA ACEVEDO GONZALES

At first, I had only heard about this legendary woman, Rachael Ortiz. Growing up in San Diego with parents who actively participated in the Chicano Movement meant spending a lot of time in Barrio Logan. My father was a muralist who painted many of the pillars in Chicano Park and my mother, a Chicana Studies professor, would take her students on tours of the park. My coming birth was announced at Chicano Park, and my brother Pablo was born on Chicano Park Day, April 22. That's how we were connected to the Barrio Logan neighborhood, and that is how we heard of Rachael Ortiz.

As a child, I mostly took for granted the beauty and culture of the neighborhood I was exposed to by my family. I never felt unsafe or concerned about being in this part of San Diego. I only later heard about the media focus on Barrio Logan as an area with high levels of crime and gang infestation and how one woman brought change to the people who lived there.

Beyond the hype, Rachael Ortiz stands out as a leader who made Logan Heights the core of her life's work, committing to positively impacting the neighborhood by addressing the issues that plagued it. Rachael is widely known as being a champion for this historic community and its residents. She is responsible for bringing in resources, creating equitable opportunities, and being a beacon of hope for marginalized youth who live there. According to an *LA Times* article that featured Rachael's work, she has come to be known in San Diego as "a woman who fought and won a personal battle against crime and drugs" (see articles.latimes.com/1986-02-03).

Born in San Diego in 1941, Rachael Ortiz was an orphan who was later adopted. She had to overcome many obstacles herself before helping others. She spent her young life in foster care and entangled in the juvenile justice system. Her involvement with "the system" would continue into her young adult and teen years as she became addicted to drugs and eventually found herself incarcerated.

She is not shy about the struggles and truth of her past. She knows that the struggles she experienced growing up and overcoming them, have made her the strong and successful woman she is today.

Rachael Ortiz, (First row, holding up UFW flag) 1968 in San Francisco, leading the march calling attention to Cesar Chavez's first fast.

Courtesy of Kurihara Photography.

Being a strong-willed person and a passionate lover of life are what got her into trouble and also got her out of it. She ultimately rejected her initial choices and wholeheartedly embraced her final decision to go the opposite way.

One move changed her life. In 1966, she relocated to San Francisco and volunteered with the United Farm Workers Union. It was there that she was given an opportunity to make some changes in her life, including leaving San Diego as a way of getting away from the circumstances that were holding her down. She became motivated by Cesar Chavez and La Causa, the cause of the United Farm Workers (UFW). But she was mostly motivated by Cesar's core beliefs about nonviolent actions and self-sacrifice. After a number of years of working with immigrants in the Bay Area, she returned to San Diego and to the community of Barrio Logan, where she would begin to effect change in the very neighborhood where she grew up and in the youth who lived there.

Rachael's greatest gift was that she did not separate herself from the young people who went to the same schools as she. She knew she had suffered the same problems and pulled the same pranks. "I grew up just like them," Rachael asserted. "And I've done the things they've done." That was only the beginning, but it was the reason why she became such an expert in being able to reach the youth she mentored.

Taking from her experience with the UFW in San Francisco, she became an activist in her own community because she was not blind to the struggles and injustices that her people endured. At first she started working as a youth organizer with the Neighborhood House Association. There, she focused on addressing the needs of young people. She continued this youth-focused work at the same time as she began volunteering at the Barrio Station. Her commitment to this work at this new place is what led her to become the executive director of the Barrio Station. This neighborhood organization focused on the support of Latino youth and families in Barrio Logan with a mission to "discourage delinquency, youth violence, gang involvement, and encourage civic responsibility and successful school performance among the youth."

Under Rachael's leadership — and with strong support from her community — she raised funds to grow services and facilities. Her vision was grand; it included a fifty thousand square-foot youth center with classrooms, studios, theater, gymnasium, and Olympic-size swimming pool. There, she was able to offer tutoring and sports activities, group counseling, and cultural activities to positively impact the lives of Chicano youth.

Rachael has the gift of making something out of nothing. She has brought in hundreds and thousands of dollars of funding for different programs she developed over the years. She works tirelessly year after year to build and sustain relationships, or to find new grants to maintain a sustainable center that is now The Barrio Station. The opportunities that she has created for youth have prevented them

Rachael Ortiz in 1972 reading the Barrio Station Newsletter.

Courtesy of The San Diego Union-Tribune.

from using drugs and following the destructive path of joining gangs. She began helping to develop them into different kinds of leaders.

Rachael created opportunities for the youth to come together with the mayor, police chief, probation officers, and city council members to have a voice. In writing this story, I asked my husband to share his experience with Rachael as mentor and leader. He was one of these kids living in Logan Heights who benefitted from opportunities Rachael offered him and his peers. He remembers Rachael inviting him to participate in a roundtable discussion with local police officers and public officials who were soliciting input from this group of young people. Rachael brought them together for their ideas on billboard messaging to their peers, encouraging them to stop using drugs. He remembers later seeing one of his ideas plastered across a billboard overlooking the freeway and thinking, "That one was my idea."

Rachael Ortiz, 1991, picketing and fasting with Barri Logan youth.

Courtesy of Barrio Station Archives.

This kind of pride instilled in others was the power of Rachael's work; she developed and created opportunities for young people in a way that could change their lives. Her plan was to create new options for them, including them in the decision-making process. She offered them something more than seeing themselves as marginalized neighborhood gangsters to becoming authors of a citywide campaign to create social change.

Other successes stem from the many volunteers, contributors, and neighborhood activists who contributed to changing the lives of the youth and children. Rachael has never forgotten them. She has demonstrated her appreciation with the countless awards she has bestowed on hundreds of people over the years. She has honored many, giving recognition to the unsung heroes of San Diego like Ramon "Chunky" Sanchez, Gloria Serrano Medina, Laura Rodriguez, Rosalia Salinas, and many others.

The success of Rachael's advocacy efforts is widely recognized. The triumphs she achieved for her community and its residents are numerous, despite the many battles she had to endure in order to effect change. As a result, she has earned countless awards herself that include the Cesar Chavez Humanitarian Award; Woman of the Year Award from the State of California Legislature; and the Dama de Distinction award; the Aztec Award by the Mexican Consulate. In 2014, Rachael Ortiz was inducted into the San Diego County Women's Hall of Fame by the Women's Museum of California.

Rachael Ortiz has gotten by because of her toughness, survival skills, and overcoming obstacles. What most people do not mention very often is her heart. Underneath the tough exterior is a soft heart. I saw it when I went to visit her in her Barrio Logan office and heard her talk about her youth and other causes. It is most noticeable when she gives recognition to others—many who have gone unrecognized—or when she gives out flowers to community service leaders at her annual banquets, as she once did for my mother; or when she stops in the middle of a strong appeal for her benefits, and shifts to serenading us with "Angel Baby," a song from the fifties whose strong nostalgia elicits memories of her youth. But her heart is most exposed every time she mentions the name of Cesar Chavez, her hero, the one who changed her life; then her voice cracks as she attempts to hold back a tear. She recovers quickly but, by then, everyone is feeling with her; there is no way that Rachael Ortiz can hide her true self or keep from revealing her heart to others.

Now, more than twenty years later, Rachael Ortiz continues in her leadership role at the Barrio Station, as well as maintaining a strong presence in the Barrio Logan community as an advocate for its residents. She exemplifies the determination and strength of a Chicana powerhouse. She is someone who, as a woman, many people admire for her determination, perseverance, and take-no-prisoners attitude. She is a true leader of mind and heart, a change agent for the Chicano youth of Barrio Logan in San Diego, which will be the living legacy of her efforts illuminated far beyond today.

About the Author:

LUCIA ACEVEDO GONZALES received the BA and MA from SDSU; she graduated with honors in the Community Based Block Counseling program (CBB) where she later taught. She has been engaged in the arts in San Diego since childhood; in the Young at Art program her work was exhibited at the Museum of Art in Balboa Park; in 1990, she won First Place in the International San Diego/Tijuana Youth History Fair. She has painted on murals with her artist father, Torero, and participated in programs with her mother Rita Sanchez, at Mesa College for Dolores Huerta and Betita Martinez. She won a grant at San Diego City College to introduce students to *Dia de los Muertos* altar-making. She lives with her husband Erik Gonzales and children, and works as senior program manager, for SAY San Diego, Social Advocacy for Youth.

*Andrea Skorepa, honored in 2013 by Latino Champions with the
Lifetime Achievement Award and again in 2016 at her retirement.*

Courtesy of Eleazar Lopez.

ANDREA SKOREPA:

EXECUTIVE DIRECTOR, CASA FAMILIAR
A Lifelong Resident of San Ysidro, the Place She Calls Home

BY MONICA MEDINA

What makes Andrea Skorepa a model for all San Diegans is her staunch belief in the town located on the international border between the United States and Mexico. As a lifelong resident of San Ysidro, California's most southern community, she advocates for it with heartfelt conviction and genuine love for the people who call it home.

"San Ysidro was like a Tom Sawyer place to grow up," she remembers fondly. "It was a small town where everyone knew everyone. We had a railroad that came through and as children we used to go and watch the trains go by. I can remember how Gypsies would come and camp on our land, have bonfires, and sing songs, and there I was, hanging out with them. My mother would say, 'You learn too much from the Gypsies.' But they inspired me because they were happy." For over 30 years, Skorepa has witnessed San Ysidro's transformation as the president and CEO of Casa Familiar. In fact, you could say she's had a hand in it.

Casa Familiar is a community-based, holistic development organization that helps individuals and families flourish by increasing their quality of life in the areas of human services, community development, recreation, technology, arts and culture, and education. Through her efforts, Skorepa has empowered thousands of San Ysidro residents to realize their own knack and know-how in helping their community flourish. "I attribute my success here," she says, "to believing the people have the answers within themselves and it's our job to enable them to use skills they already have, and polish the ones they don't."

Casa Familiar, which counts the City of San Diego Park and Recreation Department among its partners, has been working to clean up the San Ysidro Community Park, "Los Niños" Playground Project. The effort is especially meaningful to Skorepa, for the park was the first to be established by the Little Landers Colony in 1909. It is a grassroots effort, led by Casa Familiar, which plans to make it compliant with the Americans with Disabilities Act by adding ramp access and ridding it of broken sidewalks, as well as adding much-needed sand to the play area.

Skorepa's culture is very important to her and so Casa Familiar also has a strong focus on cultural arts, including a museum on its premises and *folklórico* dance classes for children. Skorepa notes, "We've always thought that one of the first things that happens in marginalized communities is that they take your culture away, your music, your art, all those kinds of things, and all you have time to do is work, work, work. But we make sure public art is available, including performances and art in parks. We have 28,000 participants a year using all our resources."

Skorepa considers that her biggest accomplishment at Casa Familiar has been to give the people of San Ysidro a voice and a seat at the table. "San Ysidro's taken seriously now," she says. "It's on everyone's radar screen. Politicians acknowledge us, and developers come and attend planning group meetings. They come to Casa for they know it's the only way to get my support, and elected officials have to earn our vote. We do get out the vote, and we do it equally. We know what moves people in different institutions."

Skorepa represents the community when it comes to the federal government's plans for the San Ysidro Port of Entry, also known as the world's busiest land border crossing. "We keep our community informed, and we want to hear from them, too," she remarks. "We have public meetings where we ask them what they want on the border. A lot of them are pedestrians and they want shorter waits. It's a problem we need to address."

Skorepa remembers a time when crossing the border was a lot simpler and waiting on long lines to cross wasn't an issue. "My grandmother had a dog, Mungo," she recalls, "and we would send him to my aunt's house in Tijuana, putting messages on him like a St. Bernard. 'We'll be there at two o'clock.' He would go to her house, she would read the note, and send one back with her answer. Mungo would go back and forth between the two countries." That's how easy it used to be.

Skorepa's career started out in community organizing through volunteerism. "I was brought up in a generation that saw the oncoming of the Peace Corps and AmeriCorps VISTA," she notes. "I joined VISTA when I was 18 because I believe in human rights, equality, and social justice kinds of issues, and I wanted to do what I could to help."

For eight weeks, Skorepa trained to be a community organizer. She soon found it was something she enjoyed doing, but when she was sent to her first assignment in Brownville, Texas, she had an epiphany. "These people were exactly the same as the people I left back home," she says. "Here I was, trying to help the poor when I realized for the first time that I was poor. So I stayed there for a year, then I came back and finished my education."

Back in San Ysidro, Skorepa became a kindergarten teacher. "I taught kindergarten because I wanted to get to children before they had all the curiosity taken out of them. But, while I was teaching I'd become curious about a child and find out more about the family. They'd ask me questions about their children and ask me for resources, and began to come to me with their problems. If I didn't know the answer, I'd tell them I'd find out. Wanting to help came naturally."

For Skorepa, being supportive meant organizing the teachers and fighting for their rights by creating a union for them. Realizing that she needed to do more, she became intrigued when she learned that Casa Familiar was in need of a new president. "I mentioned to a friend, I wish I could work there," Skorepa remembers. "And she said, 'You've been leading five-year-olds, you can do it.' She helped me write a resume and I was hired. I learned every job there so I could do them all. Now we're ushering in a new generation and it's been wonderful."

Skorepa loves her work and can't imagine being anywhere else. "I'm going to continue to share my passion with the people of San Ysidro," she says enthusiastically. "My dream is to leave San Ysidro and Casa Familiar in a position to grow and keep building a better community."

About the Author:

MONICA MEDINA's career in public broadcasting spans three decades since 1980. She joined KPBS in 1995 as director of diversity, engagement, and grants. She has spearheaded major outreach campaigns in San Diego, focusing on such issues as mental health, aging, military reintegration, children's literacy, and the annual One Book, One San Diego Initiative. She has served as project director for numerous national outreach campaigns, including project director for Latino Public Broadcasting programs like *Voces* and Equal Voice. She has received many awards, including San Diego State University's Top Twenty-Five Leadership Award.

CHAPTER 5

YOLANDA LOPEZ

GLORIA REBOLLEDO TORRES

LILIA GRACIA CASTRO

ALESSANDRA MOCTEZUMA

BERENICE BADILLO

CHAPTER 5

Chicanas in the Arts: Visual Artists

A peak period in the Chicano arts was 1965-1985. In 1990, a twenty-year retrospective opened at UCLA's Wight Gallery. It was called CARA, Chicano Art: Resistance and Affirmation, 1965-1985, the first exhibition of Chicano Art on a national scale about the Chicano Movement. San Diego artists were represented; women were represented; and in the exhibit's various themes of Chicano history and activism, a clear statement, "Chicana Feminist Visions" represented women's struggle for justice.

Art and activism defined the Chicano Movement. The two seemed to go together, making a political statement by resisting injustices suffered by the people, while affirming their Mexican and American history and identity. In 1969, both men and women gathered at the Ford Building, now the Aerospace Museum, forming a collective of artists who eventually founded the Centro Cultural de la Raza in Balboa Park. By 1970, artists, this time mostly males, became part of the Mexican muralist tradition of *Los Tres Grandes*, Mexico's three famous muralists, Siqueiros, Orozco, and Rivera. Frida Kahlo, an artist in her own right, and the wife of Diego Rivera, was not recognized until much later. Artists/activists began to paint murals on the concrete pillars under the Coronado Bridge, now Chicano Park, and in 1971 on the walls of the newly acquired Centro Cultural de la Raza. A form of resistance, they responded to the loss of the many homes wiped out when Freeway 5 and the bridge intruded into their neighborhoods; their actions were spurred on by the civil rights activity that surrounded them, and the Chicano Movement, of which they were a part.

The Mexican American people of San Diego, with support from others, had to fight for their cultural center and for the park promised them, when the City of San Diego announced a highway patrol station would be constructed under the bridge. Many of the activists who fought for Chicano Park and for the Centro Cultural were residents who were directly affected, families who lived nearby, artists and other activists involved in protests for needed community spaces, Chicano and Chicana students. These voices included a strong women's participation in acquiring these historical sites.

In this chapter, five women visual artist, tell their stories, some of them at the height of protest for equal rights during the U.S. Civil Rights Movement, others in the generation that followed, each one describing her particular struggles and triumphs.

The work of these Chicana artists/activists remains as a testament to their dedication, whether during the movement or the ongoing activities that followed. These women represent different time periods; some of them have since passed away and their stories are in chapter two: Aida Manciillas, artist and professor; and Charlotte Hernandez Terry, who painted in Chicano Park. All these artists have this in common, each one persisted in their demands for inclusion and equity, and each one represents women's legacy in the arts.

This chapter begins with Yolanda Lopez, whose art and activism exemplify the Chicana presence since the early movement days. She is important to San Diego, because she was born here and began her career here. In 1974, her work was among the first to be exhibited at the Centro Cultural gallery space in Logan Heights, and is rooted in that historical period, establishing women's artistic presence early on. Yolanda also helped young Chicanas paint a mural in Chicano Park. They called themselves "Mujeres Muralistas," after the Chicana/Latina artists in San Francisco. Since then Yolanda has become a nationally known artist; bent on dispelling stereotypes of women, she sought strong images as role models. She was part of the CARA exhibit whose catalog described her works this way, "The potential of feminist images to emancipate women is best realized in the landmark Guadalupe Series by Yolanda Lopez," helping to define women's contribution in a male dominated field. Yolanda's recent homecoming to San Diego for the Chicana exhibit at the Women's Museum of California entitled "Shoulders to Stand On," describes her legacy perfectly.

These critiques of Chicana art are important to document because for the first time Chicanas were part of a national traveling exhibit. One critic had this to say, "Chicana feminist poets, writers, artists . . .visual artists, in particular, provided a much needed dimension in Chicano art which helped to revitalize it." Self- affirmation and empowerment were the key words to describe the Chicanas, impactful words that would drive them.

In the 1980s, Gloria Rebolledo Torres' art touched many lives in San Diego: the collectors of her paintings; the many who saw her murals on walls; and the hundreds of children she reached in public schools. In 1977, a mural marathon, called Muralthon, followed Chicano Park's development, with an expansion of the art in the park initiated by the men who had begun painting together in 1970. "What seasoned the event," it has been said, "was the arrival of women" to the scene, members of Sacramento's Royal Chicano Air Force, an art group that included women. Some years later, Gloria Rebolledo, a local woman, joined forces with one of the park's founders, artist Salvador Roberto Torres, to paint in the community and to help to beautify the park. Gloria began to produce her own work. By 2006, she was honored at the Mesa College Gallery with a twenty-year retrospective, "Memories of the Rolling Hills of Old San Diego," curated by Alessandra Moctezuma, gallery director, another unveiling of what Chicanas were capable of accomplishing.

In the midst of civil rights activism and the formidable exclusivity of the Chicano mural artists, Lilia Gracia Castro decided to travel elsewhere to develop her craft. An E.O.P and MEChA student, she graduated from San Diego State University in the 1970s, traveled to Mexico City, returning periodically, until in 2014, she presented her years of success, the making of Mexican contemporary art, at an exhibit at the Centro Cultural. Lilia's story tells how she created visions that were innovative enough to bring her artistic acclaim in Mexico City, and a one-person exhibit at the Museum of Anthropology. She discovered in the earth at the ruins of the *Templo Mayor*, the roots of her artistic vision. Indigenous art had always been central to Chicano art and Lilia captured it at its source, and brought it home to San Diego, adding to the contributions made by women in the arts.

Berenice Badillo, a new generation artist, began painting as a student at Chula Vista High School, countering criticism for the Chicano art she was painting. To her, the art demonstrated worthy representations of her Mexican heritage. Her story tells how controversy turned to victory. In 1990 at Mesa College when she was only 18 years old, she was part of a Chicana Class in which she read the *Testimonio of Rigoberta Menchu*, an Indian woman who won the Nobel Peace Prize in 1993. Berenice engaged in her art, joined with the campus art committee, and designed a "Woman's Peace Mural." Since then, Berenice has painted murals all over San Diego, but her dream was to complete a mural in Chicano Park. Berenice is representative of the generation that has drawn with passion from the Chicano arts, inspired by those who came before her—something of which she is very proud.

Finding places to exhibit has always been a concern of Chicana artists. Art spaces have been very important to women who have traditionally been confined to the home. There they excelled in domestic arts like embroidery, painting on cloth, or on china, while art spaces outside the home were relegated to men. In 2001, Alessandra Moctezuma, an artist and gallery director, became instrumental in developing an exceptional art gallery space at San Diego Mesa College. Her story is one of conviction. She received an MFA from UCLA in art; painted in Los

Angeles with the late Eva Cockroft, a replica of the David Alfaro Siqueiros mural that had been erased by reactionaries to his art. She introduced Chicana Art to the Mesa College gallery, curating its first exhibit, and making Mesa College art openings a meeting place for innovative exhibitions. She extended invitations to all of San Diego, portraying a thriving presence in the arts. Not only has she opened up new spaces for other women to exhibit, her own art has been part of a number of them.

Women have indeed contributed to the murals under the bridge, to the walls at the Centro Cultural; and to the leadership of both of these spaces; they have certainly added to the reasons why these and other spaces have survived, and to the history of Chicano art in San Diego. Their narratives throughout this book, best tell their stories of overcoming challenges, persevering, and in the end, building a Chicana legacy.

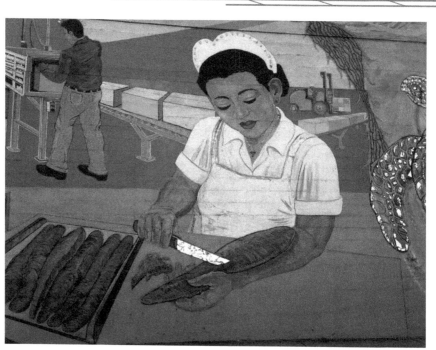

The Kelco Mural at the entry to Barrio Logan. Detail of Cannery Worker Woman on the 100 foot mural by Gloria Rebolledo and Salvador Roberto Torres.

Courtesy of Rita Sanchez.

YOLANDA LOPEZ:

NOTED CHICANA FEMINIST ARTIST

Her Guadalupe Series Challenged Stereotypes, Honored Women

BY AMERICA GONZALEZ

I feel honored to have interviewed Yolanda Lopez, such a strong Chicana artist. I would like to share my first impressions of her from 10 years ago, tell her personal story, and update it with some of her most recent challenges as an artist.

I interviewed Yolanda Lopez, well known for her Virgin of Guadalupe, series and many other works of art, including one called "Who's the Illegal Alien, Pilgrim?" It is a poster featuring an Aztec Indian, holding crumpled papers representing the Chicano response to President Carter's 1977 immigration plan. In 2006, I was a freshman in Professor Rita Sanchez's Chicana Studies class at San Diego Mesa College and my assignment was to interview a Chicana activist. I wanted to know more about Yolanda Lopez and her art because she painted the Virgin of Guadalupe in a new way. I grew up with *La Virgen* who had always been a sacred icon to me, and an important part of my faith. Back then, Yolanda's unique art interpretation with *La Virgen* running was considered very controversial, and I wanted to know more about it and the artist who created it.

Yolanda was kind enough to agree to the interview, which we conducted by email and phone conversations. After my interview with Yolanda, I realized the extent of her art and activism. Most importantly, I became aware of her concern for others who have experienced hardship; her time mentoring young artists; and, especially, that she is a talented and highly conscious artist.

Since then, Yolanda's work has grown. She has gone from being a young artist who completed her famous work in her hometown, San Diego, to becoming an important public figure in the arts. Yolanda has had many exhibits and two films that, through her art, attempt to dispel stereotypes. One such work is her video, Images of Mexicans in the Media, meant to show her young son how harmful stereotyping can be. Another exhibit, When I Think of Mexico, challenged the way the mass media depicts Mexicans and other Latin Americans.

Yolanda also worked as the director of education at the Mission Cultural Center for Latino Arts. She taught art for decades in studios and universities, including the University of California at San Diego; UC Berkeley, where she was director of the Worth Ryder Student Gallery; Mills College; and Stanford University. Yolanda's works have been purchased for permanent collections at San Francisco's de Young Museum, the Los Angeles County Museum of Art, and the Oakland Museum of California.

Yolanda Margaret Lopez is a Chicana artist, first and foremost, who helped women's rights by breaking down stereotypes and honoring hard-working women. Her series of drawings represent the Virgin of Guadalupe as seen in her mother, her grandmother, and herself. She uses her mother and grandmother as examples of hard-working women. She honors her mother with this image because her mother worked in a sewing factory for 30 years. She also honors her grandmother for her values and culture. Yolanda's own image, Portrait of the Artist as the Virgin of Guadalupe, acknowledges herself for being a runner, recognizing that not only men can become powerful athletes, but so can women. She depicts herself as the contemporary Chicana, in a very strong, energetic, and powerful way, running free. Yolanda made these drawings because she wanted Chicanas to have more positive role models. The Mexican role models women had in their lives, the Virgin of Guadalupe, La Malinche, and Sor Juana Inés de la Cruz, were not contemporary images. Not all Chicanas could easily identify themselves with these traditional images. Yolanda wanted to represent today's Chicanas and honor their work, and she did so in a very innovative way. She wanted to show society who women really are, what they are made of, and what they are capable of creating.

Yolanda was born in 1942 in San Diego, California. She grew up in the Logan Heights community where she lived with her mother, grandparents, and her two younger sisters. Yolanda is the oldest of three sisters. She is considered the favorite one, in Spanish, La Consentida. She says, "I am very lucky I didn't have any brothers, because if I had a brother he would have taken away all the attention and care from me." Yolanda believes that favoritism toward men still exists. She feels lucky in the way that her family supported her in anything she wanted to accomplish. Growing up, Yolanda had an uncle who would always help her out in school. He was also the first one to buy her paintbrushes and different colors of paint. This was a turning point in her life.

In 1961, Yolanda graduated from Lincoln High School, not knowing what to do with her life. "I had no idea how to go about studying for a career in art," she said, "I had tried to get into mechanical drawing or drafting but was turned away because girls were not allowed in those classes." Yolanda faced racism for being brown and sexism for being female, but as we see in her art, she overcame those obstacles. Four days after her graduation from high school, she decided to move to San Francisco with her uncle who had inspired her to continue her education. In the fall of 1961, she attended college and was the first generation in her family to do so. While she was in college, she worked as a nanny. "It paid well, but it was hard taking care of a little girl, and going to school," she said.

Yolanda Lopez, formal portrait, c1990. San Francisco.
Courtesy of Joe Ramos Photography.

Moving to San Francisco made Yolanda a stronger and more responsible woman. In 1966, she attended San Francisco State University (SFSU). She decided to move out of her uncle's home and become more independent. During her time at SFSU, Yolanda became more politically active. She joined the Third World Strike, a student protest that changed the university and changed her too; during this time she finally found people with her same interests. She found other smart Chicanos who wanted to succeed in life. She said, "Joining the Third World Strike was one of the best things I have ever done, because being in that group gave me power and enthusiasm to accomplish my goals. It gave me more confidence and strength to believe in myself." The strike shut down the university, but led to the establishment of Ethnic Studies at SFSU. Yolanda also became part of a support group for "Los Siete" (the seven) to make sure they got fair treatment in the courts. At that point, she decided to leave San Francisco and return to San Diego to help her community.

Upon her return to San Diego in 1971, she went back to school, later worked on the Chicano Park murals with young Chicanas, and attended the first International Women's Conference in Mexico City. By 1975, she had earned her bachelor's degree in painting and drawing from San Diego State University; in 1978, she received her master's degree from the University of California at San Diego. Soon after, in 1979, she completed "Our Lady of Guadalupe Series," which has been documented in the film, Chicano Park.

A few years later, Yolanda was discovered by Elinor Gadon, a feminist author who published Yolanda's work in her book, *The Once And Future Goddess* (1989). Yolanda was now seen as a feminist artist for her series of *La Virgen*, drawings with the purpose of breaking female stereotypes. These works were controversial because, in them, she deconstructs the sacred image and Mexico's most popular icon of the Blessed Mother, La Virgen de Guadalupe; In the Catholic religion, the Virgin is a very important spiritual figure; she is the mother of all Indians; and she is the mother of all Mexicans and the people of the Americas.

Yolanda explained that she had deconstructed the virginal image in such a way to honor Chicanas, and to sanctify everyday women and their lives' work. She said, "I chose to transform the image, using symbols of her power and virtue. I transformed them into portraits of women I knew. As Chicanos, we need to become aware of our own imagery." Yolanda was speaking up for Chicanas; she tried to show who these hard-working women were to honor them. Yolanda still believes that women should be recognized and admired for their hard work; and with her art, she has accomplished this. She continues to open doors for Chicanas to express themselves. Her art encourages activists who see her portrait of the artist as the Virgin of Guadalupe to identify with it because it honors women and makes a strong feminist statement. In 1994, Yolanda coauthored an essay with Moira Roth on "Racism and Sexism," included in *The Power of Feminist Art* (Norma Broude and Mary D. Garrard, eds. New York: H. N. Abrams). In 2008, Karen Mary Davalos wrote a book on Yolanda's life and work, titled *Yolanda M. López*, published by the University of Minnesota Press.

Yolanda now lives in San Francisco. Her only son was still living with her at the time of the interview, but has since moved out on his own. Yolanda has lost most of her immediate family. She lost her grandmother, her mother, and one of her sisters. Yolanda has also been close to death herself when she had brain surgery to remove an aneurism. Thankfully, Yolanda recovered and is in good health. When we last communicated 10 years ago, she was teaching elders about art, working in three different nursing homes. She was still drawing and selling her art. At that time, she hoped to come to San Diego and exhibit her art to college students.

Most recently, she was served an eviction notice in San Francisco, forcing her to move from the home she has lived in for 40 years. Her former husband, artist René Yañez, a cancer patient and father of her son Rio Yañez, lives in the same building and was also affected. Yolanda says in a *San Francisco Chronicle* article (June 26, 2014) that it was a very stressful time in her life as she dodged eviction process servers for three months. "They would come at all hours," she said. During this time, she decided to respond to this situation by making art. Inspired by friend and mentor Martha Rosler's 1973 art piece called "Monumental Garage Sale," Yolanda and her son Rio held a garage sale of their own, selling art and personal artifacts in preparation for their move.

Yolanda turned a difficult situation into a personal protest; she made the eviction documents an art piece. At Galería de la Raza in the Mission District, the sale turned into a conceptual performance about her own eviction. It also offered commentary on the people's permanent struggles today, as rampant evictions displace many long-term San Francisco residents. Finally, in August 2015, two nonprofits bought the building and other units from a landlord who decided to back away from the eviction, instead of selling to the city. The units will remain affordable housing and Yolanda did not have to move right away.

Yolanda Lopez tried to find role models for Chicanas, but, as we see today, she has become a role model to others. As a young Chicana myself, I now look at her as a role model, and as a feminist icon. She has broken down stereotypes by giving *La Virgen* a new meaning. She raised women's voices and also empowered them. She has opened up the political debate on immigration with her poster, questioning, "Who is the real illegal alien, Pilgrim?" Yolanda has inspired me with her art. I especially like the way she has represented Chicanas in her art. She shows how in the society in which we live, we are not just housewives, but we are also runners and hard workers. We are also smart, and we have values and morals. Yolanda has spoken for Chicanas through her actions and her art. She has given a new flavor to this new Chicana generation. Her art not only shows the truth about women, but it also shows the true meaning of Chicana power.

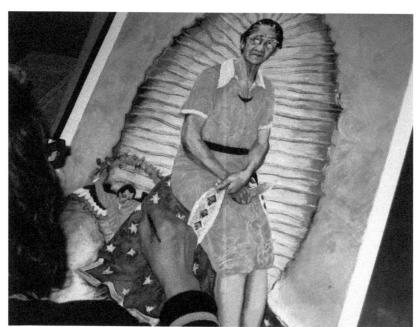

Yolanda Lopez at home with portrait of her grandmother with Virgin of Guadalupe background.

Courtesy of Sal Guereña.

About the Author:

AMERICA GONZALEZ. America came to the U.S. from Mexico in the 1980s as a two-month old baby. Her parents went to work in the fields as farm laborers, later applied for amnesty and became legal residents, and then U.S. citizens. America is a first generation college graduate. She received a B.A. from UCLA in 2009 with a major in Chicana Chicano Studies and a minor in Labor in the Workplace. She is now a social worker for the County of San Diego. A single mother, and a Certified Nursing Assistant, she is now seeking a graduate degree in nursing; America lives at home with her son Carlos.

GLORIA REBOLLEDO TORRES:

MURALIST, PAINTER AND ARTIST IN THE SCHOOLS
Painted her Memories, the Vistas and Rolling Hills of San Diego

BY MARY OTERO GONZALEZ

Gloria Rebolledo Torres recalls traveling on horseback in San Diego when there were small ranches with all kinds of animals and adobe structures dotting the landscape. She and her sisters raised goats and herded them through places untouched, long before development took over. She remembers sleeping underneath the stars, when San Diego was nothing but rolling hills and vistas as far as the eye could see.

Gloria is an artist. She is also one of the earliest residents who remembers the San Diego panorama she depicts in her art. She was born Gloria Rebolledo in 1935, a native Californian from Culver City, in the county of Los Angeles, but raised in Logan Heights in San Diego. Her family roots go back to Spain where her love of art and animals originates.

Her love of travel is as important to her as her sense of place. In fact, it is the subject of her art. And, although Gloria has resided in different places throughout San Diego County—and has traveled the United States, Canada, and Mexico—she has always returned to her Logan Heights roots.

Gloria Rebolledo Torres, painting with other artists on mural.

Courtesy of Salvador Roberto Torres.

A watershed year for Gloria was 1983. That year, she began to paint her childhood memories, almost as narratives. She was inspired to become a self-taught artist with Salvador Torres, master muralist and cofounder of world- renowned Chicano Park. Little did she know then that one day they would marry. Now her former husband, they were married twenty-three years

Her paintings, like stories, came to life on the canvases. Most of them were of her own life experiences, whether selling tamales and Mexican food or shepherding goats along the rolling hills of old San Diego. She recalls those memories of her youth as living off the land, before developers came and changed it all; before World War II erupted and her family's ranch, fairy boat, and land were confiscated to feed the U.S. Army. The story of that era unfolds, according to her uncle who visited the President of the United States Franklin Delano Roosevelt.

I now have the privilege of writing about Gloria, my friend and confidant. It was in the 1980s when I met Gloria. I was volunteering on the Chicano Park Arts Council and was just starting my career at San Diego Home Loan Counseling Center. We were at a Logan Heights land protest that the people wanted to preserve as a park. The slogans on all the signs read "All the Way to the Bay!" "Let's not stop now!" The people were shouting, "We had to fight for Chicano Park and now we want to keep this park for our children and for posterity." That park is now the Cesar Chavez Park, a people's victory, fought for and preserved by their loving efforts to build a livable neighborhood for their children. It is a park now, but at the time it was nothing but a dumping site in Barrio Logan, an eyesore and a health hazard, especially to children.

Gloria and I participated in cleaning up and watering plants in Chicano Park. We helped to keep up the condition of our neighborhood because the City of San Diego was not providing the proper maintenance. Gloria would go beyond what was expected to keep the park looking nice. She started an herb garden and planted a variety of trees. She gave the park loving care. She did all of this at a time when no one else would, and when unknowing outsiders criticized the park as being in the ghetto. She came to be known, along with Salvador, as "The Keepers of the Park."

Gloria and Salvador were married in Chicano Park in the beautiful setting that Gloria had created. The gardens she designed and the surrounding beauty attest to her love and care for the park. Not only did she marry at Chicano Park, but she participated in baptisms there and in 1990 painted a mural there as well. Gloria always felt so strongly about Chicano Park, so much so, she considered it her home.

I found Gloria's story rich with intrigue. Gloria had first married at age 16; became a mother of three; and went back to school to get her GED in order to become a cosmetologist like her mother. Her mother was her role model. She had once styled Doris Day's hair at the Coronado Hotel.

Gloria and I quickly became friends and took ceramic and sewing classes together at San Diego City College and at the Educational Cultural Complex. We both wanted to develop our artistic inclinations and had a lot of fun doing so.

Gloria is intrinsically an artist. Yet, over the years, she dedicated her life in support of her husband, Salvador, and in support of the arts in and around Chicano Park and Logan Heights. She was then 48 years old.

Gloria explains her existence as having been lived in four eras. The first she describes as living off the land in her youth; the second, living in glamour by working as a beauty operator and participating in hair-color-styling shows on the Queen Mary cruise ship in Long Beach; and the third, climbing 25-foot scaffolds, wearing coveralls, painting murals, planting xeriscapes, building kivas in Chicano Park, and setting up outdoor studios and mural living quarters. She climbed up 25-feet onto long scaffolds to help paint the 100-foot Kelco Mural with Sal in 1993. It has since been called "An evocative historical account of contributions by the peoples of Logan Heights." Her artwork has been shown alongside that of Mexican masters Diego Rivera, Frida Kahlo, David Alfaro Siqueiros, and José Clemente Orozco. She has shown and sold her art to collectors up and down the coast of California. She now considers herself living her fourth era and is still going strong.

Gloria has been on a mission since 1983 and has not stopped. I have learned to love her and appreciate her contributions to the San Diego community over the years. One of her biggest contributions—besides being known as one of the "Keepers of the Park"—is the time she has spent giving art classes to children. Gloria was selected to be in the "Young at Art Program" meant to reach 5,000 children in the San Diego Unified School District. She was one of several people hired as artists-in-residence to teach art in the schools. This program was the brainchild of Muriel Gluck, a philanthropist, who donated a million dollars so that artists and not just school teachers could teach art to children. Her vision was a resounding success.

Gloria helped produce countless art activities at Wilson Middle School and Kimberly and Sherman Elementary Schools. "At Wilson," Gloria recalled, "The school looked for the worst spots in the place and then had the children participate in beautifying those areas. In some places there were rusted pipes and so the children sanded them down and painted them in vibrant colors. At Kimberly School "we had the children paint paper murals while learning cooperation and the reasons for mural making. At Sherman Elementary the children learned to paint and make kites and were able to fly them over Golden Hill Park." Moreover, she stated, "All the children were given tours of Chicano Park and our art studios in Logan Heights, where I also taught them to work on clay and puppetry." Gloria brought passion and color and the product of her labor to the children she encountered and to their works of art. The result was a comprehensive Young at Art Exhibition at the San Diego Museum of Art.

Throughout the years, Gloria has received numerous awards for her work in the community. She even received the "keys" to the City of Coronado. Several of her students then came on a boat from Coronado, with the mayor, to visit her studio in Logan Heights. Gloria recognizes the value of her work and knows that she has done it with pure love in hopes of preserving her community's heritage through art, education, and community development.

Besides being an artist and studio maker, she is good at whatever she puts her mind to. Gloria also happens to be a great cook. More importantly, she is a pioneer of San Diego and one who has paid her dues, given the amount of work she has done for the benefit of her community. She truly believes in what she does.

I once believed that she was an undervalued asset to the San Diego Chicano community and not as appreciated as she should be. Then, in 2006, she was honored with a 20-year retrospective exhibition of her life's work at the San Diego Mesa College Gallery, under the direction of gallery curator Alessandra Moctezuma. A special program was entitled *Selected Works by Gloria Rebolledo Torres: From the Rolling Hills of Old San Diego: 1986-2006*. Gloria had several paintings that stood out in the exhibit. Each of them captured San Diego before it was developed. In one of them, "Symphony of Love," painted in 1986, she depicts herself as a young girl in 1939, serenading her goats at 7th Street and El Cajon Boulevard.

Gloria recalls herding goats from Ocean Beach to El Cajon and from San Ysidro to La Mesa, and those images became the subjects of her paintings. "In those days, there were no obstructions," she says, "So my sisters and I created our own paths." She also remembers when there were no car dealerships in Mission Valley, only beautiful Japanese gardens.

One darker work represents tragedy, recalling the brutal killing of the goats by packs of vicious wild dogs. In this black-and-white linoleum cut, the dogs are pictured wearing bow ties. They face the innocent goats as if ready to devour them. In this work, the dogs represent the corrupt political forces that have no concern for the poor and the homeless. The people who seek food or shelter are pictured as the innocent goats. They are thwarted by the powers of wealth and corruption. A memorable moment, Gloria's retrospective exhibit allowed her to tell the stories of her life that go with her paintings. It also gave San Diego the opportunity to pay homage to a loving member of its community for all that she has done.

In 2016, at 81, Gloria Rebolledo Torres is a woman of faith who continues to reside in Logan Heights. She enjoys her studio filled with her brilliant-colored art, paintings, while crocheting blankets for hire. She is enjoying her last "Hurrah Days!," as she calls them, era four, you might say. She continues working on beautifying her alley by planting flowers and gardening. She is also still seen, at times in 90 degree weather, lending a hand at Chicano Park and at surrounding mural sites along Harbor Drive and in her community.

Gloria is a loving person and I have had some of my best laughs with her, as she and I are kindred spirits. We have laughed together, cried together, worked together, and prayed together. It doesn't get any better than that.

Sunset, acrylic, 1986.

Courtesy of Gloria Rebolledo Torres.

About the Author:

MARY OTERO GONZALEZ. Mary retired in 2008 after 24 years leading the San Diego Home Loan Counseling & Education Center. She is well respected for her work with government officials, community organizations and the general public; she has spent the last six years as program manager with the City Heights Community Development Corporation; Mary is certified in community economic development by San Diego State University.

Lilia Gracia Castro, 2013, San Diego, at a Chicana Conciencia Committee meeting.

Courtesy of Rita Sanchez.

LILIA GRACIA CASTRO:

CONTEMPORARY MEXICAN ARTIST

The Templo Mayor, the Cradle of Aztec Civilization, Became Her Subject

BY NATALIA CASTAÑEDA GRACIA

Lilia Gracia Castro crossed the borders of her childhood in San Diego and became known as a respected Mexican contemporary artist. She traveled to her ancestral homeland to study at the National Institute of Fine Arts in Mexico City. She dug deep into her roots when the ruins of the Templo Mayor, the cradle of Aztec civilization, became the subject of her art. I know her story because she is my mother.

To me, she is more than an artist. My mom is a wonderful person. I see her as a tireless, determined, loving, and gentle woman. She is as admirable and exemplary for me as she is for many people. What I admire most is that she has never stopped striving to be a better person. I have seen her struggle with dignity and confidence, despite adversity.

Thanks to her, I have learned to see life from a deeper perspective, feeling more connected to the universe and to God. As a result, I have developed my own spirituality, as I have been given the respect and freedom to follow what my heart dictates. She always has had a simple, blunt, and hopeful word for me. My mom taught me what it is to feel respected and loved for who you are. Due to her loving support, I have gotten up, even when I felt I could not. She has encouraged me to struggle, persevere, and be brave in order to achieve my own dreams. She has advised me to be myself because it is a very valuable trait that requires courage. She is filled with a deep love for life and strives to make this a better world, especially through her art.

As an artist, her being is constantly renewing. Even when she feels afraid, she is studying and excelling, traveling and meeting new people, and seeing new places. She loves to have new experiences and is like an adventurous little girl with joy and humor to spread. Where she walks, she leaves a trail of friendships, fond memories, and affection. People remember her with love and pleasure because she always leaves a good impression. She is an honest woman, a woman of her word.

Lilia Gracia was born in Pilares de Nacozari, Sonora. With her parents and brothers, she immigrated to Los Angeles, California, when she was five. However, she grew up in San Diego, attending Our Lady of Guadalupe School in Logan Heights and then Castle Park High School. In 1975, she graduated from San Diego State University (SDSU) with a Bachelor's Degree in Health Science and Safety. At the age of 25, she decided that she really wanted to study art. On her own, she went to study at the University of Sonora in northern Mexico. One year later, she traveled to Mexico City, not knowing anyone there. She enrolled in the prestigious National Institute of Fine Arts, fulfilling her lifelong dream to become an artist. She graduated five years later and did so on her own, with great courage and passion.

She had always hoped to return to San Diego with her new knowledge to share with others, as she had come upon the very roots of our culture in Mexico. In the end, with over three decades of research at the National Institute of Anthropology and History, she wanted to bring to San Diego all she had learned in Mexico, fortifying our culture and establishing cultural bridges and understanding to share with others. One day she would.

Before she left San Diego for Mexico, at SDSU she was in the MEChA student organization and was an EOP student counselor. She had also joined in the community effort to acquire space for a cultural center in Balboa Park, a place where the Mexican culture and indigenous arts could be celebrated. She remembers the protests by the people and their courageous attempt to acquire the Ford Building for this purpose. She recalls, "I designed a large banner on craft paper with a serpent painted on it." Later, the people's actions resulted in the founding of the Centro Cultural de la Raza, but in another building. Lilia remembers when it was a huge water tank in Balboa Park. "It was a place where, as a girl, I could picnic with my parents and my brothers, and I could play nearby, roaming the canyons in Balboa Park after attending the museums with the whole family" she remembers fondly.

These stories tell more about my mom. For me, she is an example of life, strength, constant struggle, and survival. I honor her example in life that she so lovingly gives. From what I know, she has always been a restless being, tireless, and studious, eager for knowledge of spirit and mind. Since childhood, she has loved libraries and has learned much from reading, especially to overcome obstacles and be a better person. She is always busy, becoming a better version of herself. She is a respectable, tenacious student, the first woman in her family to graduate from a university.

I know it took years, much suffering, and hard times for her to be understood as a woman. Her parents strongly opposed and preferred that she not study art, but that she marry and settle down. However, she always fought for her right to be herself. That is why she always defends her passion and beliefs.

My mother was still an art student when the National Institute of Anthropology and History in Mexico City initiated excavations in the archaeological zone of the Templo Mayor, the cradle of Aztec civilization. She recalls proudly that, "In the mud, upon slabs of wood and structures, in contact with the ancient ruins, and among the anthropologists and archaeologists, I had the opportunity and privilege to witness a universal historical event." That moment changed my mother's life. Her art transformed from traditional to indigenous, eliciting in her, interpretations of the ancient treasures unearthed from the Mexican soil. She recalls with passion, "It seemed as if the earth itself had opened, surging forth in beauty and richness in forms, colors, textures, and symbolisms. Deeply moved, it captivated and changed me for life."

Thereafter, for a good part of her adult life, she worked at the Instituto Politécnico Nacional as a resident artist, restorer, and head of the studio for restoration, research, and production of art (taller de restauración, investigación y producción de arte), at the Exconvento de San Lorenzo Mártir, in Mexico City's Historic Center. It is one of the oldest convents in Mexico City, dating back to 1596.

When I was small, I remember I felt very proud of my mother, seeing her at work at the cloister. Other people tell stories about her too, recalling that she was always working in a small shop that smelled of paint materials, with high humidity, surrounded by books. Her studio was in a courtyard next to a historical fig tree that had thrived there since the sixteenth century.

My mother's art works always found their way, as she puts it, "to their new home." Some were bought by collectors or by the government of Mexico City; others were bought by galleries. Those who know about fine art appreciate her work because they know about the three decades of research she did with the National Institute of Anthropology and History.

My mom was always traveling back and forth, between Mexico and San Diego, since her parents, brothers, and close friends live there. She fell in love with a fellow Mexican artist and married in San Diego. I was born in San Diego in 1983, while they were both in art school.

I remember when my mom told me what it was like to be pregnant with me while painting a 100-square-meter mural. She was painting it on the third-floor stairway at the National School of Fine Arts in Mexico City. The director ordered her to get off the scaffold because it was dangerous (given the stage of her pregnancy). She refused to stop. She only responded that she "was not painting with her belly." Stubborn and tenacious, when something gets into her head, she will not let it go.

Her career as an artist has been long and plentiful. However, to me it is not just a reflection of her struggle and perseverance, but also of the quality and reliability of her work. I remember with love and joy when she had an exhibition at the Second Assembly of Representatives/ *Segunda Asamblea de Representantes* of Mexico City. She looked radiant, beautiful, smiling, full of feelings of satisfaction and joy.

Yet, she always looked forward to returning to San Diego and exhibiting her work at universities, galleries, and cultural centers. She also enjoyed giving lectures on the pre-Hispanic art of Mexico, while strengthening our identity and ties to the greatness of our Mexican culture, one of the greatest civilizations of humanity, especially in the United States where it could so easily be lost. For that reason, an invitation to have an exhibition at the Centro Cultural de la Raza, after four decades, was profoundly symbolic. Her return in 2013 was especially important because she was well aware that many people had dedicated much of their lives and effort to making the cultural center happen and to keeping it alive.

A year before graduating from art school, her now famous painting, *Chac-mol*, was one of 70 selected art pieces for the Salón Nacional de Pintura, displayed in the Diego Rivera Hall, at the Palacio Nacional de Bellas Artes in Mexico City, a major visual arts site at an international level. That same year she also exhibited at the gallery of the National Auditorium in Mexico City. An extraordinary and tenacious human being, she is like a little ant that never stops, continuing her work, aspiring to let its content be known and located where it deserves. That is my mom.

Then came her high point. In recognition of over fifty individual and collective, national and international, exhibitions and three decades of research, she was honored to have the first exhibition of contemporary art at the Museo del Templo Mayor in Mexico City's Museum of Anthropology. She was the first woman in the history of the museum and the Templo Mayor archaeological zone to exhibit at this site. With pride, she dedicated it to the women of Juárez, *las desaparecidas*, who had been kidnapped and violated. The breakthrough exhibition was a personal achievement, but also a watershed for other women like her so they could also expose their own creations.

In 2014, a homecoming to San Diego for an exhibition at the Centro Cultural de la Raza in Balboa Park brought together friends, family, and intimate encounters. But, above all, it enabled others to observe who she is today through her work. It allowed them to know her art for what it truly is: a unique contemporary view of the pre-Hispanic world, its art, and the past that help us value and understand ourselves and our present.

The story of my mom, Lilia Gracia Castro, can be told through her career as the vast and multifaceted person who has been a teacher, researcher, juror, poet, museographer, restorer, curator, and designer. She is my pride. She is also a warrior and the being whom I most love and admire.

Lilia Gracia Castro artwork, "Florecimiento," mixed media on canvas, 80x120 cm.
Courtesy of Lilia Gracia Castro.

About the Author:

NATALIA CASTAÑEDA GRACIA, Lilia Gracia Castro's daughter, was born in San Diego in 1983 and grew up in Mexico City where she attended private schools; she is mild-mannered, an avid reader, profound thinker, conscious of gender, non-violence, and defender of animal rights. She studied two years of psychology at the Claustro de Sor Juana University, and is actively preparing her thesis in linguistics at the National School of Anthropology and History.

Alessandra Moctezuma (left), 2016, Mesa College Gallery director with Pat Vine (right), art department administrator.

Courtesy of Neeko David.

ALESSANDRA MOCTEZUMA:

GALLERY DIRECTOR, SAN DIEGO MESA COLLEGE
Curates Innovative Exhibitions Including Chicana Art

BY JENNIFER VARGAS

In a world where the stigma of the "starving artist" deters many from pursuing a career in the arts, Alessandra's story shines as a beacon to prove otherwise. It's a story of the quest to find her voice. Alessandra has indeed found her voice and a new medium. At San Diego Mesa College she is a professor and director of San Diego Mesa College Gallery, as well as innovator of the Museum Studies Program.

Alessandra was a very shy child, surrounded by the vibrancy of Mexico City's art world to which her father, a filmmaker and newscaster, belonged. Her mother worked in the Museum of Anthropology and Alessandra roamed the halls of the Aztecs and Mayas. Her father was sent to Madrid as director of *Televisa* in Europe. She witnessed the changes that took place from Franco's dictatorship to a democracy. After living in Madrid for five years, she came to Los Angeles as a teenager. Upon graduation from high school, she briefly studied fashion design at the Fashion Institute (FIDM). She didn't find her calling until she took her first painting class at Santa Monica Community College and became hooked.

The traditional art training she received in Santa Monica allowed her to transfer to UCLA to pursue her desire to paint. As a Mexican immigrant kid, she had never been exposed to Chicano culture or the struggles related to it, but her increased awareness of Chicano art and interactions with organizations like MEChA opened up her vision. She was invited to participate in an exhibit where she featured her Pre-Columbian-inspired paintings.

After her plan to go to graduate school fell through, she was referred by a close friend and painting classmate to assist artist Eva Cockcroft in painting a 100-foot-long mural at the National Guard Armory in Long Beach. It became Alessandra's first mural. As she spent her summer painting in the long warm days with the at-risk youth she helped train to paint, she listened to Eva's stories of New York murals and community gardens. The rhythm of the work came naturally.

For a while, Alessandra found herself without work in the art world, until Eva referred her to Judy Baca, a Chicana muralist in need of a painting assistant. Working out of Judy's beautiful home and studio in Venice, she would spend the day painting and learning from Judy about a flurry of topics ranging from what was going on in the city, to Chicano studies, to Muralism, to Feminism, and everything in between. Artists, historians, famous athletes, and musicians were always stopping by to chat, and Alessandra felt right at home in the midst of this world.

Alessandra Moctezuma, self-portrait, artwork, "Heart of Darkness," dry point etching from a series of eight works, Journal de una mujer.

Courtesy of Alessandra Moctezuma

Judy asked Alessandra to work for her organization, the Social and Public Art Resource Center (SPARC). Alessandra grew as a painter and learned about the process of organizing an art show from start to finish, useful skills that aren't traditionally taught in art school. She was part of the team that worked on Judy's retrospective show at the Smithsonian National Museum of American Art, showcasing all of Judy's work at SPARC, which covered almost 20 years. Alessandra felt in her element, working with a team of young people at an intense pace.

After a year off of school and experience under her belt, Alessandra went back to UCLA for a three-year graduate program with a focus on printmaking and painting. She continued working almost full time at SPARC to support herself, doing her schoolwork on weekends and at night. Her goal was to teach painting after receiving her master's, which would allow her to dedicate weekends and summers to her painting.

Alessandra kept busy with an internship in the Public Arts Program for the Metropolitan Transportation Authority (MTA)—working in art projects for its light and underground rail— and participating in ADOBE LA, a group of architects and artists interested in curating exhibitions showing the Latino landscape of Los Angeles. These activities taught her about architecture, urban planning, design, and community involvement. Together they put on a show in the Museum of Contemporary Art in Los Angeles. Alessandra became an experienced and skilled artist with the ability to paint beautifully, but was at a loss when it came to incorporating her own "voice" into her paintings. At age 23, her search for her own voice had not taken her to where she could yet hear it.

During Alessandra's preparation for her final review and graduate exhibition, her mother was diagnosed with cancer; her health deteriorated abruptly from seemingly healthy to dying. As her mother went into heavy treatment, not knowing if she was going to make it past six weeks, Alessandra was offered the position of curator at SPARC and of project manager at MTA. Faced with a crossroads, Alessandra was torn between a job that gave her creative freedom and a job that offered more security; Alessandra chose the latter. She knew well enough that she needed security, and she was able to support her mother emotionally and financially for the year she survived.

Both of Alessandra's parents died six weeks apart in 1995. This sadness was followed by great happiness. She met and later married Mike Davis, author of *City of Quartz* (1990), renowned historian, and recipient of the MacArthur "Genius Award." With Mike, she taught a course at the Southern California Institute of Architecture and wrote about her activity in Los Angeles. After five years, Alessandra left MTA.

She then collaborated on the mural "Homage to Siqueiros" with her former mentor, Eva Cockcroft. The mural was painted on an exterior wall of the Self-Help Graphics original building in East Los Angeles. It was an homage to the great Mexican muralist masterpiece on Olvera Street.

In 1999, Alessandra moved to New York where her husband had been offered a job as professor at Stony Brook University and Alessandra started a doctorate in Hispanic languages and literature, aiming to go back to her plan of teaching.

Alessandra's artwork had begun to evolve into political collaborations with other artists, such as a group piece for the Garment Workers' Union in L.A. She was no longer painting for the sake of painting. Two years into her doctorate, she heard about a museum studies professor/gallery director position at San Diego Mesa College. It was her dream job, an opportunity to teach students everything she had learned through SPARC and her internships, to better prepare them for the art world. Alessandra went into the interview relaxed and calm, with the confidence that, if she was right for the job and the school was smart enough to see that, it would work out. This time she didn't worry about it, and it happened. She got the job.

Through her journey, guided by a desire to paint, Alessandra found her calling and the perfect vocation. The Museum Studies Program that Alessandra has developed is holistic in its approach, teaching students how to run a gallery and put on an art exhibit from start to finish. The program is generous in its use of the same hands-on method through which Alessandra learned, entrusting students with responsibilities and using their individual talents to work organically as a team, with Alessandra advising and guiding them. Alessandra hopes to continue her research into affordable museum studies and art programs, being proactive in advising students who hope to transfer to universities that offer more financial assistance and lower costs. She also hopes to one day find funding for students who are taking courses for credit and/or internships, understanding that not everyone can afford to work for free nor should they have to. The labor issues within the art world are important to her and relevant in the lives of art students.

In San Diego, Alessandra's involvement with students and the artist community has led her to positions in the city's art core. She serves in San Diego's Public Arts Committee and was a member of the San Diego Foundation's Arts and Culture working group, which developed and oversaw the Creative Catalyst grants. She was in the Oceanside Museum of Art Curatorial Committee, where she organized three exhibitions. She is currently a board member for the Friends of the Villa Montezuma Museum and on the advisory board for Balboa Park's nonprofit San Diego Art Institute. She has been involved in fundraising for the Gracia Molina de Pick Glass Gallery and for the SDSU Chicana Chicano Archive.

Alessandra values finding one's voice so that one's artwork can have a compass and a meaning. Finding a voice takes time and experiences; it takes living. Alessandra has found her voice and a new medium: teaching. She speaks out about important issues clouding the art world today. Her projects demonstrate kindness and generosity to aid artists in joining the art world in a just and dignified way, with a living wage and fair treatment. Life is unexpected and Alessandra's wisdom embraces this reality, and that is why she is ready to continue fighting in the name of art.

About the Author:

JENNIFER VARGAS, a San Diego native and the oldest daughter of first generation immigrants from Puebla, Mexico. She will be the first in her family to graduate from college in May 2015 with a BA in Architecture from UC Berkeley. In her work, she is interested in space as a medium to show kindness and dignity in a tangible and relevant architecture.

BERENICE BADILLO:

ARTIST FOR A NEW GENERATION

Has Left Her Mark on Walls, Hearts, and Minds of San Diego

BY PATRICIA AGUAYO

In life, there are people who interject our paths to expand horizons and challenge us to set the bar higher within ourselves. I am fortunate that this *mujer chingona*, Berenice Badillo, came into my path and gave me tools, weapons even, to liberate my own strengths. Together, Berenice and I have worked on various community art projects, murals, live painting, and performance art. Our most recent collaboration, *Chicana: Una Decisión Conciente*, was the event that sealed our sisterhood. Long before working with Berenice on any of the mentioned projects, I had been empowered by Berenice and her art work.

The first time I saw Berenice, she was live painting with two other women during a kick-off event for the "Chicano Visions: American Painters on the Verge" Exhibition. She was painting an Aztec glyph in vibrant turquoise hues. As I walked by, I stopped and watched a group

"Mural in Chicana Park," 1997, by Berenice Badillo.

Courtesy of Berenice Badillo.

of three women. They projected strength and pieces of my culture that I had not experienced before. Something within me was awakened by this moment. I felt validated in the work and moment these women were creating. I told myself I would become like one of them. I too wanted to be strong, conscious, and give back to my community through art. It was exhilarating to see women like me doing this work. They had at that time set the bar for a young Chicana who, prior to that moment, had no idea other women were doing this kind of work.

Years later, after reaching the goals I had set for myself, I sought out Berenice to collaborate with me. I have since learned something new each time we have worked together, but the biggest lesson is to be a fearless *mujer, artista, activista, sin complejos.* Berenice has advised and empowered my artistic spirit. This *mujer* will share her knowledge and convince even the most unmotivated person that all is attainable and possible. This empowerment creates the kind of sisterhood we Chicanas need to uplift one another. Berenice is the type of *mujer* who is always grinding away meticulously at a project; she leads by example. Living in a sedentary state is not acceptable when you are a self-identified Chicana who is committed to healing the community through art and activism. Currently, Berenice is an art psychotherapist and works at an outpatient clinic in Logan Heights with people who have severe and chronic mental illness.

Berenice Badillo was born in Michoacán, Mexico, and comes from a large family. Her grandmother came from a rich family, but was disowned when she married a *campesino.* Her grandfather tragically died unexpectedly, leaving her grandmother to care for twelve young children, including two sets of twins. Berenice's mother, the oldest daughter, struggled with the overwhelming responsibility to survive and help raise her brothers and sisters with little or no resources. Raised in the border city of Tijuana, then the streets of Lynwood, California, Berenice grew up with two mothers who raised her in two chapters of her life: childhood and adolescence.

Berenice set out to write the second chapter of her life by running away to San Diego at age fourteen. Having two mothers made for a certain set of obstacles common to many Chicano families regarding circumstances dealing with poverty, opportunity, and immigration. Growing up in a violent environment, she set out with the need to find and redefine her identity.

In elementary school, Berenice began to explore her creativity. It didn't take long for adults and her peers to take notice of her talent. Their reactions confirmed that she should continue to create. This gave her confidence and a positive self-esteem grew within her. She found comfort in creating, and began to escape the reality of her life circumstances and organize her emotions. Art enabled her to make sense of what she was feeling. She explains, "Art gave me purpose and hope by creating an alternative reality in which to process difficult emotions." Art is a portal to the one safe place artists can go to when they are deeply creating. It is warm, non-judgmental, and has no limits. Perhaps this is why artists escape for hours, days, and sometimes years.

By age 14, Berenice became rebellious. She was arrested for breaking into an abandoned house. By this time, she had endured physical and emotional abuse. The psychic pain and experiences of her teenage years ignited her need to explore psychology and healing. She made art to make sense of the violence in her personal life and in the communities in which she lived.

In high school, Berenice was a defiant student and would often skip classes. She felt different and didn't find herself fitting into any of the groups surrounding her. Her history and culture were not represented in her classes; therefore, she was denied the knowledge that could have empowered her identity. Looking back, Berenice realizes her rebelliousness was a cry for help.

Berenice remembers the teachers who helped her get through two classes, art and English. These teachers would not force assignments on her; on the contrary, they would allow her to make art and turn it in for credit. They found a way to meet her halfway and have her reach attainable goals. In art class, she found a sense of belonging, mostly because she could create her own world through art. She didn't have to fit into someone else's mold; she created her own. Now, she helps others do the same, in her work with marginalized populations, with homeless youth, and with people who have severe chronic illness. She meets them halfway, works at their pace, thus allowing for healing to take place during the art making process.

One of her lessons on art and activism came about in high school when she was working on an art piece as a memorial to a friend she had lost to gang violence. Her friend had been shot and killed in Barrio Logan. Her drawing had cultural images of indigenous Aztec art and Chicano barrio street culture. While she worked on the art piece, a substitute teacher criticized and censored her work without understanding the meaning, calling it worthless. Berenice's friend, activist Norma Chavez, who was involved in the student organization MEChA, helped Berenice bring up the issue at a school board meeting. The story was covered by the local media, and the drawing was displayed in the school lobby for all to see. Her art and the message it carried would not be silenced. In 1992, Berenice barely made her way through graduating from Chula Vista High School.

Hopeful and motivated, Berenice enrolled at Mesa College. Community College, which began her introduction to Chicano Studies, as it has been for many. She found herself feeling inspired, learning about a history that included her culture and Chicana identity. She got involved in MEChA and, soon after, became the co-chair. She was now leading others through activism and culture.

Berenice Badillo, Ocean View Growing Grounds Community mural event in conjunction with clients from Southeast Behavioral Health outpatient clinic, 2016.

Courtesy of Nuvia Ruland.

Her art work began to reflect the importance of social justice and Chican@ culture. During this time, she found support in her professor Rita Sanchez. Professor Sanchez was then teaching "La Chicana" class, a semester course dedicated to empowering and teaching the Chicana experience within the Chicano Movement. Professor Sanchez became one of Berenice's strongest advocates; she validated her art work and made an effort to give Berenice the resources to succeed. Sanchez knew Berenice aspired to be a muralist; she personally drove Berenice to Los Angeles to meet Chicana artist Judy Baca. "Rita was an incredibly important role model as she taught me about feminism and the worth of a woman," Berenice enthusiastically remarks. "She had in that semester challenged the traditional roles that had been engrained in my psyche."

Determined to be a muralist, Berenice transferred to Southwestern College, enrolling in Michael Schnorr's art course, another professor who would influence her path. She had heard of Schnorr, an Anglo art professor, who had painted murals at Chicano Park. She was impressed by him and his involvement in the art community, as well as his social justice projects. "I knew he was gonna be a fast ride and it was," she recounts.

Michael gave Berenice her first opportunity to teach at-risk youth in the Mark Twain Continuation School. He knew Berenice would be a great match because she was blunt, bold, and had a "drunken sailor mouth." Together, they worked with students to paint an art-fueled anti-smoking campaign targeted at youth in San Diego. This project was funded by the American Lung Association. The result included an art exhibition/installation at the children's art museum, full-size billboards, and bus stop bench advertisements. Berenice identifies this time as an important experience in her life: "It was then that I realized the power of art, when I saw and felt the glimmer of hope, the pride, ownership, and validation that our words and images provoked."

Another experience that had a great impact on Berenice was her involvement, from 1994 to 2004, with the autonomous squatter community of Maclovio Rojas in Tijuana, Mexico. Their houses were made from garage doors, discarded trash, and cardboard. "The community found itself trapped in the political grab for their right to their own land, which was surrounded by Hyundai, Samsung, and Panasonic plants. In Mexico, if you squat on the land for ten years it legally becomes yours," Berenice said. The government wanted to turn a blind eye because the land was worth money and the value would increase if further developed. "The government set out to brutally force these residents out of their land and the community led a march in protest," Berenice added. Then, Berenice, Michael, and other artists utilized their artistic talents and efforts to help bring attention to this community. They painted storefronts, made protest signs, videos, installations, paintings, and gallery exhibitions that told the story of the community, along with building a women's center and a bank. These efforts gained international attention and resulted in assistance from philanthropists and large organizations such as The Rockefeller Foundation, enabling the residents to stay on their land. The community of Maclovio Rojas successfully created their own mold by developing their land with their own vision and power.

As a Chicana artist, one of Berenice's goals was to paint a mural at Chicano Park. This is considered one of the highest honors that a Chicana@ artist can achieve. Many consider Chicano Park to be recovered land and a legacy of past, present, and future Chicanos. For many years, there was a lack of women artists painting murals at the park. Berenice sought out the support of Chicano male muralists of Chicano Park to help her and perhaps guide her in the right direction to paint her own mural at the park. These men were not open to helping her succeed. They didn't take her seriously. She faced discrimination because, as she saw it; to them, she was young, light-skinned, and a woman. In a world filled with discrimination against people of color, Berenice felt prejudice for her white skin. "Couldn't a young, light-skinned woman have an important thing to say?" she wondered.

Discrimination from Chicanos toward other Chicanos is far more common than we would like to admit. Some men—not all—within the movement do attempt to control and intimidate women. Other Chicanos are judged by their light skin and are asked to prove themselves to be true Chicanos. Berenice faced both. Although she did not get the support she had hoped for, she now had Michael Schnorr on her side; he was excited to guide and assist her.

In the summer of 1997, during the time when Chicano Park murals were being retrofitted, Berenice found herself in a hot classroom with canvas and house paint, ready to finally start her mural. Michael had left her there with the expectation that she would paint. According to Berenice, "I wanted to paint a mural that started and ended with strong women. Women that were warriors, and not naked."

That year, Berenice painted a mural at Chicano Park. The mural depicts two women of different generations attached by an umbilical cord; the older woman is at the top, ripping away layers of politics to shed light, so she can reach the younger woman below, and be able to pass the torch from generation to generation. The images in between the women represent a political arena that includes anti-immigration, racial profiling, Uncle Sam hanging the Statue of Liberty, poor education, and racism that exists in our society. The mural is far from politically correct; it is blunt and in your face. It shows the truth of our failing society and the struggle we encounter to create a better community. The forty-two-foot mural on canvas was installed on a Saturday. As per Berenice, it was "like a giant sticker with glue and pastry rollers." The process Michael had set up was, at once, a challenge and a realization of her dream. In Berenice's words, "Michael was ingenious. He saw the little spark in you and he would spin it, making the embers grow, telling everyone how amazing and talented you were, so that even you would start to believe it. What a gift he had."

This support that Berenice received from Michael Schnorr was the same kind of support and guidance that Berenice has given me. She is always open to my creative ventures, never dismisses or attempts to belittle my creative process. Like Michael, she expresses and shares my artistic potential with others. Her support has many times reminded me to rid myself of self-imposed limitations.

In 2001, Berenice acquired a Bachelor of Science degree in Human Services, followed in 2003, by a Master of Arts in Education, with a major in counseling, at San Diego State University's Community Based Block Program. In 2006, she received another M.A. in Marriage and Family Therapy from Loyola Marymount University, majoring in Clinical Art Therapy.

She currently works for the County of San Diego as an art therapist, serving lower income adults with co-occurring mental health issues. At the same time, she is working on her doctorate at Notre Dame de Namur University, currently the only Ph.D. art therapy program in the United States. If that were not enough, Berenice has dreams of one day completing another doctorate to explore "participatory action research," whose focus is on exploring what a community may need, together with its residents. That is, Berenice is bent on working with people to help them find their own liberation, adhering to the philosophy of 20th century Brazilian educator Paulo Freire. She believes that this kind of research would document the need for, and the impact of, community art therapy.

Berenice, the artist and Ph.D. candidate, hopes to center her future work on the mechanisms of change affecting individuals, groups creating murals, art programs, and literature that are relevant to Chican@s and other people of color. At present, her work is connected to the pain and healing she has experienced throughout her own life. Her contributions are much more than evangelical art or a band-aid remedy. As a master of research, she steps into the subject's role, visually and emotionally. She weaves a relationship between a person and a tangible visual manifestation of art to promote healing. Art, healing, and activism are at the core of Berenice Badillo's life work.

About the Author:

PATRICIA AGUAYO, Chicana Activist. Patricia Aguayo calls herself a community artist. She works with the Chicano Park Steering Committee and in 2012 helped restore the mural "Women Hold Up Half the Sky." She also worked on "Woman Rising," a collaborative mural, with three local San Diego artists— Berenice Badillo, Stephanie Cecilia Cervantes, and Zerina Zermeño, aka Poesia. She is responsible for co-sponsoring the notable community event called *Chicana: Una Decision Conciente* in Barrio Logan.

CHAPTER 6

VERONICA ENRIQUE

VIVIANA ENRIQUE ACOSTA

EVELYN DÍAZ CRUZ

CORAL MACFARLAND THUET

ROSA OLGA NAVARRO

CHAPTER 6

Chicanas in the Performing Arts:
Danza, Music, Teatro, Poetry

In the late 1960s, Chicanos wanted to preserve their rich Mexican heritage, and acknowledge their Hispano/Indigena ancestry. They realized that affirming their culture gave them pride in their heritage, enriched their lives and the lives of others, They celebrated their culture as a tool to bring people together, and as a basis for making social, political, and economic change. They introduced other art forms besides the visual arts, described in Chapter Five. With the Chicano Movement came a revitalization of the performing arts, attracting women to participate, to speak out, to write, and to perform.

Women participated in *ballet folklórico, danza Azteca*, Mexican and Chicano music, *teatro*, the theatre arts, and poetry. By 1965, the United Farmworkers had introduced their cause to the public with *teatro*. A time of activism for people's rights, *teatro* educated the public in the fight for better working conditions and wages. Both men and women recognized the need for a central place to gather, create and celebrate with community and family.

Women fought alongside men for needed spaces like the Centro Cultural and Chicano Park, and other spaces in the community, like Casa Salud, Voz Alta, UCSD, SDSU and other colleges and universities. These public venues proved to be the most valuable places where voices could be heard and the performing arts could flourish.

For these reasons and others, women took leadership when it came to promoting the arts, both at Chicano Park and the Centro Cultural. Since 1970, Tomasa "Tommie" Camarillo (Chapter Three) as a member of the Chicano Park Steering Committee, worked to preserve the park and the art, the people's culture; in 1975, the first guiding team of the Centro Cultural included, one woman and three men, Rosa Arreola was active in *Teatro Mestizo*, a group founded by Marcos Contreras at San Diego State in the early 1970s, and then introduced at the Centro Cultural. In 1979, another woman, director, Josie Talamantez (Chapter

Nine) developed the art gallery and increased international connections in the arts; and in 1981, Veronica Enrique became executive director, celebrating with a tenth anniversary, including music, *teatro*, and *folklórco*. Their stories tell us that Chicanas contributed significantly to the arts leadership in San Diego, and to the proliferation of the arts

Ballet Folklórico was one art form where women could be at center stage. The *ballet* appealed to audiences especially for its vibrant color, intricate costume designs, and its beauty of Mexican culture and tradition. Folklórico was the one art form where women were demanded. They were also the ones responsible for its thriving because of the discipline and commitment they applied to it. It was revived at the Ford Building, at the Centro Cultural and later at SDSU, by Herminia Enrique, who re-introduced it in the late 1960s (Chapter Two). Hermina and Julio Enrique and daughters, Veronica, Viviana, Sylvia, and Isabel, supporters of the arts followed in their mother's tradition of promoting the arts and for keeping them alive in their specific disciplines, as did Carla, Esmeralda, Teresa, Claudia, and sons Tupac, Julio Andres, and Julio Leonard.

Veronica Enrique, honored here, performed at the Centro Cultural as a girl, and then in 1981 became its executive director. Her story in this chapter shows her dedication and vision for the people.

In 1990, Viviana Enrique became the artistic director. Viviana had practically grown up at the Centro. The performing arts flourished. And like her mother, she also promoted the *Ballet Folklórico* as a way of preserving Mexicana/ Indigena culture. As artistic director, her dedication to her craft shows how a historical form can be promoted with perseverance and discipline.

Danza Azteca is an authentic art because it derives from the original Nahualtl speaking people and is celebrated as a way of preserving the Mexican Indian heritage that was deeply representative of the culture. More than entertainment, it spoke of identity and ancestry, reminding people of who they are as mestizos—giving them pride and dignity.

In this chapter, Rosa Olga Navarro's story tells how she brought her strengths as a *mestiza* woman to the dance. She considers Danza Azteca with Toltecas en Aztlán the Chicano artist collective, as one of her greatest accomplishments. Rosa Olga was one of the driving forces in reviving the Aztec dance at Chicano Park. Most of all she is proud of being a part of the artists who have accomplished so much to preserve Indigenous heritage and culture.

Many Chicanas joined the danza groups over the years. Bea Zamora (Chapter 7) as a young student discovered her Indian ancestry through danza. Today, even as a retired administrative dean, she continues to dance.

The Mexican musical tradition was richly performed by women before the Chicano Movement. One famous woman of the 1930s, Lydia Mendoza, a guitarist and singer, became known for her *Tejano, conjunto*, and traditional Mexican-American music. Chicanas of the Movement years were proud of having role models in their history and intent on reviving Mexican music. In 1969, Delia Moreno (Chapter 2) formed the Trio Moreno with her two daughters, bringing her professionalism to Chicano events. Delia overcame many obstacles and she and her daughters became the voice of the people.

Today, another performer of the traditional arts is Coral MacFarland, a professional singer. A student at SDSU in the 1970s, nearly forty years later, she began teaching the "Mexican and Chicano Music," course initiated by Jose "Pepe" Villarino in 1970. She was the first Chicana to teach the course. Her vibrant connections to Mexico and Chicano music, echo earlier performers like Lydia Mendoza, Delia Moreno, and Charlotte Hernandez-Terry, now passed away. Coral agrees with the late Delia Moreno, who in her own words believed that "our songs are meant to be passed on to the younger generation to preserve the music of our Mexican heritage."

Teatro, or *agit prop* theatre, skit or mime, as it was called, was one of the most strategic art forms used to get across the message of the Chicano Movement to audiences in communities, and colleges. It was initiated among Chicanos when a group called Teatro Campesino first began educating the public about the United Farmworkers and the Vietnam War. *Teatro* exposed injustices that led to protest in the late 1960s and1970s: Teatro Razita, Teatro Mestizo, and later, Teatro Magica Mascara, Teatro Izcalli, and Amigos del Rep. Two women were courageous enough to introduce their own version of it to the public, calling it Teatro de las Chicanas, to address the concerns of the women, dealing with racism, sexism, and exclusion. Felicitas Nuñez and her friend, Delia Ravelo co-founded Teatro de las Chicanas at SDSU. Delia Ravelo (Chapter Two) wrote the first play performed for their mothers by a group of women at SDSU, calling themselves, "Las Chicanas."

One member of the theatre group, honored here, Evelyn Diaz, was employed as the office administrator for Chicana Chicano Studies at SDSU beginning in 1974. She joined the women's theatre group when it was called Teatro Raices. After working in the Chicano Studies department for over ten years, a mother with three children, she decided to return to college. She graduated with a degree in Theatre Arts at UCLA, began to write her own plays, and is now a professor in the Theatre Arts department at the University of San Diego.

The stories in this chapter recognize the life work of many talented Chicanas whose work follows others who came before, among them, Lin Romero

(Chapter 2), one of the Taco Shop Poets. These women witnessed the people's struggles and wanted to contribute their efforts to change. Still other women made art their life's work and went on to gain significant recognition in the arts. All of them are able to tell their stories, sharing what they did at a significant moment in history, stories to be passed on to the next generation.

Photos from the First Chicana Conference 1973, Chicano Federation.
(Left to right) Top: Irene Mena; Las Chicanas
Bottom: Gloria Serrano Medina; and Yolanda Lopez with Gloria Serrano Medina.
Courtesy of Sonia Lopez.

VERONICA ENRIQUE:

DIRECTOR, CENTRO CULTURAL DE LA RAZA, 1981–1988
Her Efforts Ensured a Space Where Entire Families Could Gather

BY ZULEMA DÍAZ

> *"There is a legacy of heroines and activists in social movements and armed rebellions which Chicanas can draw from as models to emulate"*
> ~Anna Nieto Gómez

For those invested in maintaining a vibrant cultural life in our *barrios* as performers, as organizers, or as Chicana/o artists, the story of Veronica Enrique is praiseworthy; it speaks to the inclusion of Chicana activists within larger narratives about *El Movimiento* in San Diego, and the continuance of Mexican folkloric traditions within the borderlands. Her unique story and family history are intimately linked to the legacy of *Danza Azteca* and the *Ballet Folklórico en Aztlán* of Southern California. Moreover, as former executive director of the *Centro Cultural de La Raza*, Veronica Enrique's remarkable efforts in ensuring a space where entire families could learn about Mexican artistic expressions, is emblematic of the significant role that women of color fulfill as educators, leaders, healers, and culture bearers in our communities.

Now, almost 30 years after her tenure as executive director of the Centro Cultural de La Raza, Veronica Enrique acknowledges that elders have the responsibility to provide leadership and guidance to the succeeding generation. In retrospect, she also attributes community involvement and family unity as essential to nurturing talent, and providing alternative educational practices for disenfranchised members of the native communities across this hemisphere. Veronica's identity as a *Xicana* is tied to the knowledge that we are indigenous to this part of the world, and her personal history reflects the heritage of *Aztlán*. Her emphasis on safeguarding indigenous dance practices, as a committed *danzante*, uncovers the beneficial aspects of creating decolonial spaces among the borderlands which remind us that Chicana/os are native to *Aztlán*. Furthermore, documents containing detailed information regarding her tenure at the Centro

Cultural de La Raza are currently compiled and stored in the Department of Special Collections, at the University of California Santa Barbara Library.

Veronica Enrique's life-long commitment to the performing arts and social advocacy began at a fairly young age in San Antonio, Texas. Her parents, Herminia and Julio Enrique, imparted to her a profound appreciation for Mexican/Chicano artistic expressions. Ms. Enrique acknowledges that her parents' strong impulse to organize community festivals within a racially segregated society, promoted a strong sense of identity and belonging for her and her siblings. She recalls watching her mother host a series of workshops on writing, crochet, and even embroidery classes designed for kids at local parks and recreation centers. Herminia Enrique strongly believed that every person that participated in her workshops on *manualidades* had something of value to share with the society. Similarly, Veronica's father, Julio Enrique, made great efforts to organize a young men's club in San Antonio in order to strengthen ties among Mexican-American males and to promote athletic activities. The efforts made by Herminia and Julio Enrique to strengthen ties between community members, left a strong impression on Veronica and her siblings. These memories speak to the significance of nurturing inter-generational relationships, and the valuable lessons one can learn from our elders. After spending a significant part of her childhood in San Antonio, Veronica's father would eventually relocate the entire family to San Diego in order to pursue a career in the defense industry at North Island (Coronado).

Once the Enrique family relocated to San Diego in the late 1960s, they brought with them their passion for Mexican folk traditions and significant knowledge about community building. Their leadership skills and performance abilities provided an avenue for them to reestablish themselves in San Diego, and to forge relationships with an increasing population of Chicana/o activists. In San Diego, the Enrique family found a community receptive to the continuance of *zapateado* (stylized dancing), and other forms of Mexican regional dances as an integral part of Mexican festivities. However, the intent to ensure the continuance of a Mexican dance troupe did not come easy. Veronica Enrique recalls her mother having to invest countless hours sewing skirts for group members since they did not have the means to purchase costumes for the stage. After numerous fundraising events and classes offered by Veronica's two oldest sisters in National City, Herminia Enrique, eventually founded the Ballet Folklórico en Aztlán in 1967. In her own words, Veronica recounts her experiences as a *bailadora* and *danzante* during her upbringing. She states, "Thanks to the training I received from the Ballet Folklórico en Aztlán, I was taught numerous *danzas autóctonas* from different regions of Mexico. When Maestro Florencio Yescas began teaching *Danza Azteca* here in San Diego in the mid-70's, my brother, his partner, my sisters and I, learned from General Florencio and his group, *Esplendor Azteca*. Eventually, as local groups developed and transitioned, I formalized my commitment to Capitan Mario Aguilar and Danza Mexi'cayotl, and served as *Capitana del Sahumador*. Veronica's personal story not only exposes her participation in establishing significant dance groups in San Diego, but it also communicates a political ideology rooted in indigenous spirituality that was reminiscent of Chicano/a radical politics.

Veronica Enrique, 2016, performing with Danza Mexicayotl.
Courtesy of Rita Sanchez.

Veronica Enrique's involvement with the Chicana/o artistic community in the 1970s exposed her to a moment of intense political mobilization. Negotiations between activists and city officials to secure a cultural space in Balboa Park were ongoing. Veronica recalls the vacant Ford Building as being the ideal site for a cultural institution, and although Chicano muralist Salvador "Queso" Torres had the keys of the building in his possession, the plan was never approved. Subsequently, the current location of the Centro Cultural de La Raza became the alternate location.

In 1971,Veronica Enrique was selected at the age of eleven to release a dove into the air as representative of freedom and victory during the inauguration of the Centro Cultural de La Raza. One could infer that the releasing of the dove foreshadowed Enrique's career as a performer educator, since its inception, and as eventual Executive Director at the Centro Cultural from 1981 to 1988.

Veronica with braids as a young girl at Chicano Park.
Courtesy of Veronica Enriquez.

Prior to that, Veronica had spent countless weekends at the Centro Cultural de La Raza with her family attending poetry and art classes. She particularly enjoyed an art workshop on "still life" offered by a local Chicano artist named Guillermo Aranda. She claims to have been in complete disbelief that she could slowly make the "ear of corn" gradually come to life by adding layers of paint to the background. These workshops were instrumental in Veronica's life since they exposed the significance of celebrating cultural diversity, and how literacy, art, and *danza* possessed the ability to transform the lives of people living in Mexican *barrios*.

On July 11, 1981, as acting director of the Centro Cultural de La Raza, Veronica Enrique issued a welcoming statement to those attending the 10th year celebration. According to the program brochure, she stated, "As our creativity flows, with the spirit of our ancestors and the hope of our future, we open our arms to you to share the beauty of our culture on this night." That night offered many innovations and a hopeful future for the Centro Cultural under her leadership. The program included a bi-national cultural exchange project between Mexico and the United States where musicians based in Tijuana and other parts of the Mexican republic, such as *jarocho* artist Lino Chávez, participated in the anniversary event. In 1985, the Centro Cultural organized the fifteenth anniversary art exhibit, *Made in Aztlán*. A first major publication by the same title was introduced to the public. A seventy-person art exhibit included many women artists of note. Some of them are nationally known today, among them, Yolanda Lopez, Amalia Mesa Baines, Judith Baca, Diane Gamboa, and Patssi Valdez. In an article published in the *LA Times* regarding the Centro's fifteenth anniversary art exhibit, Veronica Enrique mentioned that, "We're trying to develop ourselves as an institution, and there really are no role models for us." Turning into a museum, or as she put it, a "sanctuary for Chicano art" is one possibility. This statement given by Veronica to the *L.A. Times* reporter captures her interest in building the reputation of the Centro as a legitimate institution that promotes cultural diversity by celebrating art as part of the nation's fabric. In her words, that would mean "producing, promoting and preserving Mexican, Indian and Chicano Art and Culture."

Although Veronica Enrique attributes the success of the Centro Cultural de La Raza to the efforts made by many families, the *Toltecas de Aztlán*, artists, staff, and volunteers, it is important to acknowledge that she dedicated countless hours to seeking sponsorship and to grant writing. In order to ensure the Centro as a thriving cultural institution, Veronica sought membership to various multicultural organizations where she was expected to attend meetings through various parts of California. She often had to balance motherhood with her role as executive director. Veronica recalls attending various meetings where Chicana activists, such as she, brought their children and breastfed while important negotiations were taking place.

Veronica names self-determination as one of the Centro's founding principles, along with self-respect and self-sacrifice. Previously, the cultural center was originally a volunteer organization. However, by 1985, a report in the *L.A. Times* reveals that it had an annual budget of $150,000, which paid two full-time employees, two part-time employees and four artists-in-residence. Most of the funds were obtained from COMBO, the county's combined arts funding organization; the City of San Diego; and the California Arts Council. She added, "We also received significant funding from the National Endowment for the Arts, Foundations, and Donations." In her own words, Veronica Enrique states, "We've established a track record. We've survived while other similar organizations have fallen away."

Veronica took on the new challenge of raising a family of her own. She married an artist named David Avalos whose innovative work is known in

San Diego. She and David Avalos have raised four children; two of them have been active with the Ballet Folklórico en Aztlán, and the other two who have been active with *Danza Mexicayotl*, and reside with their parents in National City. In June of 1988, Veronica resigned as the Centro's Executive Director. She was not the first woman director, but she was certainly valued for her personal investment and, as noted previously, because her entire family formed part of the Centro's founding members. Veronica is reminded how valuable that experience was, thus her determination to pass it on to other youth.

Ten years later, Veronica returned to the Centro as an invited guest for one session of the *Izcalli* program, extending her passionate commitment to do outreach among youth by teaching a Saturday school for *Izcalli*, a Nahuatl word representing awakening. This program was taught year around, and was centered on using indigenous thought and history of the Aztecs in order to invoke cultural pride among students. The four-hour class was designed to introduce to students information about Mesoamerica and concepts about Aztlán not found in traditional history books, or in school curricula within public institutions. Most of the teenagers that Veronica worked with had no knowledge of Aztlán; therefore, the classes helped spark their interest in their indigenous ancestry.

In short, Veronica Enrique's involvement with the *Centro Cultural de La Raza*, her passion for the performing arts, and her lifelong commitment to social advocacy, uncovers the prominent role that Chicanas among the borderlands, in this case San Diego, fulfill in increasing the political visibility of disenfranchised communities. The valuable lesson learned from Veronica's story is that her involvement with the Ballet Folklórico en Aztlán and *Danza Azteca* exposes dance as an integral part of social movements, and provides a possible explanation as to why, currently, these Mexican folk traditions form part of school curricula within the Sweetwater and San Diego Unified School Districts. Veronica's personal narrative communicates the experience of a Diaspora community seeking to secure and redefine a border culture that does not succumb to the pressures of U.S. cultural imperialism, but rather one that utilizes the performing arts to bridge the gap between Chicano/a and Mexican artists, and between elders and the succeeding generation of activists.

About the Author

ZULEMA DÍAZ, Ph.D Candidate, UCSD Literature; Instructor of English/ Chicana/o Studies at MiraCosta College; performance artist and member of Afro-Puerto Rican dance ensemble, Bomba Liberté.

VIVIANA ENRIQUE ACOSTA:

VOLADORA, DANCER, AND ARTISTIC DIRECTOR

Educated by Her Mother Herminia Acosta Enrique Tecihtzin

BY NANCY RODRIGUEZ

Viviana Enrique Acosta was introduced to arts and culture as a baby and, as a young girl, found herself in the midst of the Chicano Movement of the 1970s. It is no wonder that she has come to be known as the youngest, most accomplished performer, and then the artistic director at the Centro Cultural de la Raza, the premiere center for Chicano arts in San Diego. Today, with over forty years of experience, she has been recognized as historian and inducted into the San Diego County Women's Hall of Fame by the Women's Museum of California.

Viviana began engaging in her Mexican/Indigenous culture, dances, and ceremonies at a young age, educated by her mother Herminia Acosta Enrique Tecihtzin. By six months old, she was already on stage; by the time she could walk, she was in the light booth learning the technical aspects of the stage. As a child she was introduced to the ceremonies of the Danza del Venado. She learned the crafts of drawing, painting, singing, and acting, as well as the culinary arts, general building construction, and land stewardship by the time she was 10 years old.

In the 1970s, Viviana was the first child to enter the Centro Cultural de la Raza, when the keys to the building were given to the Chicano artists, becoming the first to engage in Danza Azteca in the San Diego region. At the age of 14, she was a ballet folklórico dance instructor at San Diego State University. At 17, she learned to "fly" in the ancient Volador ceremony. As a result of her courage in this performance, she was given the title of *Capitancita* and charged with maintaining this ceremony and sharing it with others. Besides that, she became one of San Diego's first Chicana experts in lighting, sound, and stage production. She performed Shakespearean roles in the Old Globe's theatrical training program. She was in the founding class of what would become known as the Visual and Performing Arts School. Most deservedly, she was one of the youngest artists to receive the California Artist-in-Residence in Communities

Maestra Viviana Enrique Acosta, 2012, Muevete Dance Studio, Lemon Grove; wearing vestuario from the region of Tamaulipas, Mexico.

Courtesy of Nancy Rodriguez.

grant, and then recognized over and over with this award for three consecutive years (1983-1985).

Viviana is best known for being a woman who has in-depth knowledge of her own individual culture, ethnic heritage, and history, and sharing these with others. As artistic director of the Ballet Folklórico en Aztlán, as *Capitana* of Danza Coyolxauhqui at the Centro Cultural, and as Two Spirit ceremonial leader, she strives to keep her culture alive and lives daily in this pursuit. She continues to teach dance with the Ballet Folklórico en Aztlán and as owner of Muévete Dance Studio in Lemon Grove, California. She has taught ballet folklórico to thousands of students at the Centro Cultural, her own studio, and Longfellow Elementary School for 14 years. Viviana currently teaches three classes at Longfellow where enrollment is always at capacity with students eager to learn Mexican folkloric dances.

Viviana's Indigenous perspective provides many girls and women with a role model so needed in our community. She has taught in workshops and lectures at all levels of the educational system in the San Diego region. She has reached thousands of residents, students, tourists, and visitors to the region, sharing her knowledge and expertise. She has also served as a cultural ambassador to visiting international diplomats and heads of state for the City of San Diego, while she was the visual and performing arts coordinator for the Centro Cultural de la Raza.

Viviana has produced and authored many dance theatre productions, plays, and musicals with her visionary spirit. She now enjoys knowing that some of her former students have their own groups and productions in the community. As curator, she has created spaces for established and upcoming artists—many of whom were women—to share their talent and voice. She gives unselfishly of her time and energy, offering her students training in ceremonies, dance, costume and set construction, acting, singing, and music as well as ceremonial land stewardship. She has offered numerous free-of-charge consulting hours for everything from park design and construction projects to assisting doctoral candidates with their dissertations. Be it mask making or wellness through dance, or intercultural communication, or on Indigenous Two Spirit Women, Viviana has been generous with sharing her expertise.

In 2015, Viviana was inducted into the San Diego County Women's Hall of Fame by the Women's Museum of California. As historian, her first response was to say that she was humbled by the recognition. Her own mother and mentor, Herminia Tecihtzin Enrique, whose spirit she keeps alive every day, was herself inducted into the Hall of Fame in 2004 for her knowledge and preservation of Mexican/Indigenous culture. Viviana's recognition passes the torch from mother to daughter. Viviana's own offering she describes as "transferring ancient knowledge and wisdom to the next generation to bring sacred traditions into fruition."

Viviana's path is a spiritual one, based on daily ceremonial life. Her courage to stand up for her Indigenous rights to maintain ceremonial dance is phenomenal. She is fearless in her determination to keep dance and ceremony alive, despite the many times she has had to overcome racism and homophobia in order to do so. She has also been known as "Bravey" since childhood. She is also the last remaining caretaker of certain sacred visions and prophecies, being a sacred culture bearer. Envisioning time and space where creativity can be offered and then making it happen, is testament to Viviana's ability to not just dream, but actually manifest. She firmly believes she is responsible for the next seven generations and strives to share her talents and wisdom with and for the betterment of the community.

About the author

NANCY RODRIGUEZ, a cultural arts activist and a co-capitana of Danza Coyolxauhqui. Currently she is a volunteer Maestra with Ballet Folklórico en Aztlán and co-producer and parent liaison at Muevete Dance Studio in Lemon Grove.

Evelyn Díaz Cruz, 2012, taken in the Vassiliadis Family Black Box Theatre for a feature story.

Courtesy of USD photographer Nick Abadilla.

EVELYN DÍAZ CRUZ:

PLAYWRIGHT AND PROFESSOR, THEATRE ARTS

"I Was Placed under Radical Scholar/Activists Who Encouraged Me"

BY JESSICA C. CORTEZ

Evelyn Díaz Cruz is known as an advocate for social justice and maintains a committed fight against racism and sexism in the arts. She is an Associate Professor of Theatre Arts at the University of San Diego where she teaches Theatre and Community, Theatre and Society, Acting, and Playwriting. She is an artist/activist with experience in writing, directing, and acting. Originally from the Bronx, New York, her study and practice of theatre is focused on community engagement by addressing issues of social justice through art. Her non-traditional approach to theatre garnered her a KPBS Hispanic Heritage Month Local Hero Award in The Arts for her contributions to the San Diego community. She is also a past recipient of the University of San Diego's Innovations in Experiential Education Award in recognition of her pedagogical approach to combining theatre and community service learning. Professor Cruz's teaching and creative scholarship reflects the University's mission of compassionate service, diversity, and social justice.

A long-time resident of San Diego, Evelyn was born and raised in the Bronx. She is a third-generation Puerto Rican and identifies as a *New Yorican* and Chicana. Stories from her youth continue to inspire and inform her work, which is Latina-centric and oftentimes focuses on the woman's body because that is the topic that young girls were forbidden to discuss. "I wanted to share stories with other women about our bodies, saying things we don't typically dare say to each other," she says. "One of those things was the myth of the maternal instinct that looms large in our communities. I have three children and each pregnancy was a decidedly different experience. I felt such guilt and shame over my differing feelings and wrote about it in *Glass Cord*, a play that was so well received by women because they could identify with it." Evelyn witnessed the emotional outpouring of women wanting to affirm their same experience; it was overwhelming and curative at the same time. "However," she continued, "I was sworn to secrecy because many women were sharing their thoughts for the first time. In the end, I shared too many tears with them." The woman's body and race are central to Evelyn's work as a means of helping women talk more openly about forbidden subjects.

Two formative moments nurtured her curiosity and set her in pursuit of her life's work. One such moment was when she was 16 years old and living with an older sister who had her own three children to provide for. During a job search, she was confronted with the stark realities of racism. Evelyn shared her experience openly with me and stated, "Growing up in New York, if you're Puerto Rican everyone knows you have at least some Black heritage, although some of us look more African than others. We even have a saying if someone is trying to deny her Black heritage: "...¿y tu abuela, dónde está?" Racism is apparent in other ways in Puerto Rican culture. Evelyn admits that, of the eight siblings in her family, she was identified and even celebrated as having the lightest complexion, a feature that would grant her more opportunities. This came into play when Evelyn was forced to "pass" as white in order to reap the benefits that whiteness afforded.

While looking for that first job at age 16, Evelyn encountered racism. She was filling out an application for a position at a Woolworth's store in Manhattan when she witnessed the white woman manager that had just given her an application deny the same application to a Black woman who arrived just minutes after Evelyn. Unable to afford losing the job, when the manager asked her if she was Italian, she could barely answer yes and then immediately felt as if she had betrayed her entire community, loved ones, and herself. Worse still was the fact that Evelyn had failed the math portion of the application and the manager fixed it for her. That transitional moment sparked her sense of awareness of white privilege, as well as her commitment to social justice that continues to inform the art she creates.

A second provocative incident occurred in the late 1970s when President Jimmy Carter created a program to help mothers get off welfare by providing them employment paid by the government's Comprehensive Employment and Training Act. Evelyn benefitted from that program. She was 21 and a single mother of two children when, as a result of her single-mother status, she was given a job as administrative assistant at San Diego State University's Chicana and Chicano Studies Department. According to Evelyn, "The world opened up to me when I was placed among radical scholars/activists who encouraged me to pursue an education and even gave me support to express myself artistically through theatre by working with Teatro Raices, an all Chicana/Latina women's *guerrilla* theatre troupe. This all-women's theatre collective grew out of the Chicano Movement— and Chicana women's civil rights movement known as *El Movimiento*." Labeled as "material feminists," the *agitprop* group's work examined class inequality, sexism, and racism from a primarily Marxist perspective. Using street theatre tactics, their work was designed to raise consciousness and inspire audiences to action. This theatre was by and for the community, and it took place wherever they were invited. Evelyn said she was "nurtured by radicals, loved, challenged, and mentored by San Diego's finest." This group's influence continues to inform and inspire Evelyn's work today.

Most recently, Evelyn's award-winning play *Glass Cord* was produced Off-Off Broadway at Latea Theatre in New York. Set on a rooftop in the Bronx during the 1970s, this play challenges the myths of the maternal instinct as something with which women must comply or else be stigmatized forever. Another original work, *Muertos: A Day of the Dead Play*, documents crossing the border through spirituality, dance, music, and communal altar creations. Evelyn has also worked and/or studied with influential theatre artists such as Marco Antonio Rodriguez (*La luz de un cigarillo*); Augusto Boal (*Theatre of the Oppressed*); Luis Valdez (*Zoot Suit, La Bamba*); and José Luis Valenzuela (*Chicano Moratorium*). She is currently working on a national multicampus play titled *Too Big*, which examines economic hardships of Generation Y.

Evelyn, like many women of her generation, pursued an education and eventual career as an artist and professor while raising three children. She graduated from UCLA and was hired by the University of San Diego (USD). At the university, Evelyn was part of a panel of Chicana activists of the U.S. Civil Rights Movement, organized by Gail Perez, professor of literature. Evelyn Diaz-Cruz, Sonia Lopez, Felicitas Nuñez, Olivia Puentes-Reynolds, and Rita Sanchez told their stories at the Social Issues Conference, in a panel discussion chaired by Professor Perez. The title of the presentation, "In Our Own Voice: the Chicana/Latina Struggle for the Education of La Raza," allowed Evelyn to tell the story of her activist journey before a public audience.

In 2015, Evelyn was the director for USD's spring production of *Twelve Angry Women*, a play by R. Rose and S. Sergel , about a first-degree murder in a seemingly open-and-shut case with 12 jurors that must weigh the evidence. In this play, deliberations grow heated and turn the jurors into 12 angry women, a searing look at the realities of our social justice system. The play and a post show "Talk Back" session provided Evelyn opportunities to display her expertise and creativity and, of course, some dynamic discussions about women and social justice.

As a professor, Evelyn Diaz-Cruz continues to engage her students in community service through theatre, both locally and most recently internationally. On a study abroad to Jamaica, she worked with young women residents at The Place of Safety, a woman's shelter. Evelyn states, "Arts education is liberation and everyone is capable of it." Evelyn's contagious energy, spirit, and authenticity come through as she continues to inspire others to more fully realize their own power.

San Diego Women's March, 2017. Top center, Norma Iglesias-Prieto, holding the "We the People" sign (by Shepard Fairey). Left to right: Patty O'Deane, Marta Sanchez, Rita Sanchez, Teyana Viscarra, Evelyn Díaz-Cruz, Lucia Acevedo Gonzales, and Jessica Cortez

Courtesy of Paul Espinosa.

About the author

JESSICA C. CORTEZ, a San Diego native and a recent graduate of the University of San Diego, Class of 2014 with a BA in Ethnic Studies and Theatre Arts, and minor in Leadership and Nonprofit Management. She is a tutor with Barrio Logan College Institute and Castle Park Elementary and an assistant for the Cesar Chavez Service Club. She is a theatre/artist activist and dances ballet folklórico.

CORAL MACFARLAND THUET:

SDSU MUSIC PROFESSOR AND PROFESSIONAL SINGER

A Talented Transfronteriza Who Captivates Young and Older Audiences

BY BERTHA HERNÁNDEZ

The audience was very attentive to the melodious voice of the redheaded woman standing before them. She not only used her voice, but also her hands and other corporal movements to get her message across. She walked from one end of the room to the other, never losing her train of thought, very assured in her delivery. She smiled at them, aware of the effect she was having. Yes, this was the beginning of yet another semester at San Diego State University, with another generation of young minds to fill with knowledge about different topics within the field of Chicana and Chicano Studies.

"I want you to meet someone," said Steve, a long-time friend of mine, "She will soon start teaching at SDSU and it would be nice if you could show her around." I joined him at a restaurant in La Jolla where Coral was performing. I, like many others present, became enthralled with her beautiful singing, of the tremendous stage presence and dominion that this woman exerted. We were introduced and that first "hello" was the preamble to a friendship that has become stronger with each passing year.

When people first meet Coral MacFarland Thuet they are oftentimes surprised that she speaks Spanish fluently. The surprise becomes magnified when she proudly says that she is from Tijuana (my *paisana*, although she was born in San Diego). Why surprised, you may ask? Well, this natural redhead is far from what most people expect—albeit stereotypically—of a Mexican woman's physical appearance; her Scottish roots are very evident. But, one needs only to speak with her about family to quickly learn that she is very proud of her Mexican heritage, of being a *transfronteriza*, of the experiences, good and bad, that life in our San Diego-Tijuana region have yielded upon her.

Coral is the typical transborder resident of yesteryear and today. It was very common then (and at present) that Tijuana residents would have their babies on the U.S. side of the border. Coral is the sixth of seven siblings. Not only did she inherit her mother's acting talent, but she was introduced to music by her father who had studied guitar with great Mexican composer Guty Cárdenas in Mexico City. In addition, her paternal grandmother and aunt sang opera. Her mother was a beautiful actress of German origin who had studied at the Goodman Theater in Chicago. On a trip there, Coral's father—born in Mina Dos Estrellas, Michoacán, of Scottish and Mexican ancestry—met her; they fell in love and married. They settled in Tijuana in the 1940s because the MacFarland brothers were established there. The brothers had traveled to Baja California to work in engineering and construction. They rebuilt Tijuana's downtown bullring, finished the Catedral de Nuestra Señora de Guadalupe, as well as many roadways. Meanwhile, Coral's mother adapted very well to the Mexican way of life. She even became one of the family's best cooks of Mexican food!

In the mid-1960s, the MacFarland family moved to Chula Vista, California. It proved very difficult for Coral to leave behind her friends, Catholic school, and a conservative Mexican lifestyle. Even though in Tijuana she experienced being "different" because of her last name and red hair, these same characteristics, but combined with her Mexicanness, made her stand out in her new public school. Since she was not fluent in English, she was mistakenly placed in classrooms for "slow" children. This was a common occurrence, given that bilingual education did not exist at the time. It took her many years to adapt to her new U.S. lifestyle, to overcome her feelings of displacement, and to break down the stereotypes of "not looking like a Mexican." Ultimately, all these experiences helped make her the strong and unique woman that she is today.

I consider Coral somewhat of a hidden musical jewel. She is an extraordinarily accomplished singer who combines jazz and Latin American music. She not only sings in English, but is just as comfortable doing so in Spanish, Portuguese, and even Ladino! She is a versatile recording artist with several CDs that include "To Another Shore" (very special to her because some of its songs' lyrics were written by her husband, Max), "Live at L'Escale," "Abriendo Puertas," and two children's albums in Spanish and English.

Coral is frequently invited to be the featured vocalist with international-caliber musicians. She has performed with the Orquesta de Baja California. She has also shared the stage with renowned jazz musicians, among them, Peter Sprague, Bob Magnusson, Gilbert Castellanos, Ramón Banda, Gary Foster, and Mundell Lowe. In addition to her singing, Coral has coproduced and performed in special musical programs: Celebrate Neruda, with Kamau Kenyatta; The Brilliance of Mexican Composers, with Allan Phillips; and Poesía, Canción y la Mujer, with Stephen O'Connor.

Coral MacFarland–Thuet, for The Real Women Project.

Courtesy of T.J. Dixon.

Her voice has also traveled the world. For example, Disney on Ice Productions selected her to sing "Beauty and the Beast" (duet with Quino, Big Mountain's vocalist) in Spanish for their worldwide Spanish-speaking audiences. She also recorded vocals for Luis Miguel, the Mexican superstar. In addition, the San Diego Padres, our local major league baseball organization, invited her to sing both the U.S. and Mexican national anthems at Petco Park. She has performed widely throughout the United States and Mexico, and one such performance stands out: singing for legendary civil rights leader Ms. Rosa Parks.

Coral's performances are always passionate, inspirational, and very authentic. She will sing with the same intensity before an audience of 20 or that of thousands. She establishes a rapport with her audiences, providing tidbits or anecdotes about the songs to be performed. She chats in Spanish and English, inviting her audiences to enjoy this journey of musical excellence.

Also a gifted actor, Coral has performed in major theater productions at the Old Globe Theater, San Diego Repertory Theater, and the Centro Cultural Tijuana. Some of her roles have highlighted her knowledge of Spanish and/or English.

There is no doubt that Coral's other passion is teaching. She has been a member of San Diego State University's Department of Chicana and Chicano Studies faculty for over seven years. She teaches oral communication, Mexican and Chicano music, and U.S./Mexico borderlands folklore. She is an integral part of the department, generously sharing her talent at sponsored events, to the enjoyment of all present. Her degree in oral communication and her music profession and sensibility are the ideal combination that makes her the perfect teacher of these courses. She also takes advantage of every opportunity—a trip to Mexico or a related seminar/workshop—to be prepared and most up to date on the topics that she teaches.

Students may often enroll in her courses only to fulfill a requirement. Many of them leave with a new sense of self, of purpose, of history. Those not of "color" will too walk away with better knowledge and awareness of our numerous Chicano/Mexicano population and its contributions and importance in the United States.

Coral truly and deeply cares about her students. Many of them are first-generation Chicana/o and/or Latina/o students who frequently struggle with their studies and life itself. She will go out of her way to accommodate and help her students succeed. I have seen her concern with this or that student who is not performing at his/her best. I have seen her delight at their accomplishments as well as her sadness at their failures. She will always believe in the best of students, rather than assuming the worst. Her students, in turn, love her! They credit her with positively impacting their lives and motivating them to accomplish their goals. They consider her unique, caring, efficient, knowledgeable, understanding. . .their list of admiring adjectives is endless.

Coral, my friend, is a wonderful woman whose sincerity and authenticity are incomparable. From my first meeting with her, her charisma was brightly evident. She always strives to become a better person and gives the best of herself. She is one of these persons who is truly humble and many times does not realize just how grand she really is. I have often wondered if she would not be a "world-renowned star" were it not for her honesty and genuineness. That lack of presumptuousness is one of her characteristics that I truly admire and appreciate—as I am sure others do too. Her friendship has become extremely important to me; I know that I can share anything with her and that I will not be judged, but understood. We regularly share our *transfronteriza* stories about our lives as we grew up to become the women that we are now. We have cried together; we have laughed together. I was blessed with three magnificent brothers, but no sisters. How lucky am I, though, that I get to choose my "sisters"?! Indeed, Coral has become my perfect sister, with her imperfections and all!

"Canta cómo los ángeles." "She sings like the angels." No doubt a cliché, but how applicable to Coral! Her love for music is undeniable. However, her love for her students is on par. When students express to her that they have learned to love their heritage, to understand their history, and to be proud of their roots because of what she taught them in her classes, I am certain that she finds these results another reason to sing.

About the Author:

BERTHA HERNÁNDEZ is an SDSU alumnus with degrees in Mexican American Studies, Journalism, and Transborder Public Administration and Governance. She is the coordinator of SDSU's Department of Chicana and Chicano Studies. She is president of the House of Mexico, a nonprofit organization, member of Balboa Park's House of Pacific Relations. In addition, she is a member of the Imperial Beach Health Center's Board of Directors.

Rosa Olga Navarro, Chicano Park.

San Diego Home/Garden Lifestyles, June 1989, in an article by Laura Walcher.
Courtesy of photographer Mary Kristen.

ROSA OLGA NAVARRO:

A LEADER, DANZA AZTECA
Has a Passion for Working with Youth

BY DIANE ORTIZ–MARTINEZ

What sets Rosa Olga Navarro apart from others is her passion for working with the youth of her community. She has educated many young women on the history that influenced her generation and on how they can influence the future. As a mother of two daughters and a long-time educator and community organizer, she has the motherly instinct that drives her to support and motivate young women. Growing up poor and becoming a mother at a young age didn't stop her from getting an education. Her drive to educate herself and establish an identity as a Chicana is inspirational. Her personal story presented here is what motivates young Chicanas to persevere despite life's challenges.

Rosa Olga considers her involvement with Toltecas en Aztlán one of her greatest accomplishments. This is a cultural organization comprised of San Diego artists, poets, and dancers that possess the strength and conviction to recapture and diffuse ancestral indigenous values. She was one of the main driving forces in reviving Aztec dancing in Chicano Park in the early 1980s. She recruited many new dancers and artists to become involved in the Barrio Logan community to bring awareness of the *Danza Azteca* culture to San Diego.

Toltecas en Aztlán, with the Chicano Park Steering Committee, organized the *Danza* celebration for 10 years. That is when Rosa traveled to Mexico and other ceremonies in Aztlán in order to reassure group leaders that the celebration would always be in April. She, thus, brought the *Danza* back to the Chicano Park Day celebration from whence it originated. Toltecas en Aztlán formed in 1975 and with the teachings of Andres Segura, *Jefe Conchero*, and Florencio Yescas, *Jefe Guerrero*. Along with Esplendor Azteca, it has received many awards for presenting a cultural experience at educational institutions, marches, protests, immigration-related events, and for serving the community in general. Rosa Olga was handed the honor of carrying the fire for Toltecas en Aztlán, due to the departure of one of its leaders, Guillermo Rosette, to New Mexico. Several years later, Rosa and her second husband Carlos Garcia were recognized formally as *jefes* during a *Cuauhtémoc* ceremony in Santa Fe, New Mexico, and the *estandarte* of the Toltecas was officially placed in their care.

Today, Rosa Olga's consciousness knows no borders. Rosa was born in Tijuana, Baja California. Her father was a sharpshooter in the Mexican Army. The members of his platoon were all native Zapotecs from the same town of Iztepec, Oaxaca. Her mother was a Chicana born in Latimer, Iowa. Her parents were repatriated to Mexico during the depression years.

Rosa, once considered a "border baby," traveled between her grandmother's house in Tijuana and her mama's in Los Angeles (L.A.) during her infancy until her mother moved the family to L.A. permanently. Later, when she was eight years old, her grandmother moved to East L.A. to take care of her and her siblings while her mother worked. Rosa was raised in East L.A. by her maternal grandmother and step dad, along with her six brothers and one sister. Her mother worked as a welder and her stepfather worked for the railroad. Their household was very poor and sometimes violent.

When crossing the border as a child, Rosa Olga recalls always declaring U.S. citizenship. Yet, she felt confused, not realizing where she was born until, eventually, as a teenager, her mother was forced to provide proof of her citizenship. At the age of 17 she became a teenage bride and mother. Three children were born from this union: daughter April, daughter Celeste, and son Ruben.

In the late 1960s, Rosa Olga became involved in the Chicano Movement for U.S. Civil Rights, through the Educational Issues Coordinating Committee (EICC) in Los Angeles. This experience introduced her to many other groups, political as well as social. She was very active in the East L.A. community during the high school "Blowouts," also known as the student walkouts for equal rights. She joined many groups that stood up for the rights of the people; all were involved in issues related to education, immigration, police brutality, and many other social problems. She was guided through this grassroots effort by some of the best teachers, such as Bert Corona from El Partido Comunista Mexicano; Abe Tapia from the Mexican American Political Association; Vahac Maridosian with EICC; and Herman Baca from the Committee for Chicano Rights. She also met many inspirational Chicanas, women from Los Angeles and San Diego. Two notable women were Alicia Escalante from the Welfare Rights Organization in L.A. and Herminia Enrique from San Diego. Rosa Olga credits these many mentors for contributing to her personal growth and political consciousness.

In 1970 her family moved to San Diego. She enrolled at San Diego City College. Joining MEChA, a Chicano student organization, was the beginning of her activism there. All the same issues from L.A. were part of the *movimiento* in San Diego. One site of great importance for this cause was Chicano Park in Logan Heights. Other central meeting places for the community were the Chicano Federation, the Neighborhood House, the South Bay Casa Hermandad General, and the MAAC Center, social service agency.

In 1973, the Chicanas from City College formed a liaison with the Chicanas from San Diego State University (SDSU). They met and worked with professors from both colleges. This was the beginning of Rosa Olga's work in the Chicana Movement, equal rights for women. For the first time she began to look at herself as a Chicana woman with her own special needs for child care as she recognized the needs of others, for example, sex education for the youth. During this time, she did not identify as a feminist. She explained it this way, "I believed that feminism was an Anglo term that I could not accept until my Chicano Raza was free from exploitation and discrimination."

The women's work led them to organize two Chicana conferences held in Logan Heights. The issues discussed were all pertinent to youth as well as to all women. Some of the work for the first Chicana conference was held at the Neighborhood House in Logan Heights, also known as the Chicano Free Clinic. Youth issues were discussed and presented by professionals as well as community residents and students. All this work done by women was meant to educate the community and demand equal rights for the people. Through it all, Rosa Olga was one of its fiercest advocates.

However, the activism of Chicanas was not always well received by their brothers; and some sisters in the movement were accused of wanting to be like white women. Rosa Olga remembers that in the eyes of some "they had shattered the pedestal of the virgin." These were turbulent times as the women had to stand up for themselves in the outside world and within their own communities.

During this epoch in her life, Rosa Olga transferred to SDSU where she graduated with a bachelor's degree and the State of California teaching credential. She accomplished all this at the same time that she worked with young girls at Balboa Elementary School, with a group called *Las Hermanitas*. Later on, when her youngest daughter became a teenager, Rosa Olga also sponsored a group called Ladies in Paradise, representing a group of *Chicanas Voluntarias*.

In early 2000, she was invited and sponsored to travel to West Germany by a group called the Four Suns. The couple in charge was Peter and Astrid Hugh. They admired and studied Native American culture. She and the Four Suns participated in a cultural exchange, with Rosa Olga representing the Aztec culture and the issues of Chicano Park. She also made a presentation at the Linden Museum in Stuttgart, Germany. In the end, she made a total of four trips to Germany.

Then, in the mid-to-late 2000s, health problems began to affect her life, one of them being the loss of her eyesight. For a couple of years, she began to depend more on the youth for assistance. Rosa Olga credits me and others when she recalls, "At that time, Diane Martinez, affectionately called *Venadita*, carried the fire for the Toltecas." Today, Rosa is grateful for all of their work.

In 2012, Rosa Olga resigned as coordinator of the *Danza* during the Chicano Park annual celebration. Rosa Olga also expresses her gratitude in this way: "I'm grateful for all my grassroots education. I believe that I never could have lived or learned this life experience even in the most prestigious universities. I have always followed and lived out my passion of working with youth."

It was because of Rosa Olga and the Toltecas that I, as a young woman, became involved in, not only the cultural, but the social political movement that involved the Chicana and Chicano community. When I faced problems concerning personal identity and feelings of not belonging in my own community, Rosa Olga would remind me of my validity that my culture affords me. She instilled in me a sense of pride and reassured me that no matter where I go in life or who might try to tell me otherwise, I should be proud of my origins.

Growing up, my mother always taught me to be conscious of my culture and my heritage as a member of the Pascua Yaqui tribe of Tucson, Arizona. I was always aware of my Native American and Mexican roots and was taught to always be proud of my heritage. When I was younger, I recall at times feeling isolated because of the ignorance I would face from classmates and friends when I expressed pride for my people and who I was. I attribute the great change I experienced to Rosa Olga and to meeting other *Danza* members. When I started *Danza Azteca* with Toltecas en Aztlán, I found that there were other people like me who were also conscious of their culture.

I believe Rosa Olga has touched the lives of many Chicanas throughout the years, identifying as a feminist during a time when the term was mostly used by white women. This was a starting point in the realization that women like Rosa Olga deserve the right to an education and a voice in the already established Chicano Movement. She has become respected in her community throughout the years for being a strong-willed woman who doesn't back down. I, along with others, have been influenced by her willingness to stand up for what is right, even in the face of men who think they know better or can do better than she. Rosa Olga is a strong woman figure for her daughters and for the many other young women she has worked with over the years. As a result, I will always be a strong Chicana woman who is capable of standing up for myself and my community. For this, I am thankful to Rosa Olga.

About the Author:

DIANE ORTIZ-MARTINEZ belongs to the Pascua Yaqui tribe of Arizona. Growing up, her mother taught her to be proud of her Native American and Mexican roots, especially as she experienced isolation because of the ignorance that she faced from classmates when she expressed pride in her people. Diane has authored the story of her mentor Rosa Olga Navarro, a leader of *Danza Azteca*. Diane is also a member of *Danza*, a student at SDSU, and a community volunteer at various Logan Heights venues that benefit the youth.

Women's March 2017, South San Diego County. Left to right: Rosalinda Arellanes, Irma Cabral Enjambre, Adela Garcia, Norma Hernandez, Norma Cazares, Mayor Mary Casillas Salas, Josie Calderon, Bea Fernandez and Joy Reyna.

Courtesy of Adela C. Garcia.

CHAPTER 7

NORMA CAZARES

ENRIQUETA CHAVEZ

MARIA GARCIA

NORMA L. HERNANDEZ

ROSALÍA SALINAS

BEATRICE ZAMORA–AGUILAR

CHAPTER 7

Chicanas in Public Education: Activist Women

This chapter includes the stories of women who graduated from college and became teachers, counselors, principals, deans, and even college presidents. As professionals they were leaders in advocating for social justice and educational reform. Influenced by the African American and other civil rights movements of the times, they were participants in the Chicano Movement to improve conditions for Mexican American students. They were among the many activists who woke up the nation to the importance of diversity in schools and colleges. They lobbied for more Chicano teachers, for Chicanas to teach women's courses, and for counselors who could provide relevant services to students.

Among the first Chicanas to teach in Chicano Studies at SDSU was Enriqueta Chavez, who was still a student at the time. Her story told here, represents only a fraction of what is held in the SDSU Special Collections Library in the Chicana and Chicano Archives among her personal papers. She is also one of the early writers whose articles were compiled as "Core Values," in the 1998 anthology *Chicana Feminist Thought, the Basic Historical Writings*. In the article, Enriqueta articulated her views on "La Chicana" in relationship to men in the Chicano Movement. It was originally published in *Regeneration* in 1971, one of the first publications of the Chicano movement. She came to San Diego from the Imperial Valley, and was one of the first Chicanas to graduate from SDSU. Her story, in part, is told by her daughter Juanita Chavez-Gordon who honors her mother for her courageous actions in working for Chicana rights in the Chicano Movement, and for her continued activism and dedication to students at Sweetwater High School District.

Women were abundant as early childhood educators, but few of them were Latinas. Chicanas began to strive for equality in these positions as teachers, principals, and administrators. Maria Garcia was raised and educated in San Diego, became a community activist, and then a school principal. She began fighting for the causes most important to the community at the same time as she was trying to complete her education. Maria became one of the first Chicanas to become a principal in the city schools of San Diego. She had taken a stand for bilingual education since 1970 while rallying for other causes with other women like her friend Laura Rodriguez, who was called the Matriarch of Chicano Park. Today, Maria has been lauded for her many interviews and narratives about the people of the Logan Heights community. She has been awarded for her accomplishments by the San Diego Historical Society, Save Our Heritage Organization, or SOHO, and in 2016 was inducted as "Historian" into the San Diego Women's Hall of Fame.

The fight for bilingual/bicultural education, so important to Chicanos/ Latinos, constituted a long struggle. During the 1970s, the fight for bilingual education became Rosalia Salinas's primary mission. A teacher at Roosevelt School, she knew that her students in San Diego's public schools needed to know and respect their Mexican culture and their primary language, Spanish, in order to develop and prosper in the world. They needed to take pride in their culture so they could be proud of themselves, allowing them to succeed. Rosalia became the president of CABE, the California Association for Bilingual Education, overseeing the group's annual conference which in San Diego drew 12,000 people. During her tenure as President of CABE, parent conferences were established across the state. Her leadership and advocacy have contributed toward policies impacting students in California. To this end, she has testified before the state legislature on issues of educational equity. For her work, Rosalia was honored with the Humanitarian Award by the Barrio Station and lauded by Assemblyman Pete Chacon.

Chicana counselors in the schools were needed to reach Spanish-speaking students. At Southwestern College, Norma Cazares mentored many students as a counselor. She set her focus on the Puente Project, an award-winning program that, for more than 25 years, has improved the college-going rate of tens of thousands of California's educationally underrepresented students. Norma helped disadvantaged students succeed in furthering their education beginning at the community college. Norma was able to reach first time college students who needed support to stay in school. They were the first in their families to graduate because of mentors like her. As a result of Norma's work, more and more Chicanas and Chicanos began to transfer to a four-year college or university. And many more Chicanas have been able to earn college degrees and return to the community as mentors and leaders of future generations. A leader in many ways, Norma became a founder of the South Bay Forum, a nonpartisan political action committee, to benefit educational, political, and economic life in San Diego.

College counseling became a high priority in order to be able to retain college students. Another counselor at Mesa and Southwestern College also made student retention a priority. Bea Zamora went from college counselor at Mesa

College to dean of students and special programs at Southwestern College. More than a dean, Bea Zamora promoted the diversity of cultures. She discovered the beauty of danza, to the extent that she joined Danza Azteca, and continues to this day. In her story she tells how she discovered her own indigenous ancestry. She met and married the leader, Mario Aguilar, and the two of them became KPBS Local Heroes, lauded for their gift of culture to the community.

San Diego has had two Chicana/Latina college presidents. Honored here is Norma Hernandez; the other was Rita Cepeda of Mesa College. Norma completed her college career as a young mother with two children. While working on her bachelor's degree at SDSU she also volunteered at the Barrio Station tutoring English and Math. She then completed a master's degree in counseling from the University of New Mexico. At Southwestern College, she went from counselor/instructor to dean of Counseling and Student Services. Then in 2003, she became the first Chicana/Latina college president at Southwestern College. She worked with others, to help build a state-of-the-art Transfer Center that is now a model for other colleges. Her story is an example of the perseverance of many Chicanas who, despite setbacks, persevered, and became successful leaders.

These stories capture just some of the women who have been activist educators who have shaped our region. Education in the elementary, middle, high schools, colleges, and universities improved because of women like these. Thanks to their activism, sacrifice, and struggle, the younger generation can benefit from their courageous efforts. They may now attend institutions of higher learning to gain more knowledge, but also to learn about their forebears and their history, and how the women managed to accomplish what they did under the most adverse conditions, at defining moments in history.

Norma Cazares, 2016, with grandsons Jacob and Joaquin.
Courtesy of photographer Krstina Neri.

NORMA CAZARES:

CO-FOUNDER, SOUTH BAY FORUM

An Educator by Training, an Activist at Heart

BY MARISSA VASQUEZ URIAS

There is an African proverb that states, "It takes a village to raise a child." In my case, it took a whole rancho to mold a scholar! I write this narrative in honor of a long-time mentor: Norma Cazares. Just as she has inspired and motivated me to persist, Norma has done the same for countless other students throughout her 27 years of service at Southwestern College.

While an educator by training, Norma is an activist at heart. In addition to her work in higher education, Norma has advocated for the need to address inequities throughout our educational pipeline. Those who know her can testify that Norma is not one to shy away from a debate. Her conviction and passion for social justice have furthered her service to our communities.

Norma Mena Cazares was born in 1951 in San Diego to Mexicano/ Chicano parents; originating from Chihuahua, Mexico, they came to the U.S. via Texas and Arizona. The second of seven siblings, she was raised in Logan Heights and Southeast San Diego. In 1969, she graduated from Lincoln High School, a predominately Black school. By the early age of 15, she was already an activist. She was recruited by Civil Rights leader George Stevens—an affirmative action officer and later elected councilman—to register people to vote. In 1968, she helped lead a walkout at Lincoln High School with Chicano and Black students who were influenced by the student walkouts of East Los Angeles, demanding equal education, bilingual classes, relevant curriculum, and faculty of color.

Norma then went on to San Diego State University, joining the Educational Opportunity Program (EOP) in 1969. She graduated with a bachelor of arts in public administration and later, in 1988, with a master of science in counseling. She continued her activism in the Chicano student movement and later in the community. She fought against proposition 187 that became law in California in 1995, denying human services, including the right to attend public schools, to undocumented immigrants. In 1996, she also protested Proposition 209, the Civil

Rights Initiative that abolished the use of affirmative action meant to remedy past discrimination against people of color.

I would meet Norma at Southwestern College where she was an academic counselor, having served there since 1989. Norma also worked as a counselor for the Puente Program. Her words still ring loud and clear: "Mija! You should consider joining the Puente Project." While I had heard of Puente as a high school student, I did not know much about it. Norma informed me that Puente was a program dedicated to supporting students who wanted to transfer to a four-year university. She encouraged me, telling me that I would also have an opportunity to visit universities, learn about scholarships, and be assigned a mentor from the community. I trusted her advice and enrolled in the program. Now, they say that some people come into our lives and quickly go, but that others stay and change us in ways never imagined. This was my experience as a community college Puentista under the guidance of Norma Cazares.

Like many students from San Diego's South Bay, I had begun my studies at our local community college, Southwestern College. Although I knew that college was important, I lacked the institutionalized cultural and social capital to navigate the education system on my own. Thankfully, I found the guidance I needed with Norma Cazares.

Thanks to mentors like Norma, the day soon came when I received my unexpected acceptance to the University of California at Berkeley. Her support was immeasurable. As the eldest of two daughters in my family, the idea of my moving 500 miles away to a university that was known for its liberalism was not what my parents had in mind when they encouraged me to apply to college. I recall crying in Norma's office when I told her about my parents' disapproval. After consoling me she said, "Don't worry, mija, I'll talk to them." And she did. Although I don't know what exactly she told them, she went out of her way to speak with my parents about this opportunity, something that no other educator had ever done for me.

At that moment, Norma became more than my mentor and academic advisor; she became my advocate. As such, she became the fierceness in my voice when all I could do was whisper. Her honesty and forthright guidance helped me get to UC Berkeley and kept me from dropping out; kept me focused when I was turned down by employers; and kept me hungry for knowledge throughout my ventures as a student pursuing master's and doctoral degree coursework. As the Puente counselor, Norma has helped countless students of underrepresented backgrounds (primarily Chicano/Latino) to reach their educational goals and transfer to four-year universities.

Norma is known as much for her college mentoring as she is for her work in the San Diego communities. Currently, her primary assignment is as coordinator and counselor of the Transfer Center at Southwestern College, a state-of-the art center mentoring students into higher education. In 1998, Norma helped found and lead the South Bay Forum (SBF), a state political action committee dedicated to addressing issues affecting the Chicano/Latino community in San Diego's South County. Since 2006, she has served as a board member for the Chancellor McGill School of Success, a transitional kindergarten–to–third-grade charter school in the South Park community. Her experiences in working with linguistically and economically diverse communities illustrate her commitment to improving the educational outcomes of all students.

Additionally, she has served as founder and primary organizer of the South Bay Leadership Symposium. For three years, she was involved with the University of California at San Diego's acquisition of the Herman Baca Chicano Archives as chair of that committee; she has been on the Community Advisory Committee for the Chief of Police of the City of Chula Vista since 2009; she has been involved in the voter registration effort of the Southwest Voter Registration and Education Project; and she has been a member of the UC San Diego Health System CEO's Community Advisory Council on Inclusion and Diversity since 2010. Her endless catalogue of volunteer efforts and leadership roles has earned her various awards, recognitions, and accolades, including the Local Hero Award from KPBS and Union Bank of California. She was honored by the Adelante Mujer 2006 organization, as Latina of the Year. Not only has Norma proven to be a [s] hero within the community, but she is also one among her family and friends.

As a Chicana activist, Norma continues to be a leader and advocate for students and our comunidad. She is a role model to many young Latinas who, like me, are eager to remain engaged in the public good. In reflecting on my journey as a community college student to now becoming a university professor, I'm reminded of all those who advocated for my success. Norma Cazares has surely been among those who have advocated the loudest.

About the Author:

MARISSA VASQUEZ URIAS, Ed.D., is an Assistant Professor in the Department of Administration, Rehabilitation, and Postsecondary Education (ARPE) at San Diego State University (SDSU). Dr. Vasquez Urias' scholarly work examines factors impacting the success of male students of color, particularly Latino and African American men, in the community college. A Chula Vista native, Dr. Vasquez Urias earned an associate degree from Southwestern College, a bachelor's degree in English from the University of California, Berkeley, a master's degree in Counseling from the University of San Diego, and an Ed.D. in Educational Leadership from San Diego State University.

Enriqueta Chavez, c1999.
Courtesy of Memo Cavada Creative Images.

ENRIQUETA CHAVEZ:

DEDICATED COUNSELOR, SOUTHBAY'S LATINA OF THE YEAR

Student Founder, San Diego State, Centro de Estudios Chicanos

BY JUANITA CHAVEZ-GORDON

My mother is Enriqueta Chavez, teacher, counselor and Chicana Activist. Growing up in Calexico, California, my mother was raised in the traditional Mexican ways. She excelled in school, both academically and in sports, so when she was offered the opportunity to attend college and leave home she jumped at it, in spite of her parents' opposition. In 1968 she was amongst the first wave of Chicano students to be recruited through the EOP (Educational Opportunity Program) and attend San Diego State (now SDSU), at a time when political unrest on college campuses seemed to be the norm.

Coming from a small town that is predominately Mexicano, my mother still vividly remembers the cultural shock she went through as a young student. Being of lighter skin and hazel eyes, peers always asked, "Are you really Mexican?" Alienated in the academic environment of the college and surrounded by political unrest, influenced by the civil rights and antiwar movements, my mother found and joined MAYA (Mexican American Youth Association) on campus, later re-named MEChA, after the Santa Barbara Conference in 1969. Through MAYA she got involved in the Chicano Movement and began to identify herself as a Chicana. Living in the dorms with other newly recruited Mexicanas and sharing similar experiences naturally united them with other young *mujeres* on campus in forming a "Las Chicanas " group. Las Chicanas group formed because, even though women were active participants in all Chicano Movement activities, they were not given the respect or acknowledgment they deserved for their work. Confronting sexism through Las Chicanas gave the women a voice and means to support one another, both politically and personally.

Of the many stories my mother has told me about those times, this is my favorite: Before we, her children, were born, my parents moved in together into an apartment near the beach. My Dad is from Sonora Texas and being the macho that he was, he expected my mom to naturally fall into the role of *la mesera, la cocinera*, and *la lavaplatos*. Boy was he in for a surprise! "I am a man from Texas and in Texas the woman cooks. You're my woman and you are going to cook for me," he demanded. His shouts were met with defiant refusal and vehement rebuttals. Eventually my mom grew tired of his insistence and accepted her comadres' offers to move in with them. Wouldn't you know it, a few days later my dad came knocking at her protectors' door (Sylvia Romero, Felicitas Nuñez, and Teresa Hoyos), begging and pleading for her to just come home and accept the domestic role society had created for her. "Nope, no and hell no! Don't you come back here cabron, until you are ready to cook" is what he got as she was supported by her friends to respond. After a few weeks of this, he missed her so much and couldn't take it anymore. He bit the bullet and signed up for cooking classes. Before he knew it he fell in love with cooking and this only made my mother fall more in love with him as he won his way back into her heart through her stomach.

Subsequently my mother, as part of the leadership of MEChA and CCHE, the Chicano Council for Higher Education, helped establish Centro de Estudios Chicanos at San Diego State. This included Mexican American Studies where she taught as a student, the Barrio Station, the Chicano Federation, the Chicano Free Clinic, and the Escuelita in Barrio Logan. CCHE was a statewide organization that came out of the Santa Barbara Conference held in 1969 and worked to implements the goals of El Plan De Santa Barbara.

After graduating with her masters degree in Counseling in 1975, my mother was hired by the Sweetwater Union High School District as one of the first Chicana counselors. My mother was never the traditional mother, but our lives were filled with exposure to art, music, culture, and social activism. She gave us a front row seat in protests, boycotts and planning meetings. I was always at awe of how she balanced being an active Chicana in the San Diego community with her super busy career as a counselor at Sweetwater High School and as coordinator of the College entrance examinations for the South Bay. I clearly recall the days when she would come home drained from her efforts at working with a student's family. Often they were distraught due to their homelessness, their immigration status, or their financial condition. But my mother loved the work she was doing.

My mother has been recognized for her work. She has been selected as counselor of the Year more than once; recognized by the Adelante Mujer South Bay; and given the Latina of the Year award in 2010.

As my mother, Enriqueta Chavez did not only impact my life by providing me the gift of a strong foundation rooted in family and tradition, but she has helped many others. Hundreds of young students from the Sweetwater Union High School District will remember her just as I do, strong, independent, loving and supportive. Today the Enriqueta Chavez papers are housed in the permanent collection of the Love Library at SDSU. They were showcased there with a reception to honor her and other contributors to the Unidos Por La Causa Traveling Exhibit that then went on display at the Logan Heights Public Library in San Diego, and then at the San Diego Mesa College Library.

About the Author:

JUANITA CHAVEZ-GORDON is a graduate of UC Berkeley; she received her B.A. with a major in Chicano Studies and a minor in Education. She lives in the San Francisco Bay Area with her husband of 19 years and two children. She has been an Aztec Dancer for 22 years and in April 2015 was received as an Ajq'ij by the local Mayan community.

Maria Garcia, 2016, when she was inducted into San Diego County Women's Hall of Fame.

Courtesy of Memo Cavada Creative Images.

MARIA GARCIA:

EDUCATOR AND HISTORIAN

She Captured the Stories of Barrio Logan Residents

BY CARRI FIERRO

In 2015, Maria Garcia was named one of six outstanding women in Senate District 40, which includes most of San Diego's South Bay. That same year, San Diego's Save Our Heritage Organization (SOHO) honored Maria for outstanding achievement in the field of historical preservation. And, in 2016, Maria was inducted as historian into the San Diego County Women's Hall of Fame. Maria is known in San Diego as an exemplary educator who has fought for the people's right to bilingual education in schools and for the people's history that she set out to preserve in San Diego's Logan Heights neighborhood.

I had the privilege of interviewing Maria for a Chicana tribute. When I met with her, she was very humble and direct. I had originally asked her questions primarily about education issues and the Latino community. Her answer was, "Everything has an effect on us, whether it is immigration, political voices, or gender relationships." She was clear that she was concerned about all aspects of life in the Chicano/Latino community. As a former principal of three different local elementary schools, she insisted, "Everything affects that child you are working with. We need to take a look at the whole picture." Her own story helps to picture how Maria became an activist educator and historian.

Born in Yuma, Arizona, Maria came to San Diego when she was just three years old. She lived in Logan Heights on 33rd and Imperial and was proud of her community. By the time she was in the fifth grade, her family had moved to Encanto where she attended Encanto Elementary School, O'Farrell Junior High School, and Morse High School.

Maria earned good grades in high school and, yet, she was encouraged to become a beautician. Despite these low expectations from the authority figures around her, she enrolled in San Diego City College during what she describes as, "a unique time," because "back in those days, it cost $12 per semester to attend community college." She started taking business classes and went to work as a teacher's aide at Logan Elementary School. She eventually changed her major to education. With some prompting and encouragement from several local area educators—two of them men who worked for the city schools, Leonard Fierro and Rafael Fernandez—she enrolled in Teacher Corps. This opportunity gave her two years of classroom experience under the direction of a master teacher. Through this program, she was mentored, valued, and supported. "Teacher Corps was one of the best experiences of my life," she recalls. Along the way, she also formed strong friendships, many of which she sustains to this day.

Her activism and exposure—from using her voice to sharpening her skills to impact the community—began in college and continued to grow after college. In 1968, she participated in the Chicano Federation Leadership program, a series of Saturday classes that lasted between eight to 10 weeks. Those classes were of great value in developing skills for community involvement. Many of the program participants went on to leadership roles in our community.

As a college student, she was one of the first elected to the Chicano Federation Board of Directors. She also became involved in Camp Oliver, where students were able to question the role or lack of support of the Catholic Church in the advancement of Latinos. She was even part of a group called Católicos por la Raza that picketed at the bishop's house. Maria recalls those experiences as necessary. "As part of the Chicano Movement during the peak days of the U.S. Civil Rights activism, we had to address our concerns at all levels, and the church was one of them. We wanted to expose the problems of discrimination in the church too." Many people were concerned that the church had been used "to keep Mexicans in their place."

In those days, she remembers that there were people who surrounded and supported you, maybe even pushed and pulled you, but always with the intention of bettering the community and the individual. "Your supporters were from different ethnic groups or from different socioeconomic groups, all willing to extend a hand," she recalled. For example, in 1970, Chicano Park and the Chicano Clinic came about and were then developed by people who worked together to expose the many injustices they experienced. Chicano Park and the Chicano Clinic exist today as a result of the demands and organizing tactics the community instigated at that time. Maria recalls, "Unfortunately, not many people with influence or power in the city of San Diego really understood the scope of the problems in the Latino community, in terms of access to healthcare, housing, and education, and so the people's presence was essential." In college and, later, through her involvement in the community and the important causes of Chicano Park and the Chicano Clinic, Maria found peers and mentors who validated her and helped her to excel.

Maria graduated with a bachelor's degree from San Diego State University and went on to receive her master's degree in multicultural education with an emphasis on bilingual education. She then became a principal for San Diego Unified School District. Her first principalship was at Baker Elementary School, followed by a principal assignment at Audubon Elementary and Emerson Bandini Elementary schools.

While Maria was a principal, she faced many challenges. She expected to influence the many areas of concern she knew were important in the schools, like discrimination, equality in education, and bilingual education, by being a voice for the underrepresented. Things were not so easy. "I had some influence," she stated, "but not to the degree I thought."

During my interview with Maria, I learned how very important it is that underrepresented communities remember that someone helped them and contributed to their success, so that the next generation also offers its support and helps others get ahead. "Not one of us has made it on our own," Maria reminds us. "We have all had help in some way from those who came before us." Maria relays how important it is for people to remember they were helped so that they may help others, because people have a tendency to ignore or forget that fact."

Maria's personal papers—"the Maria Garcia Papers"—are now housed in the San Diego State University Special Collections Library in the Chicana Chicano Archive Collection. When asked to describe some of the materials she contributed to the SDSU Chicana/o Archives, she mentioned three key areas: bilingual education, the Chicano Federation, and the Neighborhood House. These materials and other papers signify the learning and involvement she had during different periods of her activism for quality education for all people in San Diego.

The most recent driving factor surrounding her current efforts is to document the stories of Neighborhood House, which was located at 1809 National Avenue. Maria recently wrote over 54 articles on the efforts of the people who contributed and benefited from the making of this historic place. Their stories deserve to be told and their actions acknowledged.

One of Maria's narratives tells the story of Neighborhood House itself. In it, she recalls how Neighborhood House was acquired by the people of the community to be used as a clinic. Maria attended the first meetings to talk about the importance of returning this site to the people it once served. The building space had provided services to the people who lived and worked in the neighborhood. At the time of the meeting, it no longer did. The people, therefore, began to demand services in the building that had once provided them; they then decided to take over the building. Maria was at the takeover of the Neighborhood House building, along with others like Laura Rodriguez, the main actor, a grandmother and activist who had chained herself to the door as a strong statement that drew attention to their civil rights. Maria recalls that these drastic measures were necessary in order to get the attention they needed of those in charge. The people won their demand. And, the clinic is now called the "Logan Heights Family Health Center." It serves the people who live in that neighborhood.

When asked what motivated her to write the people's history, Maria remembers how she found the original cassette tapes of interviews she had done in the 1970s and was turning them over to the SDSU Chicana/o Archives. "The original 20-page paper that went with them," she said, "was for a Chicano Studies class at SDSU." She had loaned it to a local TV station and someone there lost it. She realized the interviews that she had recorded would not make sense to anyone without an explanation. "I decided to write a one-page paper explaining the tapes. Then, at a dinner event I sat next to Anna Daniels, the editor of the *San Diego Free Press*, who asked, 'What do you do now that you're retired?' I mentioned the short paper I was writing about the taped interviews and their history." A few days later, Maria got a call from Daniels asking her to write something for the newspaper. "As I started to reconstruct the story of Barrio Logan, I decided to interview others and they would tell me, 'You have to interview so and so.' From there, it grew and grew." Maria recalls that within 16 months, three of the people she had interviewed had passed away. Now, everyone from the original taped interviews is deceased. Out of this project has come her new book, *La Neighbor* (2016).

Maria has been highly regarded for her past and present efforts to recount the history of that period. In 2015, Senator Ben Hueso named her one of six outstanding women in his Senate District 40, which includes South Bay San Diego. This award was for her work in researching the history of the Logan Heights Neighborhood House. The Save Our Heritage Organization (SOHO) also honored Maria for her outstanding achievement in the field of historical preservation. This award was particularly for the series of articles she has written on the Neighborhood House in Logan Heights and the people who live there.

When asked about her core values, Maria quickly replies, "Family and friendships." "You don't abandon your family," she says with strong conviction. "And friendships are equally important to sustaining one's sense of self." The mentorships and friendships Maria has gained through her many years of contributing to San Diego have had a lasting impact and are clearly some of the anchors that keep her going. She added, "Some friends become family and you don't think about how they are not your blood because they are part of your heart."

When asked what her recommendations are for improving current conditions for San Diego's Latinos, she mentions, "We have to be careful about assuming things have changed." Although we have seen progress overall, she cautions, there is still a strong need for individuals outside the Latino community to better understand the scope of the problems that racism has placed in our communities. "We also need to remember the power of the vote," she says "We must never be too tired or too busy to vote."

Another of her core concerns is that Latino students need to be validated. "How do we make youth feel comfortable being smart?" she challenges. She observes that there is so much worry and hate among young people today: "People are not kind as they used to be." Moreover, she points out that we need to make sure parents are informed and getting basic communication from the schools. She suggests schools find ways to make updates and communication simple, relevant, and specific to the parents. For example, she would like to see better communication and coordination with parents about scholarships and financial awards for their children to attend college.

Finally, she cautions that although she is a staunch supporter of higher education, "The reality is that not all of our children end up in college." As a result, she would like to see educational programs that also find pathways to decent jobs for those students who do not go to college. Maria says, "Let's not make education a checklist," but rather, "Let's debunk stereotypes and create high expectations for all students."

As a longtime educator and historian, Maria Garcia clearly understands the urgency and scope of the issues facing the Chicano/Latino community. More importantly, she also knows how to celebrate and document the success stories as examples for future generations. Fortunately and thankfully, she is not done with her desire to create positive change for Latinos in San Diego and for underrepresented communities in general.

About the Author:

CARRI FIERRO, director of TRIO, a student outreach program at UCSD, offering college advising, financial aid, and career awareness to low income students. Born and raised in San Diego, she had close ties with her grandfather, Leonard Fierro, a Chicano educator and promoter of bilingual education at SDSU. In Chicano Studies at Mesa College she was inspired to follow in her grandfather's footprints and dedicate her career to serving underrepresented communities. In 1996, she was valedictorian of her graduating class at Mesa College; in 1998, a graduate of UCLA in Chicano Studies and American Literature; and has an M.A in Higher Education and Organizational Change. Presently she is on the San Diego State University Chicana and Chicano Archive Committee. She is married with three children.

Norma Hernandez, retired president Southwestern College.
Courtesy of Adela Garcia.

NORMA L. HERNANDEZ:

FIRST LATINA PRESIDENT OF SOUTHWESTERN COLLEGE

Bilingual-Bicultural Pride Motivated Her to Help Others

BY ADELA C. GARCIA

Norma Hernandez will be the first to tell you that her transformation from Mexicana to Chicana did not occur because she wanted a new identity. Norma was born in Tijuana, Baja California, and was the only child of José and Angelina Arce. Growing up in Tijuana and crossing the border daily to attend San Ysidro Academy, she was raised bicultural and bilingual and took great pride in being able to connect and communicate with people on both sides of the border. These skills and her determination to help others would lead her on the journey to become one of San Diego's most respected Chicanas.

After moving to San Diego as a teenager, Norma graduated from Cathedral Girls Catholic High School and then enrolled at San Diego State University (SDSU). In 1961, she married her high-school sweetheart, Jimmy Kendal, and they settled in San Diego where she gave birth to two sons, Jaime and Richard. When Norma's marriage ended, she began volunteering at her sons' school, Brooklyn Elementary. She noticed the difficulty that Mexican parents and their children had communicating with teachers and school administrators and the lack of resources available to help them. She soon found herself interpreting for these parents and students and also helping them with their paperwork.

Her excellent bilingual skills and her ability to connect with parents and school personnel were noticed. This led to a job offer as a teacher's aide in a new federally funded English as a Second Language (ESL) program. Norma traveled weekly to five schools (Brooklyn, Euclid, Central, Burbank, and Encanto) to teach ESL and visit parents' homes. This was the beginning of her interest in a career in education and her return to finish her degree.

During the early 1970s, the Chicano movement for economic and social justice was sweeping the Southwest. Groups like the Brown Berets had emerged, as Chicano activists were bringing light to the social problems affecting the Mexican-American community. While taking a sociology class at Mesa College,

Norma's professor encouraged the students to attend a community meeting at the Unitarian Church organized by the Black Panthers and the Brown Berets. Norma had first-hand knowledge of the problems facing Mexican-American families and, in her quest to find resources to help them, attended the meeting. The meeting had a significant impact on her and was a turning point in her activism and involvement in the Chicano Movement.

Norma remembers that a leader of the Brown Berets, Arturo Serrano, spoke with such eloquence and passion that she sat in amazement. "I wasn't a radical, and the speakers were a bit intimidating, but I knew they had something to offer. So, following the meeting I approached the all-male panelists Arturo, Frank Saiz, and David Rico," Norma recalls. She explained the problems she was seeing in the schools and inquired if there were resources to help Mexican-American parents. Arturo Serrano and his girlfriend, Gloria Medina, also a Brown Beret, invited her to a meeting with Chicano youth at the Boys Club in Logan Heights, a place that provided community resources..

Soon after, Norma went to work at Lincoln High School where she formed the first MEChA and there met student activist Norma Cazares who would one day become a colleague of hers.. In 1970, she started volunteering at the Barrio Station where she worked with activists Arturo Cazares, Irma Castro, and Rachael Ortiz, who were addressing the same social issues that she cared about. There, she became engaged with at-risk youth and developed programs to encourage them to stay in school. She also volunteered at Escuelita del Barrio, an alternative school, where she taught ESL. It was during this time, Norma says, that she was transformed into a Chicana.

Norma graduated from SDSU in 1972 with a bachelor's degree in Spanish and a minor in Mexican American Studies, now Chicana and Chicano Studies. That same year, she decided to pursue her master's degree in counseling and guidance at the University of New Mexico (UNM), taking part in a special program with a cohort of 24 Chicano students from the Southwestern states. This was a first-of-its-kind master's program that offered a degree in 18 months with special emphasis on the Mexican American community's needs. The program was funded under the Educational Professions Development Act (EPDA), which was enacted in 1967 and provided full funding for the participants. She said, "I had the choice of either getting my master's the long way by staying at home, or fast-tracking it by going to the University of New Mexico. Even though it was a very difficult decision to leave my sons, I felt that this was best for my family." With the support of her mother and grandmother who cared for her children, Norma left to attend UNM.

Norma recalls, "After we joined the program, we bonded with other student activists from other states. We called ourselves Los Ocho and formed a support and study group; we were getting excellent grades. Soon, we were questioning some of the curriculum and approaches to the program, while making sure all our assignments were completed." By the end of the first semester, the program director decided that Los Ocho were not coming back.

Norma considered this one of the darkest times of her life. She had left her family with great sacrifice and was now insecure about her future. As they were driving home, she kept thinking, "What am I going to say to my mother and my sons?" Once they were back in San Diego, the students garnered support from the federal-funding source and local program administration for their unjust dismissal. At the same time, they set off a whirlwind of activities to bring light to the injustice that had been committed. Since the program was federally funded, the federal government stepped in and threatened to pull the funding from the university. That got immediate attention and Los Ocho was promptly reinstated. In 1973, Norma received her master's degree in counseling and guidance from the University of New Mexico.

By 1975, opportunities for minorities had started to open up, and Norma was hired as a counselor and instructor at Southwestern College (SWC), where she began a 31-year career. She counseled students, taught personal development classes, and served as MEChA advisor. It was also during this time that she married Max Hernandez, a well-respected former union leader and non-profit executive director. At that time, Norma's outstanding counseling and management were rewarded and, in 1980, she was appointed dean of student services.

Others speak highly of her success. "Norma maintained a social justice lens on everything she did and she encouraged her team to find new and more effective ways to help minority students," says Virginia Hansen, retired SWC dean of student support services. "She significantly increased the college's outreach and implemented new programs. Among them were the Career Center, the Puente Program, the Summer Readiness Program, Outreach Services, and the Transfer Center."

The story of the Transfer Center is a major victory for Norma and others at Southwestern College and needs to be told. According to Jaime Salazar, the center's first director, before embarking on the project, "Norma would hear about a program and say, 'Learn everything you can about that program and let's bring it here and make it bigger and better.' And we did just that. Norma had the foresight to know that there was power in numbers and she used that power, having been a community activist for years with the Barrio Station. They embarked on developing an organization called the UCSD Transition Forum to increase the number of underrepresented students in higher education.

The idea for the Transfer Center was in the making and Southwestern College was at the center of the action. Southwestern invited all community colleges in Region 10 to participate in highlighting the drastic need to increase the number of minority transfer students to the universities. They hosted a regional conference, funded by Palomar College's EOP. After presentations of all the models and seeing the plans to achieve their goals, the vice president of student services at the chancellor's office liked the Southwestern College model best, even though the other projects had been in place longer. That is how the Transfer Center came about.

Norma Hernandez's successes continued and, in 1983, she was appointed vice president for student affairs. During this time, the one-stop student services center, created while Norma was a dean, was completed. That same year, the Cesar Chavez Student Services Center was inaugurated.

In 2003, Norma was appointed superintendent/president of Southwestern College, becoming the first Latina president in San Diego County. She retired in 2006, but when the college was at-risk to lose its accreditation, she came out of retirement and ran for a governing board seat. On November 2, 2010, Norma was elected to the Southwestern College Board of Trustees where she is currently serving her second term.

As a young mother, inspired by the U.S. Civil Rights activism of the 1970s, Norma overcame divorce, single parenting, and an unjust dismissal from a major university. She prevailed over all these obstacles and courageously stood her ground for equal justice. She succeeded in her efforts to obtain her education and make a difference in the Chicano/Latino community. Norma continues to do so today, standing out as an example and role model for her community, especially for young women.

About the Author:

ADELA C. GARCIA, director of the Southwestern College Foundation from 2000 to 2008 and served two terms as Foundation President. She was co-manager of Norma Hernandez's most recent campaign when Norma ran and won a seat on the SWC governing board. Adela is the Chair of MANA de San Diego's Latina Success Leadership Program and a retired IBM Business Design Consultant. Adela resides in Chula Vista, California.

ROSALÍA SALINAS:

BILINGUAL EDUCATION ACTIVIST; PAST PRESIDENT, CABE
California's Most Outspoken Advocate for Bilingual Literacy

BY SILVIA DORTA-DUQUE DE REYES

Caminante, no hay camino, se hace el camino al andar -- Antonio Machado

It was 1964. The owner of a boarding house at the University of Texas read aloud a letter from a potential resident and asked: "Do you think she is black?" Rosalía responded rhetorically, "How can you tell by her writing?" But her heart pounded with shame and regret. "I regretted that I had not yet found my voice, that I did not have the words to confront the blatant racism that allowed such an assumed exclusion, a voice that would have changed the outcome," she says. Driven by the need to find her voice and to provide others with the tools to do the same was to be one of the driving forces in Rosalía Salinas' life's work.

Since then, Rosalía has become one of California's most outspoken advocate for bilingual literacy. In 2004, she was awarded the Cesar Chavez Humanitarian Award by the Barrio Station of San Diego, in recognition of her life work for social justice and institutional change. In 2005, she was acknowledged by the California Rural Legal Counselors (CRLA), with the Cruz Reynoso-Abiscal Don Quixote Award, named for the former California Supreme Court Justice. Her personal story cannot be separated from her struggle for bilingual education in California.

Advocacy: Adding a voice to the cry -- Laurie Olsen

Rosalía Salinas has been a leader and advocate for English learners for over 40 years in San Diego and throughout California. She is known for her relentless commitment and dedication to the Chicano community and bilingual education. Her leadership and advocacy have contributed toward policies and curriculum programs impacting students statewide. To this end, she has testified before the California State Legislature on issues of educational equity on numerous occasions.

Rosalía grew up in South Texas, Laredo, where she developed a strong sense of community and always embraced the use of two languages and the dynamics of biculturalism. Her father, who had only attained a sixth grade education in México, had a tremendous work ethic and an entrepreneurial spirit. He managed to own a business by the age of 20. "He instilled in me a sense of autonomy and independence," Rosalía recalls. Her mother filled her home with the sounds of Agustín Lara and Frank Sinatra. "She was aware of the beauty in everything and surrounded our lives with joy, color, and appreciation for the arts," she says. Her mother nurtured Rosalía's sense of identity and pride in her language and culture; she strongly affirmed the importance and value of education.

> *...no te creas! ¡Créate! ¡Sé tú! Los cantos son nuestros, los rostros también...*
> *¿qué esperas? ...¡AMA!... ¡LUCHA!* -- Alurista

Then came the U.S. Civil Rights Movement. The Chicano Movement, one of the most impactful social movements of the 1960s, also came, encompassing a broad cross-section of issues, from restoration of land grants, to farm workers' rights and enhanced education, to voting and political rights. Lured by her growing passion for social justice, in 1970, Rosalía relocated to the epicenter of the movement: California. Having already taught in Texas and New York, she sought to serve as a teacher in San Diego. She recalls, "Seeking answers in education led me to the importance of not silencing the home language in students, but, rather, using it effectively to learn and gain confidence and understanding of self and others."

As a teacher and mentor in San Diego's Lincoln High School, Rosalía first sought to affirm the student's language and provide a more meaningful context for their educational experience. She knew that understanding how to access a rigorous academic course could impact students' views of themselves as scholars. Rosalía developed a U.S. History course taught in Spanish. The course highlighted the many contributions of Latinos in the United States and gave prominent status to the land and life lived in the Southwest before the U.S.-Mexico Treaty of Guadalupe Hidalgo in 1848. She also established the first Chicano Studies course, which provided students a sense of community and a unique perspective on race and cultural heritage.

Rosalía drove home the idea that "action must accompany words, which are a reflection of our values and thoughts." She established a context for gathering ideas, organizing activities, and dialoguing. A Raza Unida Club, A ballet folklórico, and a teatro formed to enhance creativity and culture. Soon, student leadership began to emerge. As students came together and began to dialogue, it expanded their understanding of the current political realities in

Rosalía Salinas, 2015, when she received the Bea Gonzales Biliteracy Award by San Diego County Office of Education.

Courtesy of Memo Cavada Creative Images.

California and how they impacted their lives. Rosalía also assembled the teatro, modeled after Luis Valdez's Teatro Campesino, where the stage served as a venue to communicate the quest for identity, self-determination, and action.

In Rosalía's effort to encourage leadership skills for high school girls and underrepresented minority groups, she also established Project STEP to encourage young girls to claim their right to access and identity. These efforts, motivated by conscious actions, Rosalía had learned since childhood. They affirmed that growing up with pride in her language and culture could be passed on to her students.

In the 1970s, Rosalía served as vice principal at Roosevelt Junior High School. As a first-year administrator, she implemented reading and math labs in Spanish. The program addressed literacy among Latino students. The results proved a reciprocal and positive correlation between achievement in primary language and English. The students were now able to learn skills and strategies in a language they understood. Then they could learn English and other content areas. She proved that "language does not exist apart from culture; every communicative encounter is a manifestation of agency and culture."

> The trust of the people in the leaders reflects the
> confidence of the leaders in the people --Paulo Freire

The urgent need for further work with English learners propelled Rosalía to focus on policy, curriculum, and professional development at the San Diego County Office of Education. She quickly realized that institutions, while established to promote a social purpose, are slow to change. Finding voice for the very students the system was meant to serve was a difficult task. She experienced the bureaucratic paperwork and endless chains of command that seemed to drown all efforts. But her determination was fueled by her commitment to providing English learners educational equity and opportunity to learn. Each day, her unwavering courage and commitment surmounted objections, criticisms, resistance, and setbacks.

Rosalía continued to engage tirelessly, serving the community at large, constantly creating alliances and strong relationships; she collaborated from within and from outside the system to forge improvements in education. She remained on the advisory committee to the superintendent at San Diego Unified School District for over 25 years. As San Diego public library commissioner, she advocated for the availability of materials in Spanish and in other languages reflective of the linguistically diverse population in San Diego.

Rosalía also deepened her service and commitment to the cause as a political activist. The opportunity to meet William Velasquez, founder of the

Southwest Voter Registration Education Project, and to see his work, fueled Rosalía's determination for political involvement. This included campaign fundraising for key candidates and getting out the vote. Even though there were losses, all efforts crystallized the need to ensure that more community members became part of the process in order to make informed decisions. She later served as president of the Chicano Democratic Association and, following Willy Velasquez's example, she focused on *tu voz, tu voto* to underscore the connection of political action and change, and to promote self-determination through voting rights.

In 1980, Rosalía played an important role in supporting assembly member Pete Chacon to enact statewide legislation in favor of bilingual education. She wanted to readdress the specific needs of English learners, after his initial legislation, the Bilingual Bicultural Education Act, had expired. In 1980, AB 507 aimed to provide English learners with English language development, core curriculum, and cross-cultural and self-concept instruction, delivered by qualified teachers. Years later, upon Rosalía's retirement, the Honorable Pete Chacon, a pioneer in California's bilingual education movement, bestowed on her a signed copy of Assembly Bill 507. On June 4, 2003, he sent her a personal note saying, "Thanks Rosalia for all the time and energy you spent over the years in support of my legislative efforts on behalf of English learners . . . Your work, and others like you, were an inspiration to me and carried me through the darkest days of extreme opposition . . . Muchisimas gracias, Pete Chacon."

In 1995, Rosalía was elected president of the California Association for Bilingual Education (CABE). In 1997, she presided over the CABE conference with the highest attendance record (over 12,000 participants) in the history of the organization.

Rosalía understood the undeniable power that parents yield, stating, "When advocating for students, the voices of their parents must be at the forefront." She realized that parents hold the highest stakes in the education of their children; yet, they were kept superficially engaged and powerless. It became very evident to Rosalía that parents needed a venue for becoming informed and able to receive vital information about the educational options for their children. "Parents," she said, "Needed to become involved at the governance level in the educational system."

Currently, Rosalía continues to serve on the board of the Parent Institute for Quality Education (PIQE) and Community Housing Works. Parents throughout the state continue to acknowledge Rosalía's affirmation of parents. Many have conveyed the impact she has had, not only on their children's education, but also on their own education and leadership. In appreciation of her vision and commitment, the parents petitioned that the CABE Conference room be renamed in her honor. Today, the parents' loyalty to her endures as "The Rosalía Salinas Parent Hospitality Room."

Rosalía Salinas (right), 1996, with Senator Barbara Boxer (left) and First Lady Hilary Clinton (center) at event in San Diego.

Courtesy of Tim Stahl Photographics.

Language is never neutral -- Paulo Freire

Rosalía has acknowledged that "leading the efforts to institutionalize bilingual education in California has been a monumental task." The call to action to create an educational system that recognizes the relationship between language and cognitive development was met with fierce opposition. The idea of bilingualism as a personal, social, economic, and national advantage was met with fear. The San Diego County Grand Jury made headlines in San Diego by declaring "bilingual education is un-American." Rosalía was outraged by this attack targeting the educational needs of the Latino community and the lack of response by educational institutions and school districts. Instead of being intimidated, she helped organize a coalition of community organizations that included Latinos, Asians, and Jewish members, to picket in front of the County Administration Building. It looked as if the initiative, called "English Language in the Public Schools," clearly meant to reject bilingual education programs. This protest was the first of many times when Rosalía had to take off her San Diego County employee hat to present herself as an advocate.

Praxis: Action That Shapes and Changes the World

In 1998, when Proposition 227 was initiated as a focused attack on language and bilingual education, Rosalía again stepped up to the plate, serving as statewide co-chair to oppose it. Years before, in 1994, Proposition 187 had set before voters an initiative to establish a state-run citizenship screening system described as "prohibiting illegal aliens from using health care, public education, and other social services in the California." Rosalía explains, "While 187 was challenged and overturned by the courts, it created a hostile environment that dehumanized immigrants. It disseminated the idea that it was righteous to deny children of a certain group access to education and health services." She further noted that Proposition 187 enabled a more focused attack on language and bilingual education. In 1998, the effects still lingered.

Sadly, Proposition 227 passed as many educators had abandoned and betrayed bilingual education. Rosalía recalls, "By passing Proposition 227, Californians voted to decide curriculum options not based on theory, but rather, on personal biased opinion." Rosalía laments that "bias is what allowed them to decide the fate of children, other than their own, and it had an immediate, detrimental, and chilling effect on the entire Latino community."

Rosalía's personal story is intricately interwoven with her passion for education. As a result of the passing of Prop 227, Rosalía was devastated. However, she was not defeated. She immediately began to rebuild and reinvigorate the few who, like her, would not turn their backs on the idea that a primary language is a valuable resource and that biliteracy was the way of the future. The first thing she did was to summon experts in the field to develop guides and compile instructional methodologies that would ensure English learners access and opportunity to learn, and that promoted teacher agency. A staff development institute and accompanying handbook titled *A Scaffold for Change* was created and disseminated statewide. It assisted teachers in examining the possibilities for working within the parameters of Proposition 227.

Another effort Rosalía made to affirm and revitalize bilingual education after Proposition 227 was the Bilingual Symposium. District leaders, teachers, and parents would be honored and recognized for their services to English learners and their continued work in bilingual education. The first celebration was on June 18, 1999, only a year after the passage of Proposition 227; nearly 200 educators attended.

Since then, the Bilingual Symposium has become a tradition in San Diego County; each year there are over 600 attendees. With renewed commitment and a sense of urgency, Rosalía collaborated with other advocates in the state to form Californians Together, a statewide coalition of parents, teachers, education advocates, and civil rights groups committed to securing equal access to quality education for all children. Californians Together has been instrumental in re-establishing bilingual education in California by institutionalizing the Seal of Biliteracy, a seal that is given to graduating high school students who meet the criteria for proficient biliteracy. The Seal of Biliteracy has now been adopted by many other states.

Rosalía Salinas has received multiple awards and recognitions throughout her years of service. Her generosity of spirit embraces all. But what sets her apart is her advocacy: her ability to courageously stand up for what is right, for defending those who are not able to defend themselves, and for facing adversity with both grace and intelligence.

Rosalía has had a tremendous impact in my life by instilling in me a sense of political awareness that is followed by purposeful action to serve and build social capital through education. Rosalía continues to make a difference in all of our lives. She creates meaning and shares vision. She communicates goals, opens spaces, and envisions possibilities. Most of all, Rosalía shares leadership and inspires leadership in others.

About the Author:

SILVIA DORTA-DUQUE DE REYES worked with Rosalía Salinas at the San Diego County Office of Education for 20 years as Spanish Language Arts Coordinator. She recently served as Expert Panel Member for the development of the California ELD Standards and subsequently as Curriculum Framework and Evaluation Criteria Committee Member for the California State Department of Education. She is well known for curriculum design, staff development, academic writing and bi-literacy.

BEATRICE ZAMORA–AGUILAR:

DEAN OF STUDENTS; CO-LEADER, DANZA MEXICAYOTL
She Heard the Drums Calling and Discovered Her True Ancestry

BY LIZZ HUERTA

For more than twenty-five years, Bea Zamora-Aguilar has reached countless students at San Diego Mesa College and Southwestern College as counselor and then as dean of counseling and student services, respectively. Her life-altering experience with Danza Azteca is the basis for the deep respect for culture she awakens in others.

When she was a student at California State University Fullerton, Bea Zamora recalls that she was making tacos for an event when she first heard the sounds of the drums and the caracol. Until that point, she had never interacted with any Native Americans. She didn't even know they were still active in their vibrant cultures. She had only read about them and believed they were just in history books.

That day, she dropped everything and ran toward the drums, as if they were calling out to her. She came across a group of dancers she had never seen before. They called themselves danzantes. She got chills as she watched them dance, although she did not know who they were. She had never seen anything like this before. It was a surreal experience for her and it brought her to tears. She watched attentively until they finished their dance and then she went back to where she had been working, not knowing that danza would soon transform her life's path.

Bea Zamora was born in San Diego and raised in an industrial neighborhood in Los Angeles. She is a second-generation Mexican-American on her mother's side and New Mexican on her father's. Coming from the barrios of Los Angeles where she grew up, she always knew she was Mexican, although she had never been to Mexico. In fact, she didn't really know what it meant to be Mexican. She grew up speaking Spanish, but not admitting her heritage. She watched the social movements of the 1960s, seeing the high school walkouts and other protests on television, while observing her parents' fear of this kind of activism. They had spoken to her about how she should never go against the government or even complain about it.

In 1972, Bea enrolled at a community college where she became involved with a group called United Mexican-American Students (UMAS). It was the precursor to MEChA, the activist students' organization that called themselves Chicanos de Aztlán. UMAS was mostly social, a way for the few Chicanos on campus to support each other, to form study groups, and to hang out together. Nevertheless, through UMAS, Bea began to get involved in the social justice issues of the time. She took her first Mexican-American history class and it opened her eyes. It was the first time she had taken a history course like this and in it discovered a history she could be proud of.

At that point, she realized that she had an obligation to educate herself in order to make a difference for those who would follow after her. It was the beginning of a life dedicated to service and education. She completed her bachelor's degree at Cal State Fullerton and moved to San Diego to pursue a master's degree at San Diego State University. Part of the reason she moved was to get away from a toxic relationship she wanted to leave behind. When she got to San Diego, things began to change for the better. She found mutual friends in the Chicano community that introduced her to her future husband, Mario Aguilar. While they were dating, Mario invited Bea to watch him perform with a dance community in which he was involved. It was the danzantes.

Little did she know that it was a love story in the making. Bea and Mario were about to find their future partners in one another. Bea told Mario about her first experience seeing the danzantes at Cal State Fullerton; Mario told her that he had been there dancing that same day. Soon, Bea began attending the danza practices, always observing, but not participating. She was shy and afraid of putting herself on display in front of an audience. Then one day she realized she didn't want to live her life on the sidelines, always the observer and never the participant. That was the day she became a danzante. She realized also that she had been called to the danza. She had never before connected with her indigenous roots but remembers always being drawn to photographs of her grandmother Beatriz, a woman with long dark braids who did her cooking in an outdoor horno. Because of danza, Bea was able to explore her Chicana identity at a whole new level. The best part of the story is that Bea and Mario soon became husband and wife.

Bea now says that danza enriched her life in ways most people cannot comprehend. Danza allowed her to walk in two worlds, the world of her everyday work life—where she was a college counselor helping students realize their potential—and a world much deeper, with a more sacred connection. Today,

Dean Beatrice Zamora, at the Intertribal Ceremonial, Gallup, New Mexico; the event has a 95 year history. Dean Zamora and her husband, Dr. Mario E. Aguilar,co-lead the group Danza Mexicayotl, one of the first traditional groups to exist in the U.S, and have been dancing there since 1980.

Courtesy of Pedro Anaya.

danza reminds her of what is essential for her, and that is her family. Bea and Mario have raised two children, Sofia and Andres, who are also in danza. Bea says that when her children were applying to college, they wrote in their application essays about how danza had shaped their lives. Bea recalls, "That is when it really hit home for me how important it was to be a part of the danza tradition."

Dean Beatrice Zamora, 2015; named Woman of the Year in Higher Education by Assembly woman Lorena Gonzalez.

Courtesy of Mario E. Aguilar.

Bea has always been known to be a hard worker. I asked Bea, if she could go back in time and "give your 20-year-old self a piece of advice, what would that be?" I was surprised to hear her response: "I would probably say, 'You know what? You don't always have to take the most difficult path; you don't always have to do the most work; you don't always have to take on the biggest challenge.'" Bea believes we all have different philosophies on why we are on this earth. She says, "I think one of the things that I'm here to do is to learn to have a little more faith and trust others." She added assuredly, "I need to trust the process more and step back a little bit."

Bea chose to pursue a career in higher education because, when she went to college, there were very few Chicanos attending. She wanted to show other students that if she made it, they could make it too. She tells students, "Most of what it takes to succeed is self-discipline and learning how to study." She tries to lead by example, showing those she works with that it's okay to speak up, to say the unpopular things, and to take a risk.

Bea says her involvement in danza taught her to listen to her heart and speak her voice. She doesn't see herself as a leader in the Chicano Movement, despite the leadership roles she has played. However, others have seen her that way. Other professors and counselors have complimented the unique ways she is able to reach students. She asks the pertinent questions and then lets the students speak. As a result, they come up with the most amazing discoveries on their own. When she manages to pose the right questions, the students seem to come up with the right answers. That way, the students prosper. As it turns out, that is truly Bea's goal as a counselor. She lives hoping to make the world a better place for the people she connects with. That is what makes her a leader.

The two major teachings in danza, she said in Spanish, are disciplina and obligación. She adds, "I know these sound like really heavy arms, but *disciplina* is about self-discipline, about being true to your word, and I've always lived that way. I always make sure that my part, the part that I have committed to, gets done." The other one is *obligación*. She considers that this is the heavy one, the obligation it takes to do things in a good way, the right way. She feels that one has the obligation to do things consistently to really impact the world. Bea believes that "as counselors, teachers, and administrators, we are laying a foundation for future generations." She includes herself. Bea went from counselor to dean of student services. "In my job, I'm the dean; I'm in this role because I'm supposed to speak my mind, and I'm supposed to make a change for students." Bea understands that most people want structure and elders to look up to, but she sees herself as a free spirit too. She adds, "I don't think it's my place to tell people how to be. Everybody should be who they are. What I really want to share is this movement I've been involved with on an educational level and also on the community level that has impacted my life, and that is Danza Azteca"

Bea strongly believes that what the danza has done for the Chicano community is very important. She adds assertively, "I think that it was the beginning of Chicanos realizing that we have roots that go back for centuries." And she believes that knowing your roots is important. She wants students to realize that "just because the United States has set borders with Mexico does not mean this is not our continent." She makes a statement of unity with other indigenous groups when she says, "From the indigenous people of Alaska, down to the tip of South America, we are really one people. For Chicanos to be able to latch onto Danza Azteca, with its vibrancy, color, and strong drums, comes the opportunity to connect to our indigenous roots. That is what is in us."

Dean Bea Zamora's words ring with cultural pride, something she believes should belong to every student. She asserts that with recent DNA studies we can look at our bloodlines and realize that most Chicanos and Latinos, or whatever they call themselves, are Mestizos, that is, of mixed blood. She wants to remind others that seventy percent of our heritage is indigenous. And that is something to be proud of. The important thing is that this socio-political-cultural Chicano Movement has allowed a few generations of Chicanos to get in touch with that fact. Dean Zamora adds, "That is what makes it an empowering movement. I love it when young people see the danza as something empowering, and not as something odd that they've never seen before."

Dean Zamora reminds us of the day she heard the drums calling her to something new: her indigenous ancestry. She says, "I had never seen anything like it before, until that day at Cal State Fullerton. Today, young ones may see the indigenous celebration and at first they may not fully understand it, but they will soon realize that it is part of their heritage." Her greatest hope is that each person is respected for the unique culture and heritage each one has, no matter what that may be. As for Bea, she has found her voice and speaks it loudly when she says, "I'm proud to be a part of that movement of people who understand our culture at the spiritual level and have let that be a guiding force."

About the Author:

LIZZ HUERTA is a poet, fiction writer and essayist from Chula Vista. Her work has appeared in *Time Online, xoJane, ZYZZYVA, The Portland Review, Ban This: Anthology of New Xican@ Writing*, and various other anthologies and magazines. She was a finalist for the Andres Montoya Poetry Prize 2011, and a 2015 Pushcart Prize nominee. Her work has appeared or is forthcoming in *Lumina, Winter Tangerine, San Diego City Beat, Read America*, and *Seven Scribes*. She is currently working on a young adult novel.

CHAPTER 8

NORMA IGLESIAS-PRIETO

GAIL PEREZ

MARTA E. SÁNCHEZ

ROSAURA SÁNCHEZ

ANGELA GARCIA-SIMS

MARIA ZUÑIGA

CHAPTER 8

First Chicana University Professors and Research Scholars

"This Civil Rights Act is a challenge to all of us to go to work in our communities and our states, in our homes and in our hearts, to eliminate the last vestiges of injustice in our beloved country. . ."

~President Johnson, 1964.

In the 1960s and 1970s, Chicanas contributed their strong voices and actions to the area of Education. They were among the first college graduates in their families and the first to become educators at schools and colleges. Since the year 2000, Latinas have earned more than half the Ph.D.s awarded to Latinos nationwide. Many had been exposed to the radical activism of the Civil Rights Movement and brought with them a new consciousness. By 1965, they had witnessed the farmworkers movement in the news. They heard a woman leader who inspired them. Dolores Huerta, a phenomenon of the sixties, exposed inhumane wages and working conditions of workers in the fields. In 1968, they also saw Chicanas protesting injustices in the schools with high school walkouts in major cities, including in Los Angeles. In 1969, a major youth conference in Denver, Colorado brought together students to talk about the problems they were facing in the schools, including one of the first Chicana caucuses. This chapter is about some of the women who were becoming politicized in this era and soon after.

Many Chicanas were among the first to leave their homes to attend college. One of them was Maria Zuñiga. She was born and raised in Logan Heights in San Diego and graduated from Our Lady of Guadalupe School ; she received her bachelor's degree from the University of San Diego in 1964; then her masters degree from UC Berkeley graduate school in 1968. Young women like Maria were about to face some of the radical moments in U.S. Civil Rights history. She arrived not long after the free speech movement had occurred on that campus and the momentum was still alive. The anti-war movement was in full swing because of the war in Vietnam. Chicanos were speaking out about how the war affected them. Maria and other students at Berkeley had their own concerns as sociology majors who had no Spanish language resources and no Chicano teachers. They decided to bring their concerns to the administration, but to do so, they had to brave the tear gas protests after the killing of four student activists at Kent State. In the end, demands were met, and Maria graduated, and went on to become one of the first Chicanas to receive a Ph.d. in Sociology.

In Southern California, Chicanas were also becoming part of a movement for higher education. In 1969, at the University of California at Santa Barbara, students, faculty, and administrators gathered at a symposium to plan a strategy to reform higher education. That historical gathering resulted in a document, called *El Plan de Santa Barbara.* Soon after, at SDSU the Centro de Estudios Chicanos was formed by students and faculty to meet the needs of Chicana and Chicano students on campus and in the community. In 1968, Mexican American courses were initiated at San Diego State and later at Mesa College. They continue today as the longest running departments.

Chicanos began to be hired at colleges and universities. Before 1970, Chicanas were hired to teach at SDSU in the newly founded Mexican American Studies. Among them were, Evangeline Bustamante Hubbard, Maria Nissley, and Maria Enriqueta Vasquez. In 1974, the Chicano Studies department began to hire its first tenure track professors, but few were granted tenure. After many years of struggle, four Chicana professors have been tenured: Norma Iglesias, Adelaida Del Castillo, Maria Ibarra, and Victoria Gonzalez. Norma Iglesias, recognized in this chapter, originally a distinguished professor at the Mexican border university of Colegio de la Frontera Norte, COLEF, joined the Chicana and Chicano Studies department at SDSU and became a full professor. Norma's story resonates as she tells how, as a young graduate student in 1985, she interviewed Mexican women workers, in *maquiladores,* labor shops supported by U.S. corporations for profit. In an unprecedented publication, she exposed the abusive system under which women were forced to work. Her scholarly work has been highly regarded and used in courses at many colleges and universities.

Chicana scholars began to graduate and be hired at other universities. UCSD had some of the first and most notable Chicana scholars. Rosaura Sanchez, a linguist, was the first Chicana hired in the Department of Literature at UCSD. Now a full professor, in 1977 she co-edited a first Chicana Journal of writings called *Essays on la Mujer,* giving young Chicanas an opportunity to publish their own research for the first time. Dr. Sanchez also published her findings, obtained from the Bancroft Library at Berkeley, the 1870s testimonios of Alta California women, in a book she authored called *Telling Identities,* breakthrough research. Rosaura and co-editor introduced Maria Amparo Ruiz de Burton, not just as the first Mexican American woman author—but the first Mexican American—to publish a novel (*The Squator and the Don*, 1895) in the United States.

Other Chicanas were being hired at major universities for the first time. Marta Sanchez came to UCSD in 1970, as a young graduate student, aspiring to obtain a Ph.D. In 1977 she was hired as assistant professor in the Department of Literature. She came to UCSD after having taught at Cal State Northridge where she was a member of the committee that founded one of the first Mexican American Studies department in the nation. Marta also has the distinction of publishing the first book of literary criticism on Chicana poetry at a time when there were few books in print for Chicano literature courses. She was also one of the first Chicanas to present her research at Modern Language Association (MLA) seminars. She served on the Board of Preuss School at UCSD, aimed at addressing the low numbers of Chicanos/Latinos and African American students in higher-education. Marta Sanchez's consistent academic work shows how Chicana scholars who were studying for a higher degree like her were expected to research, publish, and serve on committees, while also mentoring the many Chicanas/Latinas coming to the university for the first time.

Since *the Plan de Santa Barbara* symposium, departments of Chicana and Chicano Studies and Ethnic Studies have been established and now prosper in San Diego. SDSU now has a bachelor's and a master's degree in Chicana and Chicano Studies; UCSD offers an M.A. and Ph.D. in Ethnic Studies; and USD now has a Department of Ethnic Studies. At the University of San Diego, Professor Gail Perez was instrumental in establishing the first department of Ethnic Studies. Gail has been celebrated for her excellence in teaching; nominated more than once, she received the Teacher of the Year award in 2013. The first Chicana to make these inroads at USD to the extent that diversity has grown, and Dr. Perez is to be commended for building a diverse campus. She started in her English and literature courses, in her on-campus programs, and in her persistent efforts to establish ethnic studies. In 2009, she organized a seminar of local Chicana activists to speak, "In Their Own Voice," at the USD Annual Social Justice Issues Conference, as a way of presenting the earliest innovators, Chicana activists, in the movement to students and other attendees.

Women in San Diego have made important headways in the field of education. In 1994, Angela Garcia-Sims came to San Diego, after having taught at several prestigious universities. After obtaining the Ph.d in Educational Psychology at Stanford University, she was hired there as assistant director of the Stanford Urban/Rural School Training institute. She and her husband were then recruited by the Crystal City Schools in Texas, a center of Chicano activism, as directors of the Ethnic Studies Program. As a young widow, Angela came to San Diego to be the Director of Curriculum and Education in the South Bay. She fought against cultural inequities. First, she addressed the problem of signage in English-only at Old Town Park, attributing the absence of Spanish to showing disregard for Mexican culture. In an effort to acknowledge Mexican history before 1848, she helped organize the Early San Diego History Collaborative and lead the annual conferences for seven years, until 2007.

Women now have a voice in higher education, as you will see throughout these chapters. Change came because of their activism, and their willingness to speak out.

NORMA IGLESIAS-PRIETO:

PROFESSOR, CHICANA AND CHICANO STUDIES, SDSU

Interviewed and Published a Book on Women in the Labor Plants of Mexico

BY SARA SOLAIMANI

Norma Iglesias-Prieto models for other Chicanas that conscious choice says far more about who they are than does genealogical kinship. She, therefore, reminds us that being a Chicana is a serious responsibility, not the simple assumption of identity. In more scholarly terms, she describes that responsibility as "the refusal to accept the hegemonic version of transborder history and its geopolitical order." At the basis of these words is her quest for liberation from colonial mentalities.

Scholar, mother, and activist Norma Iglesias-Prieto, professor and former chair of the San Diego State University Department of Chicana and Chicano Studies, is one of the foremost border scholars in the world today. Her projects and recognitions are too many to note; it is without question that they have made a lasting stir in both Mexican and American institutions. She is perhaps most well known for developing the theoretical concept of transborder beyond its literal meaning. Iglesias Prieto has contributed much to borderlands discourse and, as a result, has reached countless Chicanas on the subject of border consciousness. She defines transborder condition as the border's imposition on the people of the so-called Third World. She further emphasizes that this definition can be as limiting for some as it is a non-issue for others. She draws from a Marxist education to a pedagogy in social anthropology at her present post in SDSU's Chicana and Chicano Studies. Iglesias Prieto's academic research, teaching, and social practice bleed drops of activism against this unjust unevenness.

The transdisciplinary fields of border and Chicana and Chicano Studies have taught Iglesias Prieto how to be a bridge or a translator that connects and complicates definitions on both sides of the border. She holds that the interrogation of borders that Gloria Anzaldúa poeticized to radical perfection opened a conversation with the Mexican *avant-garde*. Its influence from the center, stems from a dynamic system that obligates us to rethink Mexico's borders, namely that of Tijuana–San Diego. Within this reconceptualization, the subject of her scholarly work sets textual precedence. It analyzes the artistic production, audience reception, and institutional networks of the visual arts in Tijuana. In her experimental text, *Emergencias: Las artes visuales en Tijuana*, she posits that this weaving of aesthetic negotiations is a reflection and direct product of the many different possibilities used to describe the transborder condition.

Norma Iglesias-Prieto, 2010, in her garden at home.

Courtesy of Jorge Carillo.

Norma Iglesias-Prieto is an independent thinker who describes herself as a jack-of-all-trades. Born and raised in Mexico City in the 1960s and 70s, she credits her father, architect Roberto Iglesias, for helping to develop these traits in her. She strives to model these traits for her own daughters, Paloma and Andrea. They are qualities that give her the flexibility to move between occupations, empowering her to identify with the "trans" in transborder. More importantly, she has developed a serious discipline of learning the labor of each stage of production. She recalls her parents' adamancy for discipline, insisting that the Iglesias Prieto children take up a serious practice in either the visual and performing arts or music.

In 1968, Iglesias Prieto reconnected with her favorite childhood teachers, José and Azul Gordillo, after being invited to collaborate on a children's mural for Mexico's first annual Cultural Olympics. The publication that resulted from the project is titled *Lo Que el Niño Enseñó al Hombre/What the Child Taught the Man*. Iglesias Prieto's alternative pedagogy began to take shape in this very early influence. Upon graduating high school, the young student's Gramscian dream of an Italian education began to morph into a strong desire to learn more about the system of "othering" occurring on her own nation's borders, Mexico's geopolitical limitations of home. Educated in a critically active Mexican School of Anthropology at Universidad Autónoma Metropolitana, she headed for the border.

The scholar would find herself at a crossroads between *lo chicano y lo chilango*. That is, she began to define her own transborder condition through a methodological questioning of fixed notions of identity. Her groundbreaking bachelor's thesis is the product of a participant observation project in which she infiltrates the *maquiladora* system. As a result, she is able to bring the silenced narratives of women laborers to center stage. It is this research that informed her 1985 book *La flor más bella de la maquiladora/Beautiful Flowers of the Maquiladora*. In 1986, her two-volume master's thesis was published as the book *Entre yerba, polvo y plomo: Lo fronterizo visto por el cine mexicano (Between Herbs, Dust, and Lead: The Border Images in Mexican Cinema)*. It has earned distinction as one of the first in-depth analyses of audience reception to Mexican film.

In 1992, Iglesias Prieto was accepted into a communication and development doctoral program at the Universidad Complutense de Madrid. She embarked on a new adventure with her family to begin research for her dissertation "*Identidad, género y recepción cinematográfica. Danzón y su lectura por género*" ("Identity, Gender and Film Reception: Danzón and Gendered Audience Reception"). Upon returning from Spain, the young professor was invited to give several distinguished guest lectures in different departments and to sit on multiple editorial boards at universities and think tanks on both sides of the Tijuana-San Diego border. This she accomplished while continuing her own research and social practice.

In 2000, facing the impossibility of holding faculty positions in two countries, she decided to leave her 22-year post at El Colegio de la Frontera Norte (COLEF), and move to San Diego where she accepted a professorship at SDSU's Department of Chicana and Chicano Studies. Soon after, she was appointed department chair and began a collaborative process with CCS faculty to revolutionize the department's curriculum and field research opportunities for students. With this innovative transformation, she began to draw bridges between the complex growing field of Border Studies and the radical resistance and social justice plight of Chicana and Chicano Studies. For that and many other reasons, Professor Norma Iglesias-Prieto has made her mark in Border Studies today.

In 2005, the year before my son was born, I had the pleasure of meeting Professor Iglesias (whom I now address as Norma). It was my second semester in the first graduate Chicana and Chicano Studies master's degree program. It was through her criticism, pedagogic devotion, and careful mentorship that I saw my thesis, "Culture, Art and the Transborder Condition/Experience: Marcos Ramirez Erre's Art Practices," to completion and learned how to own my transborder condition. Norma models for me that being Chicana is a conscious choice and that it says far more about who I am than does genealogy. From Norma Iglesias-Prieto I have learned that being a Chicana is a serious responsibility. I was not born a Chicana and that means it is possible for me to follow Norma's path. Because of her, I have joined the Chicana feminist discursive field through conscious political standing.

About the Author:

SARA SOLAIMANI is a graduate of the SDSU Chicana and Chicano Studies Masters Degree program; she is a doctoral student in the Art History, Theory, and Criticism Ph.D program at the UCSD Department of Visual Arts. Focusing on Early Border Art History and the fractured post modernities that influenced 1980s and 90s artistic production in the region, her current work is informed by practice that operationalizes narrative to question the hegemonic neoliberal story.

GAIL PEREZ:

PROFESSOR, UNIVERSITY OF SAN DIEGO; FOUNDER ETHNIC STUDIES
Cherished Mentor and Teacher of the Year

BY GENOVEVA AGUILAR

Dr. Gail Perez was my mentor during my university years and, in many ways, a godsend that helped me survive the college experience. She has been a cherished mentor, one of the best professors I have ever had, and a true friend. Together, we were able to fight for something we both believed in: Ethnic Studies at the University of San Diego (USD).

Dr. Perez was there for me when I needed her most. Tragically, my younger brother was murdered at the age of 26, a huge loss in my life. It was not a surprise to look up and see Dr. Perez, my English professor, attending his funeral services, despite the eight years that had elapsed since I had graduated from USD. As I reflect on this trying time in my life, I cannot help but think of the one thing that my brother was missing in his life: a mentor—someone who could have steered him in the right direction. I had many mentors who helped me on the journey that is my life, but it was not until I began my studies at USD that I truly grasped the concept of what it means to have a mentor.

When I began my studies at USD, I was a lost soul. I was the first in my family to attend college and I will never forget the culture shock I experienced when I first set foot on the USD campus. During my first week, an African American transfer student whom I had just met at orientation experienced a hate crime. She and I were among the few women of color living in the dorms at the time when she told me that someone had written racial comments in her bathroom. I felt a lot of fear and anger. I realized how unprepared our university was in dealing with issues of diversity. Thanks to her courage in speaking up, some other students and I, with the guidance of another great mentor Guadalupe Corona, initiated a process for educating the campus on hate crimes and bias-motivated incidents. We advocated for changing campus policy around these issues. Becoming an advocate, activist, and organizer, however, did not happen overnight. When I first found out about this incident, I was ready to drop out, despite the long hours of personal sacrifice and hard work dedicated to my studies to ensure that I would be accepted into the university.

Then, I met Dr. Perez. There were not many students of color at USD, but the ones who were would continuously refer me to Dr. Perez, as if she were the Wizard of Oz and could make things right. I was finally able to introduce myself to her, after what seemed a lifetime to track her down. Upon entering her office, I began to cry. My feelings of loneliness and isolation immediately surfaced as I expressed to her my experience at USD as a woman of color and told how that made me feel. Her sincerity and genuine understanding of what I had been experiencing was just what I needed at the time to persevere. She knew firsthand what it was like to experience racism in San Diego. She shared with me an anecdote of her own. As a little girl, she was with her dad at the merry-go-round in Balboa Park when the ride operator looked at them and said, "spics." She told me how that made her feel. It was through Dr. Perez that I began my endeavor toward self-discovery. I was extremely happy to meet her and see that I was like her, and she was like me, a strong woman.

Dr. Perez was born in New York to Gregorio Parra Perez and Revay Pearson. She believes her parents met in Chicago at a dance club (Pérez Prado was the rage) and moved to New York. Her immigrant father lived bi-nationally and so eventually her parents divorced. That was a difficult time for her. She moved to San Diego with her mother, grandparents, and new stepfather, Nat Cordova, from Logan Heights. Although she felt privileged in many ways—her grandparents, for instance, supported her education—she was obviously of color and experienced racism. She actually had a third grade teacher who refused to teach her and another Mexicana named Elvira. Both of them sat in the back of the classroom for many weeks, ignored. She was made to feel racial distinctions at an early age and this stuck with her.

Although I did not major in English, I took several courses taught by Dr. Perez. Her door was always open and she made it a habit to be accessible to students, especially those who felt marginalized at USD. Dr. Perez was someone you could relate to because she had attended USD herself in the 1960s and 70s. It was inspiring to listen to her stories about USD during those times, for example, how she joined the antiwar movement or how she put a communist flag in her dorm's window as a way of protest. She could relate to us because she knew firsthand what it was like to attend college and also work to survive. She had lived in a modified garage during her college years and had little access to commodities. As a graduate student, she continued to support herself with work and scholarships. In the end, she was able to graduate from Stanford University with a Ph.D., debt free. She notes that much of the funding she received is no longer readily available to our generation.

Professor Gail Perez, 2009, Department of English, University of San Diego.
Courtesy of USD, College of Arts and Sciences.

Dr. Perez's wisdom has illuminated my soul. If not for Dr. Perez, I would never have served as co-chair of the student organization MEChA in my sophomore year. This organization was housed in the United Front Multicultural Center, which was very supportive of our activism at that time. I was one of the student leader activists who helped establish the Ethnic Studies major that eventually became the Ethnic Studies Department at USD. We won a hard fought battle because we dared to speak out. Dr. Perez inspired me to strive and sacrifice for what I believed in, no matter where you come from.

Teaching in the pioneering Europe and the Americas Western Civilization track at Stanford University was transformational for her. Not only did she teach on matters of race and ethnicity, something they were not entirely used to, but she and other students and faculty had to publicly defend these courses against the institution and against the media. These experiences at Stanford prepared her to give advice and guidance to those fighting for Ethnic Studies at USD.

In 1998, she and Dr. Gene Labovitz taught the first-ever introduction to Ethnic Studies course at USD. Later, they drafted proposals for, first, a minor and, then, a major in Ethnic Studies. In 2003, they hired Dr. Alberto Pulido to be the director of the new Ethnic Studies major. In addition, Dr. Perez created many new and first-time courses at USD, including Multicultural California; Chicana/o Lives; U.S. Women of Color; and Women, Land, and Justice.

Dr. Perez and I share some of the same challenges of growing up with an alcoholic parent; and only people who grew up with alcoholic parents understand that struggle. In spite of her challenges as a little girl, she made it possible for us, her students, to believe in what is right and to exercise our freedom of expression. She served as a role model of a strong independent woman. One challenge came when she was hired as an English professor. She had a bad experience with a co-worker harassing her as an "affirmative action candidate." That is, he tried to demean her inclusion at the university. According to that co-worker, Dr. Perez was too radical a professor.

Dr. Perez was the perfect fit for USD. Her teachings about taking direct action in order to create positive change helped us students embrace our First Amendment Right to protest injustice. She encouraged self-empowerment and self-determination that gave us student activists the courage to face the challenge of racism in an already challenging environment. Dr. Perez inspired us to not only get involved at our university, but in our community as well.

In my sessions with her, I shared my love for the low-income barrio I was raised in, one of the most historic barrios in San Diego and home to many Mexican American working class families. Dr. Perez introduced me to the world of gentrification and helped me understand the problems plaguing many of our communities of color whose neighborhoods are taken over for redevelopment and profit. She helped me launch a grassroots movement through an organization called Developing Unity through Resident Organizing (DURO). This community group exists to this day as Casa Vecinos Organizados (CVO) and is entirely resident run. As a community, we studied books and articles she would recommend to understand the problems. The knowledge that we gained helped us build affordable housing in our community on 22nd and Commercial Streets.

Dr. Perez's mentorship was all we needed in order to survive the realities of life and to strive to live in abundance, as we deserve. If not for her outstanding leadership, I have no doubt that I would have turned out to be another college dropout statistic. It is without question that my life path would have been disastrous and would have paralleled my brother's tragic outcome. I am extremely proud to say that I, too, have become a mentor in my own right to many of the Chicanas in our communities. I have done this as a union organizer, and within my family, and barrio. I owe it all to Dr. Perez, as I have followed in her footsteps since our first encounter. I am blessed to have met such a strong woman who has gone through the same struggles that many Chicanas face when achieving a higher education in our country, where racism and sexism still exist to this day. I still carry her advice that helped us establish Ethnic Studies: "Always do your homework and learn their—meaning other's—vocabulary. It is the only way we are going to win." And we did.

About the Author:

GENOVEVA AGUILAR is a longstanding community and labor leader who has been recognized as one of the best organizers in the San Diego region. In 2014, she was awarded the Women of the Year Award by State Assemblywoman Lorena Gonzalez; *San Diego Metro Magazine* awarded her as one of the 40 under 40 Best and Brightness Minds in San Diego. She graduated *Magna Cum Laude* from Mission Bay High School; she is first in her family to attend college, a graduate of the University of San Diego with degrees in Sociology, Spanish, and Ethnic Studies; she serves as a coordinator, SEIU-United Service Workers West, San Diego, where she empowers workers to reach their maximum potential as leaders, to organize in their worksites for better working conditions.

Marta Sánchez at UCSD, public relations announcing one of her books.
Courtesy of Paul Espinosa.

MARTA E. SÁNCHEZ:

PROFESSOR EMERITA, LITERATURE, UCSD AND ASU

Scholar/Activist: She Wrote the First Published Book of Criticism on Chicana Poetry

BY PATRICIA SANTANA

A prestigious university in one of San Diego's most affluent communities seems an unlikely place for a young, naïve, Mexican-American girl from the barrio to come of age as a Chicana activist. That is, unless you have a role model who inspires, buoys, and guides you to be the best human being you can be. Professor Marta E. Sánchez was that role model for me.

I met Professor Sánchez in 1973. That is when I learned the value of mentorship. I was a student at the University of California, San Diego, and one of my professors was Dr. Sánchez. Then, the world was in chaos—or so it seemed to my 18-year-old mind—and my identity was constantly being called into question: Am I a Mexican-American, a Chicana, or just an American? Am I supposed to be marching in rallies and partaking in sit-ins? Or, would I better serve my community by holing up in the library, studying hard, and getting good grades with the ultimate goal of a good paying job? These were the many unanswered questions I had. "Where was I in all this sociopolitical confusion?" I wondered. Then, in my freshman year I enrolled in a cultural traditions class hoping to have, once and for all, these questions answered. It was there that I met my first role model who would—perhaps unbeknownst to her—help me answer these and other questions: Professor Marta Sánchez. She was then a Ph.D. candidate and teaching assistant for the three-semester-long course. I credit her for her mentorship.

Marta E. Sánchez, daughter of Mexican immigrants, was born and raised in East Los Angeles. When her father left the home, Marta and her two brothers were raised by her mother and grandmother, two strong women. They both spoke Spanish in the home and so her home language was important to Marta.

Marta's scholarly gifts were quickly recognized in the classroom where she learned the importance of having mentors in her life. One of them, a

Dominican Sister at the Catholic school she attended, encouraged her to apply for a scholarship. Marta scored high on a national Spanish test, won the scholarship, and applied to Mount St. Mary College in Brentwood. She recalls those days. The sisters believed that "women should only be educated by other women." She took their advice. For Marta, the women's college was a good fit and, in the end, the sisters were right. She would soon have the chance to mentor other women.

Marta overcame the long commute from the East L.A. barrio in Boyle Heights to Brentwood. "I was a glutton for punishment in those days and did not mind getting up at 5 a.m. for the two-hour bus ride to school," she recalls. Eventually, Marta took a part time job after school so she could board in Brentwood. After that, there was more culture shock for the 21-year-old, living on her own in Cleveland, Ohio, where she studied at John Carroll University for a master's degree and the opportunity to teach. She then returned home to teach English and Spanish courses at California State University at Northridge.

In 1970, with the advice of a colleague, Marta pursued her doctorate at the University of California in San Diego (UCSD). She recalls some of the obstacles she met along the way. "In the comparative literature department, you have to show proficiency in three languages," and on a Ford Foundation Fellowship, Marta traveled to France: A Chicana in Paris. She had notions of being housed with the French. Instead, groups were divided according to national origin, so she was placed with other Americans. "It was a hard time," she recalls. "As much as I studied, I couldn't seem to master the language as easily as others did." She also remembers being cold, stressed, and hungry: "We had no refrigeration, so we used to put our little cartons of yogurt outside on the cool window sill. Invariably, they were taken by some other hungry student." Marta remained after her course of study, "grateful for the opportunity to travel outside of Paris" to other spots.

At UCSD, she mastered French in a seminar with Professor Jameson, who became one of her advisors. "With the help of mentors," she recalls, "I completed my language requirements." Some of her mentors in those days were Professors Joseph Sommers, Rosaura Sanchez, and Carlos Blanco. She was also able to work as a teaching assistant for Ramon Ruiz, history professor at CSU Northridge, and to teach the cultural traditions course at UCSD. "That is where I met Patricia Santana and Yolanda Guerrero," Marta rcalls.

In 1977, Marta received her Ph.D. and was hired as a professor at UCSD, one of the first Chicanas to teach at a major university. True to her love of language and literature, she taught Chicano, Latin American, and U.S. ethnic literatures.

Besides the Ford Foundation Fellowship, she was also the recipient of several other prestigious fellowships. They were awarded to her by the National

Chicano Council for Higher Education, the Rockefeller Foundation, the University of California President's Office, and the Stanford Humanities Center.

Most notably, in 1985, Marta "had the singular distinction of writing the first published book-length study of Chicana poetry." She became one of the first Chicanas to interpret the work of Chicana poets in American Literature. *Contemporary Chicana Poetry: A Critical Approach to an Emerging Literature,* published by UC Press at Berkeley, became a definitive classroom text. It is a critical analysis of poetry by women of Mexican origin in the United States and one of the first scholarly studies in the field of Chicana and Chicano studies and culture.

This is Dr. Marta Sánchez, the woman who influenced my life. Besides the profound effect Marta had on my own goals and career success, others have found her to be influential in their lives. A fellow student and now my colleague, Yolanda Guerrero, remembers that Professor Sánchez affected her life too as her first role model at UCSD. They met when, as a young professor in 1977, Marta taught an undergraduate course in Spanish on Juan Rulfo, José Revueltas, and Tomás Rivera. Yolanda was 18 years old and fresh out of high school from National City, a predominantly Hispanic community, and recalls that, "There were very few Chicanos at UCSD and I felt isolated. When I met Marta, it changed my outlook about UCSD. I now had a role model, someone to look up to and emulate." She took graduate courses on Chicano literature from Professor Sánchez, attributing her choices and area of concentration to Marta Sánchez. With many incoming Chicana/Latina students and few professors to teach them, Marta Sánchez became among the first to fill this important role as professor/mentor. She did it with tireless dedication to the many first-generation college students, away from home for the first time.

Pioneer extraordinaire, Marta Sánchez is an unassuming and gentle person with a keen intelligence and a wide intellectual range that was soon apparent to all of us. She was pivotal in my journey toward a progressive sociopolitical awakening. From my first class with her in my freshman year to later graduate seminars in Latin American and Chicano literature, Marta was one of my most important role models as I sought to understand my place in the world.

In class, Marta helped me answer the many questions with which I was struggling. She invited us to discuss controversial topics by asking questions that she wanted us to answer—Are we Mexicans with U.S. citizenship or Americans with Mexican parents?—while also urging us to go deeper and question our own conceptions about *chicanismo.* She encouraged us not only to delve into deep textual readings of the Latin American authors we were studying, but to compare these writers to writers of other cultures. "Branch out," she would say.

Marta began to explore and write about such topics herself. In 1998, the prestigious *PMLA Journal* published her "La Malinche at the Intersection: Race and Gender in Piri Thomas' Down These Mean Streets" (Vol. 113, No. 1). By 2005, she had authored another book, *"Shakin' Up" Race and Gender: Intercultural Connections in Puerto Rican, African American, and Chicano Narratives and Culture (1965-1995)* (Austin: University of Texas Press, 2005).

I remember when she challenged us to go beyond that which was comfortable for us; she wanted us to discover new cultures and compare them to our own. Whether we were analyzing Pedro Páramo by Mexican writer Juan Rulfo or *Down These Mean Streets* by the mainland Puerto Rican writer Piri Thomas, Professor Sánchez urged us to make intercultural connections, to be aware of our differences, and, more importantly, our similarities.

Her areas of expertise were not limited to the classroom. Marta authored several articles dealing with cultural diversity and identity. Among them, "Walking the Tightrope Between Two Cultures: Hispanic and Anglo-American Discourse in Family Installments" in *American Literary History* 1, 4 (Winter, 1989); and "Arturo Islas' The Rain God: An Alternative Tradition," in *American Literature* 62, 2(Spring, 1990). One of her most current works stands out. As anti-Mexican sentiment rages, Marta examines issues related to the undocumented in the United States. In 2013, she wrote, "'I May Say Wetback but I Really Mean Mojado': Migration and Translation in Ramon 'Tianguis' Perez' *Diary of an Undocumented Immigrant*" (*Perspectives: Studies in Translatology*, Vol. 22, No. 2).

Because of her well-defined scholarly approach to topics and her attention to her students, Marta instilled in me—naïve and confused as I was when I first started out at UCSD—a better understanding of my place in the university, in the community, and in the world. Her own academic success was not her only priority; her service work shows the dynamic impact that her life has had on others. At CSU Northridge, she was a member of the committee that founded Mexican American Studies and hired historian Rodolfo Acuña. At UCSD, she participated in the establishment of the Preuss Charter School on campus, for grades 6-12, aimed at addressing the low numbers of Latino and African American students in higher education; she served on its advisory board from 2000 to 2004. She was an editor for the Latinidad Series of Rutgers University Press from 2008 to 2012. One can see how her generosity through service has touched the lives of others.

In 2004, Professor Sánchez left her full-professor position at UCSD to become professor in the School of Transborder Studies at Arizona State University (ASU), hoping to open more doors for graduate students. Recruited by the university, ASU wanted her to give its graduate students a better understanding of the U.S.-Mexican transborder region. If anyone knows the arduous path of this journey, it's Marta Sánchez.

When Marta left UCSD, her colleague, Dr. Rosaura Sánchez, lauded the "dedication and commitment to teaching and mentoring that have characterized her entire career." In other words, Marta's scholarly endeavors have continued to awaken many and have opened doors to others to become professors in the field of literature or the humanities. Marta's advice to students is to "find a mentor early on." She remembers how, at an early age, the mentorship of a teacher helped her overcome her major obstacles. And she hopes others will similarly benefit.

Marta's encouragement, respect, enthusiasm, and intellect inspired me to continue my graduate studies in comparative literature and helped set the stage to my becoming a professional writer and educator. Role model, mentor, and life-long friend, Professor Sánchez is not only a pioneer, but a giant among her peers.

Marta E. Sánchez, former full professor is now retired from two universities. She is now Professor Emerita, esteemed scholar, at both UCSD and ASU. Marta represents a bold entry into the academic world of arts and letters at a time when there were few Mexican Americans and hardly any women. Her breakthrough Chicana scholarship introduced others to innovative fields of research, bringing to light the Chicano/Latino experience in literature to the forefront. Marta lives in San Diego with her husband of 30 years, Paul Espinosa, noted filmmaker. They have a daughter, Marisa Espinosa Rodríguez, a graduate of the University of San Diego, and two grandchildren, Jaime Gabriel and Paul Theodore Rodríguez.

About the Author:

PATRICIA SANTANA was born and raised in south San Diego, eighth of nine children of Mexican immigrants; has a B.A. degree, from UCSD, and an M.A. in Literature from UCLA. She teaches Spanish and is the Chair of the World Languages department at Cuyamaca College. Her first novel *Motorcycle Ride on the Sea of Tranquillity* (University of New Mexico, 2002) is the winner of the American Library Association Best Books; winner of *San Diego Magazine's* annual book award; and the winner of the Chicano/Latino Literary Award. Her second novel, *Ghosts of El Grullo* (University of New Mexico, 2008) was awarded the Premio Aztlán award, the Before Columbus American Book Award, and the San Diego Book Award. Both novels deal with the Mexican immigrant experience in the United States.

Professor Rosaura Sánchez, 2012, giving a presentation at UCSD.
Courtesy of Center for the Humanities.

ROSAURA SÁNCHEZ:

UCSD PROFESSOR OF LITERATURE AND AUTHOR
Author of breakthrough Research at U.C. Berkeley on Las Californianas

BY NANCY MADRID

I cannot express how honored I am to have the opportunity to write a tribute to Rosaura Sánchez. What I most appreciate is the experience of reading about her and talking to her, getting to know her history and some of the experiences that have shaped who she is today. I realize that her experiences also greatly shape those of my own and others. Rosaura inspires many of us to become advocates of social justice, to succeed as underrepresented students, and, of course, to be proud of our Chican@ roots and culture.

Rosaura is currently a professor of Latin American literature and Chicana literature at the University of California, San Diego (UCSD), where she has taught since 1972. She was one of the first in San Diego to contribute her work on Chican@s and to work with other underrepresented faculty and students of color. Rosaura engages students in classes on critical theory; cultural studies; third world studies; and gender studies, in both Spanish and English. She also serves as a mentor to these students and many graduate students.

Rosaura comes from a working class background in Texas. She was inspired to write by her mother and father who worked as laborers. She is a second-generation Chicana, along with her siblings Alejandro, Ruben, and Nelda. As a young girl, Rosaura picked cotton with her siblings; it was in the fields where she first felt the anger many of us are familiar with, due to the exploitation and lack of resources available in her community. In her early college career at the University of Texas at Austin during the 1960s, she was very engaged in student activism, protesting against racism, segregation, and the exclusion of Chican@ students in education.

These hands-on experiences as a student contributed to her continued activism in other areas.

Rosaura shared with me her experience of serving in the Peace Corps in the mountain ranges of Ecuador for some years after college. At the time, she wished she had studied something more practical to help the indigenous communities, rather than an education in literature, which was not as useful. However, these studies allowed Rosaura to participate in a literacy program with the Quechua-speaking indigenous groups that inspired her to continue her education in Spanish linguistics. This choice would ultimately lead her to an ability to help many more people.

Rosaura's work on critical theories is very important; it allowed her to publish books when there weren't any available in the area of Chican@ studies. She paved the way for other Chicanas to write and publish their work in Anglo-dominated spaces. In her coedited book *Essays on la Mujer*, many young women were provided the opportunity to publish important pieces that are still used today. Rosaura's work not only disrupted the domination of Anglo writers, but also broke down barriers regarding gender in Chican@ literature.

Dr. Rosaura Sánchez has written several other books and articles. In 1992 she reintroduced and coedited with Beatrice Pita, the novel, *The Squatter and the Don* by María Amparo Ruiz de Burton, for Arte Publico Press series, Recovering the U.S. Hispanic Heritage.

The Chicano literary canon had always indicated that the first Chicano novel was *Pocho* by José Antonio Villarreal. In the 1990s, Rosaura shattered that misconception with her research on the early Californios. Her breakthrough research enabled others to recognize María Amparo Ruiz de Burton as the first Chican@ author, in 1895, long before Villarreal.

Just as noteworthy is her work on early California women activists who defended and fought for their land during the U.S. invasion of the Southwest. This definitive research, oral histories by women in the Bancroft Library in Berkeley, had placed Mejicanos and our hidden written history in the institutional vaults. Rosaura was at the forefront of exposing those unknown histories, bringing them to light. In 1995, she published her scholarly research in a book called *Telling Identities*, (Houston: Arte Publico, 1995) a historical and literary analysis of these thirty 1870s testimonies of early California women.

This research by Rosaura gives insight into the Mexican American population as a conquered people, "despite being granted full rights of U.S. citizenship by the Treaty of Guadalupe Hidalgo [they] were a subordinated and marginalized national minority."

Today, I pay tribute to Rosaura for mentoring so many students like me. She was very influential in my life, helping me in graduate school, as a mentor and professor. Throughout my undergraduate career at UCSD, I never had the opportunity to take a course with Rosaura and, that, I regret. As a graduate student, I enjoyed Rosaura's Ethnic Studies class on Latina issues because it provided me a space to use my knowledge and experience as a community organizer to discuss issues regarding gender and immigration. While Rosaura was very encouraging and made us feel that our opinions were validated, I was also encouraged by her to think more critically about the material we were reading.

While in college, thinking critically changed my outlook. Rosaura's class was where I first learned about the issues on campus that would later become the topic of my master's thesis in 2012. Rosaura invited some of the women on campus who cleaned student dorms to share their stories about how many of them had been seriously injured by steam machines they were required to use. These were immigrant workers, women of color, who worked very hard cleaning the facilities on campus and caring for students. Yet, they were being asked to use a tool that was harmful because it was more economical and efficient. Rosaura encouraged us to become active in a campaign to stop the use of the steam machines. This ultimately launched a series of student petitions, protests, and advocacy in support of more humane and sustainable working conditions for workers at the UCSD campus that year.

Rosaura Sánchez.
Courtesy of Lucinda Rubio-Barrick.

Rosaura's encouragement and belief in others have helped many women. She was very helpful to me as the chair of my thesis committee during my master's program at the Center for Iberian and Latin American Studies at UCSD. I was both excited and grateful to have such a strong Chicana serve as my guide during this difficult process, particularly in an environment where there were few women like me. Rosaura helped me in ways that reached beyond advising me on my chapter outline or editing my drafts. Always encouraging, she made me feel as if I had a space in academia and helped me understand the importance and need for my work. In turn, I felt like I had a place in the university and could feel pride in both my work and my identity. As one of the few graduate students of color on campus, it was often difficult to navigate seminars and feel confident in my career. Rosaura's encouragement and faith in my writing really inspired me to speak up in my courses and in my community.

With Rosaura's encouragement, I began to make critical choices. My work exposed the contradictions that exist at UCSD and other universities. Such institutions carry the responsibility of serving as spaces that create change and encourage students to think and act at the local and global levels. Our goal as students is to come to these places and learn so that we can make the world a better place. However, Rosaura helped me to see the many inequalities still exist, specifically around janitorial workers who spend many hours not only cleaning, but also nurturing and supporting students residing in the dorms. Without Rosaura's guidance, I would not have been able to share the stories of the men and *womyn* who clean the UCSD campus, as well as the stories of the many others who are very much like them.

Rosaura described her most important role in the field of Chican@/Latin@ literature as being a teacher, mentor, and professor who has guided many graduate students like me. I would agree that her impact on students has been very profound. I have met many graduate students of color who work with Rosaura and express the same appreciation. It is important for us to have women like Rosaura in academia for many reasons. Although I completed my degree at UCSD nearly three years ago, I continue to see Rosaura as a role model and feel very supported by her. There is never a time when Rosaura doesn't encourage me to pursue a doctorate and continue my work on exposing the injustices suffered by low-wage workers. Rosaura is inspirational to me in many ways, particularly as a social justice advocate, woman of color, and also in my current role as teacher. These days, I try my best to encourage my students, particularly those who come from historically underrepresented groups, to think critically and pursue their interests related to social justice, even if nobody else is talking about it. These critical choices I attribute to having studied with Dr. Rosaura Sánchez.

About the Author:

NANCY MADRID was born in San Jacinto, California, the first in her family to graduate from college; she received a B.A. in Sociology and Latin American Studies and an M.A. at the Center for Iberian & Latin American Studies at UCSD,; her Master's Thesis Committee was chaired by Dr. Rosaura Sanchez. Nancy first taught at UCSD for the Department of Linguistics and Dimensions of Culture at Thurgood Marshall College; she currently teaches Spanish at middle and high schools. A native Spanish-speaker, Nancy proudly embraces her Mexicana roots and has a passion for critical race and gender studies, social justice, and community activism. She seeks solidarity among Immigrant wage workers and students while she continues to advocate for their rights.

ANGELA GARCIA–SIMS:

LEADER, SAN DIEGO REGIONAL HISTORY

Attributes Her Life to a Yaqui Woman Who Befriended Her Grandmother

BY NANCY TOBA–LABA

Translation by Marta Stiefel Ayala

This essay is dedicated to Angela Garcia–Sims, Ph.D. I first met Dr. Angela in 2010, when she participated in demonstrations against SB1070. (Arizona's SB 1070 required police officers to determine the immigration status of someone arrested or detained "when there is reasonable suspicion" that they are not in the U.S. legally, permitting any citizen to sue law enforcement for failure to verify the status of anyone.) As I became acquainted with her, the virtue that I admired the most was her modesty, as well as the genuineness of her words, her wisdom, and her compassion.

Angela García was born in Tucson, Arizona, into a large, not wealthy, but close and happy family. Her parents were Angelita and Bernabé García. Her father died when she was 10 years old. Her mother had to work two jobs in order to take care of four children and to pay the father's medical expenses. A few months later, she also had to pay medical bills for young Angela who suffered a ruptured appendicitis. It was at the hospital and recovering afterward at home that Angela developed her lifelong passion for reading. This love of reading would soon change her life.

Although shy, Angela earned excellent grades, so her teachers encouraged her to continue studying and supported her in her academic development. Even though she lacked a formal education, Angela's mother had learned life skills by helping her own parents run a mill and grocery store. Angela's father also had trained as a barber and had his own shop. Both parents and older siblings all expected that Angela would do well in school. She did, despite losing her father and working while attending high school. She graduated seventh in her class of 356 students and received a scholarship to the University of Arizona. Angela was the first in her family to go to college.

At the University of Arizona, she majored in English and minored in Spanish and social sciences, receiving a bachelor of arts in 1967 and a master of arts in educational psychology in 1970. While still an undergraduate, Angela was recommended to work for a doctoral student who was interviewing mothers of school children for a study at the university early childhood education center. Once she completed her program, the director recruited her at the center, doing research, teaching, and traveling to places like Alaska, Louisiana, and Georgia, to support and train educators working to change the world by radically improving schooling for diverse children.

With the encouragement of her University of Arizona colleagues, Angela enrolled in in a Ph.D. program at Stanford University. During her second year at Stanford, she accepted the position of assistant director of the Stanford Urban/Rural School Training Institute, where she met her future husband, Dr. Dennis Sims. This appointment allowed her to continue working with educators throughout the United States and Puerto Rico.

The following year, Angela and Dennis were recruited by the Crystal City Independent School District in Texas, and they moved there, as the coordinator of the Ethnic Studies program. Subsequently they moved to Lubbock, Texas, where Angela became assistant professor at Texas Tech University.

In 1977, they returned to California, to the San Francisco Bay Area where Angela became coordinator of curriculum research and evaluation for the Bay Area Bilingual Education Consortium. While there, and subsequently as administrator for the Santa Clara County Office of Education and the Eastside Union High School District, Angela continued teaching at the University of Santa Clara, San Jose State University, and the University of California at Santa Cruz. In 1992, she moved to San Diego County to join the South Bay Union School District as director of curriculum and evaluation.

Sadly, after a long illness, her husband Dennis died in 1994. His death led to a period of grief and reflection, resulting in her leaving the school district in 1996 to launch Sims and Associates Educational Services, where she headed a team of consulting educators. In 2008, Angela began to engage her energies in places that she saw inequities and cultural disregard. She joined Delta Kappa Gamma Society International (DKG), an organization dedicated to advancing personal and professional development of teachers and excellence in education.

While touring Old Town San Diego Historical Park with anthropologist Jack Williams, Angela and other members of the Eta Nu chapter of DKG saw the need for more recognition of Mexican involvement and Spanish language. "After all," Angela said, "Westminster Abbey has signs in at least seven languages and

Angela Garcia-Sims, protesting outside Joe Arpaio's jail, Phoenix, 2013; photo taken by a fellow protester with her camera.

Courtesy of Angela Garcia-Sims.

here we're within walking distance to Mexico, with many Mexican tourists, and the park signs are only in English. They need bilingual signs."

It was clearly a project that needed doing. Angela took on the task. She and her fellow educators agreed that teachers and the public in general needed to learn more about the history of San Diego before 1848. So, they decided to organize a conference on just that topic. As they met with different community and historical organizations, their enthusiasm grew, and they decided that this would be the first annual conference on Early San Diego Regional History. The conference was created to commemorate and recognize the contributions of different cultural groups who lived in the San Diego region before 1848 and, at the same time, to provide support, information, and materials for interested teachers who had little support in that period.

With Angela facilitating the project, the conference team expanded to include Joe Vasquez, education specialist and volunteer coordinator for Old Town State Historical Park; Drs. María and Reymundo Marín, founders of InterAmerican College; and Connie Puente, proprietor of El Fangango Restaurant at Old Town. Anthropologist/historian Jack Williams continued as academic member and resource. Other invaluable supporters of the team included Karl Pierce, director of education and outreach at Cabrillo National Monument; Karla Schiminsky of San Diego Unified School District; Sally Fox with the San Diego County Office of Education; a representative from the Mission Trails Park; historian Richard Griswold del Castillo, Chicano Studies history professor at SDSU; and historian Michael Gonzalez, University of San Diego.

Angela was the leader of the group that formed the Early San Diego Regional History Collaborative and the one who kept it going for seven years. She persevered, supporting the volunteers working to organize and hold the conferences and reaching out to different indigenous groups and many other new people. When asked, Angela reflected on how her activism for diversity began.

Perhaps her outreach and support of others began as a child, when she listened to her mother's stories. One story, in particular, inspired Angela, that of her family narrowly escaping disaster, only because Angela's grandmother befriended a neighbor Yaqui woman. She tells the story this way:

"My grandparents adopted my mother and returned with her to their ranchito in the state of Sonora, Mexico. My grandmother, Julia Barajas, was close to her indigenous roots in the south, so her courtesy to others extended to everyone, including a Yaqui lady who passed her fields on the way to market. Their casual greetings blossomed into friendship as the two women shared produce grown in the Barajas garden and venison caught by the Yaqui. As their friendship grew, the mutterings of the townspeople and the Yaqui rose to insults and fights due to their many differences. The townspeople began warning the Barajas about living so close to the Yaqui, urging them to move to town for greater protection against known dangerous warriors."

As "landowners," Angela's family had moved comfortably among their neighbors and the residents of the nearby pueblo. But the people who considered themselves Mejicanos, blancos, or mestizos ruled the town and country and were convinced that they were better than the Yaquis who lived in the nearby mountain. Angela recalls, "My grandparents declined moving. Their fields needed tending from dawn to after sunset. Even so, their unease grew as the summer waned.

One night, as they were about to sit down to dinner after a long day in the hot sun, my grandmother's Yaqui friend ran into their kitchen. 'Leave,' she told them. 'Don't delay to pack, just go right away! Take your daughter and go as far and fast as you can. Don't stop for anything.' Then she was gone. The Barajas immediately hitched up their wagon, got their daughter and dog, and scrambled out. They drove north all night, driven by the memory of horrors they had heard about what Yaquis did to their enemies.

After dawn, they met a large regiment of federales on horseback headed the opposite way. The commanding officer asked them where they were from. When my grandfather told him, the officer said, 'Good thing you left when you did. Last night the Yaquis came down off the mountain and razed the town and all the area around it. They killed every living thing in the area: men, women, children, dogs, cattle. Everything is ashes today.'"

Angela recalls that her mom told her that story some 60 years ago. "That Yaqui lady, a stranger whose name I don't know, is responsible for mom surviving, for my being here telling this story. How lucky I am that my grandmother reached out to befriend someone outside her own group, someone she was warned against as different and dangerous. I don't know what happened to the Yaqui lady, but I know that she loved my grandmother enough to risk her own safety to save her friend's life."

Angela's own dedication to the strangers in our midst shows in her actions and her words. "If we can send love and gratitude back in time, I send both to my grandmother and her Yaqui friend. And I give this story to you, so that you may carry it in your heart. May it light your understanding and the importance of reaching out to the other, the stranger, the person others may find threatening. May it save you, as well."

I see Angela as a compassionate, altruistic, and tireless fighter for social justice. Troubled by the anti-immigrant attacks and the brutality of immigrant detentions across the United States, she joined with other volunteers of the First Unitarian Universalist Church of San Diego to found the SOLACE Program. This is an interfaith project of "Souls Offering Loving and Compassionate Ears." SOLACE volunteers visit migrants detained at the Otay Detention Facility in southern San Diego County to relieve their isolation and express their care.

Listening to traumatic and painful stories about the dehumanizing treatment of detained immigrants—of working people, parents, children, and students—Angela asserts that all persons must be valued as an essential part of our society. As member of the First Unitarian Universalist Church of San Diego, she works with a community of people that promotes the dignity and worth of all people and rallies to make its voices heard.

Dr. Angela also volunteers as a community leader with the San Diego Organizing Project, helping with actions and programs to support communities and projects, such as the Deferred Actions for Childhood Arrivals (DACA); naturalization workshops; and door-to-door canvassing to urge underrepresented constituents to vote. Her generosity and love for others has also motivated her to share her knowledge in teaching disciplines such as feng shui, the I Ching, Chi-Gong, and Tai-Chi.

Angela refuses to accept a "cannot-be-done" attitude. She turned my life around with the fortitude she projects and the way she motivates others with words and positive actions. As she grows through life, she plants seeds of light, hope, and faith. When people like me raise our voices in defense of the oppressed, she'll say, "If we can do something, even if it is small, it will make a difference." And to that she adds, "…which is magnificent!"

About the Author:

NANCY TOBA-LABA says, "I am from Santiago de Chile. I am the daughter of the sea and the mountains. My skin was browned by the heat of the Atacama dessert. My soul is as white as Antarctica. I am from the land of the Araucanos who never surrendered. An activist since my childhood, my mother left me a legacy of great value, to be a great fighter for human rights." Nancy is an activist and volunteer in various organizations: A Reason To Survive, Society of St Vincent de Paul, and San Diego Organizing Project.

About the Translator:

MARTA STIEFEL AYALA; she was born in Argentina and grew up on her parent's farm where she and three siblings leaned to read and write; she attended Normal School and then studied psychology at the University of Cordoba. She was awarded a scholarship to study at the University of Minnesota where she graduated in 1960. There she met and married Reynaldo Ayala, Ph.D, and SDSU Professor. After raising three children, she received a Ph.D in Library Science; then she and her husband made sure that all three children received Ph.Ds. Marta has published several articles, and has been active in Reforma, a Hispanic Librarian Association.

MARIA ZUÑIGA:

PROFESSOR AND SCHOLAR ON CULTURAL COMPETENCE
She Led a Protest for Chicanos in Social Work at UC Berkeley

BY PATRICIA SANDOVAL

Maria Zuñiga was the second Chicana in the United States to receive a Ph.D. in social work and, yet, she feels that her greatest accomplishment was giving birth at an older age to her daughter Pilar. A family member once warned her that if she got her Ph.D., no man, especially a Latino, would want to marry her. She was so taken aback by the remark that she seriously considered whether the degree was worth it. In the end, she decided to pursue her doctorate even if it meant no marriage and no children.

Maria was born at San Diego's Mercy Hospital in 1942 and grew up in Barrio Logan. As a girl, she attended Our Lady of Guadalupe Grammar School. Her schoolmates were entirely non-white, 60 percent Mexican American and 40 percent African American. She saw how poverty, violence, and racism affected so many people she knew. She was especially troubled when she saw images in *Look* magazine of Blacks being dragged behind a truck or hung from a tree. These were pictures from our American South and so were shocking to her. After all, she was raised in a mixed culture. Her dentist was African American and her doctor was Japanese American. Many of her neighbors were Black families where both parents worked. Her parents had taught her to speak to everyone with respect. She remembers addressing one neighbor as Miss Connie and another as Mr. Darling, not by first names. It was a way of showing respect when she noticed that little respect was given them by others. Her formative years gave her experiences with many minority families, Japanese, Filipino, Chinese; so, it was a shock to her to witness how they were disrespected, because of their skin color, race, or ethnicity.

These formative experiences would become the baseline for Maria's future commitment to cultural competency and social justice. She had seen her mother transport Mexican mothers who were seeking help from social service agencies or translate for them, when needed. Both of Maria's parents had taught

Maria Zuñiga, 1974, Brandeis University, Boston; with outline of her Ph.D dissertation, Los Ancianos.

Courtesy of Maria Zuñiga.

her through their actions that one helped others, especially those less fortunate. So, their actions seeded her desire to become a social worker.

In 1968, Maria entered the University of California at Berkeley for her master's degree in social work. At that time, the Berkeley campus was awash in protests against the war in Vietnam; the Women's Movement was also taking a strong hold on campus. Minority students in the graduate School of Social Work had begun a Third World protest themselves. They demanded that the school recruit and support minority students to fill the gaps of professional social workers in minority communities. Maria's graduate school years were filled with student protests and demands for change. In 1970, when four students were killed by police at Kent State University in Ohio, the UC Berkeley campus was shut down by student protests and picket lines. The United States National Guard was called in and tear gas barrages were common.

During these turbulent times, Maria and three other Latino students decided to make an appointment with the provost of the university. They wanted to discuss scholarships to recruit Latinos into social work. They made the very difficult decision to cross the picket line to express their concerns and make their demands. On their way to the meeting, they were bombarded with tear gas. Maria recalls that as they ran, they had to cover their faces with their blouses and shirts to protect themselves from the fumes. In the midst of chaos and danger, they were able to meet the provost and secure funding for Latinos in social work. For this shy and self-conscious young woman, the experience helped her realize the importance of taking risks and standing up for what one believes. This success also gave her more confidence.

During this period of unrest and community organizing, Maria became even more involved in the fight for equal rights by becoming a member of Trabajadores de La Raza (TR). This organization started as a Latino/a social work group, initiated by Dr. Juan Ramos of the National Institute of Mental Health, to increase Latino professional social workers in Southwest Latino communities. As a student at Berkeley, Maria participated in a meeting that TR organized in San Jose with the deans of five schools of social work from the Southwest. She remembers how "the deans stonewalled TR's requests for funding to recruit Latinos into social work that would help them financially." With no headway, the TR members locked the deans and themselves in the hotel room where they were negotiating. "We told them no one could leave until a commitment was made," Maria says. She recalled that one of the deans was a Catholic sister. Since Maria had always gone to Catholic schools, including the Catholic University of San Diego (USD) where she received her bachelor's degree, these actions frightened her. At the same time, they also educated her, allowing her to learn how to use leverage to advocate for change.

In the end, the college deans finally met TR's conditions, committing themselves to providing resources that would enable Chicanos/Latinos/as to obtain their master's degrees. Maria recalls that some of the students, like herself, were able to go on for their doctoral degrees and became the first graduates to fill needed positions in academia that would provide for the needs of all people. These experiences enhanced her motivation for social justice and when she got her master's degree in social work, she continued to work with the chapter of Trabajadores de la Raza in San Diego.

This important advocacy group continues to function (presently named Latino Social Work Network). They later demanded that the County of San Diego pay bilingual social workers extra for carrying Spanish-speaking caseloads. This policy was adopted and still exists today. Maria continues her participation in this chapter's work, which raises funds for scholarships and provides for needy families at Christmas. Maria has also contributed to the betterment of Chicanos/Latinos in other ways; one of them is as a member of the Chicano Federation Board of Directors, a local social service agency where she has volunteered for more than twelve years.

As an academic in her field, first at Sacramento State University and then at San Diego State University's Schools of Social Work, Maria's challenge has been to teach graduate students to be culturally competent. This was especially difficult when some faculty did not often comprehend the value and critical nature of working with diverse populations in a culturally sensitive fashion. It was not unusual for the students to be more open to addressing racism than for the faculty. She found herself often advocating for students who were mistakenly viewed as less competent because of their ethnicity, or for students who faced racism or ethnocentrism in the classroom. When there was a paucity of minority graduate social work applicants, Maria stopped teaching at the graduate level. Instead, she began teaching undergraduates as a way to recruit more students into the graduate program who wanted to work in diverse communities.

Maria has helped many students, especially in human behavior courses, to recognize that being from an immigrant family, or being poor, or being a person of color, gave them expertise in knowing the difficult circumstances that many of their clients might face. If they also were bilingual, then that gave them an additional competence that they needed to value in themselves. She also shared her own experiences from her formative years, highlighting how racism can attack one's spirit, leaving the person feeling devalued and incompetent.

Maria has served in many other ways, including as a representative of National Latino Social Work faculty and on the board of directors of the Council on Social Work Education (CSWE). She co-chaired the First National Conference on Cultural Competence held by CSWE and co-authored a book on the subject, as a result, with Elaine Gutierrez and Doman Lum: Education for Multicultural Social Work Practice (Alexandria, VA: CSWE, 2004). Maria has authored many book articles on the subject. All her publications throughout her years as an academic focus on cultural competence, whether in mental health, health, work with children, or work with the elderly. In 2007, CSWE awarded Maria the Presidential Award for the innovative work she has done on cultural competence.

Respecting all cultures and knowing their unique gifts is at the center of her work. After all, her parents sacrificed to ensure she could receive a good education and Maria was bent on giving back. She says she feels as if their sacrifices to give her a Catholic education saved her life because of the nuns' dedication to excellence in teaching and their high expectations for all students starting in grammar school. However, the high school she attended had few minority students. That is when she began to experience racism, sometimes painfully, although she did not fully comprehend it. Maria believes that, because she had already built academic skills as her foundation, that allowed her to do well; for that reason, she was able to counter racism at the core and was successful doing so. She also believes that attending a Catholic university with small classes and only women students enabled her to focus on success. She is certain that if she had gone to a large university where she was only one of a few Mexican Americans, her shyness at that time, and her low self-esteem, would have derailed her.

"If I had a hammer, I'd hammer for justice, all over this land"

Maria attributes her success to her parents. She lovingly recounts, "My parents were not well educated, but each one worked very hard to ensure that my two brothers, my sister, and I would get the best education." Growing up in the fifties before the Women's Movement, it was her father who taught her that she needed to watch out for men who would try to take advantage of her because she was a woman. He told her to especially watch mechanics. "Request that the mechanic give you the part to your car that is being replaced," he advised her. "Mechanics, in particular, rip off women." Even though her father was a very traditional Mexican man, he made sure that his daughters learn to drive and take care of cars. When Maria left San Diego to drive to Brandeis University outside of Boston to study for her Ph.D., her mother gave her a St. Christopher pin for her car to protect her. Her father poked his head in the driver's window and handed her a hammer. Maria asked, "Why a hammer, Papa?" He answered defiantly, "So no one messes with you!" When Maria's father died, his neighbor told her how proud her father was of her. Maria assumed it was because of her Ph.D. The neighbor said, "Yes, he was proud of that, but he was really proud that you crossed the country three times by yourself in that Mustang of yours!"

Dr. Maria Zuñiga has used the higher education she has received to support her commitment to working with Latino families. She began to teach at Sacramento State University in 1975, while completing her dissertation. She then got married, gave birth to her daughter Pilar, and did not finish her Ph.D. until 1980. "I taught at Sacramento State for 11 years, left there in 1986, and returned to teach in San Diego," her hometown. She taught at San Diego State University for an additional 17 years. Her particular concerns have addressed the obstacles that people encounter as immigrants. Maria has helped hundreds of students graduate with their masters' degrees or doctorates to enter the workforce culturally competent, able to respect the uniqueness of all people, and able to stand up for their rights when they faced injustices. Maria retired in 2003 after 28 years of teaching.

Maria Zuñiga (right), 2002, winner of the San Diego State University Monty Award for outstanding faculty, presented by Provost Nancy Marlin (left).

Courtesy of Terry Portwood.

About the Author:

PATRICIA SANDOVAL. In 1999, Patricia received her MSW (Master of Social Work) from SDSU. She has been active in the Chicano/Latino Social Work Network, looking out for the rights of others. She worked for 15 years for the County of San Diego in Child Welfare Services. She retired and then returned to work as a medical social worker at Sharp Hospital on a per diem basis. Now she works at Sharp Barnhart Cancer Center. She has three grown children and presently cares for her mother who has Parkinson's disease.

CHAPTER 9

LINDA LEGERRETTE

CARMEN LOPEZ

OLIVIA PUENTES–REYNOLDS

CARMEN SANDOVAL

JOSIE TALAMANTEZ

CHAPTER 9

Chicana Activists Influenced by the U.S. Civil Rights Movement

The Civil Rights and Anti-War Movements unfolded across the country in the late 1960s. The California-based farmworkers' struggle, with the leadership of Cesar Chavez and Dolores Huerta, gained momentum. Students of color enrolled in colleges and universities in unprecedented numbers, made possible by the Civil Rights Act of 1964 and the Higher Education Act of 1965.

The Civil Rights Act outlawed segregation in public places and banned discrimination based on race. The Higher Education Act provided federal funds to help low-income students of color and other disadvantaged populations attend college through such programs as the Educational Opportunity Grant Program (EOP), Guaranteed Student Loan Program (GSLP), and National Defense Student Loan Program (NDSLP).

In San Diego colleges, this surge of students of color was no exception. Students from urban barrios, farmworker towns, and even suburban communities were fast enrolling in institutions of higher education. Chicano students, along with other students of color, entered colleges and universities that were unprepared to educate them. Their now-opened doors did not mean that colleges and universities were ready and willing to retain these students.

A significant number of these students had grown up in poverty and had lived in barrios that experienced high crime, unemployment, and drug abuse. Some had seen their young brothers and other male relatives drafted into war, if they had dropped out of school or did not go to college, thus not qualifying for a college deferment. Witnessing a relative or peer return from Vietnam in a body bag or missing a limb made political involvement an easy choice. The decision to become politically active was also made easier for those students with farmworker backgrounds who had worked in the fields and canneries and still had family members working there. They had something to fight for.

Institutions of higher learning were an entirely new world for the wave of incoming students of color. For example, Chicanos and Chicanas often found themselves alienated and struggling to survive both academically and psychologically. Without adequate guidance and lacking supportive structures to navigate through this new world of academics and politics, many students of color dropped out of college. However, for some that remained, movement politics in the colleges and universities influenced this new population of students. Many of them made conscious choices to become active. They wanted to work for justice in the schools and workplace. For many, it was not a difficult choice. The different political venues offered space to connect to a new reality, to find identity, and to survive the many challenges confronting them—all while committed to getting an education and continuing in the struggle for justice for their *gente*.

Many Chicana students survived college because they found mentors who believed in them. A young Linda LeGerrette, encouraged by Professor Gracia Molina de Pick at Mesa College, joined the farmworker struggle led by the late Cesar Chavez. Linda organized farmworkers along with her husband Carlos LeGerrette until they both entered San Diego State University (SDSU) in 1968 as EOP students. In late 1969, Carlos was hired as SDSU's EOP director. Later, both Linda and Carlos joined Cesar Chavez at his headquarters in Keene, California, as student volunteers. The couple worked side by side with Chavez for many years, earning five dollars a week. After Chavez's death, Linda and Carlos cofounded the Cesar Chavez Service Clubs, Inc., a school-based not-for-profit leadership development organization whose mission is to inspire young people to believe in themselves. The clubs now have a membership of 1,800 Chavistas in 59 clubs in 22 schools in San Diego.

Other Chicana students also benefitted from mentoring and joining campus organizations. Carmen Lopez attended SDSU in 1970 as an 18 year old from Imperial Valley. She became active in the Movimiento Estudiantil Chicano de Aztlan, (MEChA), a student organization. She joined marches and protests for social and economic justice organized by various Chicano Movement groups. After graduation, Carmen became one of the first bilingual psychiatric social workers for the County of San Diego, later working for the U.S. Census Bureau. Her involvement with MEChA prepared her for the work she has done since. She is presently the director of language services for the Registrar of Voters in San Diego County and has been instrumental in increasing the Latino vote in the county's 18 cities.

Membership in the Mexican American Youth Association (MAYA) at Mesa College in the fall of 1968 awakened Olivia Puentes Reynolds to her true identity. She claimed her heritage and began to identify as a Chicana. Raised by a Mexican mother and an abusive, alcoholic Anglo father, she spoke only English.

She was labeled *agringada* (acting like an Anglo woman) by Raza males in the Chicano Movement. She renamed herself "Olivia de San Diego" and in the fall of 1969 was admitted into San Diego State College (now University) under the Educational Opportunity Program. While at SDSU, Olivia and other Chicanas formed the "Las Chicanas" group. She became known for her beautiful Chicano Movement music, composing songs about people's struggles, and performed with other Chicanos. In 1996 as president of the San Diego MANA (formerly known as the Mexican American Women's National Association), her Board agreed to use a collective leadership style to develop strategies to improve the lack of local presence, voice, and opportunity for Mexican-American women, they expanded MANA's Hermanitas Program (big/little sister mentoring program). MANA was founded in 1974 to give voice to Mexican American women at the national, state, and local levels. In 1994 the national membership voted to recognize the diversity in the membership by changing its name to MANA, a National Latina Organization.

Chicanas continued to break out of traditional roles. In the mid-1970s, also at SDSU, Carmen Sandoval became MEChA historian after she refused to be the organization's secretary, a position where women traditionally had been placed. In 1979, Carmen became MEChA president. She also became president of MEChA Central in San Diego, which includes all the colleges and universities with MEChA organizations in the area. Eventually, Carmen became the district director for California Assemblyman Steve Peace, where she worked in areas critical to the people and also important to her: transportation, education, the environment, and social issues. Presently, she is public information officer/legislative liaison at the California Department of Transportation (CALTRANS).

Student activist Josie Talamantez was in Professor's Gil Robledo's Chicano Studies class at San Diego City College on April 22, 1970, when Mario Solis informed them that bulldozers were grading the land under the San Diego-Coronado Bay Bridge. She would come to join community members and other activists, including the San Diego Brown Berets, in the takeover of the land that became Chicano Park. They created a human chain to stop the construction of a highway patrol station. Talamantez graduated from the University of California at Berkeley in 1975. She worked in developing and promoting Dr. Arnoldo Solis' strategies in preventative mental health, utilizing Chicana and Chicano art with the Royal Chicano Air Force (RCAF), as documented in the 1978 President's Commission on Mental Health. Josie became the director of Centro Cultural de la Raza in San Diego's Balboa Park in 1979. As part of the Chicano Park Steering Committee, she led the process whereby in 2013 Chicano Park was designated a national historic landmark listed in the National Register of Historic Places. In 2016, the park will go before the National Landmark Committee to be designated a national landmark. She is currently working to establish a Museum and Cultural Center in Chicano Park.

The stories in this chapter give us a window to begin to understand how some Chicanas survived and thrived, at times with the support of mentors, organizations, or recently formed Chicana groups. These young women were thrust into a historical period that almost required their political engagement. Surrounded by the activism of their peers in the various political movements of the times, and often being personally affected because of the various events unfolding, (we all knew of someone that had been killed in Vietnam War), these conditions created the path that these mujeres chose to take, that of social justice for their communities.

"Chicana Tribute Wall" honoring San Diego activists at the Centro Cultural de la Raza, August 2013.

Courtesy of Richard Griswold del Castillo.

LINDA LEGERRETTE:

EARLY ACTIVIST FOR CHICANO RIGHTS AND THE UFW

Today She Honors Cesar Chavez's Life and Passes Down His Values to Young People

BY CARMEN E. QUINTANA

Linda LeGerrette was one of the first Chicana activist leaders to bring an awareness of the United Farm Workers Movement to San Diego. Her story stood out on a past UFW website, indicating she had "an almost immediate calling" to enter the farmworkers' struggle for economic justice in the fields. In it, Linda is described as "competitive, hard-driving, and well-studied." These are qualities she has modeled for other young Chicanas in the women's movement and, lately, for the Cesar Chavez Club students who she now mentors.

As early as 1966, Linda and her husband Carlos LeGerrette went to work for the United Farm Workers Movement. With the encouragement of Gracia Molina de Pick, Mejicana/Chicana activist, they attended a meeting of the local Delano grape strike support group and then volunteered their summer. That summer was to last 12 years.

Linda LeGerrette was born Linda Jogoleff in San Diego, California. She is first-generation Russian on her father's side and sixth-generation Mexican (Rodríguez) on her mother's side. She is one of seven siblings, the middle child, who learned from the older children and took care of the younger ones. Her family gave her love, encouragement, and unconditional support. Linda puts great emphasis on family values and at the center, a wealth of "family" friends, is her core pride and joy: husband Carlos; daughter Tonantzín; and grandchildren Natalie and Joseph; not to mention her two dogs Maggie and Yoyo. Her home continues to be the center of many social-justice activities, fundraisers, meetings, and bed and breakfasts. Just ask Dolores Huerta, UFW Vice President, friend, and house guest. In fact, the Le Gerrette home should be called "The South Park Center for Social Justice."

When asked to describe Linda, I immediately reflect on her immense capacity to give of herself unselfishly to both individuals and the greater community. She has a larger-than-life persona. Her passion, commitment, and tenacity permeate everything she does. Her current dedication centers on youth. She works energetically with children and young adults to imbue them with self-confidence and an assertiveness that gives them the realization that they can accomplish greatness. She lovingly surrounds herself with people who share her beliefs and commitment to a life of service and community organizing. She has learned much from historical figures with whom she has worked closely: Dolores Huerta, Cesar E. Chavez, and Sol Price. My admiration for Linda makes me want to follow her leadership and strive to be as accomplished as she, while remaining a genuine human being.

What makes Linda an incredibly genuine human being? Linda shared with me that she is a woman who is "comfortable in her own skin" and, as such, she is comfortable with both poor and wealthy people, as well as people of all colors. When one is comfortable in their skin they make others comfortable. Linda is a kind human being who does good things for other people. She wakes up every morning with a purpose. How many of us really do that?

Linda's purpose has been to consistently serve others. Not only were she and Carlos UFW volunteers in the 1960s, at that time they also reached students through a documentary film detailing their experience. The film *Yo Soy Chicano* tells the story of their involvement with the UFW, bringing consciousness to youth and to other members of the community. As newlyweds and college students, they also helped establish the first San Diego chapter of the Mexican American Youth Association MAYA (now Movimiento Estudiantil Chicanos de Aztlán–MEChA). Both have been known for their generous invitations, over the years, to their home in Golden Hill, a local landmark for political events, committee meetings, and annual birthday celebrations for their children and grandchildren.

Linda and Carlos LeGerrette founded the Cesar Chavez Service Clubs (CSC). They began with one club in 2001 to expose young students to the most important values described and lived by Cesar Chavez. In this way, they have honored his life and passed down his values to young people. Currently, in 2016, they manage 52 clubs in the San Diego School District. Linda practices the 10 club values, the same ones she expects her Chavistas to practice.

I would like to define Linda's accomplishments through those 10 values. The first two values are "Respect for Others," and "We're All Different." Linda models for all her Chavistas that we need to embrace our differences and respect each other as human beings. She teaches them to engage others with a firm handshake and direct eye contact. That, she says, manifests confidence, pride, and respect, regardless of age, color, gender, or differences. I have watched many children emulate Linda's teachings when they introduce themselves at

Linda LeGerrette, 2014, speaking at Las Mañanitas Breakfast, the JACOB'S Center, San Diego, an annual fundraiser to benefit the Cesar Chavez Clubs.

Courtesy of Carlos LeGerrette.

universities, board meetings, candidate forums, community events, and parent graduations!

Linda also practices the next two values: "Sacrifice for Others" and "Help Someone." These values are reflected in what she does every day with Chavistas, forsaking material gains and personal wealth. Each Chavista is important to her. There are no periods of time when Linda is not donating her days, nights, and weekends to prepare Chavistas to speak on behalf of teachers who are getting lay-off notices; or organizing both coordinators and Chavistas for trips they take to places like Washington, D.C., to visit the Holocaust Museum; or to Keene City, California, at Nuestra Señora de la Paz, where Cesar is buried. They also travel to places around San Diego to visit the campus of the Lawrence Family Jewish Community Center in La Jolla; and the Mo'olelo Theater in San Diego. These are just a few examples of the educational field trips that the service clubs organize for the students. The Chavistas' participation in these activities positively impacts their lives, because they become exposed to events where they, too, must learn to sacrifice their time in order to partake in social justice practices. Chavistas know the value of sacrifice and helping others because of Linda's hard work that she effectively models for them daily.

Other values are immediately evident to the Chavistas: "Be Proud" and "Be Creative." Many have watched and learned from Linda's skillful organizing strategies and creative ways of problem solving. She is reflective, intelligent, insightful, and proud of being a woman. Young female Chavistas and all the "elder" strong women are fortunate to have Linda as a mentor. She thinks outside of the box, all the while listening respectfully and reflectively to others pose solutions. Then, to watch her take decisive steps to action, organize, delegate, and execute a plan by involving everyone is truly amazing. She knows how to get things done gracefully, meticulously, and intentionally.

I asked Linda to ascribe one value to each of her own mentors. I knew it would be difficult for her, since she believes that her mentors have each exemplified, and continue to exemplify, all of the ten values. She gave Dolores Huerta the value of "Be Proud." Linda defines Huerta as a strong and intelligent woman. With 11 children and a commitment to the UFW union and the farmworkers, Dolores always made sure that her children were well cared for, while she was away making tremendous contributions to the UFW.

To the late Cesar E. Chavez, UFW President, Linda ascribed the value of "Si Se Puede." Cesar was extremely passionate about his work. Linda recalls that when he assigned anyone a task, you always knew that you were going to accomplish the task because (1) you did not want to disappoint him, (2) he believed in you and depended on you to accomplish the task, and (3) how could you ever tell someone like Cesar Chavez "I don't think I can do this?"

When Linda mentioned Sol Price—a retail magnate committed to social justice—and his influence on her, she smiled and said, "Sol was an amazing teacher and from him I learned the true spirit of giving and of "paying it forward." He had a tremendous impact on my life. The two values that should go to him are "Teach Someone" and "Knowledge is Power."

"Knowledge is Power" has got to be one of Linda's favorite values. "When you have education: culture, language, family, pride, history," she always says, "and are educated, you are in a better position to help and Teach Others." Linda is a curious person and so always asks questions for clarification and for empowering herself with knowledge to share with others. She votes for political candidates who share her beliefs. She does her homework and makes sure that candidates know who she is, what she stands for, and that they are accountable to her and the community. Chavistas learn that "arming" themselves with knowledge will lead them to make good choices, to earn respect, and to make them proud leaders like Linda.

As Chavistas become aware of the importance of who they are and what they do; they learn also that they must act without violence. Many of them come from poverty and have already known struggle. Linda reminds them, through her own experiences, that there will be times when social injustice may create conflicting thoughts, like anger, and, at times, a desire to act contrary to the value of non-violence. She repeatedly tells them that it takes more strength and courage to practice non-violence than to act out of anger or violence. It is through her modeling that Chavistas learn how important it is to make gains and progress through non-violent actions. Does Linda get upset at social injustice? Does she, as a leader, speak out against it? Does she put emphasis on her opinions? Absolutely. Always, though in her actions she is aware that she is being watched and emulated by hundreds of young hearts and minds, eager to follow in her footsteps.

Lastly, Linda believes strongly in the value of "Si Se Puede!" Through her example, Linda makes us believe that everything is possible and that becoming good human beings involves practicing all 10 values every day. She models that sacrificing for others is a good thing; empowering ourselves with knowledge will make us all teachers who help and teach others with respect and non-violence. Finally, she teaches that being proud of who we are and uniting in our differences will bring creative ways of living in peace.

Linda LeGerrette is as energetic a force as she is compassionate. She is my good friend and mentor. I admire her as a woman, teacher, and leader. She makes me laugh with her classy expletives that, in turn, fortify me to proceed with intent. Linda is a remarkable human being. The world better watch out because, if there is one powerful Linda LeGerrette, there are hundreds of Chavistas, future "Linda LeGerrettes," modeling the values of Cesar Chavez and just waiting for their turn to make Linda proud of them. Si Se Puede! It is truly an honor to write about Linda, my friend, my mentor, and my source for positive energy.

About the Author:

CARMEN E. QUINTANA, Ph.D. works as an English Language Learner coach for South Bay Community Services. She coordinates the Cesar Chavez Book Club at Castle Park Elementary School in Chula Vista, where her focus is Literacy and Knowledge is Power. She is vice president on the McGill School of Success Board; a graduate of SDSU with a doctoral degree from SDSU/Claremont McKenna. From Brawley, California she has five children. She resides with her husband, Antonio Valladolid, attorney at law, in Chula Vista.

Carmen Lopez, 2014, guest of Univision's "Despierta San Diego" talk show.

Courtesy of Marisol Rosas, News Producer, Entravision.

CARMEN LOPEZ:

SOCIAL WORKER, BILINGUAL THERAPIST, VOTER RIGHTS ACTIVIST

Her Involvement in MEChA Politicized and Changed Her Forever

BY JESSICA CORDOVA

The name "Carmen Lopez" has become synonymous with voter rights and justice. Known as Carmelita, interviews with those who knew her from childhood and college have created images, such as Carmen was the first female in the history of her junior high to become eighth-grade president; Carmen the high-energy girl, who played every sport in school and joined band, dance, swim, and, yes, debate teams in Calexico, California; Carmen, the young Chicana with the deceptively calm and measured voice, asking challenging questions in Chicano Studies classes; Carmen the Mechista who marched in solidarity with César Chávez, the farmworkers, and the grape boycott supporters.

Carmen Lopez is the youngest of four siblings, all born in Mexico, who immigrated to the Imperial Valley in California. Both of her parents were from Mexico as well. However, her father had crossed the Mexican border with his family during the 1920s to work in the copper mines and attend school in Bisbee, Arizona, as a boy. His family returned to Mexico, because the Great Depression of the 1930s worsened and Mexicanos were being deported or forced to leave due to the economic conditions. It was during this time that Carmen's parents came of age.

Her father worked as a farm implement mechanic and her mother in retail. During difficult times, they relied on family for help. To make ends meet, her mother would pick up the leftover crops from the field after the first harvest. These crops didn't meet market standards and were left discarded on the ground. She would sell the unwanted crops from the back of a truck. This memory stayed with Carmen due to the humiliation she felt when one of the farm owners accused her family of stealing watermelons, even though such gleaning of crops was a common practice at the time.

Growing up, Carmen spent some summers in Sonora on her mother's family ranch in Magdalena. She attended an all-girls Catholic high school for one year as part of her high school education in nearby Hermosillo. While there, she gained a unique experience and outlook on life, but also shared her own activism and passion for social justice with her peers. She taught English and ballet, and started the school's first newspaper in this very traditional, conservative environment. Back in Calexico, Carmen played every sport and was named best all-around athlete in high school. Carmen also liked to climb trees and ride horses. When playing baseball, people would comment that she played ball "like a boy," which was not meant as a compliment in those days. Even from a young age, Carmen was breaking the stereotypes of what women could and should do.

Coming from the sweltering Imperial Valley heat, Carmen loved attending the two-week summer camp in the Cuyamaca Mountains in San Diego County, a recreational program offered by the Neighborhood House in Calexico. "It really gave us poor families exposure to all these wonderful things that we wouldn't have been exposed to and it kept me somewhat out of trouble," Carmen reflected. These experiences nurtured a lifelong love and connection to the outdoors. There, she felt grounded in nature and still finds peace and lessons in nature.

As she looks back on her growing-up years, Carmen credits her older sister Sonia as one of the most influential people in her life. Through Sonia, Carmen was introduced to the farmworker movement while still in high school. She would accompany her sister to UFW meetings at the Armory in Calexico. Her sister and these meetings influenced her political consciousness and appreciation for the need of organized labor.

We are Border People

From Sonora, Mexico, to the desert town of Calexico, California, Carmen spent her youth crossing to and from Mexico and the United States. She says, over and over, that you have to be tough to survive and make it out of the desert. Imperial Valley has one of the highest unemployment and poverty rates in the United States. Carmen embodies that toughness and resiliency while maintaining a sense of humor, joy for life, and a deep sense of social justice.

The border is a constant in Carmen's life. Moving back and forth between both sides, between two cultures and languages, never conforming to preconceived notions of being a woman or Chicana, has shaped and driven her. "We were called Pochos on both sides of the border," she says. Her father countered that by telling her that they were just jealous because they knew two languages and could function well on both sides. He told her, "It is always better to know two languages instead of just one, Mija." Carmen also wants others to know just how much that means to her. "We're border people who grew up with bilingual, bicultural perspectives; brewing these together, we can draw upon them to make decisions. We know that there is more than one way of doing things across cultures. This great menu of cross cultures gives us the ability to exchange and reap collective solutions and ideas," Carmen told me when I interviewed her.

When talking about the border, she elaborated on how the border influenced the way she builds relationships. She said, "It doesn't feel like a vertical kind of relationship. It feels more horizontal. A vertical relationship is when the informational exchange is flowing from an uneven level, from high to low. I've tried to look at people as more horizontal than vertical because I think it puts everyone in a more equal position." Carmen believes that "sometimes you really have to fight for that horizontal relationship because you have as much to give in any culture and also to receive."

More than a friend and mentor, Carmen has treated me as someone who also has important things to share. She has given me validation and, in the process, she has become another mother figure to me. In a world of uncertainty and struggle, she has provided guidance, love, and support to many younger people like me.

Education and Schooling

Carmen began attending San Diego State University (SDSU) in 1970. She enrolled in Chicano Studies classes and was heavily involved in the Movimiento Estudiantil Chicano de Aztlan (MEChA). This involvement politicized and changed her forever. The learning was experiential; they would go to the prisons and talk to the inmates; they protested at the border; and they marched with the farmworkers. She reminisced about feeling a sisterhood with her fellow Chicanas. The women of MEChA at SDSU organized their own group, Las Chicanas, in part to counter the tendency of the men in MEChA to place women in secondary roles and to minimize the significance of their contributions. While women have always been at the forefront of struggles for self-determination and freedom, they have never been fully recognized for their work. Carmen reflected, "College was like 24 hours of total submersion. It wasn't even school; it was a life process that we were involved in. It was life; your whole life force was in teaching, in doing, in activism; there was no separation."

Carmen shared an experience that revealed the dangerous context of the time, but also fueled her fight for justice. At the National Chicano Moratorium of August 29, 1970, she recalls, "People were opening up their houses in L.A. as we were running from the tear gas and the police; they didn't even know us and they let us in their house. The shock of finding out that Ruben Salazar, a renowned Chicano newspaper reporter, had been shot down the street, was very scary and at the same time gave us more motivation."

Carmen married early in her college career and ended up leaving school to take care of her three young children. She continued her activism and worked as a social worker in a farmworker labor camp in Coachella. She would eventually go back to school on a part-time basis to earn her bachelor of arts in psychology at SDSU.

Activism and Professional History

Carmen went on to work for San Diego County Mental Health Crises Intervention and Suicide Hotline. After getting a divorce and working at various sites, she was awarded a scholarship to complete her master's in social work. She obtained her mental health clinician license from the California Board of Behavioral Sciences. Thereafter, she was promoted to senior psychiatric social worker, a licensed clinician. In 1998, the Association of Clinicians, San Diego County, recognized her as Social Worker of the Year.

Just before 2000, Carmen was recruited by the U.S. Department of Commerce to work for the Census Bureau in San Diego and Imperial counties, specifically as a partnership specialist and Spanish media liaison. Carmen traveled throughout California interviewing hard-to-reach homeless and migrant farmworkers where they lived and worked, and who had never been counted. Her work with the census broadened her perspective with respect to the specific needs of diverse communities and groups.

Whereas the approach used in mental health revolved around the individual client's needs, and why he or she experienced a crisis, Carmen now utilized the perspective of social work to understand the dynamics of different populations, namely, how different social structures and social agencies influence the individual. During the 2004 and 2007 San Diego wildfires that left many people without homes, Carmen provided mental health services to the families affected. She worked particularly with immigrant communities and migrant workers who had difficult times accessing services. Carmen looked for, and found, farmworkers who had lost their trailers in the fires. But, these trailers were not classified as "homes," so they faced barriers in obtaining the assistance others received. Carmen also intervened when people were denied services, water, and food because their immigration status or language barrier made it difficult to communicate with emergency workers. Working together with community and advocacy groups, Carmen brought attention to this discrimination and made sure people were able to access these crucial services.

Carmen returned to San Diego County Mental Health, this time to work in children's mental health. Chicanos were being severely misdiagnosed due to a lack of cultural understanding and language barriers. She stepped in to provide crucial cultural awareness, conducting special education evaluations and treatment in the schools, where many children of color were, and continue to be, siphoned into the criminal justice system. Such negligence has been considered a result of systematic racism, misdiagnosis, and a general lack of understanding the students' situations. "My jobs have been really satisfying because they have been part of who I am, and I've been lucky in that I've been passionate about it because it wasn't just a job, it was the change I wanted to live," Carmen shared.

In 2004, Carmen became the coordinator of voter outreach with the San Diego County Registrar of Voters. While all her work has been important, being in charge of voter outreach was significant because her efforts directly addressed a lawsuit by the Department of Justice against the County of San Diego with respect to the Voting Rights Act. In other words, not enough was being done by the County to make voting accessible to language minorities. For example, before the lawsuit, many polling places had no poll workers who could communicate in languages spoken by voters. Ballots were available in English only, so it was impossible for speakers of other languages to understand the issues clearly enough to vote on them. This challenging work, done by Carmen and her colleagues in voter and language outreach, has since been recognized nationally.

In sum, Carmen fought institutional discrimination, working to improve Latina/o mental health diagnosis and treatment. Moreover, she has helped increase the number of Latina/os counted by the U.S. Decennial Census of 2000. In the book Bilingual Ballots, John Tanner, former Department of Justice Attorney, reported that there was at least a 20-percent increase of Latino voters after the first year of Carmen's outreach in the County of San Diego, made up of 18 cities. Besides increasing the Latino voter numbers, she advocated to have Latino voter statistics compiled and publicly available, to make the Latino vote more visible and easier to access for political analysis.

Her work is often looked to as an example of best practices. In 2013, she presented on "Voting Rights Act/Best Practices" at the National Council of La Raza Annual Conference. Carmen is consistently on Spanish-language television, radio programs, and newspapers in the San Diego-Tijuana border region to encourage people to vote; she provides crucial voting and civic engagement information to Spanish-speaking audiences. Carmen single-handedly built the Spanish-language media program for the Registrar of Voters, knowing it was a crucial way to connect with Latino populations on the border. Carmen was honored in 2015 with the "Woman of the Year" award in the category of Civic Engagement, bestowed by the 80th Congressional District Representative Lorena Gonzalez. Ten days after receiving this award, Carmen was given the Cesar Chavez Visionary Award by the San Diego Cesar E. Chavez Commemoration Committee for her strong leadership, integrity, and work toward social justice. This award honors people who demonstrate the same values as César Chávez: hard work, helping others, and making a difference in the community. Carmen exemplifies high energy, commitment to social justice, and the value of "I Do Believe in Change."

Carmen Lopez, 2014, "getting out the vote" at U.S. Citizen & Immigration Services in Chula Vista.

Courtesy of Edwin Lin.

About the Author:

JESSICA CORDOVA, received both her BA and MA from UCSD; also an advocate for voter rights, she has worked part time as an assistant for the County of San Diego Registrar of Voters and is now employed by Center for Policy Initiatives, CPI. She was on the SDSU Chicana and Chicano Archive fundraising committee for Chicana Conciencia 2013. She is also a videographer working with Sonia Lopez on the San Diego Chicanas Oral History Project. She videoed more than one of the "Shoulders to Stand On: Chicana Narratives" panel discussions at the Women's Museum of California.

OLIVIA PUENTES-REYNOLDS:

COMMUNITY ACTIVIST; FOUNDER, CÍRCULO DE MUJERES

Working with Local Kumeyaai Provided Her with an Awareness of Her Indigenous Heritage

BY DIONNE ESPINOZA

I had the honor of meeting Olivia Puentes-Reynolds in 1996 when I began a postdoctoral fellowship at the University of California at San Diego (UCSD) in the Communication Department. I had been seeking a place to stay and, through a mutual friend, contacted Dr. Ricardo Stanton-Salazar, then a sociologist at UCSD, who was willing to rent a room in his house for a short time. While there, I was a guest at his gatherings, tertulias, and sharing of conversation, food, and music with friends, and Olivia was one of those. Little did I know that she and I would become friends for life…

That same year, Olivia was elected president of MANA (a national Latina organization), San Diego Chapter. Demonstrating Chicana leadership and mentorship, she invited several younger women in the community to become part of the MANA circle. I also learned that she had been among the pioneering Chicana activists of the student movement as a Mexican-American Youth Association (MAYA) member at San Diego Mesa College and at the regional MAYA Central, where she began to develop a rich "herstory" of community activism. She was recognized for her beautiful singing of movement and huelga songs. When she attended the historic Denver Youth Conference in 1969, she read her poetry as "Olivia de San Diego." That fall, she attended San Diego State College (now SDSU) where she was one of Las Chicanas, a circle of women activists. I also learned that she majored in economics and was a student of labor leader and scholar Clint Jencks of the film Salt of the Earth.

In the early 1990s, there was discussion among Chicano male leaders about developing a men's circle to process their experiences and gender roles from an indigenous perspective. At the same time, Olivia was involved in the beginning of Circulo de Hombres, a men's group in the San Diego area, based on her conversations with Jerry Tello of Hombres Nobles of the Los Angeles region. At her invitation, he was a presenter at the 1993 National MANA Conference in San Diego. After this meeting, Tello suggested that she consider forming a women's circle. A few years later, a women's circle came together and over time became a gathering space for community women, including Dr. Gail Perez, USD; Enriqueta Chavez, SDSU alumnus and recognized counselor in Sweetwater School District; Professor Rita Sanchez, San Diego Mesa College; and of a younger generation, Leticia Munguia, Norma Chavez, Sabrina Santiago, Fredi Avalos, Maria Figueroa, Guadalupe Corona, and me, Dionne Espinoza. Círculo de Mujeres met and shared its experiences as well as, for those who wished, participated in an Inipi ceremony made possible through Olivia's connection with local Kumeyaay indigenous communities. Her connection was a result of her 1990 research on ethnic communities within the City of El Cajon to prepare for the International Friendship Festival, a promise of Mayor Joan Shoemaker, to unite all ethnic communities in the city to share their history, food, song, dance, culture, and art. It was clear that the local indigenous community did not trust governments. It was only with assistance from Mary de Ubungco and Victor Peralta—who worked for the San Diego County Library outreach to indigenous reservations and who had earned their trust—that they agreed to participate. A few years later, local indigenous leaders organized a powwow to be part of the festival. Olivia said that this involvement provided her with a profound awareness and understanding of the local indigenous experience and deep understanding of her own indigenous heritage.

While MANA president (1996–1998), one of Olivia's priorities was to enhance and expand the Hermanitas Program. As a result, several of the new members she recruited (including me) became involved in the program (i.e., big/little sister program) and assisted its chair, Rosemarie Ponce. Together, we revamped its curriculum, which included knowing one's heritage, self-empowerment, discovery of voice, the value of an education, self-expression in poetry and written form, and songs that were taught by Olivia playing the guitar. One such song was "La Adelita," which was chosen because it was one of the few popular songs about women from the Mexican Revolution of 1910. We examined the lyrics closely, since we were considering gender roles and wanted to empower the Hermanitas to have a strong sense of self and autonomy over their lives and bodies. That is when we decided to write new words and to call the song "La nueva Adelita." I went to Olivia's home and we sat in her small office at the computer, crafting the song from a woman's perspective. We received editing assistance from Gracia Molina de Pick and Dr. Jorge Mariscal for our updated version; then, we were ready to share it. This was the final product:

"La nueva Adelita"

--Dedicada a todas las Chicanas y Mexicanas activistas que lucharon y siguen luchando por los derechos humanos y por la igualdad de nuestra gente y de todos los pueblos oprimidos, cualquiera que sea su raza, nación, género y sexualidad.

En lo alto de una abrupta serranía
Acampado se encontraba un regimiento
Unas mozas que valientes lo seguían
Porque creyeron en la revolución.

Popular entre la tropa las Adelitas
Por luchar con todo el Corazón
Y además de ser valientes eran resueltas
Y hasta todos los soldados las respetaban.

Y se oía, que decía, aquellos que
Tanto las querían…

Adelita se llama la joven
A quien recuerdo y no puedo olvidar
Eran Tías y Madres queridas
Luchando por su libertad.

Con los soldados las Adelitas
Cuidaron heridas y cocinaban
Pelearon con pistolas en las manos
Y también en las sierras murieron.

Y si Adelita viviera en este día
Y si Adelita viviera en mi lugar
Comprendería las injusticias
Y lucharía por la comunidad.

Adelita ya vive en el presente
Soy soldada valiente y sé luchar
Llevo en mi pecho la dulce esperanza
Que en mis brazos el mundo mejorará.

Que en mis brazos el mundo mejorará …
Que en mis brazos el mundo mejorará …

Paraphased by Gracia Molina de Pick
--Dedicated to all Chicanas and Mexicanas, activists who struggle and continue to struggle for human rights and the equality of our people and all the oppressed people by race, nation, gender, and sexuality.

In the high rough mountain region
young, valiant female workers who believed in the revolution found an encamped regiment and joined them.

The Adelitas were well thought of by the troops for fighting with all their heart, and besides being valiant they were determined, so much that the soldiers respected them.

And one could hear, that the soldiers said that they cherished them…

They called the young women, Adelita
The one I remember and can't forget
They were dear aunts and mothers
Fighting for liberty.

There, with the soldiers, the Adelitas took care of the soldier's wounds, cooked for them, fought with guns in the attacks, and died in the mountains.

If Adelita lived today, and she lived in my place, she'd understand today's injustices and would fight for the community.

Adelita does live today. I'm a brave soldier and I know how to fight. In my heart I hold the sweet hope that in my arms the world will get better … that in my arms the world will become well…

Words revised by Dionne Espinoza and Olivia Puentes-Reynolds on February 4, 1998, with edits by Norma Chavez and Sabrina Santiago, Círculo de Mujeres, 1998.

The Hermanitas Program continued to grow and by this time I had left for a tenure-track job elsewhere.

Under Olivia's guidance, Hermanitas and their Hermanas would march in the Cesar Chavez Parade in Logan Heights with our MANA sign. Olivia would always wear her business suit just like Tina C. de Baca, a revered activist, did in Chicano marches decades before.

Olivia Puentes-Reynolds, 2009, "Legacy of Lalo Guerrero," fundraiser for SDSU Chicana/Chicano Archive; the Barrio Station, Logan Heights; event photographed by Oliva; photo taken with her camera.

Courtesy of Olivia Puentes-Reynolds.

Olivia also shared the history of segregated Barrio Logan and the birthing of Chicano Park. The park was actualized only through community perseverance. After learning this history, the Hermanas and Hermanitas would clean Chicano Park with President Olivia carrying her grandson Zolá in a baby backpack.

Although my time in San Diego ended, I was blessed that I had the opportunity to meet so many of the Mexican-American women activists who made a difference in the San Diego community. I continued to maintain ties to the women's circle, and in the mid-2000s was honored to attend an annual reunion of Las Chicanas at Olivia's home at her invitation to me as an invited guest/daughter. There, I met many of the amazing pioneers as first-generation college students on college campuses. Within that circle I saw how they were mentors to each other as they shared their life journeys. They reminisced about their college days, their involvement in the Chicano movement, and how they raised the question about gender roles when it was not easy to do so.

A New Generation of Chicanas

I realized that in many ways the Círculo de Mujeres of the 1990s was connected to the earlier women's circle of Las Chicanas of the late 1960s. We were now generations of Chicanas creating space for self-development, collective sharing, and touchstones in our life journeys. I saw Olivia's initiation of the women's circle, her leadership as MANA president, and her involvement in indigenous ceremonies as part of the many ways that she has engaged in community building. To all this, we should not forget that she raised three daughters: Angela, Carmela, and Marisa. She was a mom who made sure her daughters participated in dance lessons and bobby-sox softball.

Olivia continues to be a doer who makes things happen. She refuses to see limits to what is possible in organizing, building community, or fundraising. Olivia has opened her home many times over the years for poetry readings, planning meetings, reunions, and talking circles, and, although retired, she continues to exemplify life-long leadership and mentorship. She is always ready to support important community issues, to sing a song or two that reminds us of our history of struggle and creativity, and to envision and implement new projects that document and represent Chicana/o communities and women.

¡Que viva Olivia de San Diego!

About the Author:

DIONNE ESPINOZA, Ph.D., Professor of Chicano Studies, Liberal Studies, and Women's, Gender & Sexuality Studies at the California State University, Los Angeles. Her teaching, research, and community engagement center on documenting, sharing, and analyzing Chicana and women of color herstories of activism, feminism, and leadership in movements for social justice. Her forthcoming monograph is *Bronze Womanhood: Mexican American Women Activists in the Chicano Movement.*

Carmen Sandoval, 2013, San Diego.
Courtesy of Roberto Pozos.

CARMEN SANDOVAL:

PUBLIC INFORMATION OFFICER/LEGISLATIVE LIAISON

She Refused to Be Called "Secretary" as the Only Woman on the MEChA Board

BY EVANGELINA BUSTAMANTE JONES

Before Carmen Sandoval dedicated herself to community service throughout San Diego County, she was an adventurous young girl with big, flashing hazel eyes who scrambled back to her Grantville home from the Padres games before the San Diego Stadium lights went off. From the early days of Padres baseball in 1969, Carmen and her sister would pick their way through a swamp, follow a trail by a creek, and cut across a car dealer lot to and from the games. Tickets then cost a dollar; one season, Carmen went to 42 games. She earned that dollar by sewing dresses for her little sister, ironing for her large family, and performing other household tasks. She loved to talk baseball, and loved to play the game too. Because Carmen, her six siblings, and parents lived in the Grantville/Mission Valley area, they saw the stadium being built, as well as Interstate 805.

How did this lively and independent young girl grow up to become so passionate about community service? Many people and keystone events shaped Carmen's perspective on the world. To begin, her immigrant parents had the determination and stamina to work and raise their large family in a land foreign to them; they had no relatives in the United States to welcome or help them. Her father proved his tenaciousness by returning to the U.S. after being deported five times, before he started a family. They had little money and had to stretch it to provide for so many children. The first time Carmen and her siblings went to Mexico to meet their relatives, she realized how profoundly fortunate she was to live in the United States. Even though she wore hand-me-downs and lived very simply, she saw that in rural Mexico, her family did not have running water, indoor plumbing, or even the most basic necessities. That first visit influenced her immensely and helped mold her view of the world.

Although born in the U.S., Carmen began kindergarten speaking only Spanish, but rapidly learned English. As she grew older, she began to see the disparity of resources between her more affluent classmates and the few students of color who attended Patrick Henry High School with her. Carmen, who had always loved school and excelled academically, also had a varsity letter in field hockey; she understood teamwork and how important it was to persevere for excellence.

On the night of her senior-year prom (which she was disappointed for not attending), she was dragged by her mother to join a church group, Acción Católica Juvenil, sponsored by Sacred Heart Church. Through this group, she got first-hand experience working on projects to help people in need. She met many wonderful friends and gained organizational skills that became the foundation for her life's work today.

As a San Diego State University (SDSU) student, Carmen was active in the student group, Movimiento Estudiantil Chicano de Aztlán (MEChA). MEChA focused on the promotion of higher education, the history and culture of the Mexican and Chicano people, and self-determination for the Chicano community. Carmen realized that through political involvement and education, change in society was possible and essential. She became the historian of MEChA, because she refused to be defined as "secretary" as the only woman on the MEChA Board. In 1979, she became chair of SDSU MEChA and later chair of MEChA Central of San Diego County. At the same time, she took numerous courses in Chicano Studies, enough to have a minor and very nearly a double major, since she yearned to learn about her Mexican roots and activist-based events in Latino history.

Upon entering SDSU, Carmen considered becoming a teacher and took a part-time job in the counseling office of an inner-city school. She became disillusioned because she saw that too many children were failing due to substandard efforts by the school's teachers. Although she was a student worker, she convinced the staff to find out why a certain fifth-grade student—who had attended that school since kindergarten—still had not learned the alphabet. This was an early sign that Carmen was persuasive and determined in her efforts to help others. By her junior year, she decided to major in public administration. She later began an internship with Community Congress, an organization that worked to improve youth services, the environment, and other social issues in various communities. Other groups, such as the Chicano Federation, Black Federation, and Union of Pan Asian Communities, were also taking similar actions and strategies to help their specific ethnic communities.

Although Carmen hoped to start her hands-on experience in a Latino nonprofit, she instead learned the ropes through the very effective Community Congress. She also proved to be quite successful in networking with key staff and volunteers. It was this organization that placed her into contact with local elected officials and new opportunities. It eventually led to her position as district director for Steve Peace when he was a member of the California Assembly.

After leaving the Legislature, Carmen worked at San Diego Transit in Community Relations; served in Parent Outreach for Casa Familiar, a community-based nonprofit in San Ysidro; and later was director of public policy with the San Diego Regional Chamber of Commerce for seven years. The issues she engaged while there were transportation and education, and the importance of requiring high schools to offer A-G courses needed to enroll in colleges and universities. As a volunteer, other boards and activities included: Girls Scouts of the USA National Board, leading a Girl Scout Troop for eight

Cesar Chavez, UFW Leader with Carmen Sandoval, c1970s.

Courtesy of Carmen Sandoval.

years; Mujeres de la Tierra (Los Angeles based); Border View of YMCA Board of Management; and UC Chancellor's Community Advisory Board. Carmen has also had a long-term involvement with the Chicano Federation in various roles, including chair of the board of directors.

Carmen volunteered with the Chula Vista Parks and Recreation Commission, examining issues to improve access to parks. This involvement led to her desire to serve on the Chula Vista City Council, which then had never had a Latino or Latina member. Her run for office did not result in victory; however, her desire to hold an elected position in order to effect change demonstrates how deeply Carmen feels about the quality of life for all community members.

More recently, she volunteered for five years with the Centro Cultural de la Raza in Balboa Park, coordinating activities, classes, and events. As its chair, Carmen helped organize art and cultural events, scheduled volunteers, and even mopped and swept when needed. She worked to rebuild relationships with other Balboa Park organizations.

Although many of Carmen's years of community service focused on Latino issues, she gets a great deal of satisfaction from her long-standing activities with the Chula Vista Rotary Club. This year Carmen is chair of the International Projects Committee and is in line to become president of her club in 2016.

One would think that Carmen does not have time left for a personal life, since she works so diligently with so many groups. But, that is not true. She is married to Jesse Fernandez and has two adult children. They enjoy sports, travel, and spending time with each other and extended family—his six brothers and sisters. And, her big, flashing hazel eyes express enthusiasm, warmth, and a zest for life. It is not hard to imagine her running home through creeks and car lots, after enjoying her Padres game.

About the Author:

EVANGELINA BUSTAMANTE JONES was one of the first full time professors to teach in the newly founded Mexican American Studies at SDSU in 1970; she grew up in Phoenix, AZ, obtaining a B. A. in Liberal Arts; an M. A. in English Education from Arizona State University; and two California teaching credentials. After 18 years of public school teaching, she earned a Ph. D. from Claremont Graduate University/San Diego State University; she enjoyed a teaching career of 42 years before retiring in 2011 as an associate professor in the Department of Policy Studies in Language and Cultural Education at SDSU; her doctoral research, "The Bicultural Teacher as Cultural Mediator," consisted of case studies of five bilingual/bicultural teachers in Calexico. Currently, Evangelina has returned to her hippie roots, creating retro-style aprons and Latino-inspired apparel which she sells at fairs.

JOSIE TALAMANTEZ:

STATE OF CALIFORNIA ARTS COUNCIL, CHIEF OF PROGRAMS AND LEGISLATIVE LIAISON

With CCSC She Received the Governor of California Award for Historic Preservation

BY ZERINA ZERMEÑO

Josephine (aka Josie) Talamantez is a Chicana trailblazer who defends and preserves our cultural identity. She is responsible for Chicano Park and its monumental murals being listed on the National Register of Historic Places. Mother of four children, she grew up Catholic as many Mexicans do, but decided to explore the indigenous road of spirituality reflective of her Yaqui heritage. I cannot begin to explain why Josie is so valuable to the Chicano community on so many levels. As her hard work prevails, future generations will be able to identify themselves with what she has preserved and archived. She has made sure that our roots remain in existence, so that we may always have our culture and voices heard. Josie does not believe in "mistakes or coincidences" and, perhaps, that is one of the reasons she has been such a trailblazer for many Chicano communities.

Josie was born and raised in what was known originally as "East End," later as Logan Heights, and now as Barrio Logan. Her family goes back in the barrio for over 100 years, beginning with her great grandmother, Concepción Verdugo Almanza. Concepción brought her children from Baja California Sur. She raised her nine children in the community of Barrio Logan. Descendant of Concepción, Sue Almanza Talamantez gave birth to Josie on August 14, 1951. Josie attended educational and cultural classes at the old Neighborhood House, Burbank Elementary School, Memorial Junior High School, and San Diego High School. Many in her family worked in the fish canneries and on the docks in Logan Heights. Josie's mother encouraged her to pursue her education before getting a job in the cannery; she did not want Josie to fall in love with money before pursuing an education. Sue was known for prioritizing education and encouraged many prominent community members to complete their educational goals, including her four children.

After finishing high school, Josie attended San Diego City College and became a student activist in the Chicano student movement. Awarded a Ford Foundation Scholarship, she then transferred to the University of California at San Diego (UCSD). Josie was very disappointed by the University's lack of diversity and activism for people's rights with which she had been constantly surrounded when attending San Diego City College. Later, Josie transferred to the University of California at Berkeley, hoping to find the same activism and energy that she sought. Although Josie's transition was difficult, she ultimately found what she wanted. Her new experience enabled her to discover new supportive preventative mental health strategies through art and history that many Chicanos and Chicanas needed. These studies helped her with the work she would do in the future.

In 1970, as a student at San Diego City College, Josie joined in demonstrations along with other community activists to save a parcel of land in Logan Heights. This land is now known as Chicano Park under the Coronado Bridge. The City of San Diego had plans for a highway patrol station under the bridge where the Logan Heights community had been promised a park. Neighborhood residents and activists protested to prevent the construction of the station. Local residents, including Josie, chained themselves to trees. They created a human chain around the bulldozers to halt the State of California and the City of San Diego. They then occupied the land for 12 consecutive days. In the end, the people were victorious.

Josie talks about her involvement with this community effort in the film, *Chicano Park*. Her passion for her neighborhood's fight for a park and for her neighborhood's upkeep shows in her voice and shines in her eyes. First, the city had cut through their neighborhood with the building of the bridge that stretched through their barrio to Coronado. These plans were successfully halted by the people of Logan Heights. Now every year, they celebrate Chicano Park Day on April 22.

Years later, Josie and other Logan Heights residents united again to protest the junkyards entering the neighborhood, and the retrofitting of the Chicano Park pillars where artists had painted murals. Artists had actively been beautifying their neighborhood park with art and plants when pollution, noise, and construction intervened. Josie explains that her "lovely barrio that was once full of family owned restaurants, businesses, cultural institutions, and *panaderías* was turning into a construction zone." These disturbances drove many residents out of their beloved Barrio Logan through the process of eminent domain. Josie was compelled to reach out to her community and fight for their neighborhood as a founding member of Chicano Park by joining the Chicano Park Steering Committee (CPSC). The committee made their voices heard to protect the park. As a result, they were able to stop the intrusions that were harming their neighborhood, the junkyards, pollution, and retrofitting. As their dedication and excitement grew, so did Chicano Park.

Josie Talamantez, 2016, San Diego.
Courtesy of Memo Cavada, Creative Images.

Josie graduated from UCSD with a BA in Sociology and from UC Berkley with an MA in History. After college, Josie worked at the Raza Recruitment Center, traveling throughout California, to find prospective students to attend Berkeley. At that time, Josie was unsure of where she would apply her knowledge gained from years of education and service. She knew she wanted to reach out to the community in a personal way. As she became interested in the mental health of our community, she took a class taught by Dr. Arnoldo Solis, the first Chicano psychiatrist in the nation at the time. She was inspired to support the concept of preventative mental health through the facilitation of spaces, promoting arts, culture, and political awareness for Chicano communities.

Josie Talamantez and Tommie Camarillo, Chicano Park.
Courtesy of Sande Lollis.

Josie also earned her wings in the Royal Chicano Air Force (RCAF). The RCAF was an arts collective that started in Sacramento to promote arts, history, and culture. It also fostered preventative mental health strategies through the arts and political activism. Furthermore, it focused on social, educational, and cultural injustices, and supported Cesar Chavez and the United Farm Workers. The RCAF served as a great support to Chicanos and Chicanas during this time of rapid shift of cultural sustainability imposed on Chicano identity. Josie traveled to different California cities to implement the RCAF and Community Mental Health

Center (CMHC) partnership model of preventative mental health services, as documented in the 1978 President's Commission on Mental Health.

From 1979 to 1981, Josie became director of the Centro Cultural de la Raza in San Diego; from 1983 to 1985, she was director of La Raza Galeria Posada in Sacramento. At the Centro Cultural, her idea was to preserve cultural artifacts with a museum of Mexicano, Chicano, and Native American art and to promote international exchanges with Mexico. She turned the Centro Cultural into a true gallery with exhibits, one by notable artist, Guadalupe Posada, and another with works by photographer, Augustin Casasola. After Josie left the Centro and the Raza Galeria, she made it to the California State Arts Council's hiring list and was offered many jobs. She took the position of artist in community that was part of the artist residency program. Although this was a big feat for Josie, she was unsure if her true purpose was to get a government job because she did not want to stray from supporting her community. However, after Josie started her new position for the State of California, she realized that she now had the power to shape policy. As a result, Josie would enable more Chicano and multicultural arts programs to preserve Chicano art, history, and culture. Josie worked in every program of the agency, lasting more than 27 years, culminating her career as part of the executive team, chief of programs, and legislative liaison. This position afforded her a great opportunity.

In 1995, Dr. Jim Fisher, cultural historian for the California Department of Transportation (Caltrans), was assigned to assess graffiti on the walls in Chicano Park. The state was awaiting Dr. Fisher's recommendation to declare the graffiti art worthless and agree with its destruction. This would allow Caltrans to continue the retrofit, a preventative measure, adding steel reinforcements harmful to the art. Dr. Fisher recognized noted San Francisco artist Rupert Garcia's work on one of the pillars and refused to give such a recommendation so eagerly awaited by state officials. Dr. Fisher only agreed to the retrofitting of the Coronado Bridge, without compromising Chicano Park or its monumental murals. Josie introduced Dr. Fisher to the community and he encouraged her to have Chicano Park listed on the National Register of Historic Places. Josie introduced the idea to the CPSC, but it was reluctant that such action would take power away from their community. Josie researched non-traditional National Register sites in efforts to appease the committee that represented Barrio Logan and the broader Chicano community. She visited and documented El Tiradito in Tucson, Arizona. El Tiradito, a shrine located on a small dirt lot, is a sacred place for the Barrio Viejo community of Tucson. During its time of listing on the National Register, the Interstate 10 freeway was being built. Its listing forced the State of Arizona to reroute the freeway around the sacred site, saving the Barrio and Downtown Tucson. She hoped the story would inspire the park committee.

Josie came to the CPSC with the great news she had encountered in El Tiradito. Although she still faced reluctance from some members, in 2012, the committee finally voted on Josie's proposal to complete the process of placing Chicano Park and the Chicano Park Monumental Murals listing on the National Register. The listing would have to be authorized by the National Historic Preservation Act of 1966 under the U.S. Department of the Interior. This effort was approved in January 2013 and then-Mayor Bob Filner held a press conference in March to announce Barrio Logan's victory. In November 2013, Josie Talamantez and the Chicano Park Steering Committee received the Governor of California's Award for Historic Preservation and also included the "Honoring of the Artists." This placing of Chicano Park and the Chicano Park Monumental Murals took vigorous work on Josie's part, since the park and murals were less than 50 years old and had to fall into special criteria for significance.

Josie has since been appointed as an advisor to the California Office of Historic Preservation (OHP). On January 28, 2015, the OHP commissioners approved the advisors' recommendations to develop a California Latino Context Statement and create a Multiple Property Registration Form (MPRF). The document and the MPRF are critical for preserving Latino cultural resources in California. She has also been appointed to the Barrio Logan Planning Committee by David Alvarez and continues to pursue her goal of creating a Chicano Park Museum and Cultural Center.

Josie Talamantez has served San Diego's Chicano neighborhoods, protecting the rights of the community members and families to have a safe, practical, and beautiful place to live and raise their children. She has served with dedication and passion as a leader and devoted advocate for preserving Chicano communities.

About the Author:

ZERINA ZERMEÑO, known as Poesia, was born and raised in the border town of San Diego. The 35 year old Xicana has been involved in the artistic expression of song and poetry for over ten years. She has supported the growth and learning of poetry by presenting at SDSU to enrich students' intellectual experience; at the Womens Museum of California for Chicanas in the Arts; at the Centro Cultural de La Raza for Enero Zapatista, celebrated annually; The Front in San Ysidro for their first annual Dia de la Mujer. Poesia also co-curated and performed spoken word for Chicana, Una Decision Conciente, an event in 2012 to honor San Diego Xicanas.

CHAPTER 10

DENISE MORENO DUCHENY

MARY CASILLAS SALAS

LORI SALDAÑA

MARIA NIETO SENOUR

TERESA PASCUAL VALLADOLID

CHAPTER 10

Community Activists as Elected Officials

The sociocultural ferment of the 1960s and 1970s opened the political landscape to a new generation of student activists. Within the anti-war, farmworker, feminist, Chicano, Black, and Native American movements, many young Chicanos—*hombres y mujeres de la Raza*—heeded the call for political action, transforming them as individuals committed to social justice

By the late 1960s, the United States counted close to 300 weekly casualties in the Vietnam War; and the economic recession was causing inflation to climb. The anti-war and other movements created political unrest at previously unseen levels and cut across ethnic and class lines. Appealing to social conservatives by promising to bring "peace with honor" to end the Vietnam War, Republican candidate Richard Nixon won the election of 1968, setting the stage for a political move to the right. The pendulum swing to the right continued well into the 1980s, with the election of Ronald Reagan in 1980. Chicanas and Chicanos continued to challenge the *status quo* and to work for change.

Leadership within the Chicano and other movements often came at a high price for Chicanas and other women of color. Some Chicanas were told that they were *agabachadas*, or acting "too white" and were not "real Chicanas" if they pushed for gender equality. The male-dominated Chicano Movement emphasized cultural nationalism, that is emphasizing our Mexican culture as the avenue for self-determination and liberation of Chicano people within the Anglo-centered United States. Chicanas who joined the Feminist Movement were labeled "sellouts," "women libbers," or in spanish *marimachas*. These labels intended to punish, silence, and discredit those Chicanas challenging the *status quo* and insisted on their political involvement. But, Chicanas continued their activism in these movements in different areas and in different roles within their communities. Some dared to call themselves Chicana feminists; others avoided any term, not sure how it would be received in whichever community or area they were working in.

As Chicana activists continued to branch out into the community, working in different areas, they came to understand the critical roles of various political entities and other institutions. They understood the necessity to run for and be elected to political office in order to bring change in laws and policies directly affecting their communities. From the onset of the Chicano Movement, Chicanas understood the important role of education in empowering their communities; therefore, running for educational boards seemed a natural starting point for many Chicanas.

Chicanas ran for public office in the 1970s—mostly at the local level— but few succeeded. In nearby Calexico, located in Imperial County, California, Mary Rangel was the first Chicana elected to the Calexico Unified School Board in 1973, followed by Gloria Nogales in 1977, who served 10 years, including as board president. In San Diego, in 1975, Hilda McFarland Inzunza ran on a slate with her husband Ralph Inzunza, Sr., for the San Ysidro Elementary School Board; both won.

Other Chicanas worked in the background to bring political empowerment to Chicano//Latino communities. Rosalia Salinas, Connie Puente, and Dolores Inzunza Arias (and husband Armando) were among those who started the San Diego Chicano Democratic Association in the 1970s. By the 1980s, we began to see more Chicanas in public office. Long-time grassroots activist Gloria Molina of Los Angeles was elected in 1982 as the first Latina assemblywoman in the history of the California legislature. In 1985, activist Hilda Solis was elected to the Rio Hondo Community College Board and, in 1992, to the California State Assembly. San Diego attorney Celia Ballesteros was appointed to the San Diego City Council in 1987, representing the 8th District on the condition that she would not run for the same seat upon completion of her tenure. These were some of the *mujeres* who laid some of the political groundwork; they became role models, and inspired those that followed.

In the 90's, Chicanas were entering a very changed political arena, where they addressed both old and new political issues facing Raza communities. In a political atmosphere increasingly becoming more anti-Mexican /Latino/ Chicano, anti-immigrant and anti-affirmative action, Chicanas continued to join the ranks as elected officials, in spite of limited financial resources and, at times, traditional cultural resistance.

Denise Moreno Ducheny grew up in Los Angeles. Her mother worked as a fashion buyer executive; her father was a member of Teamsters Local 399. Ducheny began to explore her Mexicana roots while majoring in history at Pomona College in the 1970s. She finished law school in 1979, relocated to San Diego, and opened a private practice in Barrio Logan, a largely Mexican

American/Chicano neighborhood. Denise and her husband, Al Ducheny, became community activists in the 1980s, addressing neighborhood issues. They helped to organize the Harbor View Community Council to improve parks and libraries for Logan Heights residents. In 1990, Denise became one of the first Chicanas/Latinas elected to the San Diego Community College Board of Trustees and, in 1994 she became the first Latina/Chicana woman elected to the California State Assembly. In 2000, she was elected to the California State Senate.

Mary Salas was also part of this rise in political activism. Raised in then-rural Chula Vista, California, she returned to school in the 1980s, a young divorced woman with two daughters. She credits her political success to becoming involved with the San Diego Mexican American Women's National Association (MANA), which involved her in the public arena. In 1996, Mary became the first Chicana/Latina woman elected to the Chula Vista City Council; in 2010, she was elected to the California State Assembly, representing the diverse 79th District. In 2014, Mary became the mayor of Chula Vista— with a population of 58 percent Latinos—making her the first Chicana/Latina mayor in the history of San Diego County.

Another woman found her strength in taking on environmental issues. Coming from a military household, Lori Saldaña moved frequently. Leaving friends behind must not have been easy. Playing sports and camping with her family influenced her choice of exercise science as a major at San Diego State University (SDSU). She became a student activist in the newly emerging environmental movement of the late 1980s and early 1990s. In 1990, she joined the founding board of directors of San Diego's "Earth Day," organizing and promoting the annual Earth Fair in Balboa Park. Because of her leadership in the Sierra Club and the San Diego County Democratic Central Committee, she was encouraged to run for, and was elected to, the State Assembly in 2004, representing the 76th Assembly District. While in office, she authored and coauthored bills signed into law that protected the environment, advanced equality and civil rights, and improved public safety and education.

Chicanas/Latinas ran for public office, motivated by the lack of diversity on educational boards and other offices. Educator Maria Nieto Senour, a Texas-born Chicana, was the eldest daughter whose brilliant mother had to be hospitalized because of bipolar disorder shortly after the family had moved to Detroit, Michigan when Maria was fourteen. Thus, Maria, in order to help her family, worked cleaning houses and babysitting. She lived in the Detroit housing projects and experienced racial discrimination while growing up. However, this did not stop her from pursuing her dream of obtaining an education in order to help her family. Maria, Ph.D. in hand, was hired in 1977 as a counselor educator in the Community Based Block (CBB) Multicultural Counseling and Social Justice program at SDSU. This program was dedicated to training culturally competent school counselors. She later became its first Chicana/Latina director. In 1990, she was among the first Latinas/Chicanas elected to the San Diego Community College District Broad of Trustees, where she continues to serve as board president. Her activism has made and continues to make a difference in San Diego's community.

As Chicanas became more politically active, they contributed their services as elected officials on several levels. Participation in the Chicano Student and United Farmworker movements transformed Teresa Pascual Valladolid into an activist. The young Filipina/Mexicana came to SDSU in the late 1960s from Imperial Valley—farmworker country. She began to embrace her Filipino/ Mexicano roots for the first time because of the work she was doing for farmworkers' rights; she became proud of her ancestry. Teresa graduated from college and went to work with unions, including the United Domestic Workers Union and Service Employee International Union (SEIU). In 1998, she was elected to the Southwestern College Board of Trustees. Valladolid served for 16 years, helping to bring about much-needed change to a community college situated on the U.S.-Mexican border, whose student population is majority Chicano/ Mexicano.

These courageous women entered a political arena where there were few women, Latinas/Chicanas, in particular. Chicanas have not only had to deal with the lack of economic resources to propel their campaigns and win, but have also had to challenge the socio-cultural biases attributed to Latinas/Chicanas, suggesting that they were content in staying in the background of political leadership. The mujeres in this chapter have all had a passion to bring about change and make the world a better place. Their activism continues to inspire others.

DENISE MORENO DUCHENY:

ATTORNEY FOR THE PEOPLE; STATE SENATOR

First San Diegan, First Woman, First Chicana to Chair the Assembly Budget Committee

BY NORA E. VARGAS

Against all odds, in 1994, Denise Moreno Ducheny became the first Chicana/Latina in San Diego to be elected to the California State Legislature. As chair of the budget committee, she made unprecedented gains for women, welfare rights, and immigrant rights through legislation that would improve quality of life. In 2002, she broke through traditional barriers again to win as state senator and, in 2006, she became the first woman and first Chicana/Latina to chair the Senate Committee on Budget and Fiscal Review.

I met Denise Moreno Ducheny in 1993 at a dinner hosted by the National Women's Political Caucus (NWPC). I had just graduated from the University of San Francisco and had moved back home to San Diego where I was looking for job opportunities and getting engaged in my community. NWPC's focus on changing the political landscape by getting pro-choice women elected into office—even training and supporting them in their election journey—was music to my ears. Until I attended that event and met Denise, I had no idea it would chart the direction of my professional career and enhance my love for politics. Denise filled the bill. Throughout my college course work and activism, I had yearned to connect with someone who looked like me, understood the community I came from, and had the gumption to fight for our diverse communities. I wanted to find that space within the women's movement to advocate on behalf of what I really believed in: the advancement of women of color, especially Chicanas/Latinas like me.

That night, the NWPC would showcase a San Diego Community College board member, Denise Moreno Ducheny, a candidate for the special election of the 79th Assembly District. What I knew about her was that she was a very passionate person, committed to higher education, and advocated for women to have access and a right to make decisions about their own bodies and destinies.

I also knew that she had an understanding about the interdependency of the border region and other issues relevant to our Latino community. In fact, she spoke about every one of our community issues and was fiercely determined to be an advocate for social justice. I spent the next three months volunteering on her special election campaign in an office in National City, with a small group of dedicated and committed young professionals who were determined to win. We walked precincts, knocked on doors, engaged volunteers, and even got bitten by dogs.

We worked hard every day for Denise to win that election and it paid off. On the evening of Tuesday, April 12, Denise's votes were up by a small margin, important to note, because in that election, she was the underdog against a field of four other candidates. Two of them were perceived to be, in many quarters, the front runners; they had spent thousands more funds on their campaigns than Ducheny. Denise only prevailed because of her determination and willingness to work hard and be strategic. It is a truism that every vote counts: Denise won that California State Assembly election by 27 votes.

That April 1994, Denise Moreno Ducheny was elected to the California State Assembly, representing District 79, a community largely composed of Latinos and other ethnic groups in South Bay San Diego. She won by sheer determination and dedication to the people fighting for her.

Determination is also what drove her when growing up in Southern California. She was born March 21, 1952, in Los Angeles, California, to Socorro Moreno and Jack Fitzpatrick. Her mother was also a pioneer Latina role model; she was a fashion buyer executive in an era before women were commonly full-time workers and in a field with few Latinas. It was because of her mother's executive position that Denise attended private school in her early years, as it provided full-time kindergarten classes not available in the local public school system at the time. So, she went to private school from kindergarten through eighth grade and then to a public high school.

Denise attended Pomona College, where she received a bachelor of arts in history, with scholarship aid from the Twentieth Century Fox Film Corporation available to the children of employees—her father was a long-time member of Teamsters Local 399 and worked at Fox Studios during her high school and college years. It was during her college years that she first developed a love for Mexico, her maternal heritage. She studied Spanish in Cuernavaca and traveled to many historical sites in the summer of 1973. That summer she also had the special experience of visiting with her retired grandfather, Arcadio Moreno, who had worked most of his adult life as a union carpenter in the Los Angeles area, his native land.

Following such an enriching experience in Mexico, she was able to travel to another part of the world, to Lund, Sweden, where she studied economic history. Subsequently, she graduated from Southwestern University School of Law in Los Angeles in 1979, earning a Juris Doctor (J.D.) degree, becoming the first in her family to attain both a B.A. and an advanced degree.

Following her graduation from law school, Denise moved to San Diego and opened a law practice in the underserved community of Barrio Logan. For the next 15 years, she represented South San Diego families in a general practice focused primarily on immigration and family law matters. At the same time, she accepted court appointments to represent indigent clients on appeal in criminal defense and juvenile dependency proceedings. During the 1980s and early 1990s, Denise and her husband Al Ducheny began their life-long involvement in community issues. They helped to organize the Harborview Community Council with neighbors in Barrio Logan to fight for improved parks and libraries for the residents of that community.

Her representation of immigrant families during those years eventually led Denise to run for a seat in the San Diego Community College Board in 1990. She did so to continue representing those families as they sought the district's services to learn English, to become U.S. citizens, and to provide access for their children to the higher education required to improve their career opportunities.

Now in the Assembly, Ducheny became a strong advocate for women, jobs, education, and housing. By 1997, she became chair of the State Assembly Budget Committee. With this appointment, made significant by the first Latino Speaker of the Assembly, Cruz Bustamante, whom she had assisted in obtaining that position, she broke several barriers: she was the first woman, the first San Diegan, and the first Chicana/Latina appointed.

She served as chair of the Assembly Budget Committee between 1997 and 2000, and as vice-chair in 1996. As assemblywoman and the first Latina ever to be appointed to such a powerful position, she was in charge of developing and overseeing the state's $100-billion spending plan. She also served on numerous other committees, including Water, Parks and Wildlife; Housing; and Environmental Safety and Toxic Materials. She also served as chair of the Select Committee on California-Mexico Affairs; cochair of the Special Committee on Welfare Reform; vice-chair of the Joint Legislative Budget Committee, and vice-chair of the Latino Legislative Caucus. In these positions, the people had a spokesperson that understood and fought for their concerns.

Denise authored landmark legislation during her time as the people's assemblywoman. The CalWorks Welfare Reform Act of 1997 assisted many in the transition from welfare to work; the College Affordability Act rolled back student fees at the University of California (UC), California State University (CSU), and community college systems for the first time in 13 years. The Reverse Mortgage bill provided protection to senior homeowners and consumers; the California Public School Library Act provided additional funding for school libraries; and the Indian Child Welfare Act protected the role of tribes to participate in juvenile court proceedings pertaining to the welfare of children of tribal members. Her legislation also established the California Office of Binational Border Health to coordinate efforts to improve public health outcomes in our binational region. She assisted her communities with the help they needed.

All of these achievements that Denise accomplished as assemblywoman, from 1994 to 2000, prepared her to win another unprecedented election in 2002 as California State Senator. A newly drawn district that encompassed California's border with Mexico—Imperial County, the eastern Coachella Valley portion of Riverside County, and southern San Diego County—allowed her to have an even greater impact for change.

Most importantly, during her career in the Senate from 2002 to 2010, Senator Ducheny continued to be a strong advocate for women, jobs, education, and housing. She again broke through traditional barriers to become the first woman and first Chicana/Latina to chair the Senate Committee on Budget and Fiscal Review in 2006. Her committee assignments in the Senate extended to include agriculture, transportation, and the judiciary, among many others.

Throughout her tenure in the State Legislature, Denise paid close attention to border issues and built closer relationships with Mexico, particularly our Baja California neighbors, a primary focus of her work. While a member of the State Assembly, through her work with the Council of State Governments-West, she launched a series of binational meetings among state legislators of the 10 U.S.-Mexico border states that eventually became known as the Border Legislative Conference. In 2010, her last year in the State Senate, Denise was honored to chair that Conference.

At the first of two special occasions in the late 1990s, she met with a small group of other U.S. local elected officials of Mexican ancestry. The second time Denise was invited to Los Pinos in Mexico City, she was in the company of then recently elected California Governor Gray Davis. They participated in a meeting that was significant to begin repairing the damage to the California-Mexico relations as a result of the 1994 passage of Proposition 187, the largely unconstitutional attack on California immigrant families.

There is no doubt that Denise has left a lasting impact in San Diego's South Bay, and in all of California, as a local attorney for the people, a community activist for their causes, as California Assemblywoman, and as State Senator. She

Denise Moreno Ducheny, 2002–2010, as State Senator.
Courtesy of Office of the California State Senate.

has also helped pave the way for future Chicana/Latina leaders and continues to inspire us to reach new heights.

My fondest memories of Denise are during those early campaign days when I first supported and believed in her. That experience showed me that the underdog candidate can win with the right vision, teamwork, and determination. Denise Ducheny is the best example of those strengths. She simply powered through those hard times and rallied her team, always with the people of her community foremost in her mind. Our community needs committed leaders like her, voices bent on advocating for the people.

Senator Ducheny served two terms in the Senate, and left office only due to term limits. However, she has never stopped serving her community. In the summer of 2014, her efforts of over 25 years to foster improved relations between governments of the United States and Mexico, and in defense of immigrant rights, were recognized by the Mexican government. The Mexican ambassador to the United States bestowed upon her the prestigious Ohtli Award, the highest honor awarded by that government to non-Mexican citizens. She was proud to be nominated by her former colleagues in the National Association of Latino Appointed and Elected Officials (NALEO).

In the Fall of 2014, President Barack Obama appointed Denise to a key administrative post: the U.S. Public Member/Border Resident position on the U.S.-Mexico Board of Directors for the Border Environment Cooperation Commission (BECC) and the North American Development Bank (NADBANK). She also serves on the nonprofit boards of the North American Research Partnership and the Children's Council of the Children's Advocacy Institute.

Currently, Denise is senior policy advisor with the Center for U.S.-Mexican Studies at the University of California at San Diego (UCSD), School of Global Policy and Strategy. She also serves as a lecturer in UCSD's Urban Studies and Planning Program, where she shares her knowledge acquired over her years in elected office with a new generation. In these positions, she continues to work for improved understanding of the binational region of the Three Californias, and to improve government-to-government relationships between the United States and Mexico.

Denise now resides in Imperial Beach with her husband Al Ducheny, her greatest supporter, campaign manager, and husband of over thirty-five years.

About the Author:

NORA E. VARGAS is a dynamic and accomplished leader in non-profit management, government, politics, and public policy. Since 2009, Ms. Vargas has served as the Vice President of Community & Government Relations for Planned Parenthood of the Pacific Southwest. She has committed her career to advancing an agenda of inclusion, and many of her endeavors have served as models across the United States

MARY CASILLAS SALAS:

MAYOR, CITY OF CHULA VISTA; FORMER ASSEMBLY WOMAN

The First Chicana/Latina Elected to City Council and Then Mayor

BY AIDA BUSTOS

The story of Chula Vista Mayor Mary Casillas Salas is about the enduring power of Latina friendship that embraces, sustains, and inspires. That story begins when her husband suddenly left her, upending her tranquil life as a stay-at-home mother who had married just out of high school. Overnight, she had to construct a new life for herself and her two daughters. Her rebirth was her enrollment in college at the age of 37.

Mary's experience as an older student led her to a nonprofit organization just starting out called MANA de San Diego, a national women's organization. It was there that she met Bea Fernandez, Elisa Sanchez, Olivia Puentes Reynolds, Adela Garcia, and many other Latinas whose friendship still sustains Mary today. They welcomed her into the group and immediately assigned her volunteer work.

MANA mentors young Latinas, encouraging them to go college and develop careers. It was a message that resonated with Mary. "I didn't feel that I had a purpose, until I joined that organization," she said. "I believed in MANA's work and vision. My best friends are still my MANA friends from back then."

At the time, one of the organization's goals was to diversify public boards and commissions. Mary applied for a spot in Chula Vista's Civil Service Commission and, to her surprise, was selected. She began to learn about the intricacies of city policies—and was hooked on public service.

In 1996, her friends encouraged Mary to run for office in the Chula Vista City Council.

What happened next was nothing less than "Latina power unleashed," she recalled. The friends, joined by dozens of volunteers, turned Mary's garage into a bustling campaign headquarters. Day after day, they wrote voters, built lawn signs, and walked precincts. They raised money, too, surpassing the establishment candidate by several thousand dollars.

Mary won the election, which she said reflected the community's interest in having a qualified and prepared Latina on the City Council. Mary was the first Chicana/Latina elected to the council and the first woman to be elected by a vote of the people rather than appointed. Though she won her historic City Council race by 10 percentage points, serving would be another challenge from day one.

The city had changed dramatically since Mary was born in 1948, when Chula Vista had about 10,000 residents. Her parents, Paula and Nicolaz Casillas, had raised Mary and her two sisters in the rural southwest neighborhood of Harborside. The houses were surrounded by fields, where lettuce and other produce were grown and sent out by trains that rumbled through the area, blasting their horns and shaking the family's house. Her neighborhood was predominately white, save for a handful of Mexican families like hers. "When I started kindergarten at Harborside School, I was the only Mexican kid in class," Mary said. The city's demographics began to shift in the 1970s, with the arrival of mostly Mexican immigrant families. By the 2010 Census, Chula Vista's population was 58 percent Latino.

Mary's family and friends had jammed the council chambers for her swearing-in ceremony. But the mayor abruptly decided not to allow Mary to address the crowd, breaking with the tradition of council members taking the podium. Undaunted, Mary took the microphone, faced the crowd and delivered her remarks to "those who really mattered: the people of Chula Vista."

After the ceremony, three of her friends—Delia Talamantez, Julie Rocha, and Norma Cazares—intercepted the mayor. "Mary was duly elected and you treated her rudely," they told her. "We're her friends and supporters. We will be watching to see that she is given the full respect of her office."

By 2002, in the middle of her second term at the City Council, Mary ran for mayor of Chula Vista. "I really felt that I was best suited to be the mayor of my city," she said. "I really felt that I could do a better job, that I understood my community a whole lot more than my opponent." After a hard-fought campaign, she lost. "It was heart-breaking because I felt that I let down so many friends and volunteers that had given their all to support my candidacy," she recalled. "I thought at that time, 'I'm never going to run for public office again.'"

The Democratic Party leaders in Sacramento, however, had another idea. They had taken note of her strong record of community service and recruited her to run for the 79th Assembly District. With their help—and backed once more by her friends—she won, serving in Sacramento as assemblywoman until 2010.

That successful race was followed by a bruising one, which pitted her against a fellow Democrat for a state Senate seat, a contest she lost. "It was awful at the time," she reminisced. "In retrospect, it was the best thing that could ever have happened. My true passion was always serving the community I loved."

Backed by her core group of amigas—and the broad group of supporters she had picked up in two decades of public service—she decided to run for mayor of Chula Vista. Mary Salas was elected mayor of her hometown in December 2014. "That's all I wanted to do," she said.

Mary Casillas Salas, Mayor of Chula Vista.
Courtesy of City of Chula Vista Mayor's Office;
photograph by Ian Trotter, Chula Vista Photo.

Her mother was at her side when Mary took the oath of office as Chula Vista's mayor. "My life is filled with the love of my 92-year-old mother; my sisters Gloria and Alicia; my two daughters Michele and Sara; and my grandchildren. I am a woman fulfilled," Mary expressed.

Her friends are never far away nor the cause that brought them together initially. Mary often responds to their requests to speak to young Latinas. "I love encouraging them," she said, urging them to consider careers beyond the well-worn ones. "I tell them to think about public administration," she said. "We don't have a lot of city managers that are Latino. It could be a wonderful career for them."

Mary Salas, Mayor of Chula Vista, 2015, delivering the State of the City address.
Courtesy of Bob Hoffman.

As a Chicana/Latina mayor—the first in San Diego County—Mary values the city's location on the border and its residents. She considers them assets for the city to advance. She champions the effort to bring a university that prepares graduates for international commerce and reaches out to Tijuana metropolitan leaders to work together. These efforts will help to grow the region's economy, tapping Chula Vista's young, diverse population.

The smaller acts of friendship continue to sustain her. "I bounce things off of her," she said of Bea Fernandez. "She is someone who is wise, pragmatic, and funny. Always the true friend who tells you like it is and not how you want it to be."

About the Author:

AIDA BUSTOS is a *fronteriza*. Born in San Diego, she has lived and worked on both sides of the U.S.-Mexico divide. Captivated by the power of words, she's been writing stories since elementary school. As a journalist and bilingual communication specialist, she tells the stories of individuals and organizations making an impact in the border region. She is a founding partner at CIMA, a bilingual communications agency; a staff writer for *Southern Cross*, of the San Diego Diocese; and professor of digital journalism at City College.

LORI SALDAÑA:

FORMER ASSEMBLY WOMAN; LEGISLATOR OF THE YEAR

On the Founding Board of San Diego's Earth Day; Helped Organize the Balboa Park Fair

BY CASSIE MORTON ROCHIN

Lori Saldaña, San Diego political activist and legislator, is an advocate for women, military families, the underrepresented, and the environment. She takes pride in her Latino heritage and the support she and her sisters received from their parents to keep them focused on their education. She stands out as a role model, especially for young women. She was elected as California State Assemblywoman, with over 40 percent of the vote, and was named legislator of the year more than once.

In 2004, Latinos received unprecedented attention from both presidential campaigns. Various groups sponsored voter registration and get-out-the-vote drives. But no campaign was more enthusiastic than the one for California State Assembly. In San Diego, a young Latina woman caused the stir. Among others, Chicana/Latina activists saw a woman like themselves running for higher office and they were ready to join the campaign to fight for her election. To add to that, she was a local, born and bred in San Diego.

Lori Saldaña was born in 1958. Her family, typical of military families in those days, moved frequently. After her father's retirement from the Marine Corps in 1964, he moved the family back to San Diego. He worked as a reporter for 25 years with The San Diego Evening Tribune. His daughters benefited greatly, as he regularly took them to the El Cortez Hotel to await election results. Thereafter, in high school, Lori began volunteering in political campaigns.

Her father Frank Saldaña was a first-generation U.S. citizen, born in Los Angeles. A career marine, he served in World War II and Korea. His father Angelo (Lori's grandfather) came from Panama, while his mother Aurelia Garcia (Lori's grandmother) came to the U.S. from Baja California when it was still a territory— not yet a state—of Mexico. Because of her, Lori says, "My heritage runs deep into

Mexico." Aurelia's father, Juan Antonia Garcia, had been a comandante in the Mexican Revolution.

Lori's mother, Virginia, was of Norwegian descent by way of Minnesota. She met Frank in California, while on vacation with friends. She had worked in banking to support herself as a single mom before meeting and marrying Lori's father. With Lori's birth, the third of four daughters, Virginia took up motherhood full time and participated as a PTA volunteer. As a result of her hands-on mothering, all four daughters graduated from college, the first generation in the family to do so!

Lori grew up playing sports, so she pursued a degree in exercise science at San Diego State University (SDSU). There, she became active in the emerging environmental movement by pushing for recycling bins on campus. She also worked in the Women's Studies Department where she developed an interest in the treatment of women in the workplace and in society. On top of this, she was leading backpacking, rock climbing, and canoe trips into the California wilderness through The Leisure Connection, an SDSU on-campus program. She also took a "Conservation of Wildlife" class and completed the docent training program at the San Diego Natural History Museum.

Lori had always been interested in the outdoors and wildlife, having camped with her family. These college classes and outings spiked her interest in conservation, connecting her campus activism in recycling with the impact that trash had on the environment. In 1990, she was on the founding board of directors of San Diego's "Earth Day" and helped promote and organize the first Earth Fair in Balboa Park that year.

After she graduated, she began teaching sports, computer science, and women's studies. She was a coach at San Diego City College, Clairemont High School, Hoover High School, and Madison High School. Later, she worked as a professor and administrator in the San Diego Community College District where she taught Business Information Technology. She also managed Department of Labor grants used to provide technical skills and training to "at–risk" students from economically depressed communities. At the University of California at San Diego (UCSD), School of Communication, she taught "Computers and Communication" and at SDSU, her alma mater, she taught "Sex, Power, and Politics."

In 1992, Lori married Dr. Tim Baumgartner, an oceanographer. The couple lived in Baja California where he was a researcher for the Mexican government. "We met at UCSD while Tim was on a sabbatical at Scripps Institution of Oceanography," Lori said. "I accompanied him to conferences and took an interest in research on climate change and its impact on fisheries." Lori recognized the key role of politics in conservation and began to write responses to environmental impact reports related to cross-border issues.

Several key moments led to her election to the Assembly. Lori worked with the Sierra Club, and was a plaintiff in a lawsuit on the Border Wastewater Treatment Center. She served on their executive committee as chapter chair and took on other leadership roles from 1993 to 1997, including chair of the Political Committee, which interviewed candidates for elected office.

Lori Saldaña, 2012 election campaign.
Courtesy of Miriam Rafferty.

After leaving the Sierra Club, all of her enthusiastic political activism would lead to her own election. In 1997, she was encouraged to volunteer on the San Diego County Democratic Central Committee and with the executive board; she also served as vice-president of the Pacific Beach Democratic Club.

In 1999, after becoming more involved in water quality programs on both sides of the U.S.-Mexican border, Lori was appointed to the Border Environment Cooperation Commission by President Bill Clinton and served until 2003. That same year, she was awarded a Research Fellowship on Cross-border Environmental Programs at the UCSD Center for U.S.-Mexico Studies. During this time she volunteered on various political campaigns of several local leaders until 2002, when she was encouraged to run for office herself.

Lori Saldaña ran for Mayor of San Diego in 2016.
Courtesy of Michael Kreizenbeck, campaign manager.

In 2004, following a vigorous campaign and much community support—especially from many enthusiastic young SDSU Chicana/Latina students who knew they were witnessing history—Lori Saldaña, a woman and a Latina, had been elected by unprecedented margins to the California State Assembly. She would represent San Diego's 76th Assembly District. That year, she had the fourth highest district voter turnout in California. "I knew it was because of so many dedicated activists who cared about their communities and the environment," Lori said. During her six years of service, Lori's commitment to the causes of her campaign never waned. She was elected chair of the Women's Caucus and became Speaker Pro Tempore, a position that allowed her to preside over the Assembly floor sessions.

Her dedication to the causes most dear to her and her supporters showed in her proposals. "I could now act on those important measures that the people were asking for," Lori recalled. She authored and coauthored several landmark bills signed into law, including bills to protect the environment, advance equality and civil rights, and improve public safety and education.

In 2006, she coauthored AB 32—the "Greenhouse Reduction Act"—that mandated the reduction of greenhouse gas emissions with the goal of returning to 1990 levels; a bill to improved funding, educational opportunities, and support for children with disabilities; and another interstate compact, to provide additional counseling support for students from military families who transfer from state to state.

An innovator and champion of people's rights, Lori coauthored the nation's first "Marriage Equality" bill (AB 848) and in September 2005 she was the only San Diego Assembly member to support the measure. In 2007, she also authored AB 1103, which mandated disclosure of energy consumption, encouraging increased efficiency in commercial buildings, while promoting smart, green energy, and construction policies. In her concern for the elderly, she authored other laws to ensure adequate state funding for affordable housing for seniors and measures to protect their investments in long-term care insurance.

Along with her passion for the environment, for women, and for the elderly, Lori Saldaña is proud of having involved young people in the process. She hired and relied on young staff and interns for her six years in office. Through this diverse and extensive experience in political activism and legislative work, Lori is proudest of her relationship with young people. "Of all of the accomplishments," Lori says, "I'm grateful for being able to provide positive learning and leadership experience for young people in my office." Lori strongly believes that their participation gave them policy experience in many areas, helping to create the next generation of community and state leaders.

About the Author:

CASSIE MORTON ROCHIN. Born and raised in Georgia, Cassie developed an early interest in cultures, and majored in cultural anthropology with an emphasis in Meso-America at UCLA. She then got a degree in rehabilitation counseling at SDSU. After marriage to her first husband and raising three children, she returned to the workplace at San Diego Community College District, where she served as a counselor and dean. She and Lori worked together on one of these large grant projects, addressing out of school youth in mid-city San Diego. Married again, Cassie is now retired, works part time as a counselor at City College, and lives in San Diego with her husband, Refugio Rochin. She enjoys volunteer service related to foster youth in California, as well as in Africa, empowering village women with budgets and planning.

Maria Nieto Senour, 2016, San Diego.
Courtesy of Cesar Gumapas.

MARIA NIETO SENOUR:

PRESIDENT SAN DIEGO COMMUNITY COLLEGE BOARD
A Perfect Fit for CBB Leadership: Generous, Compassionate, Diverse

BY ANDREA ARAGOZA

Dr. Maria Nieto Senour is a prominent Chicana leader, educator, and activist in the San Diego community. She taught for 37 years and served as program director of the Community Based Block (CBB) Multicultural Counseling and Social Justice Education Program. Her sights have always focused on diversity and social justice. That is the reason she also decided to run for San Diego Community College District Board of Trustees. No Latina had ever been elected until she and Denise Ducheny ran in 1990. After 25 years as a board member, Maria is now the board president.

Maria's personal journey is inspiring because it illustrates what is possible, even when faced with obstacles. Her story is dear to my heart because she is my mother and her history has shaped my life in many ways.

Maria grew up learning the values of diversity early on. She also saw the benefits of sharing with one another—music and food, for example—in a multicultural setting with diverse people. This sharing of culture and the obstacles she faced may be what made her the compassionate leader she is today.

My mother was born on July 20, 1943, in San Antonio, Texas, into a working-class Mexican-American family. She is the second of four children and the eldest daughter. Her mother Josefina was a brilliant, dedicated, and witty woman who always pursued her dreams. Her father Pedro was soft-spoken, humble, hard-working, playful, and generous. Josefina and Pedro met at a restaurant in Austin, Texas, where she worked as a waitress and he played guitar in a trio. They both described the encounter as love at first sight and soon after were married. They opened "Casa Loma" with family, the first integrated restaurant in Austin, Texas. Many well-known musicians, including Count Basie and Ruth Brown, were Casa Loma customers, because, regardless of race, the entire band could eat together without fear of discrimination.

However, the Nieto family moved frequently in search of better opportunities. Thus, throughout her childhood, Maria experienced a great deal of instability, which included living in three different cities, moving to dozens of homes, and attending ten different schools, including four different high schools. When Maria was 14, her mother was diagnosed with bipolar disorder and hospitalized for most of the subsequent 12 years. While her father worked three part-time jobs, Maria cleaned houses, babysat, and sold snacks at the concession stand at a movie theater.

Through it all, she earned her high school diploma in Detroit at the age of 16. Despite her father's concerns, Maria enrolled in college with the hope that she could eventually support her family and help them move out of the Detroit housing projects where they lived for several years. She attended Marygrove College in Detroit with help from a Ford Foundation scholarship she earned. My mother remembers having to borrow her classmates' books when they weren't using them. She managed to graduate with a bachelor's degree in art and education while working as a live-in nanny and housekeeper for a family with seven children.

After teaching art to elementary school students for three years, my mother earned her master's degree in counseling from the University of Toledo, later followed by her Ph.D. in counselor education from Wayne State University. That is when she met and married my father, Robert Senour, while they were both earning their doctoral degrees. They relocated to California in 1970. She worked as an elementary school counselor in Redlands, California; a psychologist at the University of California, Riverside; a visiting professor at the University of Redlands; and went on to found and teach in the Counselor Education Program at California State University, San Bernardino. During this time, my younger brother Jon Carlos and I were born.

In 1977, she took the position with the Community Based Block (CBB) Multicultural Counseling and Social Justice Education program within the Department of Counseling and School Psychology at San Diego State University (SDSU). It was in CBB that she discovered what would be her true calling. To know CBB is to know Maria.

In teaching for CBB, Maria became part of one of the most innovative faculty groups in the country in the field of counseling, particularly in the specialization of multicultural counseling and education. The CBB program attracts students who have a passion for working independently and cooperatively with individuals from ethnically and culturally diverse groups, a perfect fit for

Maria. Since its inception in 1973, CBB has awarded master's degrees in the counseling field to more people of color than any other program in California, and probably the entire country. CBB graduates describe their experience in the program as transformational, something of which Maria is extremely proud.

I am a graduate of the CBB program myself, and can honestly say that it changed my life.

Because of my mother, CBB has permeated every aspect of my life for as long as I can remember. My brother and I had the unique privilege of growing up around CBB, listening to group discussions about racism, sexism, homophobia, or presentations about counseling theories. I have fond memories of watching my mother stand in her familiar "flamingo" pose (one foot propped up on the opposite knee), while teaching in the center of a circle of students. At a very young age, I knew that my mother had a gift, and it was a gift she was imparting to other people, including me.

However, it wasn't until I was a CBB student myself that I truly understood my mother's mastery of the art of teaching, counseling, and the process of gaining self-awareness and promoting change. She has the ability to facilitate a group from seemingly unsolvable conflict to meaningful resolution, all the while gently identifying a person's positive and unintended negative influences on the group's interpersonal dynamics. One of the best gifts of my mother being a CBB faculty member is that I watched her fall in love with cohorts of students year after year. Each time new members were joining our CBB family, and often my own family, for life. In 2009, with the support of a diverse group of her loving former CBB students, my mother took care of her terminally ill husband, Denny Ollerman, my stepfather and a former SDSU faculty member in CBB, who died in 2010.

I remember the hard times, but I also remember the laughter. My mother and her family have a gift for finding humor in just about anything. We laugh with and at ourselves and at each other. Growing up, I looked forward to family gatherings because there was always lots of laughter, music, singing, and delicious food.

In addition to her CBB work, my mother has been an activist in both the university and community. At SDSU, she advocated for increasing the number of local students admitted to the university. She also worked on changing the personnel promotion process so that the faculty's work in mentoring underrepresented students and their service to the community count toward promotion and tenure. She published the first authoritative scholarly book chapter on the "Psychology of the Chicana." She has since authored and coauthored publications on issues ranging from Chicana/Latina/Mexican-American mental health, to "CBB as a Site of Praxis and Social Justice" (*Journal of Praxis in Multicultural Education*, Fall 2008). My mother certainly inspired me and my fellow CBB students to fight for social justice!

My mother's passion to educate others about working with Latinos and other underrepresented groups may partially come from her own experience of starting elementary school without speaking English, and from the racism she encountered on a daily basis in Texas segregated neighborhoods. After moving into one predominantly white neighborhood, stones and tomatoes were thrown at her family's house. In school, children who spoke Spanish would have their mouths washed out with soap. Despite these painful memories, my mother believed that change was possible, and she has worked tirelessly to make it happen.

That my mother was one of the first-ever Latinas elected to the San Diego Community College District Board of Trustees impacted my life. The timing was excellent because it was the first time I was eligible to vote; I had the privilege of voting for my mom! She has since been reelected every four years, most recently in November 2014. As a trustee, she has advocated for students of all ages, as well as for increasing staff and student diversity and success. She helped create a district policy that requires everyone who works or studies in the district to be culturally competent, that is, to be aware of other people's culture and values. One of her current goals is to bring credit courses to incarcerated people to help them gain marketable skills for when they reenter society.

My mother's many honors and awards include SDSU Professor of the Year; she received an SDSU top 25 award given to university and community leaders by then-SDSU President Stephen Weber for "Contributions to Transformational Change in San Diego." In May 2010, she was awarded SDSU's first Faculty Diversity Award.

To accomplish all of this, my mother has some defining characteristics. Like her mother, she dreams big and takes risks. Like her father, she works hard while still maintaining a sense of playfulness. She has the ability to focus intensely on something or someone. As her daughter, I remember feeling very special when I was with her, as she asked me many questions about my life, showing real interest in every detail. She interacts in the same way with my husband Dean, my brother Jon Carlos, and his new wife Briana. She gives that same intense focus to her students and to her work. My mother is also incredibly talented. When she has free time, she loves to paint and create stained-glass pieces. She also has a gift for music, which runs in the family. After listening to a song a few times, she'll know the lyrics and will recall them years later. As my husband says, she is one in a million! One of my mother's favorite songs is "The Impossible Dream" from the play Man of La Mancha. The ideals this song expresses match her fervor to help create a better world.

Maria Nieto Senour, 1983, Committee on Chicano Rights (CCR), 17 mile "Walk for Rights," from Our Lady of Guadalupe, San Ysidro to U.S./Mexico border in opposition to proposed Simpson/Mazzoli immigration bill.

Courtesy of Herman Baca.

About the Author:

ANDREA ARAGOZA, author of her mother Maria Nieto Senour's story. Andrea is an adult school counselor in the Sweetwater Union High School District and the proud mother of Isabella, 12, and Elias, 9. Andrea is carrying on the tradition of activism both in her career and at her children's schools.

Teresa Pascual Valladolid, 2013, San Diego.
Courtesy of David Valladolid.

TERESA PASCUAL VALLADOLID:

TRUSTEE, SOUTHWESTERN COLLEGE; LABOR RELATIONS ADVOCATE

Phenomenal Woman: Activist for MEChA, Matapang, and UFW

BY MAITE VALLADOLID GUZMAN AND EVITA VALLADOLID TAUFAASAU

We already knew that Teresa Pascual Valladolid was an advocate for the poor, the undocumented, and workers. Then we found even better language, using more poetic terms, by three women authors whose words suit her perfectly and help us tell her story.

Clarissa Pinkola Estes, author of *Women Who Run With the Wolves*, says, "Within every woman there is a wild and natural creature, a powerful force, filled with good instincts, passionate, creative, and ageless-knowing. Her name is Wild Woman, but she is an endangered species." We believe our mother encompasses and demonstrates all aspects of these qualities. As her daughters, we have had the privilege of being loved, guided, and supported by a *womyn* who has always remained true to herself and has allowed her "Wild Woman" to emerge. Teresa has not only been a powerful mother and *womyn* to us, but she has also been a significant mentor to many other individuals.

Teresa is a very accomplished *womyn* with many achievements. But, what most people don't get to see is the beauty, love, grace, and, yet, fierce attitude our mother carries within herself each day. Her involvements and work have not been easy tasks, but she has done them all almost effortlessly. She has managed this in a society that pits *womyn* against each other when they should be working together to encourage one another. Teresa has been an exemplary role model for us and many young *womyn*. Throughout all of life's conflicts and drama, Teresa models such beautiful characteristics. She never takes anything personally, allowing things to roll off her shoulders. She holds her head up high and continues on her journey to provide quality education and make this a better world for all human beings.

Author Diane Mariechild describes "A woman as the full circle. Within her is the power to create, nurture, and transform." Teresa contains all these elements of the circle. To begin, Teresa came from very humble beginnings, born to migrant farmworker parents; her father came from the Philippines and her mother from Mexico. Her parents both sacrificed much to come to the United States, not only for themselves but for their future family. They met in Imperial Valley working in the fields and packing sheds. As the eldest of six children, Teresa blazed the path for her siblings in a white racist society where assimilation was pushed on people of color. It was a time when young girls strived to be more "American," renouncing their cultural identity. Our mother shared with us that in her effort to belong, she would put baby powder on her skin so she would appear lighter.

Teresa was always a hard worker. Every summer, her parents would take her and some of her siblings to work in the fields to help support the family. However, they also stressed the importance of getting a good education to make a better living. They didn't want their children to enslave themselves to such a laborious, thankless job.

Little did Teresa know that the seed planted by her parents would soon affect her own experiences and the rest of her life journey. She would be transformed in such a way that she would "create, nurture, and transform" not only herself and family, but others in the community around her.

Teresa first attended community college at Imperial Valley College and then transferred to San Diego State University (SDSU). She was the first in her family to attend college, with many of her siblings to follow. It was during her SDSU days where that seed began to grow; Teresa became empowered and proud of her Mestiza culture. The memories of her childhood summers in the fields also began to bring forth a new perspective of not only the inequalities in her community, but of all the injustices prevalent in the world. She began to truly understand and appreciate her parent's teachings, the value of an education, the importance of activism, and making a difference for our people—all people, no matter who they are or where they come from.

Author and Poet Laureate, Maya Angelou, describes a Phenomenal Woman as someone "who ought to make you proud." In the words of this famous author, Teresa is a "Phenomenal Woman." She was one of the many founders of the Movimiento Estudiantil Chicano de Aztlán (MEChA) in San Diego. She was also a founder of Matapang, a social justice Filipino student group at SDSU. In fact, she was very involved in the Chicano Movement for equal justice and civil rights and, at the same time, became actively involved in the Cesar Chavez United Farm Worker Movement (UFW). In addition, Teresa, along with many beautiful and amazing Chicanos and African-Americans, brought together these two powerful movements during the Chicano and African-American Civil Rights Movements of the 1960s-1970s; in doing so, they overcame much potential strife.

After graduating from SDSU with a bachelor of arts degree in Mexican-American Studies, she was hired by the TRIO Program, part of the SDSU Educational Opportunity Program (EOP), where she worked for over five years. While working at SDSU, Teresa met her match, David Valladolid, an activist for social justice like her. They were married in the 1980s; they had two beautiful daughters, Maite and Evita.

Words like creative, nurturing, and phenomenal, from the authors mentioned here, best describe our mother. Besides raising us, she has worked in the community for over 45 years, dedicating her life, heart, and passion to empower many individuals. Although she still resides in San Diego, she did not fail to return to her home community to help organize farmworkers for better working conditions in Imperial County and throughout California. Teresa would drive three days out of the work week to the Imperial Valley to support the farmworkers, inspiring them and giving them a voice.

Teresa's dedication is evident in the work she has done. She is a *womyn* who has contributed much to organized labor causes, having worked more than 27 years for the American Federation of State, County and Municipal Employees (AFSCME), United Domestic Workers, and the Service Employees International Union (SEIU). She also served on the UCLA Labor Center Advisory Board. Then, in the past six years, Teresa has worked as a labor relations advocate at the University of California, San Diego (UCSD).

During the time Teresa has been an advocate for labor rights, she has also worked for women's rights, voter rights, and immigrant rights. Over the years, Teresa has been involved in many organizations and many boards. For women's rights and voter rights, they include MANA, a national women's organization; League of Women Voters; Southwest Voter Registration and Education Project; Get out the Vote Campaign, San Diego; and Latino Vote USA in San Diego, where she was co-chair in 1996.

Teresa also works hard for immigrant rights and equal education. She served at the Center for Migrant Services Board of Directors and is a member of the Filipino Rights Organization. She has had the privilege of being a keynote speaker for the Asian and Pacific Islander Student Alliance at UCSD. Other student organizations she has participated in, because she has cared so much about equal rights in education, were the Chicano/Latino Coalition at Southwestern College and the Association of Chicana Activists (ACHA) at SDSU.

Teresa has also been a guest lecturer for the Graduate School for Social Planning and Policy at UCSD; the Mexican American Studies Department at SDSU; the Chicano/Latino Graduation at San Diego City College; and for the First Annual Filipino Education Summit at Chula Vista. She has also served on the SDSU Academic Review Committee and the Chicano Federation Board of Directors. She is a member of the South Bay Forum and the American Civil Liberties Union (ACLU).

In 1998, Teresa was elected to the Southwestern Community College Board of Trustees and served for 16 years. It is important to acknowledge the great achievements that were attained during her extensive term. She was a dedicated and tireless worker, attending hundreds of events and meetings at the college, in addition to the required monthly board meeting. During her tenure, Southwestern opened three new Higher Education Centers in National City, Otay Mesa, and San Ysidro; the college's DeVore Stadium was renovated. Teresa was instrumental in the passing of two general obligation bonds, one worth more than $500 million in construction for the college and the other, a resolution to rename the college mascot the Jaguars, instead of the Apaches, out of respect for indigenous cultures.

Although she was very involved in the community, Teresa was also the nurturer creator; she still found time to give us, her daughters, a loving, well-rounded, and active childhood. She was a soccer mom, a ballet mom, a gymnastics mom, a tutor, and so much more. She attended countless school field trips, yet always made sure dinner was on the table every night. She did all of this, while working more than your typical eight-to-five job. All of her community involvement, while taking care of us, makes her nothing less than incredible. She was and is our role model, our hero, our friend; she has molded us into the beautiful and loving *womyn* and mothers that we are today. She showed us that even with all the hurdles in life, you can do anything you set your mind to.

Our mother has overcome obstacle after obstacle since she was a child. And that is why the words of America's poet laureate, Maya Angelou, sound so much like our mother. We know better than anyone that our mother is a "Phenomenal Woman."

About the Authors:

MAITE VALLADOLID GUZMAN: mother, wife, daughter, sister, aunt, niece and granddaughter. M.A. in Education, SDSU, with a specialization in multicultural counseling–Community Based Block Program. Currently a Family Support Partner (FSP) for the Non-Profit Organization, SAY San Diego; and EVITA VALLADOLID TAUFAASAU: wife and proud mother of two. Previous Credit Union Financial Representative; currently full-time wife and mom.

PART III: THE FUTURE

TODAY'S ACTIVISTS INSPIRED BY THE PREVIOUS GENERATION

CHAPTER 11

CARMEN CHAVEZ

GUADALUPE CORONA

NORMA CHÁVEZ PETERSON

ADRIANA JASSO

CONSUELO MANRÍQUEZ

ELSA SEVILLA

CHAPTER 11

Chicanas for Innovative Change and Public Service

In these last two chapters, the reader will learn about Chicana activists who are making a difference in the community today. Some of them come from immigrant backgrounds that have both influenced and inspired their determination to seek justice for their communities. Their lives were affected by the Civil Rights Movement and the women who came before them.

As the Civil Rights Movement began to take on a different momentum in the United States, along with various other movements of the late 1970s, the 1980s gave the illusion that there had been some change in the political and socioeconomic spheres for people of color and women. It appeared to be the era when people of color and women became more visible in mainstream jobs. Programs like affirmative action had helped open up employment and educational opportunities, but with some backlash. For instance, as early as 1978, in the landmark case of the Regents of the University of California vs. Bakke, the U.S. Supreme Court ruled that using racial quotas in the admissions process was unconstitutional (Marin and Horn. *Realizing Bakke's Legacy: Affirmative Action, Equal Opportunity, and Access to Higher Education.* Stylus Publishing, 2008).

This "push back" of affirmative action programs and other civil rights gains continued well into the nineties and to the present. The Civil Rights Act of 1964 required educational institutions receiving federal monies to make efforts to balance diversity or face losing such funding. As a result, more Chicanos /Latinos were becoming teachers, doctors, lawyers, and other professionals; however, their percentages were disproportionate to their populations. Thus, for the majority of people of color, their social, economic, and political status had changed little by the 1980s. Young people of color still had the highest school dropout rates, made up the majority of the defendants in the criminal justice system, were the lowest-paid wage earners, and had very little political representation (Bean and Tienda. *The Hispanic Population of the United States.* Russell Sage, 1987).

By the 1990s, racism in the United States had become more sophisticated and discreet as a response to the Civil Rights Act of 1964. It had become illegal to discriminate on the basis of race, color, religion, sex, and national origins in public facilities and private businesses. Even so, affirmative action programs continued to be challenged and dismantled and anti-immigrant views again began to resurface.

In 1994, California's Proposition 187, known as the "Save Our State" initiative, was passed by voters. It sought to establish a state-run citizenship system to prohibit undocumented persons, labeled "illegal aliens," from using health care, public education, and other services in California (Ramirez. "Multicultural Empowerment." *Stanford Law Review*, 1995.) However, the proposition would eventually be declared unconstitutional by a federal district court. All these conditions brought forth a new generation of Chicana activists seeking justice, having been inspired by their own experiences and by those who came before them, whether their families, mentors, or other Chicanas/Latinas. By focusing their activism on different issues affecting their communities, Chicanas continued moving forward in their efforts to make our society gentler, more compassionate, and equitable.

Chicanas who grew up in segregated neighborhoods still graduated from college and developed professional skills that would benefit their communities. One of them is Carmen Chavez, now a practicing attorney, who was raised in different *barrios* throughout San Diego. Like her parents, she learned the importance of getting involved and giving back to her community. She became aware as a child that people were treated differently due to their racial or economic status. In high school, she came to understand more fully how poverty could determine a person's educational access and life choices. As a result, she became an activist while a student at San Diego State University (SDSU) and was inspired to study law. Carmen is now director of Casa Cornelia Law Center in San Diego, a Catholic faith-based nonprofit organization that provides free legal services to indigents, especially children, within immigrant communities who suffer from human and civil rights violations.

Chicana student activists would again organize women's support groups at the college level in the 1990's. Dr. Guadalupe Rodriguez Corona, first in her family to go to college, understood the value of sacrifice and commitment. When her parents divorced, as the eldest of four children, she became a second mother to her siblings because her mother was always working to make ends meet. As a young student activist at SDSU in the 1990s, Guadalupe embraced her feminist identity and voice through political involvement in the student organization, MEChA, Movimiento Estudiantil Chicanos de Aztlán. She also saw the need for a Chicana organization committed to empowering, mentoring, and providing leadership among women. In 1991, she became co-founder of the Association of Chicana Activists (ACHA). She received a B.A. in Humanities and Mexican American Studies, with a minor in Women's Studies; a master's in Leadership Studies; and a doctorate in Educational Leadership. She is presently director of Equity, Diversity, and Inclusion at Southwestern College in Chula Vista.

Other Chicanas have thrived, even while facing discrimination as immigrants, and have persevered to become advocates for immigrant populations. Coming to the United States at age 14, and undocumented, Adriana Jasso quickly found out that she was not fully accepted in this country. Unafraid, she threw herself into the campaign against the anti-immigrant Proposition 187. This was in 1994 when she was still in high school in Oxnard, California. An honor student, she helped organize student walkouts throughout Ventura County to call attention to immigrant rights. She graduated from the University of California at San Diego (UCSD) with a B.A. and an M.A., and is now coordinator of the U.S.-Mexico Border Program for the American Friends Service Committee of San Diego which works with border issues ranging from illegal government detentions and deportations to human rights violations.

Some publicly well-recognized Chicanas like Norma Chavez have been inspired by their hard-working immigrant mothers who sought a better life for their children. Norma's mother came to this country with her seven children, spoke no English, and sometimes had to work three jobs in order to provide for them. Despite many obstacles, Norma became a leader at a young age. She saw the importance of organizing a MEChA organization as early as junior high school to engage her peers in community issues. After graduating from high school, she attended UCSD, but dropped out after marrying and becoming a young mother. Getting divorced motivated Norma to work harder to complete her degree at San Diego State where she continued to work on community issues as a student activist. After graduating and working at several jobs, she became cofounder and executive director of Justice Overcoming Boundaries (JOB), a network of faith, educational, business, and labor partners working together to advance social justice in San Diego. In 2012, Norma became the first Chicana executive director of the ACLU, a national organization dedicated to protecting people's civil rights.

Other immigrants have become important educational and cultural leaders through hard work and dedication. Consuelo "Chelo" Manriquez came to San Diego as a young girl via Mexicali and Tijuana, Baja California, Mexico. In addition to being an educator, publisher, and founder of Calaca Press, she is also an artist and activist. Consuelo became principal of the School for the Performing Arts in the San Diego Unified School District, and later, principal of King-Chavez Community High School. Today, she continues to play an active role in organizations, seeking to promote quality education for diverse communities, such as Educate for the Future. She is also a member of the CPSC (Chicano Park Steering Committee) and still finds time to organize events to commemorate International Women's Day every year.

Another educational and cultural leader, well known in San Diego as a television personality is Elsa Sevilla. Elsa's mother encouraged each one of her children to seek a career. Growing up with four brothers, and the youngest of four girls, Elsa had to figure out quickly how to make her presence known. Her love of journalism and her ethnic identity took her on a journey whereby she has become the present host of the KPBS television program "San Diego's Historic Places" and the cofounder of Sevilla Productions, a family owned business. Elsa credits her mother, sisters, and MANA San Diego, a women's national organization, for much of her success. Elsa continues to make documentaries through her company and helps raise scholarship funds to benefit local Latinas seeking an education. She also encourages and mentors journalism students as well as new journalists in television.

The stories featured in this section show brilliant and successful immigrant women, or the daughters of immigrants, who have contributed much to the quality and fabric of society.

CARMEN CHAVEZ:

CEO, CASA CORNELIA LAW CENTER/IMMIGRANT RIGHTS
Her Voice and Actions Work for Justice with Compassion

BY VERONICA BONILLA

Carmen Chavez's dream to become an attorney grew from her desire to help others.

Her motivation developed from observing her parents actively engage in their community. She learned early on that giving and sharing were essential elements to a meaningful life. In college, she was chairperson of the student organization MEChA, Movimiento Estudiantil Chicano de Aztlán; an organizer of high school conferences for Latinos and Latinas entering higher education; a participant in the Chicano Leadership Camp; and a board member of the Chicano Federation of San Diego County. Her dream to study law was realized with the help of mentors who encouraged her.

In 2000, as a result of her dedication at Casa Cornelia Law Center, Carmen received the Equal Justice Works Fellowship, which allowed her to continue her public service work. Behind it all is her passion for representing in immigration court, children who have been abused, abandoned, and neglected; immigrant victims of domestic violence; and asylum seekers. Today, she is president and CEO of Casa Cornelia Law Center and well known as an involved activist for law and social justice, especially for the rights of children.

I could write more about all of her accomplishments and the journey that led her to where she is today. I could mention the obstacles she has overcome, the motivations that drive her, and all the awards and nominations she has received. They are all impressive and she is deserving of all of them. However, what I find most admirable about Carmen Chavez is more basic, accessible, and easily overlooked. These traits are more everlasting, consistent, and unbreakable, and very few people possess them. They are what, above all, sets her apart from other leaders. She is a good and humble woman. These traits are behind the faith that led Carmen to take the first step toward fulfilling her dream to become an attorney.

I met Carmen Chavez in 2012 when I began volunteering at Casa Cornelia Law Center. She is the CEO of the nonprofit immigration law center that serves many people who have no legal resources. From the beginning, Carmen was very engaging and has remained the same throughout the time that I have known her. Over time, I have gotten to know her a bit better, mostly as a leader and role model. She maintains her professionalism at all times as well as a sense of humor. I have seen her in countless interactions with people from all walks of life, including volunteers, attorneys, delivery personnel, and even the janitor, because sometimes she stays at work very late. From where I sit, I can hear her sing and laugh in her office. The one characteristic that stands out is that she treats everyone the same. That quality adds to her integrity.

To better illustrate where and how her legacy began, Carmen was born and raised in San Diego; she grew up in San Ysidro, City Heights, and other areas heavily populated by Mexican families. Her parents were both hard working, strong individuals who looked out for the benefit of the community. Her mother is very extroverted and flamboyant; her father is more reserved, but just as involved in helping others. Through their example, Carmen saw generosity and concern for the welfare of the community, not limited to self-interest or just the family unit. This good example nurtured from childhood has followed her since then. Carmen expresses it this way, "Giving is a necessity for the soul and we as humans have many needs, but the power of giving can be transformational."

Her greatest observations of human nature began early. As a child, Carmen became aware that certain people were treated with indifference and lack of respect as a result of their circumstances. In high school, she saw divisions delineated by cliques and, although she could have been a part of those groups, she did not want to promote separations. She also became aware of the deficiencies in the educational system and the lack of support for at-risk youth. She responded with great concern and tells the story well. "I wanted to do something to help, but I did not know how," she says. "As a teenager my mother took me to a Latina leadership conference." It was at that conference that Carmen met a Latina judge and was "immediately drawn to the idea of becoming an empowered woman like her." As she listened to the judge speak eloquently and passionately, she said to herself, "I want to be like her!" She took the first step in that direction, visualizing herself as the woman she wanted to be. She later became involved in protests and demonstrations that expressed disapproval of the educational system's deficiencies she had observed. It was during this time that Carmen's leadership began to develop.

At first, she considered herself a very shy person, but noticed that others saw in her the ability to communicate assertively and effectively. They would encourage her to address the crowds; it was that demonstration of confidence by her colleagues that transformed her from a shy person to an outspoken leader. Carmen simply allowed herself to become an instrument of justice, not by mere ambition, but as a necessary step that enabled her to become the voice of the unheard.

Carmen Chavez, CEO Casa Cornelia.
Courtesy of Laura Radack.

Among the many interactions that influenced Carmen, in 1988 she met Cesar Chavez, the nonviolent leader of the United Farmworkers Union (UFW). She simply described him as "a good and humble man." She noticed that he did not need to say much to convey his message. She saw him as a man who inspired many with his presence, his actions, and few words. She admired Cesar Chavez as the main figure of the nonviolent Civil Rights Movement who worked to improve the working and living conditions of farm workers and their families.

He was the leader who first established the National Farm Workers Association and initiated numerous demonstrations until he gained the attention necessary to make change possible.

Carmen saw Cesar Chavez, along with the strength and leadership of Dolores Huerta, UFW, United Farm Worker leaders, as advocates for nonviolence and education. These two leaders educated the people at public events and also spoke to students about justice, education, and nonviolence. It was one of those presentations that Carmen, as a student leader, coordinated at her college campus. However, she faced opposition from the Associated Student Council, since some of the students were the children of California growers whose lives were affected by the boycotts and protests of the UFW Movement. Nevertheless, Carmen proceeded with the program. With persistence and diligence, her student organization succeeded in bringing the presentation to campus. She vividly remembers introducing Dolores Huerta to a large and enthusiastic crowd at San Diego State University. This experience continued to foster an incessant need in her to pursue justice and equality for those in vulnerable circumstances.

Carmen continued her education. After graduating from college, she began working for the County of San Diego as a benefits analyst. She once again became aware of discriminatory behaviors against disadvantaged persons, and her desire to change those practices continued. Carmen recalls that employees in her office would demonstrate irritation and lack of empathy for the clients in need. They were in a position to help, but when clients called them, they would openly show signs of annoyance. Carmen was perplexed by the negative attitudes of workers in positions of authority who showed very little compassion for the people they were there to serve. At this point, becoming a lawyer seemed to be the appropriate career for the goals she had in mind. After many trials and obstacles, with the encouragement of a mentor, she remained on her true path.

Her major obstacle—as it has been for many others with similar backgrounds—was the lack of information and experience. Some children grow up surrounded by professionals in different fields and are generally encouraged to pursue higher education. Others grow up under different circumstances, surrounded by teen pregnancy, gang violence, and even drugs. The people in their lives may be laborers, gardeners, security guards, caretakers, or domestic workers. They might also face high school counselors who believe it would be a waste of government aid to send kids from low-income neighborhoods to institutions of higher education. It is harder for people like these to gain access to someone who has successfully navigated the educational system and is willing to share that invaluable knowledge. Although Carmen knew she wanted to be an attorney, she did not know how to pursue her goal. That is why she is eternally grateful to Ann Durst, a mentor who shared valuable information with her, encouraging her to try again, to study harder, and to go forth with her plan to become a lawyer.

Just as there were friends and cheerleaders who guided her along, Carmen now consistently does the same for countless students, volunteers, staff, and clients. By sharing her experiences and setting an exceptional example for others, she has made lasting impressions. She shared with me stories about former volunteers who told her that they had gone to law school because she had transformed their hopes into determination. Some even chose Loyola Law School because that is where Carmen received her degree. She recently heard from a former intern who is currently working for a U.S. Senator. The list goes on of people who have succeeded in their careers because their lives were touched by Carmen's words and presence. They see her as a good leader. They recognize that she moves forward with passion because that is her purpose in life. Carmen is grateful for their appreciation.

She also values letters she receives from the people she serves who are most vulnerable, clients who were given an opportunity to start a new life. They share their gratitude with her. One of them said, "While I was in detention two and half years ago, I lost everything and beyond that all my hope! And then one day someone said, 'If you lose money, you lose one thing. If you lose health, you lose something. If you lose hope, you lose everything.'" Carmen understands their suffering. These letters remind her how important the work is of Casa Cornelia. Another person wrote, "I can't find a way to start, but I would like to thank you for being so helpful to me. You have opened the road that was dark for me. I was scared to walk through it with my girls but thanks to you and all your help that dark road now has light and I'm not so scared to start walking. Thanks for all your hard work."

These letters also remind us that the world needs more leaders like Carmen who are willing to stand in the front lines, because extraordinary leadership is easy to follow.

So, what is it about Carmen that makes her different? In her many interactions, I have noticed that she stays true to one thing: she treats everyone with respect and fairness. Not only does she treat people equally, but she makes every client, every member, and every contributor feel like an important and unique part of the organization and the mission. Carmen introduces everyone not only by name, but by all the things she admires about that person. She wants everyone to understand that giving is a necessity for the soul and sharing gives us a reason to live; it gives us hope to work for something bigger than ourselves, a cause, a selfless contribution that will benefit both the giver and the receiver.

Carmen leads by example. By demonstrating her commitment every minute of the day, she has that ability to convey a message in a few words. Most recently her greatest concerns are with the President's Executive Order on immigration. She said,

"We share the anguish of many as we consider the consequences of the President 's Executive Orders impacting immigrants and refugees. . . Policy change will require the detention of all undocumented persons seeking refuge at the border, including the hundreds of unaccompanied children and asylum seekers who depend on us."

A letter from Casa Cornelia described the Immigration Courts as currently having a backload of some 500,000 cases. Detaining thousands more while they await a hearing will, in effect, result in prolonged detention—not for criminals but for victims. Carmen's concern is that "these measures will stigmatize and marginalize the already vulnerable communities that make up our client base."

Carmen continues to give her all, building on what she has achieved with hard work, dedication, and compassion. She can talk to anyone as if they were a close friend, a special individual, or just as a person deserving of attention and respect. She can comfort a crying mother, a battered victim of crime, or an asylee who speaks little English, and restore their hope. She understands that Casa Cornelia is only able to provide quality legal protection for immigrant victims of human and civil rights violations. Even so, her words are reassuring, honest, and generous. They confirm that she has surpassed her goal of becoming an empowered professional woman. She is, above all, a good and humble woman.

About the Author:

VERONICA BONILLA is a proud veteran of the United States Marine Corps. She is a graduate of San Diego State University with a degree in Spanish and Chicana and Chicano Studies. Veronica currently works as a legal assistant in the Human Trafficking Program at Casa Cornelia Law Center.

GUADALUPE CORONA:

DIRECTOR OF EQUITY, DIVERSITY AND INCLUSION AT SOUTHWESTERN COLLEGE

Cofounder of ACHA, Association of Chicana Activists

BY VENUS MOLINA

To know Dr. Guadalupe Rodriguez Corona is to know sacrifice, commitment, and success.

When I asked Guadalupe how she identified herself, she responded, "*Soy Chicana Fronteriza.* I am from both sides of the border, not only Mexicana or only American.*"

Guadalupe was born in National City in 1971 to immigrant Mexican parents, her mother from Culiacán, Sinaloa, and her father from Autlán de Navarro, Jalisco. Her family relocated to Tijuana, Mexico after her birth, moving in with her father's family because of economic necessity. In 1977, the family crossed the border back to the United States and stayed in South San Diego for a few years. Guadalupe started school at Otay Elementary School, which then had a bilingual program that helped her transition into the English language.

In the early 1980s, her father—a carpenter by trade who worked in construction—was hired to take care of an avocado ranch in Escondido, California, where he moved his family. Guadalupe started her high school education at Orange Glen High School. Although it was mostly a white student body, Orange Glen had a Migrant Education Program for students like Guadalupe. Migrant Education Programs assist and support migrant children and their families in school contexts such as academics, counseling, and social experiences.

Guadalupe's mother joined the Migrant Education Parent Committee and in time became more involved in her children's education. With her mother's support, Guadalupe excelled academically. The Migrant Education Program provided opportunities to visit colleges. It was during a visit to San Diego State University for the Movimiento Estudiantil Chicano de Aztlán (MEChA) High School Conference that she made a decision to go to college. She recalls that when

Guadalupe Corona, official photo KPBS Hispanic Heritage Month, Local Heroes Award.

Courtesy of Melissa Jacobs.

she approached her high school counselor about taking classes in order to go to college, he told her, "Why waste your time? You migrant girls get pregnant at 15." Determined to get the required college courses, she and her mother persisted until the counselor agreed to enroll her in the appropriate classes.

During her youth, her father would leave her mother to go live in Tijuana. Guadalupe and her mother had to then figure out how they would live on welfare and food stamps. The family moved back to South San Diego shortly afterward. In spite of her mother working full time to support the family, they lived in poverty. Guadalupe remembers accompanying her mother to the welfare office, helping her obtain assistance to make ends meet, and serving as her mother's interpreter. She recalls how her mother was creative in using government cheese to feed her and her siblings. Most importantly, her mother reminded Guadalupe how angry she would get when they would claim to have lost her mother's documents after hours of waiting to get support from government agencies. Her mother told her,

"You were so angry that you said you were going to work really hard so that others would not have to be treated this way." Guadalupe enrolled at Montgomery High School, which historically had a student population of predominantly Filipino and Mexican American students. In her sophomore year, she joined MEChA, the student organization that promoted mostly culturally relevant activities. It was during this time that Guadalupe was part of the group that founded the first Spanish-language newspaper in the history of the school, *La Voz Azteca*. Furthermore, the newspaper experience empowered Guadalupe to seek a student government position at Montgomery High School. An important life changing experience for this young *Chicanita* was the day she was elected vice president of the student body. She had won an election against the current class president— the quarterback of the football team—although she was the new kid at the school. She was so inspiring to others that many students came out at 7 a.m. the day of the election to support her; this group of student leaders she didn't know were led by one student who wanted to support her. She had taken the time to organize a group of students to stuff lockers that morning with flyers saying, "Vote for an Aztec; vote for Guadalupe Corona." This event marked Guadalupe's life forever. To know you can inspire change and get people out to do something about it has been Guadalupe's legacy.

A short time later, Guadalupe and her family moved again to another area in San Diego County, this time to Spring Valley. At Mount Miguel High School, Guadalupe got involved with MEChA again, and became part of the leadership team. She shared an experience from that time, remembering how MEChA, along with other ethnic student organizations, planned a major multicultural event to raise money for scholarships. However, the school principal would not allow the event to take place. Thus, Guadalupe and some of her MEChA peers sought the help from then Assembly member Peter Chacon, who represented the 77th District; and Gus Chavez, then director of the Educational Opportunity Program (EOP) at San Diego State University. With the assistance of Irma Muñoz, who worked at Chacon's office, the event took place, but by then all the other groups had dropped out due to the political upheaval that had transpired. This incident was a critical point in Guadalupe's life. As a young Chicana, she learned about the power people can have when they organize for social justice.

First in her family to go to college, Guadalupe entered San Diego State University in 1989, with her eye on becoming a journalist. That spring semester, she became chairwoman of MEChA, and then got married in her second year. In 1991, with the help of Chicana and Chicano Studies Professor Isidro Ortiz, Guadalupe attended the National Education for Women's Leadership Conference sponsored by the Center for American Women in Politics (CAWP) where she met influential feminists like Gloria Steinem and Bella Abzug. Identifying herself as a Chicana feminist, Guadalupe cofounded the Association of Chicana Activists (AChA) along with Silvia Bustamante, Martha Cervantes, Dr. Rosa Hernandez, Maria Del Carmen Mendez, Lorena T. Valenzuela, and Teresa Zamora that same year at SDSU. AChA is a Chicana organization with the purpose of "empowering, mentoring, and providing leadership in the community."

Guadalupe's political involvement would eventually branch out to work with students of color coalitions that led to her being elected executive vice president of the SDSU Associated Student Body (ASB) in 1992. She credits other women like Carmen Chavez and Cynthia Rico for their encouragement and mentoring. Guadalupe was the first woman to run for and win this position—while six months pregnant, carrying 21 units, and later, taking care of a newborn. Besides that, as executive vice president of finance, she helped oversee a 6.5 million-dollar budget. Guadalupe served the ASB in different positions throughout her years at SDSU until 1995.

After receiving a bachelor's degree in humanities with a Mexican American studies focus and a minor in women's studies from SDSU, Guadalupe enrolled at the University of San Diego (USD) to work on her master's in leadership studies and was also hired as a graduate assistant. That same year, she cofounded AChA at USD, and in 1997 she earned a master's in leadership studies. Continuing her community involvement, in 1999 she became vice chair and later president of the board of directors at Centro Cultural de la Raza in San Diego.

In 2002, she became assistant director of the United Front Multicultural Center and later its director at USD. During her ten-year tenure at the United Front Multicultural Center, Guadalupe not only worked to support students to succeed academically, but engaged them in social issues confronting the university and the community.

Hate crimes seemed to be running rampant at this time, from USD where racial slurs were being posted at the campus against people of color, to Imperial Beach where undocumented people were being killed. Guadalupe was always at the forefront to confront the issues by organizing and working with all stakeholders to bring diversity, policy change, and to push back hate culture. Today she concludes that the 1990s represent the decade of diversity for students of color at universities; students of color ran for and were elected to student government, and an ethnic studies major was implemented and later became a department at USD.

In 2007, Guadalupe became system wide director of the Latino/a Achievement Initiative at Alliant International University. In 2010, she received her doctorate in leadership studies from the University of San Diego. In 2015, she became director of the office of International Students and Student Scholars at Alliant University.

Tackling issues of racism, inequality, and discrimination are points of passion for this dedicated woman. Her service in these areas makes her an integral part of our progress. Not only is she an advocate for the Latino community, but she has worked extensively for the advancement and advocacy of the underprivileged and underserved of all racial, ethnic, and socioeconomic backgrounds. Her level of academic success stands as a testament to her drive and gumption. Currently, Guadalupe is the Director of Equity, Inclusion, and Diversity for Southwestern Community College in Chula Vista, California. There, she continues to inspire young students to pursue their dreams of a higher education. She is personally committed to the South Bay community, where her roots help her to lead a very important department at Southwestern College.

Guadalupe has worked tirelessly to overcome obstacles and barriers set by family, society, and school in order to pursue a higher education that has not only led to her personal success, but also allows her the opportunity to give back to her community. She has not only paved the way for Chicanas/Latinas, but for all community members of different backgrounds. This has made her an inspiration to those who dream of rising above their circumstances and who want to make a positive impact in the world, especially because she did it all while raising two sons. What do you call a woman that takes on challenges head on? I would say *chingona*, a hard driving, assertive Chicana.

Guadalupe Corona, ACHA (Association of Chicana Activists) Women's March at SDSU.

Courtesy of Guadalupe Corona.

About the Author:

VENUS MOLINA is Director of Community Affairs and Government Relations for the Jacobs Center for Neighborhood Innovation; Vice-President of MANA of San Diego; graduate of the University of San Diego in International Relations; and member of the Harvard Business Club of San Diego.

Norma Chavez Peterson, director ACLU.

Courtesy of Marcia Shields.

NORMA CHÁVEZ PETERSON:

FIRST CHICANA EXECUTIVE DIRECTOR FOR ACLU, SAN DIEGO AND IMPERIAL COUNTIES

Her Dream is to Create a World Where There is True Equity, Respect and Dignity for All

BY BIANCA BOYER

Norma Chávez Peterson is a beautiful Chicana role model. An immigrant herself, she is a powerful advocate for immigrant rights. I admire her as a woman and feel blessed to have worked with her in the past. Norma has a vision for San Diego and the experience to carry it out. She is dedicated to the community she lives in, and she wants to make San Diego a better place to live. The reason: Norma cares about people. She talks to people, informs them, and finds answers to help make the quality of life better for those in the daily struggle. Working together with community and with other people who seek justice, Norma believes change is possible. She believes that change can be made for immigration reform, educational equality, women's reproductive rights, and keeping youth out of the prison system. Her big dream is focused on creating a world where there is true equity, and where respect and dignity exist for all human beings.

How is she able to accomplish such a monumental task? Norma is the executive director of the American Civil Liberties Union in San Diego and Imperial Counties. In this capacity, she is discovering that all things are possible when people work together for human rights. Many people who have seen her in action trust her judgment in her continued support for equal protection for all people under the law. They already know her experience, energy, and passion. Building "people power" is her strength. She makes others feel part of a collective struggle by finding individual voices and uniting them in a common cause apart from alienation, to keep them from feeling alone.

I first met Norma in Logan Heights at an Immigration Task Force meeting sponsored through Justice Overcoming Boundaries (JOB), a nonprofit interfaith community based organization that works to advance social justice in San

Diego. The first thing I noticed about her was her very genuine smile. That is the authentic reception we got when she greeted my *tía*, my dad Cesar Lopez, and me. My family loved her; I could tell by the hugs they gave each other.

At that time, Norma and my family invited me to a meeting concerning naturalization workshops. These workshops were to assist immigrants with legal permanent resident status, ones who had been in the country for a long time, to begin the difficult process of applying for U.S. citizenship. At the workshop, I learned how to help people fill out the paperwork and anything else that was required as part of the legalization process. Also attending the meetings were community activists, lawyers, teachers, students, counselors, and people of all ages who wanted to contribute to this needed service in our neighborhoods.

For more than two decades, Norma has played a key role in many organizing and mobilization efforts, including the largest pro-immigration march in the history of San Diego called the "March for Dignity, Respect, and Hope." That 2006 march stood against the passage of the Sensenbrenner Bill HR4437, and in support of a real path to citizenship and legalization for the close to 12 million undocumented immigrants living in the United States.

Recently, Norma and I met near Mesa College where one of Norma's daughters attends school. Knowing the kind of work she does at ACLU, and the work she does at home in partnership with her husband, raising three daughters, I asked, "How do you do it all?" She laughed and answered, "I ask myself, 'How did *my mom* do it all? How did she manage to clean, work, cook, take care of seven kids, as a single mother and an immigrant in a new country, not speaking English?'" She continued, "I get my strength from my mom and seeing how she worked so hard. Sometimes she would have three jobs. She wanted us to have a better life. We were poor and we had no father in the home; we all could have easily gone down a destructive path. But I found an outlet for financial stress and turned it into determination, and for me, that was school. My mom taught us that "education is the key to success and freedom." Norma says her mother is her best example and inspiration for working hard.

Norma was born in La Piedad, Michoacán, Mexico, in 1974. Norma's father, a migrant worker in the 60s and 70s, came to the U.S. to work, leaving her mother, Esperanza, and his children to live with their maternal grandmother, Felicitas, in her improvised rancho. Eventually he established another family in Baja California Norte. After struggling to provide for basic needs for her children at the rancho, Norma's mother decided to come to *El Norte* (the U.S.). Norma and five of her six siblings were brought to the United States by her mother, temporally settling in Santa Barbara, California. Her mother worked multiple jobs to be able to support herself and her children and had to rely on the oldest child, Juanita, who had come to this country at the age to 16, to be the second source of income and also the second parent. Norma's mother worked packing avocados, cleaning hotel rooms, laboring in factories, and even in the fields. They were undocumented, living in the country without the required papers until they were granted legalization in 1986. Through the Immigration Reform and Control Act (Simpson–Mazzoli Act), legalization opened many doors for Norma's family. It ultimately created the opportunities for her and her siblings to become administrators in higher education, academic professionals, accomplished community organizers, advocates, educators, law enforcement professionals, and small business owners.

Norma's social consciousness began to develop when she was in junior high school and had the opportunity to visit the high school and first learned about a student organization called MEChA, Movimiento Estudiantil Chicano de Aztlán. It was during those teenage years, that Norma was searching for a sense of identity, trying to figure out how she, her family and her people fit into the narrative of this country. Norma, along with her friend Patty Curioca, worked with others to start a MEChA chapter at Chula Vista Junior High School. Norma went on to attend Chula Vista High School, where she continued her involvement with MEChA. It was during this period that she was exposed to progressive Chicana/o students from San Diego State University. These students began to introduce her to Chicano literature and history. She began to attend protests against police and border patrol abuses with the late Roberto Martinez, the revered director of the U.S.–Mexico Border Program for the American Friends Service Committee. Attending these demonstrations, becoming friends with politicized college students, and becoming an active MEChA leader, led Norma to her career in nonprofit social justice work.

She got married right after high school, attended the University of San Diego, and in 1993 gave birth to her oldest daughter, Monica Metzeri Alvarado. Soon thereafter, Norma left USD and later divorced. After attending community college, she went on to San Diego State University, graduating with a major in political science and a minor in Chicana and Chicano studies. Her journey was not easy, but she was determined to finish school and continue her community involvement through work in the nonprofit sector.

In 1995 she went to work for LISC Americorps initiative, a local support corporation, and worked on affordable housing and resident leadership programs at the Hacienda Townhomes on 17th street in what is now East Village. She was then hired at the MAAC Project where she was mentored by then executive director Roger Cazares. By her mid-twenties she was a supervisor overseeing all of the resident leadership and other program work that took place at the MAAC Project's affordable housing communities throughout San Diego County. After eight years, in 2004 Norma left to become cofounder and executive director of JOB (Justice Overcoming Boundaries) a network of faith, community, education, business, and labor partners working together to advance social justice in San Diego County, addressing economic justice, affordable housing, educational equity, immigrant rights, and racial justice.

In October 2007, during the disastrous s wildfires that engulfed parts of San Diego, one incident led to the deportation of an undocumented family from the Qualcomm Stadium evacuation site. Norma, along with JOB, helped mobilize dozens of volunteers to come to the aid of immigrants as interpreters, advocates, and legal observers in San Diego County. The result of the field operation led to the publication of a report and policy recommendations in partnership with the ACLU of San Diego and Imperial Counties titled, "Firestorm: Treatment of Vulnerable Populations During San Diego Wildfires." This collaboration is what initially connected Norma to the San Diego ACLU. Her commitment and dedication to social justice, and her extensive work experience in the nonprofit, led to Norma being hired as organizing director for the San Diego office in 2012. After being with the organization for only a year and half, ACLU conducted a national executive director search. Although initially hesitant to apply, Norma was hired as the first Latina executive director of the ACLU of San Diego and Imperial Counties in September 2013.

As director of the ACLU, Norma has built relationships and bridges with diverse groups of people and organizations to advocate for priority issues. She relates to poor communities of color in a deep way because of her own experiences. She advocates for undocumented immigrants to come out of the shadows because she can relate to their problems personally. Love and compassion drive her spirit. She is not only a strong advocate for immigrant rights, but also a champion for criminal justice reform, voting rights, all civil rights, and human rights. Her organization addresses these issues through strategic litigation, legislative advocacy, and community education and organizing.

Through it all, Norma has learned to find balance with staying healthy, working and being a wife, mother, and daughter. She has her work, her husband, Tommy "Shamroc" Peterson, and their blended family; although she admits, "Finding time to fit everything into one day can be a challenge." Keeping her spirituality in perspective allows her to maintain her peace; staying positive is what motivates her daily. She says that she also keeps in mind that "quality, not quantity" is best when she spends time with her children. "It's better to be present and engaged," she has learned while raising two younger daughters, Tehya and Amaya, and supporting her older daughter Monica, who graduated from college this year. She realizes that there will always be new challenges.

Ironically, it took a nationwide search to find the perfect candidate for the ACLU position of executive director for San Diego and Imperial Valley Counties. Norma Chavez Peterson has decades of work in San Diego's most vulnerable communities and has built a reputation of working in a collaborative way, building progressive power and leading with integrity. These are only some of the reasons she was the number one choice to be hired as executive director of the American Civil Liberties Union of San Diego and Imperial Valley and a few of the reasons that San Diego, especially the Latino community, is so proud of our *mujer* who gives us strength through her hard work and her unsurpassed love for others. Norma Chávez Peterson, thank you.

Norma Chavez Peterson with daughter Amaya at Izcalli's Dia de Los Muertos, the Jacob's Center, 2015.

Courtesy of Esperanza Chavez.

About the Author:

BIANCA BOYER is a reentry student at San Diego Mesa College where she is preparing to transfer to the university. She has volunteered with U.S. Citizenship Workshops as a member of the San Diego Immigration Task Force. She has been instrumental in introducing young students to programs and curriculum for Cesar Chavez Day at Longfellow School where her children attend. She brought Ramon "Chunky" Sanchez and his music to the students; and has provided materials for the school to enhance their resources for the important State of California holiday. She lives in San Diego with her husband Brandon Boyer and two children, Tatiana and Triston.

Adriana Jasso, at home.
Courtesy of Harry Simon.

ADRIANA JASSO:

IMMIGRANT RIGHTS ADVOCATE, AMERICAN FRIENDS SERVICE COMMITTEE

Adriana's Empathy for the Value of Human Life Transcends All Borders

BY KATHLEEN ROBLES

Adriana Jasso's story starts out like that of many others who made their way into the United States by risking life and limb to cross the border, without the opportunity to secure appropriate documentation. Where it becomes unique is with the path her life took beyond that moment. Her compassion is for those in similar challenging circumstances. With resiliency for navigating through a system where the deck was clearly stacked against her, she has undeniably prevailed. Adriana's empathy for the value of human life transcends all borders; her kindness, experience, and resilience have touched and changed the lives of many. She is a true Chicana activist—empowered and transformed by her own struggles, trials, and tribulations—one who helps guide and encourage others to find their own way and their own voice.

Adriana was born in 1974 and was raised in the village of San Vicente de Tuna Agria, Romita, Guanajuato, Mexico. She is the second oldest of five children born to María de la Luz Meza and Serafín Jasso. The village operated on the concept of *milpa* farming, where each of the five extended families that comprised the population of approximately 150 residents (all related) had their own piece of the communal land. The main crops were *maíz* and *frijoles*.

Her father was rarely present during this phase of her life because he had gone to secure employment as a farmworker in the Ventura County and Fresno areas of California. He returned only twice per year to visit. Both of Adriana's grandfathers were *braceros*, guest workers in the United States, and her father followed naturally in their footsteps.

In her early years, Adriana was raised mainly by her mother. According to Adriana, the opportunities in her home village were becoming fewer. In addition, the nearest middle school was three hours away. "My mother had grown tired of raising us kids alone and wanted something better for us," Adriana said. "She made the trip to Tijuana with my oldest brother, then 14, and my youngest brother, two and a half, to cross over into the United States and join my father." Adriana's middle brother, younger sister, and she were left behind. They were raised by family, until funding could be saved up to send for them.

When the time came for Adriana and her two remaining siblings to join the rest of the family in the U.S., her father went to help the three children make the risky trek across. She recounts, "Crossing into the Unites States was a very awakening experience." Not only was it the four of them, but the group consisted of 15 people in total. When they got to the location selected for crossing, they were instructed to form a line. While Border Patrol agents were being distracted, the group had to make a run for it—200 meters—to an area near Imperial Beach, California.

On the U.S. side, her brother informed her dad that he needed to use the restroom, but the Border Patrol was milling close by. So, her father quickly lifted her and her sister into a dumpster for safe cover, and took his son to the restroom. He was stopped and questioned by an agent; he showed his green card and was let go. When the coast was clear, he retrieved the two girls from the dumpster and met up with his brother, who was waiting for them; he drove them north to Oxnard, California, where her mother and two brothers were awaiting their arrival.

Adriana began attending ninth grade at Channel Islands High School, which had a population of 3,000 students. She experienced a major transition from her small hometown community where she was related to everyone, to the new "city life," where many changes were unfolding. Speaking no English, Adriana had to partake in an English learners program. This was the first time she had been separated from her sister, who was 13 years old and enrolled in middle school. She was also re-acclimating with her mother and two of her brothers, after a yearlong separation, as well as adjusting to living with her father on a full-time basis. She described all of this as a very emotional time in her life.

The first summer following her freshman year, her father purchased a van and took the entire family to Fresno to pick grapes. She explained that he wanted his children to know what it was like to labor in the fields and to experience the physically and mentally tiring conditions of a farmworker. He rented a small trailer for a month and a half, near the fields. Adriana said without question, "it was the most painful summer of my existence. I resented my father at the time for doing that to us and for saying, 'This is what I told you the *Norte* looked like.'" She later came to respect his decision and to thank him for the "powerful educational lesson."

In 1992–1993, Adriana's senior year in high school, Pete Wilson was the governor of California when Proposition 187, meant to deny public services to immigrants, was placed on the ballot, although it was later declared unconstitutional. In the meantime, it became a heated topic, resulting in blame being placed on undocumented Mexicans for various perceived social issues. "I became very upset by the unfairness of the argument and statements being made," Adriana said. Her English teacher, Bill Terrazas, employed what she described as a "radical and incredibly conscious teaching style." He implemented Paolo Freire's critical pedagogy principles in the classroom. His students were English-language learners and "excluded barrio youth." "Mr. Terrazas actively, passionately, and without fear or apology, taught us to bring our voices to the classroom," Adriana remembers. "This served as the catalyst and turning point of my life."

Adriana began to take part in efforts that reflected her new consciousness. Organizing a Latino associated student body, or ASB, was one of her first goals. She felt that many high school activities, including ASB, were geared solely toward Anglos. Though the Latino ASB was rejected by the high school administration, Adriana found mentors outside of her high school. She received a scholarship from Future Leaders of America to travel to Washington, D.C. Her sister received an award as well. They were part of a group of 75 students from the United States and 75 students from Mexico scheduled to meet up at a conference in Washington D.C. The irony of this particular situation is that Adriana was working to facilitate change in a system that had historically marginalized and excluded specific students. Yet, when she and her sister were unable to provide social security numbers on the day of the White House tour, they were left behind, unsupervised, to fend for themselves. The entire group and chaperone staff went into the White House, while the two sisters were instructed to walk around outside and return at 5 p.m. when the tour was over.

Adriana graduated from Channel Islands High School in 1993, at a time when anti-immigration was percolating throughout the United States, and she could feel the escalating effects of being undocumented. She had built relationships beyond the high school walls with mentors who had been part of the United Farmworkers Union (UFW) in the 1970s and teachers who had after-school and theater programs. She had more contacts than the average student. She enrolled in Oxnard Community College from 1993 to 1997, while awaiting her immigration papers to be approved.

Her immigration process became longer and more costly because Adriana had turned 18. She took a part-time job to help cover expenses. One of her post-high school dreams was to attend the University of California at San Diego (UCSD). This dream began after a high school varsity cross-country match where her coach took the team on a tour of the UCSD college campus. Fulfilling this dream started with a move in 1997 to San Diego and an interest in community work, including issues involving the border. She was accepted to UCSD and began classes in Latin American studies, with an interest in Spanish literature, at one of the six undergraduate campuses, Thurgood Marshall College. In 2002, Adriana graduated with a double major in Latin American studies and Spanish literature.

After taking a year off from school, Adriana completed a master's program at UCSD from 2004 to 2006, receiving a degree and teaching credential in elementary education. She was involved in various capacities at the community level and was politically active with many key people instrumental in the Chicano Movement within the San Diego area. One of the most influential was Ernesto Bustillos (Chicano activist, teacher, community organizer, and founding member of Unión del Barrio) whom she met in 1995, while participating in the *Marcha*, commemorating the 25th anniversary of the National Chicano Moratorium Committee (NCMC), in Los Angeles. She became a member of Unión del Barrio and remains one to this day, in a volunteer capacity.

Adriana also became interested in the work of the American Friends Service Committee (AFSC) and their U.S.- Mexico Border Program. In the early 2000s, the AFSC held community dialogs regarding U.S. Border Patrol raids on the San Diego Trolley. Following the attacks of 9/11 (2001), the Border Patrol heightened its monitoring of people riding the trolleys. The AFSC was involved in documenting incidents of abuse by the Border Patrol. In 2002-2003, Adriana began coordinating community efforts and got closer to the work of the AFSC. By the time she had finished her master's program, the AFSC suggested she apply for a position that had become available. She landed the job and has been employed with them ever since. She now resides in San Diego with her husband and teenage daughter.

Adriana loves her job. The primary focus of the AFSC is documenting those incidents of abuse committed against any community member at the hands of a federal agent. Some past incidents have led to loss of life. Proximity to the border in San Diego creates a much larger presence of Border Patrol. Adriana's work with the AFSC helps address these issues and others such as militarization of the border and its effects in relation to documentation of abuse; providing community accompaniment; legislative work; and alliance building—working with other organizations on similar immigration issues.

Adriana is well versed in the challenges that come with immigration as a result of her grandparents, parents, and her own firsthand experiences. These provide her with the strength and compassion to help others who are facing their own challenges involving immigration. She says she sees herself staying with the AFSC and expressed these sentiments, "I couldn't be in a better place with a more incredible group of human beings." Her hope is for a policy change in immigration that will take place at the federal level for those who have been repressed by the system. Current immigration law does not allow for people who are already in the United States as undocumented to fix their status. Adriana says, "There must be a dramatic change in federal policy that will honor and see the humanity in people who were born outside the borders of the United States."

Adriana's compassion shows in her concern for others. It touches the hearts of those who are most concerned with immigrant rights when she says, "Through my experiences, I have learned that collective experiences are much more telling than an individual life. Due to our proximity to the border, we have a responsibility to making sure that our experiences become collective and that we participate in community collectively. It becomes instrumental for finding collective answers to our problems as a community that will benefit all of us together."

About the Author:

KATHLEEN ROBLES has a master's degree in anthropology/museum studies from San Diego State University and is a Ph.D. candidate in the SDSU/CGU Joint Doctoral Program in Education. She has taught anthropology courses at San Diego City College and Grossmont College for many years. She also has experience in documenting the culture, history, and politics of Chicano mural art and is co-director of the Chicano Park Historical Documentation Project. She has curated several Día de los Muertos installations and provided lectures on the subject at various locations throughout San Diego. She is a member of the SDSU Chicana/o Archive Committee.

Consuelo Manríquez, Speaking out for justice.
Courtesy of Brent E. Beltran.

CONSUELO MANRÍQUEZ:

LEADER IN STUDENT ACHIEVEMENT, SAN DIEGO SCHOOLS
Long time Editor, Community Leader, and Publisher

BY LETICIA HERNÁNDEZ-LINARES

Dr. Consuelo Manríquez not only finds the path forward, she forges the path itself and clears the dust for others. A trailblazer, a tremendous force, Consuelo is renowned for leaving no challenge dismissed, no obstacle unturned. When I met Consuelo, she was teaching full-time at Memorial Junior High School in Barrio Logan; attending graduate school for her third degree; and, on the side, creating opportunities for Chicano and Latino writers as co-founder and co-owner of Calaca Press, an independent Chicano small press dedicated to publishing the works of socially conscious bilingual writers. A long-time educator, community leader, publisher, art collector, event producer, community organizer, among many other things, Dr. Manríquez invokes the Superwoman Chicana image, as she juggles various roles and attacks multiple issues on a superhero level.

At this writing, Dr. Manríquez was the principal of King Chavez Community High School, a dynamic leader and seasoned educator committed to equity and social justice. Her greatest success as principal of this diverse high school was accelerating the development and achievement of all of her students, in particular, English-language learners. She is known for cultivating school communities that challenge and motivate a diverse group of students, teachers, and staff.

The fourth of five children born to Antonieta Solórzano and Arnulfo Manríquez, Consuelo was born in Mexicali, Baja California. At four years old, she moved to San Antonio del Mar, and attended school in Playas de Tijuana for eight years. The school was run by nuns who introduced her to one of her all-time favorite writers, Sor Juana Inés de la Cruz. Sor Juana was a seventeenth-century nun and writer who advocated for women's rights, and her example clearly inspired Consuelo as a little girl. The move on August 3, 1981, to San Ysidro, California, proved to be among the first major obstacles in her life.

Consuelo was thirteen years old when her family moved across the border. Only a handful of years later, in 1989, Consuelo began teaching at a Catholic school for girls, Immaculate Heart of Mary in Los Angeles. She later returned to San Diego to pursue a bilingual teaching credential. Her middle school teaching career included English as a Second Language, or ESL, Spanish, and technology classes. In 2007, she accepted her first appointment as vice-principal at Correia Middle School. In 2009, she became a high school principal.

A dual citizen of both Mexico and the United States, Consuelo has obtained multiple degrees throughout her career as an educator: a bachelor's degree in Spanish from the University of San Diego (USD); a bilingual teaching credential and master of arts degree in Spanish from San Diego State University (SDSU); and, finally, a doctorate in education, with a specialty in turnaround schools. When she is not pursuing degrees, she raises funds for important causes. I recall when, in less than two years, she raised $24,000 in bus fare scholarships for her students at the school for Media, Visual, and Performing Arts (MVPA) at San Diego High School. An unprecedented gesture, she began this campaign to aid students with bus fares when she realized that many of them were missing school because they could not afford to pay for the bus ride.

Upon her arrival, MVPA was categorized as one of the lowest 5% schools in the nation. Under her leadership, the school reorganized, made major changes, and by year two, made headline news, boasting the district's biggest gains in academic achievement. For Consuelo, where there are resources and solutions, there also has to be art. The MVPA Mariachi Program performed, for the first time, at Balboa Theater—one of the most historic theaters in San Diego, two years in a row.

Fostering a deep commitment to social justice, human rights, and the arts, Consuelo has played active roles in various organizations such as the Chicano Park Steering Committee (CPSC)—where she began volunteering in 1995—the Voz Alta Project, and the Red CalacArts Collective, just to name a few. She began her long career as an activist and community leader with groups like the Raza Rights Coalition and Unión del Barrio. Ensuring the vitality and success of Chicano Park Day has become a constant in her activism. Moreover, since 1998, she has organized over 100 cultural events, including annual celebrations honoring Women's History Month and Día de los Muertos. She continues to participate in the Chicano Park effort to this day, and organizes annual fundraisers for Chicano Park Day, raising thousands of dollars, even hosting events at her own home.

Speaking of home, it was out of her very own home that Consuelo cofounded the press that would publish over thirty titles. As a bilingual teacher, Consuelo struggled to find relevant literature for her students. When she used a friend's poem in her Spanish for Spanish-Speakers class and saw the special connection that her students made, she decided to create the books she couldn't find on bookshelves or at conferences. A year after she was married, she used the down payment for a house to finance the Calaca Press launch, while her father invested in a new computer for the publication of the first book. In 1998, Calaca Press published *Bus Stops and Other Poems* by Manuel Velez. Consuelo was the head of the Calaca Press *familia*.

While her ex-husband took care of design and publishing, she worked every intersession and summer to keep Calaca Press solvent. When she finally bought a home in National City in 2001, it became the community hub for Chicano Park, Chicano artists, and Calaca Press writers. These events at her home came to life with musicians, artists, and *comida Mexicana* that she cooked herself, donating her labors for different causes, to the delight of those who attended the large community gatherings. One event at her home benefitted San Diego State University's Chicana and Chicano Archive. It included performers, a live auction, art sale, a tour of the beautiful art inside and outside the house, and of course, Chelo's signature dish, *birria*, that no one can quite duplicate,

Consuelo Manríquez, holding picket sign at rally.
Courtesy of Brent E. Beltran.

Day of the Dead was one of Consuelo's beloved dad's favorite holidays and, as she recalls, "*Calacas* were always part of my life." The *Calaca* skeleton, representing *la muerte* or the transitory meaning of life in Mexican culture, became synonymous with community. The house itself, where many well-known Chicano artists painted a mural and poets passed through and recorded their poems, became known as *Calacalandia*. Everyone was welcome at *Calacalandia*. You just needed art, or an appreciation of it, in order to be a part.

One invitation no one ever received, however, was to celebrate Consuelo's birthday. She decided to celebrate it each March, on International Women's Day instead of her own birth date. For Consuelo, that day is never just about her and, yet, for the rest of us, it is all because of her.

It turns out that the National City house Consuelo loved so much and called her cacoon, was sold after her divorce. She launched a new press shortly after that she named *Caliposas*, to bring together her *calacas*, her love of butterflies, and her Mexicali/California roots. As she makes plans for *Caliposas* Press, she is most proud of having completed her doctorate and having endured the transition of divorce, all while executing her first principalship. When she was not busy at the job of leading King Chavez Community High School, making 80+ burritos for volunteers, hosting Chicano Park Day, and on adventures with her countless family and friends, she was writing from a faraway part of the world.

Reflecting on her most enduring influences, Consuelo credits her growth as a teacher in part, to Linda Taggart-Fregoso, an English Language Arts teacher at Memorial Junior High School who encouraged her to attend conferences and integrate technology in the classroom. She is also grateful to master teacher, the late Ernesto Bustillos, as a key figure in her development as an activist and leader.

She continues to volunteer for CPSC and moderate important events, like the fall 2016 fundraiser for the documentary film about "Chunky" Ramon Sanchez, produced by Paul Espinosa at Barrio X, at which Chunky was present; and then sadly, soon after, at the Memorial Celebration for his passing, held in Chicano Park, where thousands gathered to honor him.

Today, Dr. Manriquez is associate director of communications and operations at Darnall Charter School in San Diego. A dynamic leader and seasoned educator committed to equity and social justice, one thing is sure, she is building community wherever she goes. She is a *caliposa* in flight.

About the Author:

LETICIA HERNÁNDEZ-LINARES, an award-winning writer and community leader, has performed her poem songs throughout the country and in El Salvador. Published widely, her writing has appeared in newspapers, literary journals, and anthologies, some of which include *Street Art San Francisco*, *This Bridge We Call Home*, and *U.S. Latino Literature Today*. Her first poetry collection, *Mucha Muchacha, Too Much Girl*, is forthcoming from Tía Chucha Press.

ELSA SEVILLA:

DIRECTOR AND HOST, KPBS "SAN DIEGO'S HISTORIC PLACES"

Her Work Represents Her Heritage and Her Desire for Responsible Storytelling

BY EVA SALAS

San Diego's documentary storyteller, Elsa Sevilla, strives to educate and inform the community about the history of the region. You might catch her on KPBS TV, with her warm voice and dignified air, telling intriguing stories of the past on her television show, "San Diego's Historic Places."

Elsa thrives because of the responsibility she feels for being ethnically diverse and because of her desire for responsible storytelling. She began her journey as documentary producer, with stories about the Indians, then the Spanish friars, and the *conquistadores* who arrived in Baja and Alta California during the eighteenth century, contributing to the making of San Diego.

As a child, Elsa was always intrigued by how government, politics, and the economy functioned. Even then, she knew that a journalism career would give her the opportunity to learn about all these topics and much more. With such an interest in how things worked, Elsa also fell in love with writing, reading, and history. While Elsa knew that journalism would allow her to be in the middle of many big stories, her career would also come with big responsibilities, educating the public on local events and history. Childhood was a curious time for Elsa, who grew up in a large family with seven siblings in Southeast San Diego. It was also a difficult time, learning English for the first time and adapting to a new life. Born in Tijuana, Baja California, Mexico, to U.S. born parents, Fermín Martínez and Isadora Montoya, the family returned to the United States in the early 1970s.

Growing up alongside four brothers gave Elsa a competitive edge and taught her not to give up. Her mother was tough and wanted her children to succeed, making sure each of them chose a career. But it was Elsa's three older sisters who, in many ways, paved the path for her to choose higher education.

Elsa Sevilla, host of San Diego's Historic Places.
Courtesy of Memo Cavada, Creative Images.

Attending Southwestern College and then San Diego State University, Elsa would get her first career job at KGTV 10. It was at Channel 10, she says, where she learned everything, from researching difficult topics, finding people to interview, to writing, producing, editing, reporting, and even anchoring. In addition, Elsa researched causes she cared about and thus reported on homelessness, mental illness, suicide prevention, and the wild fires that devastated San Diego.

Elsa won three Emmy nominations for her investigative journalism: she exposed the child sex trade along the San Diego-Mexico border; uncovered Alzheimer's breakthrough research in San Diego; and revealed an unknown history of local historic theaters. She credits some of the news photographers and reporters she met at work as important influences, especially Guillermo Sevilla. They were married and raised two children. Since then, the two began working side by side, creating their own video production company, Sevilla Productions.

Establishing a company, juggling a journalism career, producing monthly documentaries, and raising a family proved to be demanding endeavors. It wasn't until after their children, Samantha and Julian, were born that Elsa came into her own. She felt a sense of empowerment and determination to be professionally successful. Elsa was motivated to do what she loved best. She continued to be a storyteller in balance with family life.

In 2008, Elsa became the creator, producer, and television host of her own show, "San Diego's Historic Places." Elsa would be the first woman journalist to become a KPBS TV independent video producer. With her unique vision, she was able to create a very successful documentary series. The program is entertaining and educational; it teaches San Diegans about the region's history, showing historic black and white photographs of the people dating back to the 1700s. Her program is one of the top-rated in local programming among KPBS TV viewers.

In 2010, the City of San Diego's Board for Historic Preservation recognized Elsa for her KPBS documentary series. Her work has surpassed the production of more than sixty documentaries on local history, thus far. Elsa coordinates every detail of her TV documentary series from start to finish, producing six documentaries yearly.

All this experience has helped Elsa establish the company and bring it to a higher level of production, creating new partnerships with the San Diego History Center, KPBS TV, and others. Besides "San Diego's Historic Places," Elsa has been producing videos for local colleges, universities, casinos, and nonprofits for the past 16 years.

In 2013, Elsa was awarded the *San Diego Union-Tribune's* "Business Leader Award" for her small business contributions. She has been nominated for *San Diego Magazine's* "Latinos Making a Difference" and "Woman of the Year" awards and for *San Diego Business Journal's* "Women Who Mean Business" award.

Elsa also mentors and encourages young journalism students and journalists in the television news field. Giving back to those in need is a big part of Elsa's life. She has helped young Latinos find a successful career path through higher education. Every year, through Sevilla Productions, Elsa donates *pro bono* services to local nonprofit organizations. Elsa also helps organizations with promotional videos to increase their sales, fundraising, and services to the region.

Elsa has served on the MANA of San Diego board for five consecutive years. It is a national women's association and one she credits for her early formation. She has also been responsible for raising thousands of dollars in scholarship money awarded to local Latinas pursuing higher education. And, she has been instrumental in coordinating yearly women's business conferences for MANA members. Elsa says, "For me, the goal in life is to live it to the fullest and share it with others." Elsa acknowledges those TV journalists, small business colleagues, and many of the MANA women who have had a positive impact on her life and career.

Elsa Sevilla has gained numerous awards for the work she has done during her 25-year career in broadcast television news and production. She responds gratefully, "I am most thankful to my mother, Isidra Montoya, who raised eight children, making sure each one of us chose a career."

Elsa has not been spared the challenges and obstacles of today's complicated world, but what she has taken away has made her stronger and wiser. She finds an end use to experience: pass along our knowledge to our children and our community so they too can succeed in life.

About the Author:

EVA SALAS is a home-based graphic designer, and owner of her own business, Aplomb Media. She grew up bilingual and bicultural on the southernmost border of California where she lives with her husband, Michael Ornelas and three adult children. An avid cyclist, she is part of a large extended family. She has been a long-time supporter of the Chicana/Chicano studies mission at Mesa College, since it was first founded in 1970s, as her husband served a member of the department for nearly forty years. Recently she was nominated for an Orchid's Award as Architect/Designer of the Heritage Museum photographic display in the Chula Vista Library, commemorating "The Great Flood of 2016."

CHAPTER 12

FREDI AVALOS

VIRGINIA ESCALANTE

IRENE LARA

ELVA SALINAS

CHAPTER 12

A New Generation of Chicana Scholars

People of color in the United States have always understood that marketable skills and degrees in higher education are a path to economic, political, and social equity for their communities. However, it was not until the late 1960s, that many believed these goals were attainable. Because of the civil rights movements and the ongoing political turmoil of the country at that time, some Chicanos made gains by embracing militancy as a means to achieve economic, social, and political equity. For instance, in 1968, Chicana and Chicano high school students staged walk-outs in the streets of Los Angeles protesting inferior education (see Garcia. *Blowout! Sal Castro and the Chicano Struggle for Educational Justice*. University of North Carolina, 2011). In 1963 in New Mexico, Reis Lopez Tijerina incorporated the Alianza Federal de Mercedes, an organization to address the dispossession of Spanish land grants that lead to active protests, bringing attention to the historic injustices suffered by the New Mexican people. (see *Chicano! History of the Mexican American Civil Rights Movement*. Video. NLCC, 1996). Protests and demonstrations in the colleges and universities across America, forced educational institutions to become more accessible to Chicanos, as people of color.

Many Chicanas embraced education as a tool of empowerment, fortifying themselves against family, cultural, and societal expectations. Education also meant rediscovering and reclaiming a heritage that gave back the culture, pride, and identity that some had lost or learned to reject due to the lack of resources in the schools and colleges. As a result, more Chicanas began to earn degrees in higher education. Chicana empowerment translated not only to economic self-reliance, but also to educating oneself as a means of giving back and by taking on leadership in the areas critical to one's community. As one new generation Chicana, artist Patricia Aguayo, reminded us a few years ago, "Ser Chicana" comes with the responsibility to give back to our communities, something that early Chicana activists promoted, and that the women in this final chapter are continuing to do.

A generation of Chicana educators and professional scholars is now addressing the many complex issues facing their communities through various avenues. They must now navigate through a more complex world than those who came before them. It is a different world because they live in the digital age, making communication and access faster and easier. Yet, in many ways, they are confronting a world similar to that of their mothers, one where racism, sexism, and income inequality determined their place in society. Despite the challenges, these women continue to go against the odds to make a difference, not only in their own communities, but in the world.

One of these women is Fredia (Fredi) Avalos. She is one of many Chicanas who has now earned a Ph.D. While excelling, she is part of a group that is also facing new challenges in academia. Fredi knew from a young age that she would be a fighter. Her father, a professional boxer, taught her to never back down in defense of those who are oppressed. Justice, she learned early in life, did not come without a struggle. As a result of her upbringing, she is engaged in the many human rights battles facing Chicanos/Latinos today.

As a new generation Chicana activist, she has tackled issues in keeping with new technology. In 1996, she traveled to Chiapas, Mexico, to study the Zapatista Movement, an Indigenous *guerrilla* resistance movement, eventually completing her doctoral dissertation on international digital revolutions. Fredi also worked her way up the corporate environments as a public relations professional. Today, she is a writer, community scholar, communication consultant, media strategist, and a professor at California State University at San Marcos in the Department of Communications. Her activism in protecting Chicano/Latino human rights from violations has been widely recognized.

Indeed, in this new generation, more Chicana women are acquiring doctoral degrees, which in higher education speaks to their intelligence, dedication, and tenacity. Against all odds, Chicanas have shown their power and strength to overcome. They have surpassed all expectations and achieved excellence.

Another example of this kind of woman is Dr. Virginia Escalante. She was born and raised in the small town of Eloy, Arizona. As a child, she, along with her family, worked in the fields to survive. She would eventually graduate as the salutatorian of her high school graduating class. After teaching high school English and journalism for eight years in Ajo and Tucson, she decided to follow her heart and work as a journalist. While working for the *Los Angeles Times*, she became a member of a team that was awarded the Pulitzer Prize's "Gold Medal for Meritorious Public Service" as a contributing writer in "Southern

California's Latino Community" series. Thereafter, she would return to her *alma mater*, the University of Arizona, as an assistant professor of journalism and advisor to produce, implement, and develop a bilingual student newspaper, *El Independiente*. At San Diego Mesa College, she took on the job as the initiator and advisor of *The Mesa Press*. Presently, she is professor of English at San Diego City College and the project director/manager of the SDCC Book Fair that is held every year.

Another Chicana with a Ph.D. graduated from the University of California at Berkeley to become the first Chicana professor of women's studies at San Diego State University. Chicanas have always been in a unique position to talk about spirituality and health because of their closeness to their indigenous ancestry. Irene Lara's exploration into indigenous spirituality has provided exciting perspectives for the current generation. With her scholarly approach to the work of *curanderas*, indigenous women healers, she has recently co-edited an anthology, *Fleshing the Spirit: Spirituality and Activism in Chicana, Latina and Indigenous Women's Lives* (2014). She developed a new mentoring paradigm she borrowed from Indigenous women's knowledge, traditions, and healing practices to encourage her students to develop themselves as *curandera*/scholar activists to examine and consider their scholarship as a healing work for the 21st century, *el sexto sol*. Her work shows them a new way to heal themselves as well as their communities from their historically imposed traumas in order to uplift and bring personal, social, and ecological balance.

Like other women, Chicanas/Latinas have been encouraged to study in traditional areas where women are expected to achieve. However, many have gone on to fulfill other goals for themselves, breaking stereotypes along the way. Elva Salinas has broken many barriers, leaving behind others' expectations for women, while seeking her own goals and dreams. A role model for the new generation, she is known to her Chicano students at San Diego City College as *La Profe* because she does not fit the mold as a traditional professor. Elva, once a hairdresser, turned English professor/activist, continues to be a role model and an inspiration to her students. Even as a full-time professor at SDCC, with all of its responsibilities, she is known for mentoring those students most in need. Recognized at the "Ser Chicana: Una Decisión Consciente" event in 2012, she has also received the Latina Leadership Award, the Golden Apple Award, and the KPBS Local Heroes Award. These are but a few testaments to her commitment to our communities.

Whether the issues that Chicana professors face today are educational inequality for students of color, biased media coverage, immigration enforcement, or other issues, these arenas—with their ever-changing policies and laws—will not deter them. As activist/educators, they continue to work at making change possible, eradicating injustices, and uplifting our communities. In spite of the challenges, these women insist on working against the odds to make a difference in the lives of others, not only those in their own communities, but for all.

FREDI AVALOS:

PROFESSOR CSUSM, CULTURAL AND MEDIA STUDIES/LEADERSHIP

Human Rights Activist, Writer, Communications Consultant, and Media Strategist,

BY KAREN GUZMXN

> You have been telling the people that this is the Eleventh Hour, now you must go back and tell the people that this is the Hour. And there are things to be considered…Where are you living? What are you doing? What are your relationships? Are you in right relation? Where is your water? Know your garden. It is time to speak your Truth. Create your community. Be good to each other. And do not look outside yourself for the leader.
>
> -- attributed to an unnamed Hopi elder,
> Hopi Nation, Oraibi, Arizona

My name is Karen GuzmXn and I have been asked to write the story of my friend, teacher, and mentor, Dr. Fredi Avalos. Fredia (Fredi) Martinez Avalos was born in Logan Heights, San Diego, California. Her family had been there for 100 years until her father, who served in the U.S. Army Air Force, benefitted from the G.I. bill and insisted their family move into Paradise Hills, a newly developed suburb. Fredi described it as "a bright and shiny neighborhood." However, residents did not want Mexican Americans to purchase property there and made it difficult for them to do so. Not until her father produced three additional references from his white employers were Fredi's family finally able to move in.

Fredi was a very quiet, thoughtful, shy child who learned at a very young age to negotiate life in a loving, but very dysfunctional family, and to live life on the edge. She did not have a carefree childhood, but rather one where she took care of everyone else. This overwhelming responsibility, placed on a large majority of young *mujeres* in our community, is something that helped Fredi understand early on what feminists call male privilege and socially constructed gender roles. While her father was her greatest hero, he was also a man of his time. He believed that women should be treated equally in the workforce, but he did not practice equality in his own home. Yet his progressive politics and his love were key in developing the woman Fredi grew up to be. These conflicting and almost contradicting dynamics are something that many of us women can understand.

Growing up in an alcoholic home, Fredi learned to live with constant uncertainty. She always understood that life could change instantly and not necessarily for the better. This also allowed her to become a great strategist. She understands how her parents' flawed, but loving humanity, helped make her who she is today. Her now deceased father, a union organizer and professional boxer, might have indeed inspired Fredi to be a fighter for the long run. Even to this day, Fredi continues to put in countless hours and her wholehearted energy in the service of many social justice and human rights issues that impact our communities. She quotes the lyrics from songwriter Leonard Cohen to help explain her understanding and love of her family: "Even though it all went wrong, I'll stand before the Lord of Song with nothing on my tongue but, Hallelujah."

She grew up singing songs of the Mexican Revolution, taught by her mother, Antonia Zatarin, also a passionate supporter of human rights. As a young girl, influenced not only by the politics of her time, but also by the politics of her parents, Fredi developed as an activist at a very early age. In fact, her first demonstration was actually a sit-in she organized in her Catholic school during the sixth grade. It was to fight against the unfair and excessive homework assignments the nuns were demanding of her and her peers. She encouraged her peers to stage the sit-in outside of class and to sign a petition demanding their concerns be heard. Her 15-minute direct action resulted in a school suspension, but it did not discourage her from trying to make the world a more equitable place.

As a teenager, leaving Catholic elementary school and going into public high school, Fredi was overwhelmed by a whole new sense of freedom. By the end of her sophomore year, Fredi was taking advanced classes; yet, she was a total hellion. She met her first husband at age 16, and two years later began what was to be a 27-year marriage. Looking back on this time, she feels that part of this decision was based upon wanting to get out of her house. Fredi started working diverse jobs and helped put her first husband through school. In her thirties, she went back to school and found the space to come back to herself and to her political activism. She became very involved in a variety of social justice issues, where her heart had always been. Among her many acts of activism, Fredi was a cofounder of Developing Unity through Resident Organizing (D.U.R.O.) during the first onslaught of gentrification in Barrio Logan and Sherman Heights. Although the battle for decent housing continues in the area, D.U.R.O. had a lasting legacy of activism in the inner cities of San Diego.

Fredi Avalos, 2016 at home in Vista.
Courtesy of Mark Day.

Eventually, Fredi wrote her master's thesis on the Zapatistas, a Mexican guerilla group and their use of the internet. Later, she was one of only 200 Americans invited to the Zapatista *Encuentro* in Chiapas. She now looks back at her life as B.C. (before Chiapas) and A.C. (after Chiapas), because this gave her a transformative perspective. She realizes that "in the twenty-first century, social change will not come from the actions of charismatic leader, but will emerge from a network of leaders, shared power, and a flattening of organizational hierarchies." Fredi went on to get her doctorate in Cultural and Media Studies from Claremont Graduate University in Los Angeles County, completing her dissertation on International Digital Revolutions. She continued to organize around human rights violations of Latina and Latinos in San Diego, gaining credibility and recognition for her tireless work.

Today, Dr. Fredi Avalos, is a professor at CSU San Marcos, where she nurtures and leads students in activism. For instance, in 2010, she and her students created a media campaign against then Congressman Brian Bilbray who had declared that you could tell undocumented immigrants by looking at their "shoes." While local and national news cameras rolled, the protesters delivered hundreds of shoes to Bilbray asking him to identify those that belonged to "illegals." The campaign, and others like it, helped many young people learn to use media in creative ways in the struggle for social justice.

Fredi considers it a true badge of honor that the nativist minutemen organization, which-harassed the Latino population in North County for many years, named her a "Most Wanted Enemy" on its website. For over six years, she and her second husband Mark Day, a recognized social justice activist and filmmaker, worked tirelessly with a small group of committed individuals "to stop the intimidation and hostility the community was experiencing at the hands of racist organized vigilantes." Indeed, many of Fredi's friends and colleagues often use the word "fearless" to describe her approach to activism.

Her Legacy as an Activist

In addition to being a professor at CSU San Marcos, Dr. Fredi Avalos is a very well-accomplished human rights activist, a writer, communication consultant, media strategist, and fundraiser. She is an inspiration to countless people in North County and greater San Diego County. She is the faculty fellow in diversity and cultural intelligence and the director of the Engaging Diverse Dialogue Initiative. Her work as the director of the Difficult Dialogue Project of North County has helped to bring diverse people together to help heal a region ridden with racial tension. As a consultant and a keynote speaker in the area of cultural intelligence, she has worked with corporations, non-profit organizations, churches, universities, and San Diego County school districts. She is the recipient of many awards and recognitions for her teaching, scholarship, and activism and serves on several community advisory boards. Recently, she was named a "Woman who Moves the City" by *San Diego Magazine*. Her editorial and opinion pieces have appeared in *The San Diego Union-Tribune*, the *Los Angeles Times*, *La Prensa*, *Hispanic Link*, and *San Diego Free Press*. In 2013, her essay "Bread and Roses Too" was published in the *Social Justice Journal*.

For those of us in the movement, we are very familiar with the concept of burning out, given the very modest salaries of jobs in the social justice arena, and with the ostracism one encounters in a white, capitalist, and patriarchal society. This is why Fredi's long legacy of human rights activism speaks volumes about her dedication and work ethic; it provides youth activists some comfort knowing that they can count on her for advice, wisdom, and affirmation to continue in the struggle.

Most recently, Fredi's interests have turned toward justice and support for the thousands of unaccompanied minors from Central America who are seeking asylum from the horrors of war, rape, oppression, and poverty. Currently, she and her students are working with a Syrian American refugee relief organization to assist the millions of displaced children by sending supplies and other materials to Europe and the Middle East. At a more local level, Fredi is a recognized leader in the struggle against police brutality in the City of Vista in the North County region of San Diego.

Over the years, Fredi has experienced many victories, but warns us that "we must be ready to accept defeats." When asked about what might have possibly discouraged her from pursuing a life as a human rights activist, Fredi believes that there will be many such moments not only in activism, but in life. "You win some, but you must be ready to lose most… so when you're an activist, it's a matter of learning to negotiate the dark moments," she shared over dinner, recalling a morose loss while doing anti-gentrification work in the inner city and the many years of organizing in Vista, where the issue of police brutality is barely getting federal or public attention. She added, "Even when it might appear that you have lost a battle, you may have planted some seeds for future actions." As she finished her sentence, I noticed Fredi held her hands together as though she were swimming through many profound thoughts. September 11, 2001, was one of those darkest moments; she continued, "For human rights activists, this was a very dark moment. I knew that despite whatever struggles we had before, things were going to get much worse. I could feel the fear and see the turn toward fascism."

Fredi explained that coming to terms with a new world order after 9/11 was very difficult. During this time, her 27-year marriage came to an end. Everything she had ever known since her early adolescence—in every way possible, personally and publicly—was gone when those planes smashed into those twin towers in New York City. However, you learn that struggle is the basis for a meaningful existence and you learn to embrace it. While there are victories, they are short lived. Still, you keep doing the work, because you cannot *not* do it. The love you have for others and the vision you hold will always keep you going through this ebb and flow. "The struggle for justice has no end point. It is not a zero sum game," she says.

Fredi has learned to fly freely in order to avoid disappointment and hold ultimate agency in her work. She saw that instead of belonging to one organization, institution, or structure, she developed more as a human rights "freelancer," to be loosely coupled with organizations. This "strategic essentialism" allowed Fredi to come together with other people and form alliances temporarily to get things done, ultimately allowing her to complete many of her goals. This postmodern organizing philosophy taught Fredi that because everything is so fluid politically and identity-wise, you will often find that some of the same people who aligned with you on one issue, will be on the opposite side the next week.

Understanding activism this way, she said, helps make it easier to deal with fragmentation in a postmodern world. Often, this fragmentation consequently forces people with intersectional and marginalized identities to compromise one or more of their social identities. This may constrain their ability to gain access to certain spaces that focus on the liberation of another one of their identities. This perspective has taught her to negotiate these spaces strategically, rather than be entrenched in an ideological prison. In her lifetime, this fluidness has allowed her to work on an array of social justice issues she was passionate about, and to effect change in some things rather than try to do everything. Fredi's ability to organize and connect temporary *ad-hoc* groups is a successful tactic of hers. She feels that this is due to all the connections she's made and all the people she can bring together because she herself has occupied so many spaces. She explained that just as freelancers do certain kinds of arts, her activism is also specific: addressing human rights violations of Latinos and children. This is why she can organize a highly successful fund-raiser and successful marketing campaign to support the hundreds of unaccompanied minor children fleeing Central America.

Despite all her activism, Fredi is first and foremost a teacher. She has mentored countless students and young activists and organizers. Childless, but not without children, she has been a mother to many people, helping direct so many of us. She has left her students with a sense of their own power and voice. She has taught her students to seek a meaning that goes beyond consumerism. In a time when so many powerful forces try to wrestle us from our humanity, Fredi has and continues to prepare generations for the battles of today. She has helped empower young women of color to occupy spaces, to speak truth, and to get over the fear of being powerful. She has guided students to find meaning in suffering so that their lives are not compromised or without hope. Above all, she teaches youth to think for themselves so that they can respond appropriately to the issues of our time. After all, as the Hopi prophecy says, we are in the eleventh hour.

Like an artist who must explore and master specific mediums or who is known for a specific artistic technique, activists too must discover and develop their talents, concentrate their interests, and work to become experts in specific social justice issues to gain credibility. Activists use their activism to manifest the values they feel inside and the hope they have for the world. Artists are normally perceived less seriously than other professions and are taken for granted. Oftentimes, some of the most amazing artists barely make ends meet and may not even see how popular their work becomes in their life span. Likewise, activists may put in a lifetime of struggle without seeing their full victory. And just as artists leave beautiful work behind for the rest of the world to enjoy until the end of time, so do activists. Activists continue to create and leave behind so much beauty in a world that grows colder. It is something that must not stop, because it brings so much color into this black-and-white world.

I had never perceived activism as something beautiful, but listening to Fredi helped change my entire perspective. Fredi has created so much beauty in a dark world. She has provoked, provided insight, and changed the lives of the many people who observe her work, just like the impact we can receive from a powerful piece of art. She has left and will continue to leave something beautiful behind in this world and in the hearts of those around her. For that reason, I thank Fredi Avalos for making my world much more colorful, more creative, more inspiring.

About the Author:

KAREN GUZMXN spells her name with an X, her unique statement; she is an LGBTQ immigrant and feminist living in San Diego. She is a senior at California State University at San Marcos. Karen will graduate with a bachelor's degree in Women's Studies and a minor in philosophy. She also works at CSU San Marcos where she organizes for the California Faculty Association (CFA). She is a member of the San Diego Dream Team and Feminists Unite. She serves on the National Leadership Committee for United We Dream, the nation's largest immigrant youth-led organization. Karen enjoys playing the guitar, watching documentaries, and walking in nature.

Virginia Escalante, Professor, San Diego City College.
Courtesy of Ernesto Collosi.

VIRGINIA ESCALANTE:

PROFESSOR AND PULITZER PRIZE WINNING JOURNALIST

From the Fields of Arizona to University Professor

BY TEYANA L. VISCARRA

The daughter of field workers, seemingly bereft of opportunity, a young Chicana becomes a high school teacher and award-winning writer for the *Los Angeles Times*, a member of a Pulitzer Prize winning team. She then became a university journalism professor, and the adviser for an award-winning college newspaper, *The Mesa Press*, and is currently director for the San Diego City College International Book Fair. If you had any doubts about the children of farm laborers in the United States making it out of the fields and into higher education, you have not met Virginia Escalante.

Virginia has a vibrant and intelligent presence, hard to match when mixed with her uplifting sense of humor and down-to-earth personality. She would *not* be the first one to tell the story of her challenges or her victories. And, yet, you can sense that she is proud and grateful. These qualities show in the way she treats others. She has since used her talents and accomplishments to encourage students to find the way to success, just as others helped her.

These traits that shine in her have not gone unnoticed.

Her high school inducted her into the Santa Cruz Valley Union High School Hall of Fame in 2012. It all started there when Virginia was barely a teenager. She served as editor of the newspaper and yearbook, and won numerous awards in several subjects, including chemistry and English. She was also named "Girl of the Year" and was chosen as salutatorian of her graduating class. It's no wonder that her students get the hopeful message from her, "You can do anything you set your mind to." Virginia is living proof. She was a different kinda girl.

"My family worked in the fields because that's how we survived," she explains.

Born and raised in the small Arizona town of Eloy, she was a field worker as a child. As a high school senior, Virginia attributes her growing consciousness and ability to succeed to "a wonderful adviser and mentor, a Cuban exile," she recalls. "He paved the way, taught me not to be afraid, and to trust myself," something she is now bent on doing for others.

She attended the University of Arizona in Tucson, majoring in education and English. The printer's ink in her blood, she minored in journalism. She then taught at a small-town high school. "I started teaching at 21," she said. "At the time, I didn't know how to pace myself, so after eight years, I burned out." She remembers, however, "that the experience was tremendous. But it was time for me to get back to my first love, a job where I could write every day."

After teaching high school English and journalism in Ajo and Tucson, Arizona, in the 1970s, Virginia attended a training program for minority journalists at the University of California at Berkeley. After that, she became a reporter at the *Stockton Record* for 16 months and then at the *Los Angeles Times*.

A turn of events and a perfect opportunity at the *Los Angeles Times* led her to become a member of a reporting team that produced a series on Chicano issues called "Southern California's Latino Community." For this timely and innovative effort, the team was awarded the Pulitzer Prize, the "Gold Medal for Meritorious Public Service." Virginia was cited for her contributions to the series. Her first-person account compared her own memories as a child field worker to those of contemporary farm laborers, and was singled out in the nomination. Virginia recalls the reporting team and how "we were all proud of the series, feeling it had served as a real community resource."

After six years, Virginia was recruited by her alma mater, the University of Arizona, to advise students in producing a Spanish-language newspaper. An assistant professor of journalism, she now taught and served as adviser to the bilingual newspaper, *El Independiente*, which covered the City of South Tucson. In 1990, Escalante was recognized for her university efforts with a Community Service Award from *Chicanos Por La Causa* for her "perseverance, invaluable contributions, and commitment to our youth." She also received the University of Arizona Hispanic Alumni Award for "indefatigable teaching efforts and academic excellence." After that, Virginia returned to California and entered the doctoral program at the University of California at San Diego (UCSD) with many accolades. There, she became a UCSD fellow when she was awarded a UCSD President's Dissertation Fellowship, the UC Mexus Dissertation Grant for Chicano Studies, and the Ruben Salazar Award for Most Outstanding Journalism Candidate. In addition, she was also named a Freedom Forum Journalism Scholar—a graduate scholarship awarded by the Freedom Forum in Arlington, Virginia—and granted the Graduate Communications Scholarship from the Mexican American Legal Defense and Education Fund.

Virginia's firsthand experience plus her more recent research are the essence of her doctoral dissertation at UCSD. Her research focuses on Spanish-language media. She talks about her reasons for writing it and how important it is to provide diversity in the media. "Spanish-language press has a long history dating back to when the Southwest was part of Mexico," she said. "I'm happy to be able to contribute something to journalism with history that isn't as well known or even compiled on this side of the border."

After her graduate studies, Escalante remained in San Diego, where she taught English, journalism, and Chicano Studies, first at San Diego Mesa College for six years, and then at San Diego City College where she is presently.

At Mesa College, in a 2002 interview with *WE*, an online college district magazine, Virginia stressed that, "One of the reasons I decided to come here was the integrated campus." She said, "I didn't want to be the only brown person in the classrooms, whether behind the podium or sitting in a chair. I wanted to be in a learning environment that represented society."

At Mesa, she was adviser to the campus newspaper, *The Mesa Press*, which won several local, regional, and national awards. She also taught English composition from a Chicano perspective, and pressed her English and journalism students to seek diverse viewpoints. She stressed that diversity—in the newsroom and in news coverage—is "an issue of national importance in mass media."

The Mesa Press went on to win many awards. It placed second nationally at the prestigious "Best of Show in College Media" at the Associated Collegiate Press/Media Advisers Conference in Washington, D.C. *The Mesa Press* also won first place overall for "Best College Newspaper" in the Society of Professional Journalists' San Diego competition and another first place for its "9-11 News Coverage." And what an honor that was, both for her and her students, as well as for San Diego Mesa College.

Virginia Escalante is now full professor of English at San Diego City College where she has been teaching and working in other capacities as well since 2005. She continues to expand her student audience, while teaching writing across the curriculum and as director of the San Diego City College International Book Fair. In the latter position, Virginia is a "long-time facilitator for cultural interaction and expansion." Virginia also believes that the book fair "plays an important function in this pedagogy, exposing both students and residents to the work of national and international authors and artists."

When the former director of the book fair stepped down from that position, Virginia volunteered for the role because it is such an integral part of the school's curriculum. It provides students with the opportunity to meet and interact with the authors, "which enriches their understanding and appreciation of the literature they read in the classroom." The fair also serves as a resource for faculty who also strive to enhance their own teaching and intellectual development. It also builds community, something Virginia cares about.

Virginia has constructed her approach to teaching and working from experiences on both sides of the education system, both as a Ph.D. candidate and college professor. She is still thinking about how she can help others, especially her students. So, the question at the forefront is how can her academia and life experiences and accomplishments help create a forum for others to succeed?

Virginia Escalante, high school teacher, reporter, graduate student, and professor speaks from the places where she grew up, so that the students—some very much like her who did not always have the best access to educational excellence—become the beneficiaries. That is why she emphasizes the resources that make up San Diego's "vibrant, multicultural community in music, art, literature, film, and other forms." The community, she hopes, will provide more affordable cultural events that will serve all segments. "The arts should be accessible to all," she says, "rather than for the sole purview of the affluent."

As she has demonstrated, the journey through journalism and academia has led Virginia to assume a role where she has been able to apply her personal experiences as well as her skills to create a forum for others to do the same.

About the Author:

TEYANA L. VISCARRA, an activist for social justice most recently made the harsh winter pilgrimage as "water protector" at Standing Rock, North Dakota. She received her masters from Fuller Theological Seminary in Pasadena; a certificate in Leadership and Community Development from Harvard Divinity School. She competes as an ultrarunner athlete in hopes to inspire young girls/women to go the distance of their dreams. As an innovator in her regiment of hill running, she calls Gravity Training, she has been acknowledged in the *U.S. News and World Report, Los Angeles Times, Shape magazine, Allure,* and *The New York Times.* Her work continues as a private and high school (Pacific Palisades and Arcadia) running coach.

IRENE LARA:

FIRST CHICANA PROFESSOR IN SDSU WOMEN'S STUDIES
Author, Healer, and Scholar of Curanderismo

BY MARIA FIGUEROA

D r. Irene Lara is my friend, *comadre*, sister, godmother to my children, colleague, and fellow Chicana scholar activist. Like the Greek origins of her name, Irene embodies peace in all aspects of her physical being. Her gentle demeanor, however, should not be confused with passivity or disengagement. On the contrary, her peaceful nature is Irene's powerful medicine, one that was predetermined from the day she traveled through her mother's birth canal and made her way to the light of this mother earth.

It feels very natural to talk about Irene as a mother of many things. A biological life-giving mother she is for certain, having given birth to two beautiful, inquisitive, and cheerful daughters Belén and Xóchitl. Alongside her life partner, Raúl, she lovingly guides her daughters into complete and complex beings, oftentimes modeling within context the tumultuous task known as parenting. Perhaps this explains my strong-felt desire to have her stand before the presence of our ancestors as my children's godmother with full confidence in the knowledge that she would love and honor them as her own.

As I was brainstorming for this narrative, I recalled the first time I met Irene. I was newly commencing my community college teaching career, when I ventured onto a solo-trip through the Sonoran desert with the destination being a National Association of Chicana and Chicano Studies (NACCS) Conference in Tucson, Arizona. The year was 2001. Tucson was a place I had yet to visit and making the journey in my newly purchased vehicle as a woman alone was quite liberating. It was a *Thelma & Louise* sort of premise, only I was both a brown-skinned Thelma *and* Louise. In our recollections, this was a pivotal NACCS for both Irene and me. She was on the verge of completing her Ph.D. dissertation from UC Berkeley and moving back home to the borderlands of Tijuana, BC–Chula Vista, CA. Our mutual friend Gail Perez, one of the few Chicana professors in San Diego at the time, who was also in attendance at NACCS, encouraged me to attend a panel focusing on spirituality and healing. This had only been my second NACCS so I wasn't privy to the sorts of topics explored or discussed in NACCS outside of "Chicano nationalism" politics. So, a panel on spirituality and healing intrigued me. I attended. When the panel finished, Gail formally introduced Irene and me to each other; since then, our friendship has evolved into a *comadrazgo*, almost a blood-like kin relationship of chosen family, founded on mutual respect and admiration.

There is a prominent *dicho* (saying) in the Mexican familial tradition that says, "*Dime con quién andas y te diré quién eres*," which loosely translates to "tell me with whom you keep company and I'll know who you are." Irene, my friend and colleague, is someone with whom I enjoy keeping company. A blossoming fifteen-year friendship has nurtured a strong professional/collegial relationship. If there was ever any moral truth in the aforementioned proverb, I eagerly embrace a healthy moral compass and feel fortunate to be mentored by the accolades of my colleague. Shaped by her gentle and peaceful ways, Irene masterfully nurtures the strongest qualities of those who surround her, be they her students, colleagues, friends, or family. She listens, acknowledges, observes, cares wholeheartedly, honors, and directs. These traits are certainly those Irene has learned and accessed from the multiple influential Chicana *Indígena curanderas* she has interviewed, such as the late Elena Avila, author of *Woman Who Glows in the Dark* (1999); Madre Sarita, who cofounded the first *espiritualista* temple in San Diego; and cultural educator Grace Alvarez Sesma. The many exchanges between her and these *curanderas* have led Dr. Lara to embark upon spiritual academic work foregrounding the groundbreaking anthology, *Fleshing the Spirit: Spirituality and Activism in Chicana, Latina, and Indigenous Women's Lives* (2014), which she coedited with Dr. Elisia Facio. Irene describes the publication of this text as a birthing journey of sorts, midwifed by many along the way.

Today, Irene is distinctive in her field as the first Chicana to be tenured in the Women's Studies department at San Diego State University. She has now coedited two books; the most recent is *Women in Culture: An Intersectional Anthology of Gender and Women's Studies* (Scott et al. 2017). She believes, "We write the books we need to read; we create the communities we need to be a part of," not so much to gain admiration, but to forge our personal and collective paths of *conocimiento*, as Gloria Anzaldúa would say. She also believes that "individualism in our culture isolates us from one another by promoting the idea that each of us should be a stand-alone star. In community, our visions of love, justice, healing, and well-being can more powerfully be embodied."

Defining her project further tells the uniqueness of what Irene has achieved: to write as spiritual beings *and* scholars, thinkers, and healers. A descendant of women of color writers who, to adapt Cherríe Moraga's words,

Irene Lara, 2015 at SDSU, near the Koi Pond.

Courtesy of Ginger Shoulders.

"theor[ize from] the flesh" (1981), she calls this work a fleshing of the spirit and a spiriting of the flesh with the aims of healing the western secular divide between body, mind, and spirit and decolonizing sexuality and spirituality.

Irene sees spirituality as reclaiming ourselves apart from the institutions that can be tremendously oppressive. S/spirit is what makes us feel whole on the path of being fulfilled; it promotes liberation, taken from us by a colonial legacy that disregards the roots of our indigenous ancestry. In addition to many other Chicana writers who form part of her intellectual genealogy—such as Ana Castillo, Laura Pérez, Lara Medina, and Inés Hernández-Avila—Irene recognizes Gloria Anzaldúa's influence, especially her book *Borderlands/La Frontera* (1987) and her essay on the path of *conocimiento* (2002). As a teacher, Irene furthers this engagement with indigenous approaches to *conocimiento* (knowledge) constructed from all of our senses. It is discerned through our intuition, through listening to S/spirit—*conocimiento* as a path of survival—of creating deep bonds with people; grounded in nature, humanity, social justice, and an ecological (re)awakening that we are related to all of life. The project is also unique in the university in that it acknowledges the original people of the land, our own ancestors.

Dr. Lara believes that healing is what brings us together. She applies her *curandera* healer knowledge by inviting students to think about how their scholarly methods and research content can heal their wounds of academic trauma and suture the splits between the cultures of home and school, between our bodies, minds, and spirits demanded by dominant forms of education. Her efforts have resulted in the creation of a new, explicitly decolonial feminist mentor paradigm—*Femtoring*—where by borrowing from Chicana, Latina, and Indigenous Women's healing practices, her students are encouraged to partake, examine, and consider their scholarship as healing work (Gonzalez et al. 2015). The *Femtoring* paradigm invites the possibility of seeing Chicana Latina Indigenous women as *curandera* scholars on a path to healing themselves and creating healing stories (Levins Morales 1998). Several of her students have confirmed that "Profe" Lara literally saved their souls. Her students enthusiastically confirm that her classes and her teaching methods rooted in indigenous epistemologies are a place where storytelling, active listening, and heart-led experiences are honored and create a space for these young Chicanas to reconnect with themselves. Dr. Irene Lara, *doctora de filosofía, profesora*, is also a healer.

Irene has also saved my soul. Irene's friendship and gentle guidance led me back to my soul in the aftermath of a life-changing event. She and her family provided my son and me, her *ahijado*, (godson) a refuge where we could lick our wounds and begin anew. Inhabiting her space, while temporarily, provided me with an intimate glimpse of her ability to challenge the centuries' old dichotomies, which split the scholar's natural inclination to be whole where the home space occupied by parenting and familial roles is obviously divorced from the space of academia.

Over sips of coffee, *tecitos*, and communal cooking of vegetarian enchiladas, I recognized Irene's relentless desire to live a praxis way of life where her academic scholar self was not divorced from her partner or mother self and vice versa. Instead, her life's work as scholar, mother, and thinking/feeling *sentipensante* (Rendón 2009) takes on an energy associated with the *Mexica* mother earth deity, Coatlicue. A life abounding and simultaneous cleanser of life, Coatlicue's image of the double-headed serpent with talon feet visually reminds us of the balance necessary for the survival of all living entities. The balance is in the talons, representative of the sky, and the serpent, representative of the earth. Without balance, without harmony in nature, the possibility of reproduction, whether it be physical life or of ideas, is impossible. Hence, for those who engage her work, Irene's academic creations echo the energetic proprieties of Coatlicue's *fuerza*, force or power, where we are challenged to consider the spiritual consequences of splitting the self, as well as the spiritual consequences of living out of harmony with the earth.

Thus, the significance of Healing Splits is very important to her. Indeed, her project includes acknowledging one of the worst splits of which women must be aware: the madonna/whore, or "virtuous *virgen*/pagan *puta*," split (Lara 2008, 2014). This oppositional binary labels us as deviant. Thus, we are unworthy of being treated with dignity, if we do not comply with the patriarchal and colonial concepts devised to keep women separated from one another and from being their whole selves.

Ultimately, the focus of Dr. Lara's project, her scholarship and teaching is to validate indigenous knowledge and give honor to the idea of place. That is, the story of America by colonizers is misinformed; America is an occupied land base. The project exposes this, bringing awareness to the people and their struggles that persist. Drawing from the knowledge of her ancestors and passing it on to her students is both life-giving and redeeming.

"*Dime con quién andas y te diré quién eres*" reminds me that I am in good company with my friend, *colega, comadre*, and fellow Chicana scholar activist. She and I, like all those who have been blessed to cross her path, are each other's *In Lak'ech*, the Mayan indigenous concept that reminds all of us: "*tú eres mi otro yo*/you are my other me."

Works Cited

Anzaldúa, Gloria. *Borderlands/La Frontera: The New Mestiza*. Aunt Lute Books, 1987.

---. "Now Let Us Shift…the Path of conocimiento…Inner Work, Public Acts." *This Bridge We Call Home: Radical Visions for Transformation*, edited by Gloria E. Anzaldúa and AnaLouise Keating, Routledge, 2002, 540-578.

Avila, Elena, and Joy Parker. *Woman Who Glows in the Dark: A Curandera Reveals Traditional Aztec Secrets of Physical and Spiritual Health*. J.P. Tarcher/Putnam, 1999.

Facio, Elisa, and Irene Lara, editors. *Fleshing the Spirit: Spirituality and Activism in Chicana, Latina, and Indigenous Women's Lives*. U of Arizona P, 2014.

Gonzalez, Alejandra, Irene Lara, Carolina Prado, Sophia Rivera, and Carmen Rodriguez. "Passing the Sage: CuranderaScholarActivists in Academia." *Chicana/Latina Studies: The Journal of Mujeres Activas en Letras y Cambio Social*, vol. 15, no. 1, 2015, pp. 110-155.

Lara, Irene. "'Goddess' of the *Américas* in the Decolonial Imaginary: Beyond the Virtuous *Virgen*/Pagan *Puta* Dichotomy." *Feminist Studies*, vol. 34, no. 1/2, 2008, pp. 99–127.

---. "Sensing the Serpent in the Mother, Dando a luz la Madre Serpiente: Chicana Spirituality, Sexuality, and Mamihood." *Fleshing the Spirit: Spirituality and Activism in Chicana, Latina, and Indigenous Women's Lives*, edited by Elisa Facio and Irene Lara, U of Arizona P, 2014, pp. 113–34.

Levins Morales, Aurora. *Medicine Stories: History, Culture, and the Politics of Integrity.* Southend P, 1998.

Moraga, Cherríe, and Gloria Anzaldúa, editors. *This Bridge Called My Back: Writings by Radical Women of Color.* Persephone P, 1981.

Rendón, Laura I. *Sentipensante (Sensing/Thinking) Pedagogy: Educating for Wholeness, Social Justice and Liberation.* Stylus, 2009.

Scott, Bonnie Kime, Susan Cayleff, Anne Donadey, and Irene Lara, editors. *Women in Culture: An Intersectional Anthology of Gender and Women's Studies.* Wiley-Blackwell, 2017.

About the Author:

MARIA FIGUEROA is professor of English at MiraCosta Community College. In 2005, she taught one of the first courses for Chicanas at San Diego City College when they had no courses for Mexican American women. She authored "Toward a Spiritual Pedagogy along the Borderlands" in the book *Fleshing the Spirit*, coedited by Elisa Facio and Irene Lara (2014). Both Maria and Irene have presented their work at the Gracia Molina de Pick Feminist Seminars at San Diego Mesa College. Maria is the mother of two children.

ELVA SALINAS:

PROFESSOR OF ENGLISH; SAN DIEGO CITY COLLEGE
Faculty of the Year Award; KPBS Local Hero

BY JAZMIN MORELOS

Professor Elva Salinas is my heroine and this ode is a reflection of the way I see and feel about her. This is my personal gift and declaration of gratitude, respect and admiration for someone who has provided so many with much needed balance, guidance, and perspective in their lives. If *La Profe* were a precious gem, she would be Tanzanite because she is extremely rare and can be found only once every few decades, and doubtlessly with time her value increases.

Throughout history names such as Cleopatra, Mozart, and Garcia-Marquez have been immortalized through poetry, literature, and music. These names have become symbols, representations, and identification markers of people, places and time periods. We all go by a name, whether imposed on us by our parents or a self-chosen alias. Throughout our life we build a reputation attached to that name and it follows us wherever we go. All names are attached to the past, the present and the future, and can therefore tell stories about who that person is.

When I see or hear the name Elva Salinas, I recall beautiful memories of the journey I have traveled to become the woman that I am today. The last decade of my life was filled with her influence in the form of education, love, wisdom, laughter and inspiration. To me, she is more than just Elva; she is Professor Salinas, also known as *La Profe.* The letters that make up this *linda chicana's* name say something about her character: She is an Educator; a Lover; Virtuous by birth; a fearless Activist; she is Smart; Amazing; a Leader; Inspiring; Nurturing; Adventurous; *and of course*, Sexy.

I had heard about a Professor Salinas, who walked and fought alongside her students and her community, but I had yet to meet what seemed to be a mythological creature. The stories I heard about her seemed too good to be true. I first met *La Profe* in July 2005 while battling the *Minute-Mensos*, or Minutemen, a vigilante, anti-immigrant group. She was hard to miss with her red curls

Elva Salinas, Professor, English, San Diego City College.
Courtesy of Aisha Salinas.

flowing through the driver's window, or with the loud thumps coming out of her older model mini-van speeding through the rocky dirt road. When we finally met, it was a match made in heaven. She immediately became my mentor, my friend, my cheerleader and most importantly, my *familia*. I enrolled in her college courses and watched this vibrant woman in action. Her devotion to teaching her students how to think and write critically, filled me with admiration and gratitude. Until I met her, I hadn't met another person who exuded so much vitality and so nurturing a spirit.

Now I understood what students meant when they talked about her. Professor Salinas gave us the wings, allowing us to grow, making us see our value, and awakening our dreams. She has also seen some of her students' dreams come true in various ways, through sustainability movements, recycling, environmentalism, food justice, growing their own gardens, taking on some land, growing corn, promoting free trade coffee. She watched one group called CAFE form, making great strides.

Elva's passion for her students is what leads to their transformation. In Elva's own words, coming from an interview I had with her, "Transformation happens when students can tell us *their* stories; when they are introduced to the scholarly works of *their* own culture; to Pulitzer Prize winning authors; to the poetry of Latin America; the stories of the Aztecs, and the Mayan *Popol Vu*. It awakens *their* voices and they feel empowered." The more I've gotten to know her, the more I see how valuable her contributions are to society.

I am grateful that she has shared very personal stories with those in need of important life lessons. Whenever I feel helpless in a challenging situation I always remember the stories she shared with me about her childhood. She turned hurt into humor to help others when she told me that as children, she and her brother made a game out of killing *cucarachas* in the middle of the night. I vividly remember the cute dimple formed by her smile when she shared this story with me. It was no longer a sad or painful story; it was empowering. Her stories taught me lessons about humility, life, self-love, and personal growth.

This remarkable *mujer* has proven to be good at anything she tries, thus explaining her excellent track record of achievements. She graduated high school with honors despite being discriminated by the *gueras envidiosas*, envious ones. She then went on to become a cosmetologist and within sixteen years she had gone from adjunct professor at San Diego City College, to professor, to chair of the Cosmetology Department; she then went on to receive a master's degree in English, making the cross over into teaching English and Chicano Studies courses. Not only did she succeed in doing all of this in such a short amount of time, but she also somehow managed to give birth and raise three beautiful children.

A full professor of English at San Diego City College, she became part of thirteen committees. In her role as a professor, she has presented at more than 100 conferences and workshops; has developed faculty professional development courses; and has won several prestigious honors. It seems every other year she is bestowed with some kind of recognition, and at this rate soon she'll be more famous than Shakira. Besides the KPBS Local Heroes Award, other awards include San Diego State University *Chicana Conciencia*: Past, Present and Future tribute; *Chicana Conciente* Educator Award; Latina Leadership Award; Faculty of the Year, Golden Apple Award; among many others. Besides her fame, which follows her wherever she goes and with great reason, she can face obstacles with equal dignity.

In the hardest times she still comes through. She recalls when a budget crises hit the community colleges, "Morale became low with budget cuts and things changed; there was a faculty freeze, and courses were cut." Still, she centered on basic skills courses to assure student transfer to the State Colleges and UC systems which were also affected. She recalled that in classes of thirty, only two or three students were accepted to transfer. Again, she continued "to fight for reallocating resources for the future of our children, for the future of our country."

I once heard a rumor that the sun was worried that *La Profe*'s radiance and warmth would replace him, but she assured him they could have a bigger impact if they joined forces. He liked her idea so much that he decided to bless her with an additional gift, her contagious smile and laughter. Besides her radiant smile, she is a guide, a mentor, a positive instigator, a believer in the goodness of humankind, and, the life of the party—a wild and free spirited soul who I respect and admire. More importantly, she is a strong force behind creative change and action. Elva recalled a time when professors had access to faculty development programs to help students who wanted to give up. She took advantage of the aid offered to teachers. A Title 5 Serving Grant to Hispanic Institutions helped to create positive change for students with the focus on student retention and success. Elva recalls that "Faculty could learn to reach students so they that were not constantly looked at from a deficit model." Some students seemed to always be told, "You don't have this; you don't have that; you don't speak English well enough; your culture is different; your language is different." She tried the opposite approach.

Her example taught me that praxis is a way of life; it's not just some meaningless word that often appears in the texts she uses. Professor Salinas lives her life in the service of seeking truth and freedom, and the dignity of all humans. She is always ready to act. It could be for student interventions instead of letting students drop out. If they feel like giving up, she may just ask, "What is going on with you?" to help students. She reminds them, "Your ancestors paid highly the price with their lives, with their blood and sweat in the Civil Rights Movement. You deserve this education." That way, she says, "They learn self-efficacy: their education belongs to them, not to the faculty, and not to the administration."

To me she is a vibrant star whose light illuminates the darkest hearts and corners of San Diego City College. She parades the campus confidently with an entourage of admirers and followers: to and from classes; to committee meetings; to writing grants so low-income students have a better chance at succeeding in life; to making time to listen to a distressed student who needs a sympathetic ear; to attending every single event in the life of her three children; to being Elva Salinas to the maximum power—and then more.

If *La Profe* were a season she would be eternal spring because her touch encourages the blossoming of human potential, in all its colorful beauty and splendor. If she were a flower, she would be a hardy and resilient desert rose from her homeland, Deming, New Mexico, one that could survive and thrive in any environment. If she were an animal she would be an Aztec jaguar from Aztlán, constantly guarding and nurturing her *crias*—whether her own children, unofficially adopted children, or friends. If I had to give her a nickname, I would definitely name her *La Transformer* because she can go from chasing *minute-mensos* on the rugged border, to wearing stylish high heels, a cute *falda*, a skirt matching her passion-red manicure and pedicure. Though respectful and polite, if you cross her the wrong way, you will definitely be greeted and politely put back in place by an educated and fierce *chola*.

Most recently she took her passions to the extreme, along with all her other commitments and challenges. *La Profe* decided to run for San Diego's Grossmont Union High School Board of Directors. In the midst of one of the most divisive national presidential campaigns, in 2016 she was the first Chicana/Latina to be elected to the local school board, beating the incumbent republican trustee.

If there were a saying that best describes Professor Elva Salinas' approach to life, it would definitely be, "When life gives you lemons, make lemonade," because she turns obstacles into opportunities and dead ends into roads of infinite possibilities.

About the Author:

JAZMIN MORELOS holds an M.A. in Communication Studies from San Francisco State University. She is a mother, a photographer, videographer, life enthusiast. She has worked on immigrant rights issues and focuses on the immigrant experience. She grew up in Tijuana, but has made the Bay Area her home for the last decade. Currently she is working on a campaign normalizing breastfeeding in public through art and education.

Editor Profile

Rita Sanchez

Rita Sanchez, 2013, at home.
Courtesy of Zerina Zermeño.

Rita Sanchez always had a passion for writing and reading ever since she was a girl. During the turbulent sixties she centered this love of books on studying for a degree in literature. Then as an English and Chicano Studies professor she used her profession as a way to reach hundreds like herself, first generation college students to help them graduate from college.

Born and raised in San Bernardino's west side to a working class family, her ancestral roots run deep in New Mexico before the pilgrims when the land was Indian and Spanish. In the early 1900s, her grandfather moved his wife and children to California with the railroad. Her father, Leonides Sanchez worked for the Santa Fe and there spoke up for workers rights ending discriminatory practices. Seventh of eleven children, Rita attributes her drive for justice to her father, and her love of learning to her mother Macedonia Acuña's great wisdom of teaching her children to read and to introducing them to the library at a young age.

At first, a journalism major, Rita was assistant editor of *The Tyro Weekly News* at San Bernardino High School. She won the Winifred Martin Journalism Award given in a citywide competition by the *San Bernardino Sun Telegram* which enabled her to go away to San Jose State College in 1956. She always recognized that she was following in the footsteps of her older sisters, Josephine, Theresa, and Mary, serious students, whom she considers her greatest mentors.

As a young Catholic girl she married a student in her freshman year; and with great dreams for their future, worked full time to put him through college and law school, while raising two daughters. Sadly, they were divorced ten years later, a period of heartbreak, then recovery, which Rita attributes to her family, her faith, and the Civil Rights Movement. Never giving up her dream to finish college, in 1968 she took to heart the words of Dolores Huerta, Cesar Chavez, and Bobbie Kennedy who said, "This generation cannot afford to waste its substance and its hope on the struggles of the past." As a reentry mother, she made the honor roll at Foothill Community College in Palo Alto, and went on to graduate from Stanford University with a B.A. and M.A. in English.

Very soon, Rita committed to helping others to graduate, a mandate given to the Mexican American students who had made it thus far. With civil rights activism at its peak in 1970, Rita was recruited by her English professor, author and activist, Arturo Islas, to join the Chicano Affairs Advisory Committee to the President of Stanford. As a result, she served on the hiring committee to select its director, Cecilia Burciaga, whose long career at Stanford benefitted many incoming Chicana and Chicano students, while Rita herself determinedly began to prepare for her own career, knowing she must as a young mother.

As a graduate student, Rita applied for the Stanford Chicano Fellowship, proposing to teach the first course for Mexican American women who were attending the university in great numbers following the Civil Rights Act of 1964. The first woman fellow, she also proposed a course in writing specifically to orient the many incoming Mexican American freshmen, and then proposed a women's journal, *Imagenes de la Chicana*, published at Stanford in 1973.

In the midst of all the activism and finding herself at home with daughters to raise, she challenged her students to write as another way of protesting the injustices they were experiencing in education that dismissed their culture and history. Recognizing the value of writing and publishing as revolutionary, her 1970's essay, "Chicana Writer Breaking Out of Silence," became her focus. It was later reprinted as, "Writing as a Revolutionary Act," its dominant theme; and then republished in *Chicana Feminist Thought, The Basic Historical Writings* (1997).

In 1974, she was recruited to teach English in the Department of Mexican American Studies at San Diego State University, the first woman tenure track professor; she wrote the department's "Mission Statement;" taught Chicana Studies; and in 1976, with the help of Chicanas on campus, like Elizabeth Alvarado, EOP Counselor, edited another student journal at SDSU she called *Visión de la Mujer de La Raza*, to honor Stanford friend and colleague, Antonia Castañeda who taught the first woman's course at the University of Washington.

In 1976 she entered the Ph.D. program at UCSD, on a Ford Foundation Fellowship, essentially working 3 full time jobs, teaching at SDSU, working on her doctorate at UCSD; and raising two more children. After ten years at SDSU, in 1990 she began teaching English and literature at San Diego Mesa College, and responded to a MALDEF (Mexican American Legal Defense Fund) objection to the low numbers of student transfers. As a writing instructor, Rita became Mesa's and then UCSD's best advocate teaching writing required to transfer, enabling students to graduate in higher education. She also taught the Chicana course; wrote the curriculum to articulate it as a transfer course required at SDSU; was lauded for her significant contribution as author of the Chicano Studies department's self study for accreditation; and revised Mesa's once broad multicultural course requirement to read, "cultures which have been historically excluded because of race, class, ethnicity, or gender," and as first woman chair of Chicano Studies, proposed the department's name change to Chicana and Chicano Studies. Her activism led to significant policy changes to benefit students and effect change.

Rita, now retired is grateful for the opportunity to document Chicana civil rights activism and to have contributed her essay, "Chicanas in the Arts, 1970–1995" to the book *Chicano San Diego* (2007). Recently she was keynote speaker at the Gracia Molina de Pick Feminist Lecture series. The title she borrowed from her activist essay, calling it "Writing As a Revolutionary Act: A Chicana's Journey."

Rita was inducted into the San Diego County Women's Hall of Fame as Activist in 2010 at the Women's Museum of California. After a 30 year career as college professor, Rita continues to write for publication, to research her family history; and to spend time with her four children, Lisa La Rossa, Teyana Viscarra, Lucia Gonzales, and Pablo Acevedo, all activists in their own right; and with her husband of over twenty years, Professor Richard Griswold del Castillo and his family; between them they have eleven grandchildren, and two great-grandchildren. Together the two of them have devoted their retirement to collecting the personal papers of San Diego's civil rights activists for the Archives of SDSU's Special Collections Library, and to volunteering for Encuentro, a Catholic ministry for Latinos.

Editor Profile

Sonia Amelia Lopez

Sonia Amelia Lopez was born into a family whose ancestors immigrated to California and Arizona in the mid-1800s, 1920s, and 1950's; the latter period continued its demand for Mexican cheap labor, which coincided with this country's unprecedented economic and political prosperity. Originally from the Mexican state of Sonora, Sonia's immediate family was no different from other immigrants seeking a better economic life. Her

Sonia Amelia Lopez, 2009, San Diego.
Courtesy of Amelia A. Hinojosa, daughter.

mother, three siblings, and Sonia joined her father in Heber, California where he found work as a mechanic of farm machinery. Sonia's family would settle in Calexico, California, where the majority of the population was and still is comprised of *Mexicano* migrant workers. Calexico borders Mexicali, the capital city of Baja California, and is situated in the Imperial Valley desert. Once irrigation was introduced to the Imperial Valley, its farmlands became some of the most successful agricultural lands globally. These lands were developed and harvested by mostly Filipino and Mexican agricultural workers allowed into the United States to assist farmers though the federal Bracero Program of the 1940's and 1950's.

Sonia's interests in the disenfranchisement and political agency of Mexicans on this side of the border inspired her activism in the Chicano Student Movement of the late sixties and early seventies, although she grew critical of its sexism and fought for gender equity by creating and teaching Chicana studies courses and by writing and making presentations on the importance of Chicana issues. She joined the student group MEChA at San Diego State College participated in Cesar Chávez's farmworker union picket lines, and worked with the Chicano Council for Higher Education (CHHE), which sought to implement El Plan De Santa Barbara and its recruitment and retention of Chicana/o students in colleges and universities throughout the state.

In 1970 she transferred to Sacramento State University and was accepted into the Mexican American Education Project with a full scholarship, a program conceived and directed by Esteban Arvizu to train bilingual teachers. That same year, as part of the Sacramento contingent, along with others such as the Royal Chicano Air Force (RCAF), Sonia marched in many statewide moratoriums against the Vietnam War. She would also become part of Teatro Jalapeños, directed by Jose Montoya, which performed and depicted the plight and struggle of Chicano and Mexicano people.

In 1972 she graduated with a B.A. in Ethnic Studies and a minor in Education and was hired as a full-time lecturer in the Department of Mexican American Studies at San Diego State College where she developed and taught the first ethnic women studies course titled "La Chicana," and taught community-organizing classes at San Diego City College. She also published the article, "The Role of the Chicana Within the Student Movement" in *Essays on La Mujer*, one of the first anthologies on Chicana women (Chicano Studies Center Publications, UCLA, 1977); later reprinted in *Chicana Feminist Thought: The Basic Historical Writings* (N.Y.: Routledge, 1997). Her courses emphasized community involvement by linking student projects with the cultural, social, economic, and political development of Latino communities. In 1973, in collaboration with San Diego City College, San Diego State College, Chicana MEChA students, and community members, Sonia participated in the organization of the First Annual High School Chicana Conference in San Diego, with Isabel Rodriguez of Los Angeles and local leader Gloria Serrano as keynote speakers.

In 1976, Sonia would go on to earn a masters in Counseling from San Diego State University (SDSU) and become a counselor at Calexico High School, her alma mater. While there she was instrumental in helping elect Education Board member Gloria Nogales, establishing a counseling center, increasing the counseling staff, and recruiting Raza teachers. In 1980's , she worked as a counselor at Southwestern College, San Diego City College, and for SDSU's Imperial Valley Campus to provide educational and job-training resources to a diverse population of unemployed and disenfranchised students, including newly released prisoners and those living on reservations.

She went on to work for the Sweetwater Union High School District to work with at-risk youth in National City, Chula Vista, Imperial Beach, San Ysidro, and parts of south San Diego. In 1993 she helped found the Adelante Mujer Conference of the South Bay, which focused on at-risk Latina students and their mothers. In 2009, she retired after returning to alternative education for four years; and in 2013 the Adelante Mujer Committee of South Bay recognized Sonia for her commitment to community service and to promoting higher education for young Latina women.

In 2014 Sonia's long history of leadership and community work was recognized once again when she was inducted into the San Diego County Women's Hall of Fame by the Women's Museum of California, for her community activism, including her efforts to empower women through education and for documenting Chicana history.

Throughout her life, Sonia has not only worked for the equality of Chicanas, but for the equality of all groups regardless of their social, political, economic, gender, and racial status. She continues to work with issues confronting undocumented migrants and is an active member of the SDSU Love Library's Special Collections, Chicana and Chicano Archive Committee, dedicated to preserving Chicana/o history. Both as a student and professional, Sonia has actively sought to bring change to conditions that exploit and oppress Latinos.

Sonia is the mother of three children, Amelia, Anita, and Mark Hinojosa, and lives in San Diego with her brother Cesar Lopez, writer, artist and poet, who was an activist during the Chicano Movement of the late 60's and 70's.

Selected Bibliography

Chapter 1:

Chicano Park. Directed by Marilyn Mulford, produced by Marilyn Mulford and Mario Barrera, written by Juan Felipe Herrera, et al. New York Cinema Guild, 1989.

Garin, Nina. "Tina C. de Baca, 79, Long Time Chicana Activst." *San Diego Union-Tribune*, 6 Nov. 2012, B-4.

Sainz, Pablo J. "Celebrating the Life of Marta Sotomayor." *La Prensa San Diego*, 12 July 2013, 1.

Sevilla, Gracia. "Laura Rodriguez, Cornerstone of the Barrio." *San Diego Union-Tribune*, 2 May 1991, B-1.

Sotomayor, Marta. "The Hispanic Elderly and The Intergenerational Family." *Journal of Children in Contemporary Society*, vol. 20, no. 3-4, 1989, pp. 55-65.

---. Personal Papers. Chicana and Chicano Archives and Special Collections. San Diego State University Libraries.

Sotomayor, Marta, and Alejandro Garcia, editors. *Elderly Latinos: Issues and Solutions for the 21st Century*. National Hispanic Council on Aging, 1993.

Chapter 2:

Allatson, Paul. "Reading the Taco Shop Poets in the Crossroads of Chicano Postnationalism." *Rethinking Chicana/o Literature Through Food*, edited by Nieves Pascual Soler and Meredith E. Abarca, Palgrave Macmillan, 2013.

Andrade, Gloria, and Richard Rodriguez. "Teresa Urrea: Her Life as it Affected the Mexican-U.S. Frontier." *Quinto Sol/El Grito Publications*, vol. 5, no. 4, 1972, pp. 48-68.

Brookman, Phillip, and Guillermo Gomez-Peña, editors. *Made in Aztlán, 15th Anniversary*. Centro Cultural de la Raza, 1986.

García, Laura E., Sandra M. Gutierrez, and Felicitas Nuñez, editors. *Teatro Chicana: A Collective Memoir and Selected Plays*. Forward by Yolanda Broyles-Gonzalez, U of Texas P, 2008. Chicana Matters.

Hernandez-Terry, Charlotte. Personal Papers. Chicana and Chicano Archives and Special Collections. San Diego State University Libraries.

Mancillas, Aida. "The Citizen Artist." *The Citizen Artist: 20 Years of Art in the Public Arena*, edited by Linda Frye Burnham, et al., Critical P, 1998.

Moraga, Cherrie, and Gloria Anzaldúa, editors. *This Bridge Called My Back, Writings by Radical Women of Color*. 1981, 4th ed., SUNY, 2015.

Moreno, Delia. Personal Papers. Chicana and Chicano Archives and Special Collections. San Diego State University Libraries.

Romero, Lin. *Happy Songs, Bleeding Hearts (Rostros de Amerindias: A Series of Indigenous Xicano Journeys)*. Toltecas en Aztlán, 1974.

Tecihtzin. *Chia: A Powerful Recuerdo*. Tochtli Publishing, 1996.

Chapter 3:

Molina-Enríquez, Gracia. *Mujeres en la historia, historias de mujeres: una revisión de la historia de México a través de la participación de las mujeres*. Salsipuedes Ediciones, 2009.

Molina de Pick, Gracia. Personal Papers. Chicana and Chicano Archives and Special Collections. San Diego State University Libraries.

Puente, Connie. Personal Papers. Chicana and Chicano Archives and Special Collections, San Diego State University Libraries.

Chapter 4:

Alfonso, Mirna. "Barrio Station: Youth Center Curbs Crime and Puts Youngsters on the Right Path." *Los Angeles Times*, 2 Feb. 1986.

Castro, Irma. Personal Papers. Chicana and Chicano Archives and Special Collections. San Diego State University Libraries.

Chapter 5:

Cockcroft, Eva Sperling, and Holly Barnet-Sánchez, editors. *Signs From the Heart: California Chicano Murals*. U of New Mexico P, 1993.

Davalos, Karen Mary. *Yolanda M. López*. U of Minnesota P, 2008.

Gadon, Elinor W. *The Once And Future Goddess, A Symbol For Our Time*. Harper and Row, 1989.

Griswold del Castillo, Richard, Teresa McKenna, and Yvonne Yarbro-Bejarano, editors. *CARA: Chicano Art: Resistance and Affirmation, 1965-1985*. UCLA Wight Gallery, 1991.

López, Yolanda M., and Moira Roth. "Social Protest: Racism and Sexism." *The Power of Feminist Art*, edited by Norma Broude and Mary D. Garrard, H. N. Abrams, 2008, pp. 140-157.

Mesa-Bains, Amalia, Tomas Ybarra-Frausto, and Shifra Goldman. *Signs From the Heart, California Chicano Murals*. SPARC, 1990.

"Twenty-foot Mural." Installation piece by Berenice Badillo. *La Prensa San Diego*, 14 Sept. 2012, p. 4.

Chapter 6:

Chavez-Arteaga, Alicia. *Las Mujeres De Teatro Izcalli: Transformative Stories of Healing and Resistance.* Thesis, San Diego State U, 2012.

Diaz Cruz, Evelyn. "The Glass Cord." First performed in New York, 2012.

———. "MUERTOS: A Day of the Dead Play." First performed at USD, 2012.

MacFarland-Thuet, Coral. *Abriendo Puertas.* Innerfocusmusic, 2000.

———. *To Another Shore.* Webster's Last Word, 1999.

Chapter 7:

Chavez, Enriqueta. Personal Papers. Chicana and Chicano Archives and Special Collections. San Diego State University Libraries.

García, Maria E. "The Complete History of Neighborhood House in Logan Heights Series." *San Diego Free Press*, 2 Feb. 2017, sandiegofreepress.org/category/columns/history-of-neighborhood-house/.

———. *La Neighbor: A Settlement House in Logan Heights.* San Diego Printers, 2016.

———. Personal Papers. Chicana and Chicano Archives and Special Collections. San Diego State University Libraries.

Huerta, Lizz. *I Succubus.* Lumina, 2016.

Chapter 8:

García-Sims, Angela. Personal Papers. Chicana and Chicano Archives and Special Collections. San Diego State University Libraries.

Gutierrez, Elaine, Doman Lum, and Maria Zuñiga. *Education for Multicultural Social Work Practice.* CSWE, 2004.

Huerta, Alvaro, Norma Iglesias Prieto, and Donathan Brown, editors. *Contemporary Issues for People of Color Surviving and Thriving in the U.S. Today, vol. 4: Immigration and Migration.* ABC-CLIO Greenwood, 2016.

Iglesias-Prieto, Norma. *Emergencias las Artes Visuales en Tijuana. Volume I. Los contextos glocales y la creatividad.* Consejo Nacional para la Cultura y las Artes, Centro Cultural Tijuana, and Baja California: Universidad Autónoma, 2008.

———. "Female Images in Mexican Border Cinema." *Americas and Latinas.* Working Group on Women in Gender, Center for Latin American Studies, Stanford U, 2000, pp. 28–36.

———. *Beautiful Flowers of the Maquiladora: Life Histories of Women Workers in Tijuana.* U of Texas P, 1985. Spanish Version: *La flor más bella de la maquiladora.* SEP-Cultura-CEFNOMEX, 1997.

Perez, Gail. "Ana Castillo as Santera." *A Reader In Latina Feminist Theology: Religion and Justice*, edited by Maria Pilar Aquino, Daisy C. Machado, and Jeanette Rodriguez, U of Texas P, 2002, pp. 53–79.

Ruiz de Burton, María Amparo. *The Squatter and the Don*. Introduction by Rosaura Sanchez and Beatrice Pita, Arte Publico, 2012.

Sanchez, Marta E. *Contemporary Chicana Poetry: A Critical Approach to an Emerging Literature*. U of California P, 1985.

---. *Shakin' Up Race and Gender: Intercultural Connections in Puerto Rican, AfricaAmerican, and Chicano Narratives and Culture (1965-1995)*. U of Texas P, 2005.

---. Personal Papers. Chicana and Chicano Archives and Special Collections. San Diego State University Libraries.

Sanchez, Rosaura. *Telling Identities: the Californio testimonios*. U of Minnesota P, 1995.

Sanchez, Rosaura, and Rosa Martinez Cruz, editors. *Essays on La Mujer*. UCLA, 1977.

Santana, Patricia. *Motorcycle Ride on the Sea of Tranquility*. U of New Mexico P, 2002.

---. *Ghosts of El Grullo*. U of New Mexico P, 2008.

Chapter 9:

Espinoza, Dionne, and Lorena Oropeza. *Enriqueta Vasquez and the Chicano Movement: Writings from El Grito del Norte*. Arte Publico, 2006.

MANA San Diego Papers. Chicana and Chicano Archives and Special Collections. San Diego State University Libraries.

Puentes-Reynolds, Olivia. *Brown is Beautiful*. Poetry presentation. Unpublished. Chicano Youth Conference, 1969.

Sandoval, Carmen. Personal Papers. Chicana and Chicano Archives and Special Collections. San Diego State University Libraries.

Chapter 10:

Angelou, Maya. *Phenomenal Woman: Four Poems Celebrating Women*. Random House, 1995.

Butler-Byrd, Nola, Jesus Nieto, and Maria Nieto-Senour. "Community Based Block as a Site of Praxis and Social Justice." *Journal of Praxis in Multicultural Education*, vol. 3, no. 1, 2008, pp. 17-38.

Mariechild, Diane. *Mother Wit*. Harper Collins, 1981.

Nieto-Senour, Maria. Personal Papers. Chicana and Chicano Archives and Special Collections. San Diego State University Libraries.

---. "Psychology of the Chicana." *Chicano Psychology*, edited by Joe Martinez and Richard Mendoza, Academic Press, 1977. Reprinted in *Female Psychology: the Emerging Self*, edited by S. Cox, St. Martins Press, 1981.

Pinkola Estes, Clarissa. *Women Who Run With the Wolves: Myths and Stories of the Wild Woman Archetype*. Ballentine, 1996.

Chapter 11:

Avalos, Fredi. "Bread and Roses Too." *Social Justice*, vol. 39, no. 2-3, 2012, pp. 128-9.

Bean, Frank, and Marta Tienda. *The Hispanic Population of the United States*. Russell Sage, 1987.

Franco, Jean. "Sor Juana Ines de la Cruz." *Plotting Women; Gender and Representation in Mexico*, Columbia UP, 1989, pp. 23-54.

Freire, Paolo. *Pedagogy of the Oppressed*. Herder & Herder, 1970.

Hernandez-Linares, Leticia. *Mucha Muchacha, Too Much Girl, Poems*, Tia Chucha P, 2015.

Marin, Patricia, and Catherine Horn. *Realizing Bakke's Legacy: Affirmative Action, Equal Opportunity, and Access to Higher Education*. Stylus P, 2008.

Chapter 12:

Facio, Elisa, and Irene Lara. *Fleshing the Spirit: Spirituality and Activism in Chicana, Latina, and Indigenous Women's Lives*. U of Arizona P, 2014.

Figueroa-Chacon, Maria. "Toward a Spiritual Pedagogy Along the Borderlands." *Fleshing the Spirit: Spirituality and Activism in Chicana, Latina, and Indigenous Women's Lives*, edited by Elisa Facio and Irene Lara, U of Arizona P, 2014, pp. 34-42.

Galan, Hector, producer. *Chicano! History of the Mexican American Civil Rights Movement*. Galan Productions, 1996.

García, Mario. *Blowout! Sal Castro and the Chicano Struggle for Educational Justice*. U of North Carolina P, 2011.

Ramirez, Deborah. "Multicultural Empowerment: It's Not Just Black and White Anymore." *Stanford Law Review*, vol. 47, no. 5, 1995, pp. 957-992.

Scott, Bonnie K., Susan E. Cayleff, Anne Donadey, and Irene Lara. *Women in Culture: An Intersectional Anthology for Gender and Women's Studies*. John Wiley & Sons, 2017.

Editors' Annotated Selections in Chicana Studies:

Anzaldúa, Gloria. *Borderlands/La Frontera: The New Mestiza*. Aunt Lute, 1987.

> Gloria Anzaldúa was a Chicana-tejana-lesbian-feminist poet, theorist, and fiction writer from South Texas. In addition to authoring *Borderlands/La Frontera*, she was the editor of the critical anthology *Making Face/Making Soul: Haciendo Caras* (1990), and co-editor of *This Bridge Called My Back* (1981). She passed away in 2004 and was honored around the world for shedding visionary light on the Chicana experience by receiving the National Assn. for Chicana and Chicano (NACCS) Studies Scholar Award in 2005.

Berelowitz, JoAnne. "Las Comadres: A Feminist Collective Negotiates a New Paradigm for Women at the U.S./Mexico Border." *Genders*, vol. 28 (1998).

In the spring of 1988 a group of women artists and activists in the contiguous border cities of San Diego and Tijuana established a collective which they later named *Las Comadres* . . . for the production of a powerful, socially-committed art. In1990, at the Centro Cultural de la Raza in San Diego their efforts culminated in a performance and installation that embodied their ideas and attracted national attention, including invitations to perform at art spaces both in and beyond San Diego.

Blackwell, Maylei. *¡Chicana Power! Contested Histories of Feminism in the Chicano Movement*. Chicana Matters Series, edited by Deena J. González and Antonia Castañeda, U of Texas P, 2011.

¡Chicana Power! provides a critical genealogy of pioneering Chicana activist and theorist Anna NietoGomez and the *Hijas de Cuauhtémoc*, one of the first Latina feminist organizations, who together with other Chicana activists forged an autonomous space for women's political participation and challenged the gendered confines of Chicano nationalism in the movement and in the formation of the field of Chicana studies."

Broyles-González, Yolanda. *Lydia Mendoza's Life in Music: Norteño Tejano Legacies/ La historia de Lydia Mendoza*. Oxford UP, 2001.

This is a bilingual English and Spanish presentation of Lydia Mendoza's *historia* as an interview between the artist and the author, concluding with an extended essay on the significance of her singing career and her place in Tejana music and Chicana studies. Her career encompassed a sixty-year period from the 1920s well into the 1980s. Her status as a working-class idol continues to this day, making her one of the most long-standing performers in the history of the recording industry and a champion in Chicana/o music.

Castañeda, Antonia, Tomas Ybarra-Frausto, and Joseph Sommers. *Literatura Chicana*. Prentice Hall, 1972.

One of the first books on Chicano culture published in the United States. It Includes various references to Mexican American cultural icons and identity at a time when the people were beginning to explore their own values and history and could read something about themselves in print.

Chavez-Arteaga, Alicia. *Las Mujeres De Teatro Izcalli: Transformative Stories of Healing and Resistance*. Masters Thesis, San Diego State U, 2012.

A feminist oral history, narrating and analyzing the experiences and activism of nine women members of the Chicana/Chicano comedy troupe Teatro Izcalli based in San Diego with: Alicia Chavez-Arteaga, Cristina "Tina" Nuñez-Medina, Maria Santos-Ochoa, Claudia Cuevas-Ramirez, Olympia Andrade Beltran, Veronica Burgess, Iyari Arteaga, Michelle Tellez, and Maria Figueroa-Chacon. The work shows the ways the women *teatristas* healed and empowered themselves and their communities by employing decolonizing feminist perspectives.

Cotera, Maria. *Chicana Por Mi Raza*. Digital Memory Collective: Interviews with Chicanas/Latinas, chicanapormiraza.org.

Digital curriculum initiated at the University of Michigan, organized around capturing important Chicana and Latina voices from the long Civil Rights Era. *Chicana por mi Raza* is first and foremost an oral history project with over 150 oral histories, as well as over 5000 digitized supporting archival records.

Del Castillo, Adelaida. "Malintzín Tenepal: A Preliminary Look into a NewPerspective." *Chicana Feminist Thought: the Basic Historical Writings*, edited by Alma M. García, Routledge, 1997, p. 26.

> Del Castillo authored influential historical writings: "La Visión Chicana" in *Encuentro Feminil* (1974), the first Chicana feminist journal; and "Malintzín Tenepal: A Preliminary Look Into A New Perspective" in *Essays on La Mujer* (UCLA 1977).

García, Alma M. editor. *Chicana Feminist Thought: the Basic Historical Writings*. Routledge, 1997.

> *Chicana Feminist Thought* brings together the voices of Chicana poets, writers, and activists who reflect upon the Chicana Feminist Movement that began in the late 1960s. With energy and passion, this scholarly anthology documents the personal and collective political struggles of Chicana feminists.

García, Diana. *When Living Was a Labor Camp*. U of Arizona P, 2000.

> Garcia's first collection of poems pays tribute to the migrant labor camps of California and to the *campesinos* of California's San Joaquin Valley, their daily joys and sorrows. Called "Bold, political, and familial, García's poems gift the reader with a sense of earth, struggle, and pride—each line filled with the sounds of agrarian music, from mariachi melodies to repatriation revolts. Embodied with such spirit, her poems rise with the convictions of power and equality."

Griswold del Castillo, Richard, editor. *Chicano San Diego: Cultural Space and the Struggle for Survival*. U of Arizona P, 2007.

> This collection of essays, by three women and four men, all activist scholars, shows how the Spanish-speaking people of San Diego have a long, complicated, and rich history, and how as Chicanas and Chicanos, have created their own cultural spaces; it explores what is unique about San Diego's Mexican American History. Sensitive to issues of gender, it also pays attention to immigration, and other political areas important to the people.

Heidenreich, Linda, and Antonia I. Castañeda, editors. *Three Decades of Engendering History: The Collected Works of Antonia Castañeda*. U of North Texas P, 2014.

> For over three decades the work of Antonia I. Castañeda has shaped the fields of Western History and Chicana Studies; selected works with original interviews with Luz Maria Gordillo, with an introduction by Deena J. Gonzalez.

Ibarra, María de la Luz. "Mexican Immigrant Women and the New Domestic Labor." *Human Organization*, vol. 59, no. 4, 2000, pp. 452-64.

> The focus of this article is on Mexican immigrant women who form part of a "new" domestic labor in Santa Barbara, California. Two case studies—one of a "labor contractor" and the other of an "elderly care provider"—illustrate some of what the emerging, polarized categories are, the qualitatively distinct labor process associated with each, and some of the differences and similarities between the *Mexicanas* who undertake domestic employment.

Lopez, Sonia. "The Role of the Chicana Within the Student Movement." *Essays on La Mujer*, edited by Rosaura Sanchez and Rosa Martinez Cruz, U of California Los Angeles, 1977, pp. 16-29.

> In an important pioneering collection of Chicana feminist writings, the articles introduce concepts and topics of particular interest to analysis of the Chicana within

her particular historical, political social, and economic context. Lopez's essay introduces women's unique struggles with male dominance in leadership roles which Chicanas began to identify and address in order to demand change.

---. "The Role of the Chicana Within the Student Movement." *Chicana Feminist Thought: the Basic Historical Writings*, edited by Alma M. Garcia, Routledge, 1997, pp. 100–106.

Chicano students, inspired by the militancy of the Black Movement and political activities of Chicanos in the *barrios* and agricultural fields, directed their activity toward forming student organizations on college campuses. This essay examines the political development of Chicanas within the student movement, which led many to initiate a process by which they could begin to resolve inconsistencies between male and female roles.

---. Personal Papers. Chicana and Chicano Archives and Special Collections. San Diego State University Libraries.

Of special interest is a 1973 oral interview totaling approximately 64 minutes with Lopez discussing a wide range of topics including: the political environment of Calexico and the Imperial Valley; gender rights and expectations within Mexican-American families and communities; and differences in culture within the U.S. compared to Mexico; the relation of the women's liberation movement to the Chicano liberation movement; and Mexican machismo and the debate over terminology, "Mexican-American" versus "Chicano."

Martinez, Elizabeth "Betita." *500 Years of Chicana History/500 años de la mujer Chicana*. Bilingual Edition, Rutgers UP, 2007.

500 Years of Chicana Women's History is a powerful story of Mexican American Women in pictures and text. It describes their struggle, resistance, and achievements. The book is described as having "a remarkable combination of scholarship and youthful appeal."

---. *De Colores Means All of Us: Latina Views for a Multi-Colored Century*. Forward by Angela Davis, Southend P, 1997.

Elizabeth "Betita" Martinez (born 1925) is a Chicana feminist and a long-time community organizer, activist, author, and educator. Revered by Chicanas for her committed work relative to Chicana/Chicano struggles; she has written numerous books and articles on different topics relating to social movements in the Americas.

NietoGomez, Anna. "Chicana Feminism." *Encuentro Feminil*, vol. 1, no. 3–5, 1974.

In 1974 Anna NietoGomez founded *Encuentro Feminil*, a feminist journal; she recognized that the Women's Movement in the United States was not a unified movement. In 1972, she promoted the earliest discussions on Chicana feminism, noting the lack of recognition Chicanas received, and the negative attitudes towards a Chicana Caucus at the National Women's Political Caucus Convention, which she argued promoted maternalism and racism.

Perez, Gail. "Women Hold Up Half of Chicano Park." *La Prensa San Diego*, 12 July 2012, A1.

From a series of related articles on the Chicano Park mural restoration, this one addresses the women of Chicano Park, and like the others is based on personal interviews by Gail Perez with the artists who painted in the park beginning in 1970.

The *Prensa* articles begin with Part I,"Through Our Blood: Historic Restoration of Chicano Park Murals Begins" 8 July 2011; and Part II, by Gail Perez and David Avalos, "Revitalization Not Restoration: A People's Art," 15 July 2011.

Rodriguez, Maggie Rivas-Rodriguez. *Mexican Americans and World War II*. U of Texas P, 2005.

A celebration of the overlooked contributions of the 750,000 *Mexican American* veterans of the "Greatest Generation," initiated by Rivas-Rodriguez, Professor of Journalism at the University of Texas at Austin. In 1999, she launched the U.S. Latino and Latina World War II Oral History Project, which has since gathered nearly 1,000 interviews with men and women from all over the country, resulting in publications, presentations, and conferences.

Sanchez, Rita. "Chicana Writer, Breaking Out of Silence." *Chicana Feminist Thought: the Basic Historical Writings*, edited by Alma M. Garcia, Routledge, 1997, pp. 66–70.

Reprinted from a 1976 article in *De Colores* 3:3 (1977), later published as "Writing as a Revolutionary Act," for *Visión de la Mujer*, a journal of student writings she edited and then had published at San Diego State with the help of SDSU Women activists of that time period, Eliabeth Alvarado Diana Borrego, and Maria Elena Avila.

———. "Chicanas in the Arts, 1970–1995." *Chicano San Diego: Cultural Space and theStruggle for Justice*, edited by Richard Griswold del Castillo, U of Arizona P, 2007.

The essay reflects on thirty years of Chicana involvement in the arts in San Diego; also an exploration into the many ways in which Chicanas have contributed to the arts at a time when full participation was denied them. Specific examples provide ample evidence of women's engaging presence even before the Chicano Movement reached its peak in the 1970s.

———. "Remembrance and Discovery: The Five Sanchez Brothers." *Mexican Americans and World War II*, edited by Maggie Rivas-Rodriguez, U of Texas P, 2005, pp. 1–40.

"Remembrance and Discovery" is a journey into Rita Sanchez's childhood memories, with reflections on her Mexican American family's participation on the home front and on the battlefield during World War II; includes stories about four aunts who were workers for the war industry, later called Rosie the Riveters; and expanded research from the National Archives (NARA) in Washington, D.C. on her uncles, her father's brothers; documenting the actual places where they fought, and ultimately gave their lives for their country.

———. *The Rita Sanchez Papers*, 1956–2013. Green Library, Stanford University.

The collections pertains to her early years in San Bernardino; her education at Stanford; her teaching career at San Diego State University and San Diego Mesa College, her interest in Chicano/Chicana artists and activists, and the Chicano Movement; included are her own writings, class papers, articles, correspondence, publications, audio and videotapes, journals, photographs, including her Sanchez y Acuña family history, and other materials. Repository: Stanford University, Department of Special Collections and University Archives.

CPSIA information can be obtained
at www.ICGtesting.com
Printed in the USA
FSHW01n0051090918
51918FS